INTERNATIONAL
DEBT REPORT
2024

T0398727

Data for this book are available in the World Bank's Development Data Hub at https://datacatalog.worldbank.org/int/search/dataset/0038015/international-debt-statistics.

Scan to see this book and prior editions.

INTERNATIONAL DEBT REPORT 2024

Contents

Foreword	*ix*
Acknowledgments	*xiii*
Introduction	*xv*
Key Takeaways	*xvii*
Abbreviations	*xxi*

PART 1. Overview — 1

Chapter 1. Analyses of External Debt Stocks and Debt Flows as of End-2023 — 3
- Trends in External Debt Stock, 2013–23 — 3
- Debt Ratios and Debt Resolutions — 16
- Debt Servicing Burdens of LMICs, 2013–23 — 22
- Trends in External Debt Flows, 2013–23 — 29
- Trends in Net Transfers on External Debt, 2013–23 — 40
- Note — 47
- References — 47

Chapter 2. The Macroeconomic and Debt Outlook for 2024 and Beyond — 49
- Introduction — 49
- Macroeconomic Outlook and Risks — 49
- Debt Outlook and Risks — 52
- References — 56

Chapter 3. The Debt Transparency Agenda: Moving It Forward — 57
- Introduction — 57
- Borrower Countries — 58
- Creditor Countries — 62
- The International Community — 66
- Notes — 69
- References — 69

PART 2. Aggregate and Country Tables — 71

All Low- and Middle-Income Countries	73
East Asia and Pacific	74
Europe and Central Asia	75
Latin America and the Caribbean	76
Middle East and North Africa	77
South Asia	78
Sub-Saharan Africa	79
Afghanistan	80
Albania	81
Algeria	82
Angola	83
Argentina	84
Armenia	85
Azerbaijan	86
Bangladesh	87
Belarus	88
Belize	89
Benin	90
Bhutan	91
Bolivia	92
Bosnia and Herzegovina	93
Botswana	94
Brazil	95
Burkina Faso	96
Burundi	97
Cabo Verde	98
Cambodia	99
Cameroon	100
Central African Republic	101
Chad	102
China	103
Colombia	104
Comoros	105
Congo, Democratic Republic of	106
Congo, Republic of	107
Costa Rica	108
Côte d'Ivoire	109
Djibouti	110
Dominica	111

Dominican Republic	112	Nigeria	161
Ecuador	113	North Macedonia	162
Egypt, Arab Republic of	114	Pakistan	163
El Salvador	115	Papua New Guinea	164
Eritrea	116	Paraguay	165
Eswatini	117	Peru	166
Ethiopia	118	Philippines	167
Fiji	119	Rwanda	168
Gabon	120	Samoa	169
Gambia, The	121	São Tomé and Príncipe	170
Georgia	122	Senegal	171
Ghana	123	Serbia	172
Grenada	124	Sierra Leone	173
Guatemala	125	Solomon Islands	174
Guinea	126	Somalia	175
Guinea-Bissau	127	South Africa	176
Guyana	128	Sri Lanka	177
Haiti	129	St. Lucia	178
Honduras	130	St. Vincent and the Grenadines	179
India	131	Sudan	180
Indonesia	132	Suriname	181
Iran, Islamic Republic of	133	Syrian Arab Republic	182
Iraq	134	Tajikistan	183
Jamaica	135	Tanzania	184
Jordan	136	Thailand	185
Kazakhstan	137	Timor-Leste	186
Kenya	138	Togo	187
Kosovo	139	Tonga	188
Kyrgyz Republic	140	Tunisia	189
Lao People's Democratic Republic	141	Türkiye	190
Lebanon	142	Turkmenistan	191
Lesotho	143	Uganda	192
Liberia	144	Ukraine	193
Madagascar	145	Uzbekistan	194
Malawi	146	Vanuatu	195
Maldives	147	Viet Nam	196
Mali	148	Yemen, Republic of	197
Mauritania	149	Zambia	198
Mauritius	150	Zimbabwe	199
Mexico	151		
Moldova	152	**APPENDIX**	201
Mongolia	153		
Montenegro	154	**Data Sources**	203
Morocco	155		
Mozambique	156	**Country Groups**	205
Myanmar	157	Regional Groups	205
Nepal	158	Income Groups	206
Nicaragua	159		
Niger	160	**Glossary**	207

BOXES

1.1 External Debt Data: Concepts, Sources, and Coverage 5

1.2 Understanding Bilateral Currency Swap Lines 7

1.3 IMF and World Bank Efforts to Assist with Crises 12

1.4 Debt Resolutions in Low- and Middle-Income Countries 17

1.5 World Bank Income and Lending Classifications Used in *International Debt Report 2024* 20

1.6 Allocation of the International Monetary Fund's Special Drawing Rights in 2023 25

1.7 Debt-for-Climate Swaps 34

1.8 Government Expenditures and External Debt Service in Developing Countries 44

3.1 How China Lends 65

FIGURES

1.1 Creditor Composition of External Debt Stock in Low- and Middle-Income Countries, 2013–23 5

1.2 External Debt Stock of Low- and Middle-Income Countries, 2013–23 9

1.3 Creditor Composition of Low- and Middle-Income Countries' (excluding China) Long-Term Public and Publicly Guaranteed External Debt, 2013–23 10

1.4 GNI Growth versus New World Bank Commitments as a Share of GNI, Low- and Middle-Income Countries, 1971–2023 11

1.5 Creditor Composition of IDA-Eligible Countries' Long-Term Public and Publicly Guaranteed External Debt during Crises, 2006–23 15

1.6 External Debt-to-GNI Ratios for Low- and Middle-Income Countries (excluding China) and IDA-Eligible Countries, 2013–23 17

B1.4.1 Evolution of the Risk of External Debt Distress 18

B1.5.1 Number of Low- and Middle-Income Countries Covered in *International Debt Report 2024*, by FY2025 Income and Lending Group 21

1.7 Variable Interest Rates and Interest Payments on Long-Term Debt of Low- and Middle-Income Countries (excluding China), by Creditor Type, 2020–23 23

1.8 Average Terms on New External Debt Commitments for Low- and Middle-Income Countries (excluding China), by Creditor Type, 2013–23 24

B1.6.1 SDR Allocations as a Share of International Reserves, by Region, 2023 26

1.9 Interest Payments on Public and Publicly Guaranteed Debt of Low- and Middle-Income Countries, by Region and Creditor Type, 2013–23 26

1.10 IDA-Eligible Countries' Interest Payments on External Debt, by Creditor Type, 2013–23 27

1.11 Average Terms of Commitments of External Public and Publicly Guaranteed Debt to IDA-Eligible Countries, by Creditor Type, Average 2013–23 28

1.12 Net Debt Inflows in Low- and Middle-Income Countries, by Maturity, 2013–23   29

1.13 Long-Term External Debt Flows to Low- and Middle-Income Countries (excluding China), by Borrower Type, 2021–23   32

1.14 Bond Flows to Low- and Middle-Income Countries (excluding China), by Borrower Type, 2022–23   34

1.15 Net Flows to IDA-Eligible Countries, by Region and Creditor Type, 2023   38

1.16 Net Equity Inflows and External Debt Flows to Low- and Middle-Income Countries, 2013–23   39

1.17 Long-Term Net Transfers on External Debt in Low-and Middle-Income Countries (excluding China), by Debtor Type, 2013–23   41

1.18 Long-Term Net Transfers on Public and Publicly Guaranteed External Debt in Low- and Middle-Income Countries (excluding China), by Creditor Type, 2013–23   42

1.19 Debt Flows on Public and Publicly Guaranteed Debt in IDA-Eligible Countries, by Creditor Type, 2021–23   43

1.20 Net Transfers on Public and Publicly Guaranteed Debt in IDA-Eligible Countries, by Creditor Type, 2021–23   44

B1.8.1 Government Expenditures and External Debt Service Comparison, 2018–23   46

2.1 Percent Change in Gross Domestic Product, 2021–26   50

2.2 Interest Payments on Total External Debt as a Share of GNI, 2013–23   53

2.3 Composition of Government Revenues as a Share of GDP, 2010s vs. 2020s   55

3.1 Public Debt Disclosure by IDA-Eligible Countries, Access and Coverage, 2020 vs. 2023   59

3.2 Reporting Timetable for Debtor Reporting System Countries, 2019–23   60

TABLES

1.1 External Debt Stock of Low- and Middle-Income Countries, 2013–23   4

1.2 Net Debt Inflows to IDA-Eligible Countries, 2013–23   36

Foreword

It was a bold idea, boosted by a snappy slogan: "billions to trillions." A decade ago, in an era when private capital was gushing into developing economies, governments and development institutions figured it was exactly what was needed to turbocharge progress on poverty reduction and other development goals. "The good news is that, globally, there are ample savings, amounting to US$17 trillion, and liquidity is at historical highs," read a key World Bank strategy document of the time.

That proved to be a fantasy. Since 2022, foreign private creditors have extracted nearly US$141 billion more in debt service payments from public sector borrowers in developing economies than they disbursed in new financing. As this report documents, that withdrawal has upended the financing landscape for development. For two years in a row now, the external creditors of developing economies have been pulling out more than they have been putting in—with one striking exception. The World Bank and other multilateral institutions pumped in nearly US$85 billion more in 2022 and 2023 than they collected in debt service payments.

That has thrust some multilateral institutions into a role they were never designed to play—as lenders of last resort, deploying scarce long-term development finance to compensate for the exit of other creditors. Last year, multilateral institutions accounted for about 20 percent of the long-term external debt stock of developing economies, five points higher than in 2019. The World Bank's International Development Association (IDA) now accounts for nearly half of the development aid going from multilateral institutions to the 26 poorest countries. In 2023, the World Bank accounted for fully a third of the overall net debt inflows going into IDA-eligible countries—US$16.7 billion, more than three times the volume a decade ago.

That reflects a broken financing system. Capital—both public and private—is essential for development. Long-term progress *will* depend to an important degree on restarting the capital flows that most developing countries enjoyed in the first decade of this century. But the risk-reward balance cannot be allowed to remain as lopsided as it is today, with multilateral institutions and government creditors bearing nearly all the risk and private creditors reaping nearly all the rewards.

When global interest rates skyrocketed in 2022 and 2023 and debt distress rose in the poorest countries, the World Bank followed its usual practice. It shifted from providing low-interest loans to providing grants to countries at high risk of distress. It increased its overall financing for these countries, typically over terms ranging from 30 to 50 years. But private creditors headed for the exits, more than fully compensated by high interest rates for the investment risks they had taken. In the absence of a predictable global system for restructuring debt, most countries facing distress opted to tough it out rather than default and risk being cut off indefinitely from global capital markets. In some cases, new financing arriving from the World Bank promptly went out to pay off private creditors.

In 2023, developing countries spent a record US$1.4 trillion just to service their debt. That amounted to nearly 4 percent of their gross national income. Ballooning interest payments accounted for most of the increase in overall debt-service payments. Principal repayments remained stable at about US$951 billion, but interest payments surged by more than a third to about US$406 billion.

The result, for many developing countries, has been a devastating diversion of resources away from areas critical for long-term growth and development such as health and education. The squeeze on the poorest and most vulnerable countries—those eligible to borrow from IDA—has been especially fierce. Their interest payments on external debt have quadrupled since 2013, hitting an all-time high of US$34.6 billion in 2023.

On average, interest payments now amount to nearly 6 percent of the export earnings of IDA-eligible countries—a level that has not been seen since 1999. For some countries, the percentages range from 10 to as much as 38. No wonder that more than half of IDA-eligible countries are either in debt distress or at high risk of it. No wonder that private creditors have been retreating even as multilateral financing increases.

These facts imply a metastasizing solvency crisis that continues to be misdiagnosed as a liquidity problem in many of the poorest countries. It is easy to kick the can down the road, to provide these countries just enough financing to help them meet their immediate repayment obligations. But that simply extends their purgatory. These countries will need to grow at a faster clip if they are to shrink their debt burdens—and they will need much more investment if growth is to accelerate. Neither is likely given the size of their debt burdens: their ability to repay will never be restored.

It's time to face the reality: the poorest countries facing debt distress need debt relief if they are to have a shot at lasting prosperity. A twenty-first century global system is needed to ensure fair play in lending to all developing economies.

Sovereign borrowers deserve at least *some* of the protections that are routinely afforded to debt-strapped businesses and individuals under national bankruptcy laws. Private creditors that make risky, high-interest loans to poor countries ought to bear a fair share of the cost when the bet goes bad.

In an era of great international mistrust, it will be a struggle to establish these precepts. But without them, all major development goals will remain in peril—perhaps as much of a fantasy as "billions to trillions."

Indermit S. Gill
Senior Vice President and Chief Economist
The World Bank Group

Acknowledgments

This volume was prepared by the World Bank's Debt Statistics Team of the Development Data Group, comprising Parul Agarwal, Arzu Aytekin Balibek, Kifaye Didem Bayar, Matthew Benjamin, Sylvie Kabaziga Bishweka, Wendy Huang, Chineze Olive Okafor, Malvina Pollock, Prateek Samal, João Miguel Falcao Pinto Da Silva, Rubena Sukaj, Tin Yu To, and Rasiel Vellos. The work was carried out under the management of Evis Rucaj and the direction of Haishan Fu. The team was assisted by Nancy Kebe.

The overview was prepared by the Debt Statistics Team, with contributions from Yan Bai from the Price Statistics Team and Shijie Shi and Naotaka Sugawara with guidance from M. Ayhan Kose and Carlos Arteta from the Development Economics Prospects Group.

Valuable guidance was provided by Indermit S. Gill, senior vice president and chief economist of the World Bank Group, and Haishan Fu, chief statistician of the World Bank and director of the Development Data Group. Constructive feedback was provided by Brian R. Pinto, former senior advisor at the World Bank. The Development Economics Vice Presidency; Macroeconomics, Trade and Investment Global Practice; Development Finance Vice Presidency; and Development Economics Prospects Group of the World Bank provided helpful feedback on the overview. The final statistics were reviewed by country economists from the Macroeconomics, Trade and Investment Global Practice.

The cover was designed by Parul Agarwal and Bill Pragluski. Mark McClure, Jewel McFadden, and Orlando Mota coordinated the publication and dissemination of this volume. Kristen Milhollin, Karolina Ordon, Joseph Rebello, Shane Kimo Romig, and Mariana Lozzi Teixeira managed the communications surrounding the release. .

The accompanying International Debt Statistics electronic products were prepared with support from a team led by Kunal Patel, Ramgopal Erabelly, and Sebastian Ariel Dolber, and comprising Yuliyan Nikolaev Bogdanov, Rajesh Kumar Danda, Svetoslava Georgieva Dimitrova, and Tsvetelina Nikolova Stefanova.

Introduction

As the global COVID-19 pandemic of 2020–22 recedes into history, its impact on the debt burdens of low- and middle-income countries (LMICs)—and particularly the world's poorest countries—remains. Policies implemented to deal with the pandemic, many of which are still largely in place, continue to strain the budgets of these countries, which tend to rely heavily on external financing from official and private creditors to fund their social and fiscal priorities.

LMICs accumulated significant debt during the pandemic years to fund massively expanded health services and compensate for dramatically reduced economic activity and government income. That accumulation continued apace in 2023, with LMICs adding another US$633.1 billion to their debt stock, an 8.1 percent increase over the 2020 level. Consequently, LMICs' debt currently stands at a record US$8.8 trillion. The increase was proportionally larger for the poorest nations—those eligible for assistance from the International Development Association—where external debt has risen 17.9 percent since the onset of the pandemic in 2020 and now stands at a record US$1.1 trillion.

LMICs now have significantly higher debt levels overall than in the decade that preceded the pandemic, and servicing that debt has become an ever-larger burden on their economies and limited resources. In 2023, LMICs spent 3.7 percent of their gross national income to service their debt, including 1.1 percent of gross national income on interest payments alone, which was the highest amount of the past two decades. Such increased debt service burdens have a significant negative impact on spending by those governments on other priorities. A recent World Bank statistical analysis shows that, when debt service burdens rise, the levels of spending on agriculture, the environment, and education fall; this report quantifies those spending decreases.

The composition of external borrowing has also changed since the onset of the pandemic. As private creditors became risk averse and pulled back on lending to LMICs, multilateral creditors—particularly the World Bank—stepped in to provide support. In 2023, LMICs owed 15 percent of their overall external debt to multilateral institutions, a significant 4-percentage-point increase from prepandemic levels. Although private creditors increased lending to LMICs in 2023, net debt outflows from LMICs to bondholders— US$1.2 billion in 2023—indicate that investor confidence has yet to return to prepandemic levels.

Pandemic-induced economic bottlenecks across the globe, coupled with fiscal policy actions taken by governments in reaction to COVID-19, helped drive global inflation higher while reducing fiscal space for many countries, especially LMICs. Moreover, monetary policy actions in response to rising global prices—by central banks of high-income countries in particular—drove interest rates much higher. This rise in global rates significantly increased debt service burdens for LMICs' existing long-term debt contracted on variable rates—interest payments on long-term variable rate loans were 14 percent of long-term debt service in 2023, up from 10 percent the previous year—while rendering new external borrowing more expensive. Although global rates look likely to begin falling soon, they remain high and continue to put pressure on LMICs' budgets, and the increase in debt servicing costs is expected to moderate only gradually as global interest rates decline.

On a positive note, LMICs' economies are growing again, with average growth of 4.2 percent so far in 2024 that is expected to remain relatively stable over the next two years. Because of an increase in activity among commodity exporters and some stabilization in fragile economies, growth in low-income countries is expected to be even higher. This higher, steadier growth should provide LMICs with some measure of relief to manage their rising debt service burdens.

Still, the risks remain. They include an escalation of armed conflicts, further trade fragmentation, persistent global inflation, a weakening of global risk appetite, and weak growth in major LMICs, especially China. Any one of these factors could drive debt burdens higher for many LMICs.

For this reason, accurately tracking LMICs' debt levels and debt trends is more important today than ever. Diagnosis is a large part of any cure, and the international community can address debt vulnerabilities and debt distress levels only if it has the data to show precisely how much debt borrowers carry and how it is evolving. To that end, the World Bank, other multilateral institutions, debtor and creditor country governments, and academia are working together to increase debt transparency among LMICs, including crucial reconciliation of the claims of Group of Seven countries and other members of the Paris Club with debtor records. Although much remains to be done, remarkable progress has already been made to further the debt transparency agenda.

The COVID-19 pandemic did significant damage to economies around the world. Although global economic activity has rebounded strongly, the debt incurred in the process—particularly by LMICs—remains. Much work must therefore be done to bring LMICs' debt levels and debt service burdens back to a reasonable and manageable position.

Key Takeaways

Debt servicing costs of low- and middle-income countries (LMICs), excluding China, reached an all-time high in 2023, double the level of a decade ago. Higher external debt levels—which also increased to an all-time high in 2023, to US$8.8 trillion (including China)—coupled with elevated interest rates posed new and challenging debt burdens for these countries. Overall debt levels continued to rise as a result of accumulated borrowing during the pandemic and were exacerbated by financial pressures in its aftermath: notably, a sharp rise in global interest rates, depreciating local currencies, and uncertainty surrounding global economic growth.

In addition, the data indicate that the composition of LMICs' external borrowing has changed markedly since the onset of the pandemic, with multilateral creditors significantly increasing their share of lending to LMICs amid slower lending growth from private creditors.

Key takeaways from the 2023 data include the following:

- The total debt servicing costs (principal plus interest payments) of all LMICs reached an all-time high of US$1.4 trillion in 2023. For LMICs, excluding China, debt servicing costs climbed to a record of US$971.1 billion in 2023, an increase of 19.7 percent over the previous year and more than double the amounts seen a decade ago. These historically challenging debt service costs were due to record debt levels, interest rates at a two-decade high, and depreciation of local currencies against a strong US dollar.
- Since the onset of the pandemic, multilateral lenders have become the central financial lifeline for LMICs amid a slowing of private lending. The composition of LMICs' external debt portfolios has changed significantly since 2019 as multilateral creditors—including the International Monetary Fund, the World Bank, and regional development banks—stepped up and assumed the role of providers of emergency relief and balance of payments support in times of crisis. Borrowing from private creditors fell sharply because of adverse market conditions, investor retreat from frontier markets, and—in countries eligible for International Development Association (IDA) assistance—a concentration on borrowing from official creditors on concessional terms to support debt sustainability.
- Official multilateral creditors have been positive contributors to net transfers to LMICs throughout the past decade, offering concessional financing at low interest rates, long maturities, and support for countries through times

of shocks that have negatively affected their economies since 2019. By contrast, and excluding China, net transfers from private creditors to public sector entities in LMICs have been negative and have resulted instead in a withdrawal by this creditor base for the past three years. Net transfers on external debt owed to bondholders turned negative in 2020 and, despite a significant improvement, remained negative at US$13.8 billion in 2023.

- Debt stock owed to multilateral creditors rose 6.8 percent to US$1.3 trillion in 2023, whereas debt stock owed to private creditors increased just 0.8 percent. This contrast mirrors the increases in multilateral lending during other periods of economic crisis, including during the 2008–09 financial crisis, when debt stock owed to multilateral institutions grew at five times the pace of lending by private creditors. Multilateral creditors have played an even more pronounced role in IDA-eligible countries: their debt stock to these countries increased 10.1 percent in 2023 to US$400.8 billion. The World Bank accounted for US$170.8 billion, or 42.6 percent, of that debt stock.

- Total external debt stock of LMICs hit at an all-time high of US$8.8 trillion in 2023, up 2.4 percent from the previous year. This rise was driven by a 3.4 percent increase in short-term debt stock (with maturity of less than one year), to US$2.3 trillion, and a 2.0 percent rise in long-term debt stock, to US$6.5 trillion. Long-term public and publicly guaranteed external debt rose 3.6 percent to US$3.8 trillion, whereas long-term private nonguaranteed debt remained unchanged. China's external debt stock fell for a second consecutive year, decreasing 1.1 percent to US$2.4 trillion. China accounts for more than 27 percent of the total debt stock of LMICs.

- For all LMICs (excluding China), external debt stock rose 3.8 percent to US$6.4 trillion in 2023. Yet debt burdens, which measure debt relative to gross national income (GNI), were broadly unchanged, at 34.4 percent, because of a 6.3 percent increase in the dollar value of LMICs' combined GNI in 2023 and a smaller, 3.8 percent increase in debt stocks. Debt burdens in the poorest countries, those eligible for IDA resources, continued to rise in 2023, however, increasing by 1.9 percentage points to an average of 40.6 percent of GNI, as the rise in their debt stock outpaced their GNI growth. The pandemic and its aftermath have hit these countries hardest, and the increase in their debt burdens has diverted resources away from other critical areas, including social services and infrastructure development; negatively affected economic growth; and exacerbated debt vulnerabilities in many of them.

- Combined World Bank and International Monetary Fund long-term debt stock to LMICs has risen 63.1 percent since before the pandemic, more than nine times the growth of private lending to LMICs over the period. Debt stock owed by LMICs (excluding China) to the World Bank's International Bank for Reconstruction and Development and IDA was US$421.8 billion in 2023, equivalent to 34.0 percent of all multilateral creditors.

- Because of the monetary tightening of recent years, interest payments on public and private debt increased across all regions in 2023. New commitments to LMICs (excluding China) also became more expensive: interest rates on new loans from official creditors increased 2.1 percentage points to 4.09 percent in 2023, and rates on loans from private creditors increased 1.37 percentage points to 6.0 percent, the highest level since 2008. Both interest payments and rates look likely to mitigate going forward as many central banks have begun to ease policy.

In addition to the release of the 2023 external debt data from the International Debt Statistics database, this edition of the *International Debt Report*

- Provides analysis of the near-term macroeconomic outlook and risks LMICs face amid changing global financial conditions and what they portend for these countries' debt burdens and vulnerabilities going forward;
- Examines the ability of the smallest and poorest countries, many of which have underdeveloped domestic financial systems and lack access to global capital markets, to carry debt and sustain larger-than-ever debt service burdens; and
- Identifies steps and efforts that governments of debtor and creditor countries, together with the international community, have undertaken to move the debt transparency agenda forward, with support from research and input from academia.

Abbreviations

AFESD	Arab Fund for Economic and Social Development
BCIE	Central American Bank for Economic Integration
BCSL	bilateral currency swap line
BDEAC	Development Bank of the Central African States
ComSec	Commonwealth Secretariat
DRS	Debtor Reporting System
EBRD	European Bank for Reconstruction and Development
EIB	European Investment Bank
FDI	foreign direct investment
FY	fiscal year
G-7	Group of Seven
G-20	Group of Twenty
GDP	gross domestic product
GNI	gross national income
HIPC	Heavily Indebted Poor Countries
IBRD	International Bank for Reconstruction and Development
IDA	International Development Association
IDB	Inter-American Development Bank
IDS	International Debt Statistics
IFAD	International Fund for Agricultural Development
IMF	International Monetary Fund
LICs	low-income countries
LMICs	low- and middle-income countries
MICs	middle-income countries
OPEC	Organization of the Petroleum Exporting Countries
PPA	performance and policy action
PPG	public and publicly guaranteed
PNG	private nonguaranteed
RBI	Reserve Bank of India

SDRs	special drawing rights
SOE	state-owned enterprise
TDB	Eastern and Southern African Trade and Development Bank
UNCTAD	UN Trade and Development

All dollar amounts are in US dollars unless otherwise indicated.

PART 1
Overview

1. Analyses of External Debt Stocks and Debt Flows as of End-2023

Trends in External Debt Stock, 2013–23

Total external debt stock of low- and middle-income countries (LMICs) increased 2.4 percent in 2023, to US$8.8 trillion. The increase signaled a return to the upward long-term trend that has persisted in this group of countries over the last two decades, disrupted slightly by decreases in 2015 and 2022 (table 1.1). The 2023 increase in external debt stock[1] highlights the elevated indebtedness pressures these countries face in the aftermath of the COVID-19 pandemic, including inflationary pressures, high interest rates, depreciating local currencies, and uncertainty over global economic growth.

Tight monetary policy in high-income countries has pushed interest rates to their highest level in two decades, and central banks have kept rates elevated in an effort to ease inflationary pressures. Higher global interest rates have augmented interest expenses on existing debt obligations contracted at variable rates and have made newly contracted borrowing more expensive for LMICs. This expense has diverted resources away from other critical areas, including social services and infrastructure development, and has negatively affected economic growth.

From a maturity standpoint, the increase in total debt stock of LMICs was driven by an increase in both short- and long-term debt in 2023: short-term debt stock increased 3.4 percent, to US$2.3 trillion, and long-term debt stock increased 2.0 percent to US$6.5 trillion. Excluding a slight decrease in 2022, short-term debt stock has been rising since 2016 (figure 1.1). LMICs' increased reliance on short-term debt resulted from countries' needs to cover liquidity requirements, especially during times of economic uncertainty when short-term debt was used as a flexible financing option, and during periods of external debt shocks when countries increased short-term debt as a response to urgent funding requirements and to the lack of long-term external funding. The use of short-term debt was also a debt management policy response to prevailing high interest rates, as countries opted for lower-cost debt with shorter maturities to avoid the higher interest costs of long-term commitments. (Refer to box 1.1 for definitions of short-term debt and other concepts used in this report.)

Table 1.1 External Debt Stock of Low- and Middle-Income Countries, 2013–23

US$ (billion)

	2013	2014	2015	2016	2017	2018	2019	2020	2021	2022	2023
Debt stock	5,712.6	6,290.7	5,901.5	6,124.8	6,884.9	7,381.9	7,753.7	8,173.4	8,819.3	8,630.7	8,836.5
Long-term	3,850.8	4,268.0	4,370.5	4,641.8	5,076.1	5,354.0	5,705.2	6,111.6	6,478.2	6,366.6	6,495.9
Official creditors	998.5	1,005.3	1,031.5	1,088.8	1,190.8	1,268.6	1,331.3	1,498.5	1,700.0	1,732.0	1,822.9
Bilateral	367.0	371.4	377.8	404.3	443.4	470.2	477.4	508.0	504.0	492.4	499.0
Multilateral	631.5	634.0	653.7	684.5	747.4	798.4	853.9	990.5	1,196.0	1,239.5	1,323.9
World Bank	264.3	269.1	278.6	289.3	312.5	322.1	340.5	376.2	388.8	406.5	437.2
IMF	106.1	97.9	100.7	104.0	114.7	142.2	162.3	215.3	387.6	382.2	382.8
Private creditors	2,852.3	3,262.7	3,339.0	3,553.0	3,885.3	4,085.4	4,373.9	4,613.1	4,778.2	4,634.7	4,673.0
Bonds	1,017.3	1,211.9	1,237.2	1,351.0	1,641.4	1,762.5	1,976.6	2,198.2	2,298.8	2,162.0	2,140.7
Banks and other private	1,835.0	2,050.8	2,101.8	2,202.0	2,243.8	2,322.9	2,397.3	2,414.9	2,479.3	2,472.6	2,532.3
Short-term	1,861.8	2,022.7	1,531.0	1,483.0	1,808.8	2,028.0	2,048.4	2,061.9	2,341.1	2,264.0	2,340.6
Memorandum item											
Long-term PPG	1,942.3	2,139.3	2,201.0	2,362.1	2,668.4	2,903.4	3,112.0	3,400.2	3,716.1	3,699.6	3,832.6
Long-term PNG	1,908.5	2,128.7	2,169.5	2,279.7	2,407.7	2,450.6	2,593.2	2,711.4	2,762.1	2,667.0	2,663.2

Sources: World Bank International Debt Statistics database, International Monetary Fund, and Bank for International Settlements.
Note: World Bank includes IBRD and IDA; IMF includes use of credit and SDR allocations; IBRD = International Bank for Reconstruction and Development; IDA = International Development Association; IMF = International Monetary Fund; PNG = private nonguaranteed; PPG = public and publicly guaranteed; SDR = special drawing right.

The rise in the long-term debt stock component was mostly driven by an increase in obligations to multilateral creditors, which rose 6.8 percent in 2023 to US$1.3 trillion and were equivalent to 20.4 percent of total long-term debt stock. Multilateral institutions continued to provide support while lending by other creditor groups has yet to return to prepandemic levels. In 2023, the debt stock of bilateral creditors increased 1.3 percent to US$499 billion, whereas private creditors' debt stock increased 0.8 percent to US$4.7 trillion. Debt stock of bilateral creditors increased in 2023 after a two-year decline as creditor governments returned to lending to LMICs and continued to diversify the mix of bilateral lending instruments, including bilateral currency swap lines (box 1.2). Central banks' use of bilateral currency swap lines has risen in the aftermath of the pandemic to help facilitate trade and serve as a safety net to provide temporary balance of payments support.

Figure 1.1 Creditor Composition of External Debt Stock in Low- and Middle-Income Countries, 2013–23

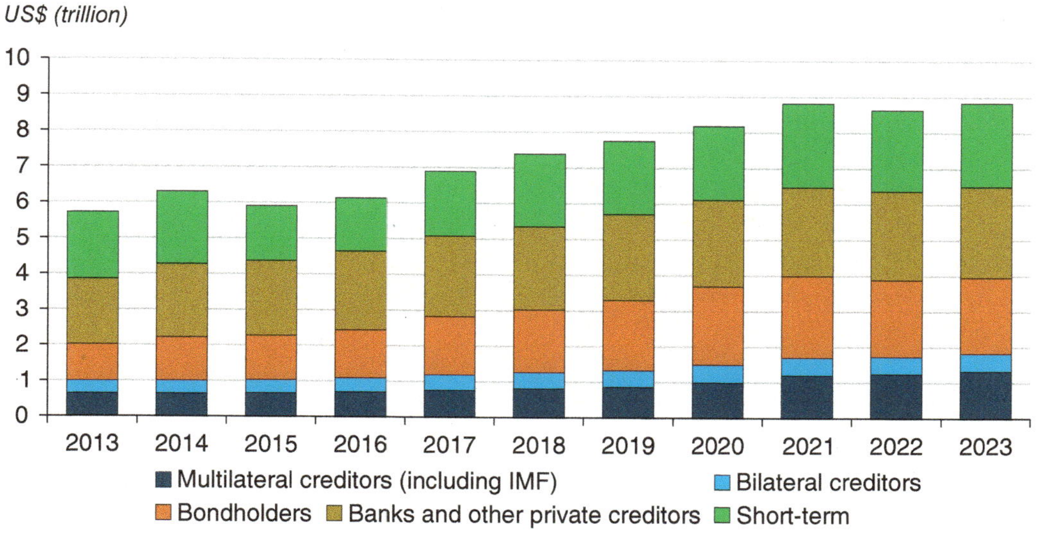

US$ (trillion)

Source: World Bank International Debt Statistics database.
Note: IMF = International Monetary Fund.

Box 1.1 External Debt Data: Concepts, Sources, and Coverage

This report presents data and analysis on external debt for 119 low- and middle-income countries and Guyana. The primary source for these data is reports to the World Bank's Debtor Reporting System (DRS) from member countries that have received either International Bank for Reconstruction and Development loans or International Development Association credits and have outstanding obligations to the World Bank. The DRS, instituted in 1951, has its origins in the World Bank's need to monitor and assess the financial position of its borrowers. Comprehensive information on data sources and the methodology used to compile the statistics presented in this report can be found in the appendix under "Data Sources." The following describes the key concepts and data sources.

- The DRS follows international standards and defines *external debt* as the outstanding amount of actual current liabilities in both domestic and foreign currency that require payment(s) of principal and/or interest by the debtor at some point(s) in the future and that are owed to nonresidents by residents of an economy. The sum of principal and interest payments is defined as *debt service*.

(Box continues on next page)

Box 1.1 External Debt Data: Concepts, Sources, and Coverage (*continued*)

- The *total external debt* of a country is the sum of public and publicly guaranteed debt, private nonguaranteed debt, and short-term debt.

- *Public and publicly guaranteed external debt* comprises long-term external obligations (maturities of over one year) of all public debtors, including debt held by the central government and by state-owned enterprises. Data are collected on a loan-by-loan basis through the DRS. Reporting countries submit quarterly reports on new loan commitments and annual reports on loan status and transactions (new commitments, gross disbursements, principal, and interest payments).

- *Private nonguaranteed debt* comprises long-term external obligations of private debtors that are not guaranteed by a public entity. The DRS has covered private nonguaranteed debt since 1973; however, for this category of debt data, the annual status and transactions (gross disbursements, principal, and interest payments) are reported in aggregate.

- *Short-term debt* is defined as debt with an original maturity of one year or less and is not covered under DRS reporting requirements. However, most DRS reporters provide an annual report on outstanding short-term debt stocks on a voluntary basis. For countries that do not provide these data, information on their short-term debt is drawn from the Quarterly External Debt Statistics database, a joint World Bank–International Monetary Fund initiative, wherein data are compiled and reported by countries' central banks, along with data compiled by the Bank for International Settlements.

All debt data reported to the DRS are validated against—and, when appropriate, supplemented by—data from other sources. These additional data include the Balance of Payments and International Investment Position statistics, Quarterly External Debt Statistics, information published on official government websites, reports from the International Monetary Fund, regional development banks, the Organisation for Economic Co-operation and Development, the Bank for International Settlements, and websites and annual publications of lending agencies.

Box 1.2 Understanding Bilateral Currency Swap Lines

Bilateral currency swap lines (BCSLs) are not a new tool for central banks. Currency swap lines in their current form date to the 1960s, though they became much more prevalent in the wake of the global financial crisis of 2007–08, which disrupted global financial markets and threatened liquidity crises for banks worldwide. More recently BCSLs helped stabilize market conditions in the wake of the COVID-19 pandemic.

Historically, BCSLs have been used for three main objectives: (a) to defend a currency peg system such as Bretton Woods; (b) to act as a global liquidity backstop in times of crises or market turmoil; and (c) to enhance the international use of a domestic currency (for example, the Chinese renminbi).

How they work. A BCSL is an agreement between two central banks to exchange currencies. Such agreements allow a central bank to exchange its own currency for the equivalent amount of the counterpart central bank's currency in order to provide foreign currency liquidity to domestic commercial banks or to hold as reserves to meet temporary balance of payments needs. BCSLs typically have a three-year renewable term, but some extend to five years or can be open-ended for BCSLs between advanced economies like the United Kingdom and the United States. When a BCSL is used—that is, drawn upon—the two central banks involved swap currencies, providing their own currency in exchange for an equivalent amount in their counterpart's currency. The swap is based on the exchange rate at the time of transaction, and the swap back at a specified date in the future uses the same exchange rate as the first swap transaction. The swap back may be within as little as one day but more typically occurs three months later; in a few exceptional cases, a swap line has been extended to six months or one year. Because the terms of the second transaction are set in advance, fluctuations in exchange rates during the period have no impact on repayment.

Accounting and disclosure. From an accounting perspective, only draws on BCSLs count as gross international reserves because reserve assets must be available and under control of a country's monetary authorities. Foreign exchange resources that could be obtained under BCSLs are contingent foreign exchange resources because they do not constitute existing claims.[a] Draws on BCSLs used to support central bank liquidity operations and settled without recourse to government financing are excluded from public debt statistics and from Debtor Reporting System data. However, draws on BCSLs that are used for balance of payments support are considered to be public debt, and the Debtor Reporting System records the draw on the BCSL as debt outstanding to the bilateral creditor that extended the BCSL based on information reported to the Debtor Reporting System by the central bank.[b] Information on BCSL agreements' terms and sizes

(Box continues on next page)

Box 1.2 Understanding Bilateral Currency Swap Lines (*continued*)

is generally available in central bank publications, though details of draws and repayment terms are more limited and may be confidential.

Swap lines extended by China and India. Although initially done primarily between central banks of advanced economies, BCSLs have recently become common for other large economies like China and India to promote trade and regional cooperation. The People's Bank of China established its first BCSL in 2008 and since then has concluded over 40 agreements with high-income economies and low- and middle-income countries worldwide. Currently, 31 of those agreements are active. In 2022 and 2023, the People's Bank of China converted its BCSL with Hong Kong SAR, China, to a long-standing arrangement, signed a BCSL with Saudi Arabia, and renewed agreements it had with the European Central Bank, Indonesia, Singapore, and the United Arab Emirates. The total amount available on China's BCSLs was about ¥4.16 trillion (US$586 billion) at end-2023, but the amount drawn was much smaller, ¥114.9 billion (US$16 billion), or less than 3 percent of the amount available (PBOC 2024). Low- and middle-income countries with draws on their BCSLs with China at end-2023 included Mongolia and Pakistan.

The Reserve Bank of India (RBI) offers BCSLs to its neighbors under the South Asian Association for Regional Cooperation currency swap facility. This facility was implemented in 2012 to help meet the region's short-term foreign exchange liquidity and balance of payments needs.[c] RBI's BCSLs usually have a three-year term, and RBI can offer swaps in euros, Indian rupees, and US dollars. Bhutan, the Maldives, and Sri Lanka have used the facility and established swap lines with RBI and have drawn on those swap lines at various dates between 2012 and 2023, including during the COVID-19 pandemic. The BCSLs in place in 2023 were Bhutan and the Maldives, each equivalent to US$200 million, and Sri Lanka, equivalent to US$400 million. At end-2023, the BCSLs for Bhutan and Sri Lanka were fully drawn.

a. This definition is consistent with accounting for an International Monetary Fund Flexible Credit Line in Balance of Payments statistics.
b. This practice is consistent with IMF (2018) and IMF (2022).
c. All countries in the South Asia region are members of the South Asian Association for Regional Cooperation.

China, the largest borrower among LMICs, accounting for 27.4 percent of the combined end-2023 debt stock of LMICs, offset the rising debt stock trend (figure 1.2). Albeit at a slower pace, China's total debt stock position fell for the second year in a row in 2023, decreasing 1.1 percent to US$2.4 trillion. China's short-term debt stock as a share of total debt stock is the highest among LMICs,

Figure 1.2 **External Debt Stock of Low- and Middle-Income Countries, 2013–23**

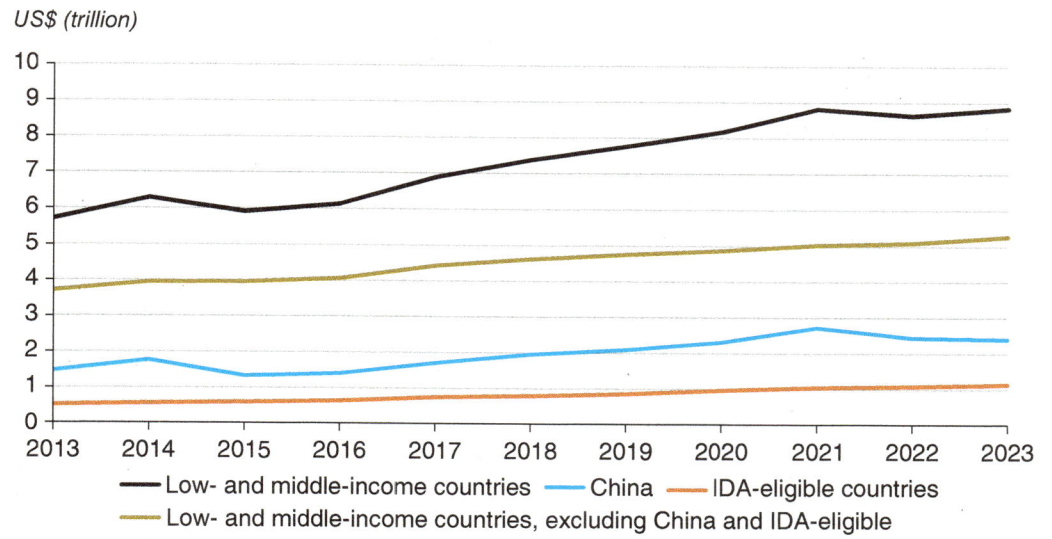

US$ (trillion)

Source: World Bank International Debt Statistics database.
Note: IDA = International Development Association.

at 53.2 percent, rendering its economy almost equally affected by fluctuations in short- and long-term debt stock. In 2023, China's short-term debt stock bounced back and increased 1.8 percent to US$1.3 trillion, whereas long-term debt stock decreased for the second year in a row, falling 4.2 percent to US$1.1 trillion. The contraction in long-term debt was attributable to an 8.1 percent decrease in borrowing from the private nonguaranteed (PNG) sector of the economy, to US$616.2 billion in 2023. PNG debt from bondholders decreased 10.9 percent to US$268.0 billion, and PNG debt from commercial banks and other private creditors decreased 5.8 percent to US$348.2 billion. Along with the decreasing debt stock position, economic growth in China has slowed over the past two years, mostly driven by a slowdown in the real estate sector.

The total debt stock of LMICs excluding China increased at a faster pace of 3.8 percent, to US$6.4 trillion in 2023. For this group of countries, short-term debt stock increased for the third year in a row, by 5.5 percent to US$1.1 trillion, highlighting the procyclical nature of these obligations because they have remained positive since the outflow experienced in 2020. Excluding a slight 0.3 percent decrease in 2022, long-term debt stock has been on an upward trajectory since 2006. In 2023, it increased 3.5 percent to US$5.4 trillion because of an increase in long-term public and publicly guaranteed (PPG) debt stock of 4.0 percent to US$3.3 trillion and an increase in PNG debt stock of 2.5 percent to US$2.0 trillion (figure 1.3).

Figure 1.3 Creditor Composition of Low- and Middle-Income Countries' (excluding China) Long-Term Public and Publicly Guaranteed External Debt, 2013–23

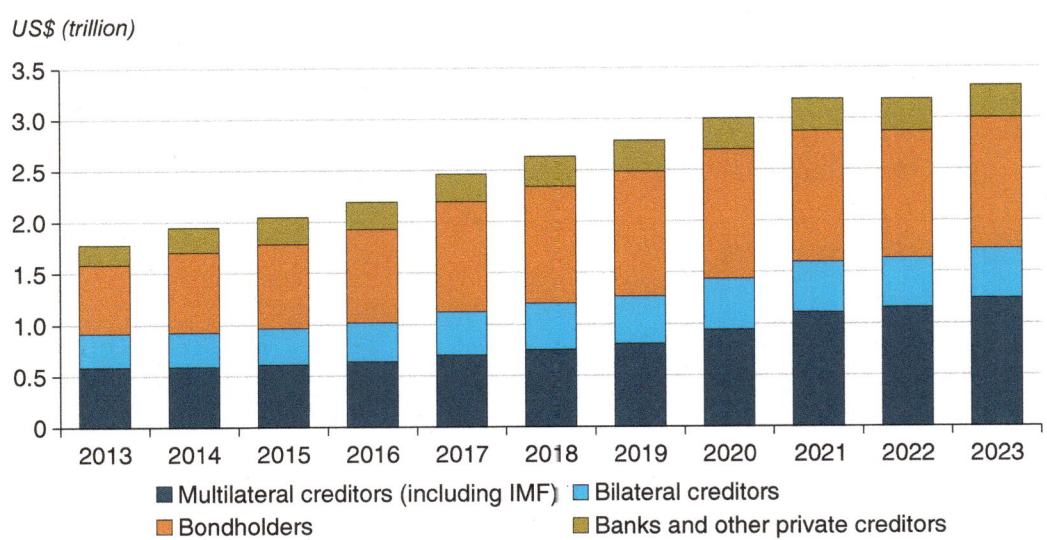

US$ (trillion)

Multilateral creditors (including IMF) ■ Bilateral creditors
Bondholders ■ Banks and other private creditors

Source: World Bank International Debt Statistics database.
Note: IMF = International Monetary Fund.

From the creditor perspective, the rise in PPG debt stock was driven by a 7.3 percent increase in multilateral debt, which underscores the role of multilateral organizations in supporting countries during periods of uncertainty and debt restructuring operations through the provision of net positive flows. Consequently, the share of multilateral debt stock (compared to total debt stock) for LMICs excluding China has increased steadily, from an average of 13.7 percent during the 2013–19 period before the pandemic to 19.3 percent in 2023.

Historically, LMICs excluding China have relied on financing from the five largest traditional multilateral institutions: the International Monetary Fund (IMF), which accounts for a 26.9 percent share of total multilateral debt stock in 2023, the World Bank (accounting for 34.0 percent: 18.1 percent for International Bank for Reconstruction and Development [IBRD] and 15.9 percent for International Development Association [IDA]), the Asian Development Bank (10.3 percent), the Inter-American Development Bank (7.9 percent), and the African Development Bank (3.7 percent). Of the multilateral institutions that lend to LMICs, the Asian Infrastructure Investment Bank (recently founded in 2016), the European Union, and the African Export-Import Bank have scaled up their cumulative financing the most rapidly over the last five years.

The World Bank has increasingly stepped up its role as a multilateral creditor and has performed the role of lender of last resort, compensating for declines in financing from the private sector. International institutions have a long and established history of official lending during periods of economic crises in countries. Through its concessional lending window, the World Bank's IDA has been supporting countries facing higher risk of debt distress by providing ex post but also implicit ex ante debt relief and financial support. Most IDA credits carry a zero or very low interest rate, and repayments typically extend over 30–50 years; however, more than one-third of IDA-eligible countries receive all or part of their IDA resources in the form of grants that carry no repayments in the future. Whereas IDA focuses on the most impoverished nations, the World Bank's other lending arm, IBRD, has played a crucial role in coordinating responses to regional and global challenges by providing loans and financial services to middle-income and creditworthy low-income countries (figure 1.4). IBRD was created to support countries rebuilding after World War II and has continued its crisis and emergency support through increased lending to countries affected by other crises since then, including the 2008–09 financial crisis, the 2014 Ebola outbreak, and the COVID-19 pandemic. Since inception, IBRD and IDA lending has responded positively to adverse external shocks affecting the economies of countries eligible for such financing, and this countercyclical lending has been a recurring and stabilizing response to dramatic drops in economic growth in these economies over the years.

Figure 1.4 GNI Growth versus New World Bank Commitments as a Share of GNI, Low- and Middle-Income Countries, 1971–2023

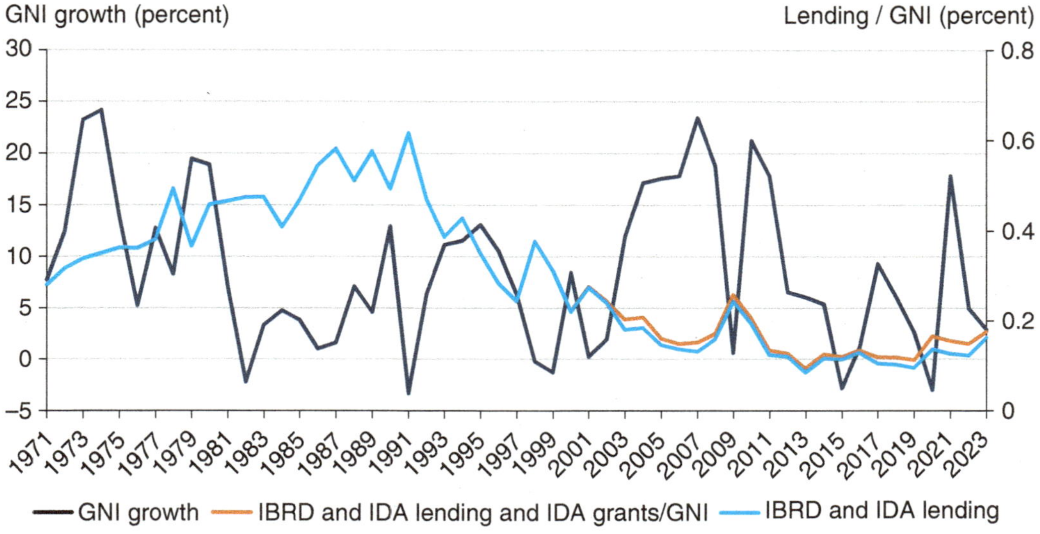

Source: World Bank International Debt Statistics database.
Note: GNI = gross national income; IBRD = International Bank for Reconstruction and Development; IDA = International Development Association

The World Bank is actively pursuing strategies to scale up its lending capacity while maintaining its AAA credit rating through capital optimization. These strategies include several distinct efforts: (a) increasing the power of guarantees that World Bank shareholders can provide to boost lending, which will mobilize larger amounts of financing with lower risk exposure and more favorable terms, allowing for a broader reach in critical areas such as education, agriculture, and health; (b) raising hybrid capital from shareholders and other development partners, which allows investment in bonds with special leveraging potential, where every dollar of hybrid capital can amplify lending capacity sixfold over 10 years; (c) extracting more value from callable capital by widening the terms and conditions under which the World Bank can call on shareholders; and (d) moving forward with the IDA Crisis Facility, which will provide concessional finance for IDA-eligible countries in times of crisis and ensure that vital resources are available when most needed (refer to box 1.3 for a discussion of the IMF and World Bank instruments and joint efforts to assist with crises).

Box 1.3 IMF and World Bank Efforts to Assist with Crises

In light of global crises, the International Monetary Fund (IMF) and the World Bank have engaged in the following recent joint efforts to assist countries in their response:

- *Global Sovereign Debt Roundtable.* Co-chaired by the Group of Twenty, the IMF, and the World Bank, this group includes official bilateral creditors (both traditional creditor members of the Paris Club and new creditors), private creditors, and borrowing countries. It aims to build greater common understanding among key stakeholders on debt sustainability and debt restructuring challenges, and ways to address them, focusing on technical matters like restructuring timelines, information sharing, domestic debt treatment (including holdings by nonresidents), assessing comparability of treatment, engaging with credit rating agencies, and suspending debt service.

- *Joint IMF/World Bank Statement.* In September 2023, the IMF managing director and the World Bank president issued a joint statement on deepening their partnership to help resolve global crises. Among other commitments on climate and digital transition, the two institutions will enhance support for debt management and transparency, revise the Low-Income Countries Debt Sustainability Framework, and improve the Common Framework.

- *Enhanced Cooperation Framework for Climate Action.* Through the Resilience and Sustainability Facility, the IMF and the World Bank will support countries in advancing their climate change efforts by aiding policy reforms, offering technical assistance and financing, and helping to mobilize additional climate finance via country-led platforms. Madagascar is the first country to benefit from this framework.

(Box continues on next page)

Box 1.3 IMF and World Bank Efforts to Assist with Crises (*continued*)

These new initiatives build on longstanding efforts, including the IMF–World Bank multipronged approach to address debt vulnerabilities (IMF 2020), the Heavily Indebted Poor Countries and Multilateral Debt Relief initiatives,[a] and the Debt Service Suspension Initiative/Common Framework (World Bank Group and IMF 2021).

Each institution also offers its own resources to assist countries.

World Bank. The new Expanded Crisis Preparedness and Response Toolkit aims to better support countries navigating future crises. It features the Rapid Response Option, which enables countries to quickly repurpose unused World Bank financing for emergency needs. The toolkit also offers greater flexibility for countries to secure contingent resources for future crises and provides faster access to new financing during disasters. Countries can now feature catastrophe bonds, insurance, and other risk management products, allowing access to needed funding without incurring additional debt. Last, Climate Resilient Debt Clauses now allow small states to pause debt repayments on existing loans during crises, enabling them to focus on recovery efforts.

This new initiative is the latest in the World Bank's ongoing efforts to help borrowers tackle development and financial challenges during crises. Other instruments include the following:

- *Crisis Response Window.* Established in 2011, it provides International Development Association (IDA) countries with additional resources for severe natural disasters, public health emergencies, economic crises, and food insecurity.

- *Private Sector Window.* Launched in 2017, it combines IDA resources with International Finance Corporation/Multilateral Investment Guarantee Agency support to attract sustainable private sector investment in IDA and fragile and conflict-affected situation countries through four facilities: the Blended Finance Facility, the Local Currency Facility, the Risk Mitigation Facility, and the Multilateral Investment Guarantee Agency Guarantee Facility.

Additionally, the World Bank has offered the Disaster Risk Financing and Insurance program to reduce disaster costs and Development Policy Loans with Catastrophic Drawdown Options for both International Bank for Reconstruction and Development and IDA countries under varying terms.

IMF. The new Food Shock Window under the Rapid Credit Facility and Rapid Financing Instrument provides extra emergency funding for countries with urgent balance of payments needs due to food insecurities, cereal export disruptions, and/or rising food import costs. Access is capped at 50 percent of quota, in addition

(Box continues on next page)

Box 1.3 IMF and World Bank Efforts to Assist with Crises (*continued*)

to current Rapid Credit Facility and Rapid Financing Instrument limits. Beneficiaries include Burkina Faso, Guinea, Haiti, Malawi, South Sudan, and Ukraine.

The IMF's new lending arm, the Resilience and Sustainability Trust, offers long-term support for climate change, pandemic preparedness, and other sustainability issues. Loans feature a 20-year maturity, a grace period of 10.5 years, and an interest rate with a modest margin over the three-month special drawing rights rate. The most favorable terms are given to the poorest countries through a tiered interest structure. This initiative builds on established IMF efforts, such as the Catastrophe Containment and Relief Trust, established in 2015 to offer debt relief to the poorest nations affected by severe natural or public health disasters.

a. IMF, "Debt Relief under the Heavily Indebted Poor Countries (HIPC) Initiative," https://www.imf.org/en/About/Factsheets/Sheets/2023/Debt-relief-under-the-heavily -indebted-poor-countries-initiative-HIPC.

Apart from debt stock owed to multilateral creditors, increases were recorded in the PPG debt stock owed to bilateral creditors and private creditors for LMICs excluding China. PPG debt stock owed to bilateral creditors increased 1.6 percent to US$486.9 billion in 2023, rebounding after decreasing for the past two years. PPG debt stock owed to private creditors including bondholders, commercial banks, and other private creditors also rebounded in 2023, increasing 2.4 percent to US$1.6 trillion. In 2023, PPG bond financing showed signs of recovery, increasing 2.8 percent to US$1.3 trillion, and PPG financing from commercial banks and other private creditors increased 0.6 percent to US$314.0 billion.

The 2023 recovery in PPG debt stock was not fully matched in the PNG sector economy for this group of countries, where the PNG debt stock owed to commercial banks and other private creditors recorded an increase of 4.0 percent, to US$1.8 trillion, but PNG debt stock owed to bondholders decreased for the second year in a row by 6.2 percent, to US$271 billion. The decrease indicates that—despite signs of recovery in the PPG sector—overall tight financing market conditions, constrained supply from international capital markets, and elevated credit risks persist and reflect a decrease in investor confidence. Countries that have historically relied on these flows for new or existing financing needs will continue to face difficulties and vulnerabilities if this trend continues. The recovery of bond financing has been slow because of a deterioration in credit ratings for some LMIC borrowers, which prevented these borrowers from accessing the market. In addition, amid high global interest rates, some creditworthy borrowers have postponed borrowing via new bond issuances in order to avoid paying higher spreads than they have contracted in the past.

In 2023, the rise in debt stock of the world's poorest countries—those eligible for IDA concessional financing (designated as IDA-eligible countries)—outpaced the rise in other LMICs. It increased by 4.8 percent to an all-time high of US$1.1 trillion. The combined debt stock of IDA-eligible countries has been on an uninterrupted upward trend since 2007, yet gross national income was stagnant in 2023, raising concerns about debt vulnerability and sustainability for this group of countries. Long-term debt stock increased 6.4 percent to US$1.0 trillion, composed of the PPG portion, which increased 6.6 percent to US$780.3 billion, and the PNG component, which increased 5.9 percent to US$246.7 billion. The increase in long-term debt was offset by the decrease in the short-term stock, which contracted 7.9 percent to US$109.3 billion in 2023. Multilateral creditors played an even more pronounced and important role for this group of countries: multilateral debt stock increased 10.1 percent to US$400.8 billion in 2023 (figure 1.5). Reliance on multilateral institutions continued to increase in 2023, and the ratio of multilateral debt to long-term debt stock rose from 37.7 percent in 2022 to 39.0 percent in 2023. Debt owed to the World Bank (IBRD and IDA) increased 12 percent to an all-time high of US$170.8 billion in 2023, more than twice the comparable figure of a decade ago. Despite the increase, the World Bank share of multilateral debt stock, 42.6 percent in 2023, was slightly below the 44.5 percent decade average.

Figure 1.5 Creditor Composition of IDA-Eligible Countries' Long-Term Public and Publicly Guaranteed External Debt during Crises, 2006–23

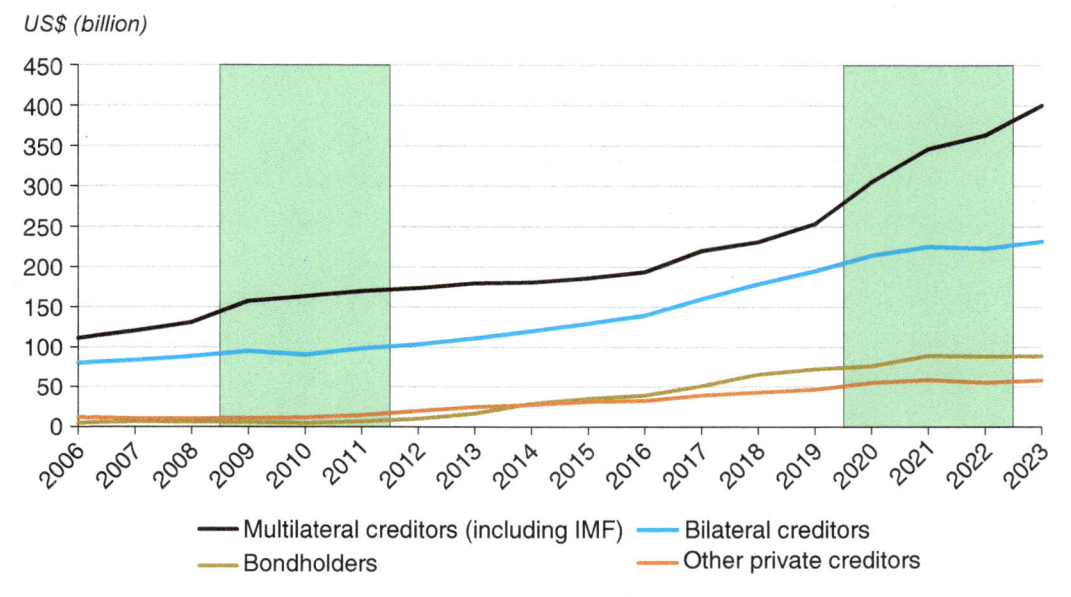

US$ (billion)

Source: World Bank International Debt Statistics database.
Note: Shaded green areas indicate periods of crises. IDA = International Development Association; IMF = International Monetary Fund.

Debt Ratios and Debt Resolutions

Despite economic uncertainty, inflation worries, and high interest rates, economic growth among LMICs as measured by gross national income (GNI) in nominal terms proved to be resilient in 2023. The debt-to-GNI ratio for LMICs excluding China remained steady (decreasing by only 0.8 percentage point) at 34.4 percent in 2023. The ratio has shown a declining trend since reaching a two-decade high of 41.8 percent in 2020. The steadiness in 2023 reflected an increase in the US dollar value of LMICs' combined GNI (not including China), which rose 6.3 percent to US$18.6 trillion, coupled with a 3.8 percent increase in debt stock.

Countries eligible for IDA assistance showed a different pattern. The debt-to-GNI ratio of IDA-eligible countries increased by 1.9 percentage points in 2023 to 40.6 percent, higher than the average 40.2 percent recorded in the aftermath of the pandemic in 2020–21 (figure 1.6). The increase in the ratio was attributable to the 4.8 percent increase in total debt stock to US$1.1 trillion, as GNI remained steady, rising just 0.1 percent to US$2.8 trillion in 2023. The most significant improvement in the ratio took place in low-income countries, all of which are eligible for IDA assistance. Similar to the wider group of IDA-eligible countries, the low-income group also saw the combined level of its debt stock increase 3.8 percent in 2023, to an all-time high of US$232.0 billion. Despite the increase in total debt stock, the debt-to-GNI ratio ameliorated for this group of countries, decreasing 7.9 percentage points to 37.3 percent. The improvement was the result of a record rise in the combined GNI of low-income countries, which increased 25.7 percent to US$621.3 billion, with Sudan, Ethiopia, and Niger leading the trend.

Middle-income countries (not including China), composed of a mix of countries having access to both IBRD and IDA resources, saw a slight improvement in their debt-to-GNI ratio in 2023, which decreased 0.7 percentage point to 34.3 percent. Overall, the surge in global debt accumulation has led to liquidity and sustainability issues in LMICs, resulting in elevated requests for debt repayment suspensions and debt rescheduling agreements, as the percent of IDA-eligible countries at high risk of debt distress or in debt distress has doubled since 2015 (box 1.4).

Figure 1.6 External Debt-to-GNI Ratios for Low- and Middle-Income Countries (excluding China) and IDA-Eligible Countries, 2013–23

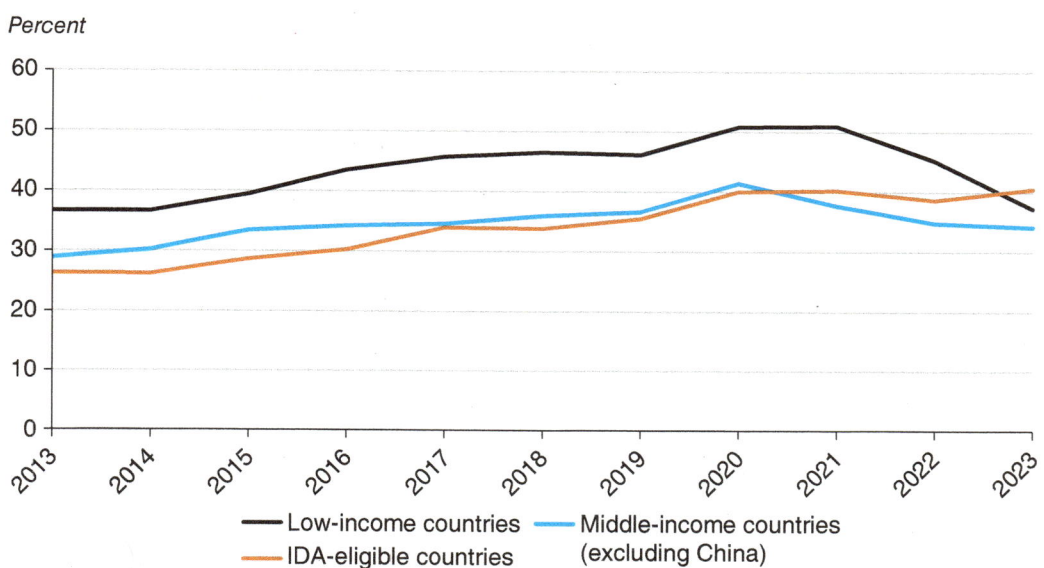

Percent

Low-income countries
Middle-income countries (excluding China)
IDA-eligible countries

Source: World Bank International Debt Statistics database.
Note: GNI = gross national income; IDA = International Development Association.

Box 1.4 Debt Resolutions in Low- and Middle-Income Countries

The surge in global debt accumulation has led to liquidity and sustainability issues in low- and middle-income countries, resulting in elevated requests for debt repayment suspensions and debt rescheduling agreements as the percent of countries eligible for International Development Association resources and at high risk of debt distress or in debt distress has doubled since 2015 (figure B1.4.1). Some progress has been made toward sovereign debt resolutions in the context of the Group of Twenty Common Framework, the Paris Club, and bondholders.[a] Within the Common Framework, Chad was the first country to conclude an agreement with its bilateral creditors in October 2022, and with private creditors including Glencore PLC shortly thereafter. In 2023, Zambia became the second country to conclude a debt restructuring agreement, reaching a milestone agreement with bilateral creditors, including China, to restructure US$6.3 billion. It reached a subsequent formal agreement with its sovereign bondholders in March 2024 on the restructuring of US$3 billion.

(Box continues on next page)

Box 1.4 Debt Resolutions in Low- and Middle-Income Countries (*continued*)

Figure B1.4.1 Evolution of the Risk of External Debt Distress

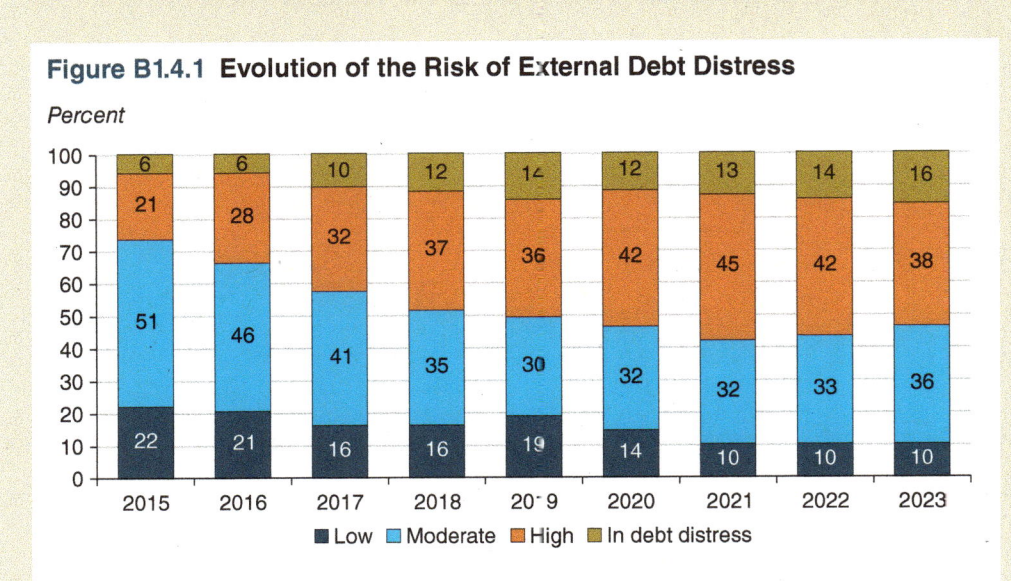

Percent

	Low	Moderate	High	In debt distress
2015	22	51	21	6
2016	21	46	28	6
2017	16	41	32	10
2018	16	35	37	12
2019	19	30	36	14
2020	14	32	42	12
2021	10	32	45	13
2022	10	33	42	14
2023	10	36	38	16

Source: World Bank–International Monetary Fund, Low-Income Countries Debt Sustainability Analysis database.

Ethiopia and Ghana also achieved progress under the Common Framework. In November 2023, Ethiopia reached a temporary debt service suspension agreement with its official bilateral creditors and is currently in the process of negotiating with its bondholders to restructure its sole sovereign bond maturing in 2024, worth US$1 billion. In early December 2022, the government of Ghana launched the first stage of the Domestic Debt Exchange Program, a voluntary approach designed to reduce debt servicing costs and extend the maturity of domestic bonds. It completed the first stage in February 2024 and extended the program into a second phase to include Cocobills issued by Cocobod, US-denominated domestic debt, pension funds' holdings of government bonds, and nonmarketable debt held by the Bank of Ghana (IMF 2024). In June 2024, Ghana signed an agreement with its official creditors to restructure US$5.4 billion, and it has also reached a preliminary agreement in principle to restructure US$13 billion in obligations owed to its international bondholders.

With regard to the Paris Club, Sri Lanka sealed a debt restructuring agreement with its official creditors in June 2024 through the Official Creditor Committee and a separate bilateral agreement with China, in an effort to restore debt sustainability. In July 2023, the Sri Lankan government approved a domestic debt restructuring plan that will convert treasury bills and provisional advances into longer maturity treasury bonds, the superannuation funds' holdings of treasury bonds into longer-term maturities, and commercial banks' selected local law foreign currency–

(Box continues on next page)

> ### Box 1.4 Debt Resolutions in Low- and Middle-Income Countries (*continued*)
>
> denominated claims on the government into rupee debt instruments (IMF 2023). The authorities are also in the process of reaching an agreement to restructure US$12.5 billion owed to international bondholders.
>
> In December 2023, Somalia reached Completion Point under the enhanced Heavily Indebted Poor Countries Initiative. The achievement of this milestone reduces the country's external debt to sustainable levels and allows Somalia to reenter international markets and regain access to new external financing. Suriname also finalized an agreement with its bondholders in November 2023 to reschedule its two outstanding dollar-denominated bonds to a new US$650 million 10-year amortizing bond, with an additional US$10 million issued to cover fees and expenses of the bondholder committee. In September 2024, Ukraine became the latest country to successfully reach an agreement with its bondholders to restructure US$20 billion in international bonds. The agreement follows the two-year bond moratorium agreed upon in 2022.
>
> a. This information is current through September 15, 2024.

The World Bank uses GNI for operational purposes because GNI includes net income received from abroad, unlike the gross domestic product measure, which counts only income received from domestic sources. Member countries' relative poverty is measured in relation to GNI per capita, and this measure underpins the annual income classification published by the IBRD and IDA operational cutoff (US$1,335 per capita for fiscal year 2025) and the IBRD and IDA lending terms (interest rate and maturity) for specified borrowers (box 1.5).

The ratio of debt stock to export earnings deteriorated in 2023, increasing 4.7 percentage points to 116.9 percent for LMICs excluding China. After rebounding from the pandemic and reaching an all-time high in 2022, export earnings from goods, services, and primary income remained steady in 2023 (decreasing just 0.4 percent) at US$5.5 trillion for this group of countries, whereas debt stock increased 3.8 percent to US$6.4 trillion. In 2023, these earnings remained steady despite the negative effects of geopolitical tensions, trade fragmentation, and ever-changing regulatory environments. IDA-eligible countries also saw a deterioration of their debt stock-to-export ratio, which increased 6.6 percentage points, to 190.2 percent. This deterioration was the result of the 4.8 percent increase in debt stock obligations in 2023, which outpaced the 1.2 percent increase in export earnings, to US$597.5 billion.

Box 1.5 World Bank Income and Lending Classifications Used in *International Debt Report 2024*

The World Bank classifies economies by income level for analytical purposes (to broadly group countries by level of development) and operational purposes (to determine their Financial Terms and Conditions of Bank Financing). This report presents data for 119 low- and middle-income countries and Guyana (the only high-income country eligible for International Development Association [IDA] resources) reporting to the World Bank Debtor Reporting System. Twenty-four of these countries are classified as low-income, with per capita income of US$1,145 or below; 95 countries are classified as middle-income, with per capita income greater than US$1,145 and less than US$14,005; and one country, Guyana, is classified as high-income, with per capita income of US$14,006 or more.[a]

Income classifications are updated annually at the start of the World Bank fiscal year (July 1) on the basis of gross national income per capita for the previous year. This year Bulgaria and the Russian Federation were reclassified from middle-income to high-income. Gross national income is expressed in US dollars and determined by conversion factors derived according to the Atlas methodology.[b] Forty-eight of the middle-income countries covered in this report are eligible only for nonconcessional loans from the International Bank for Reconstruction and Development (IBRD), and are referred to as IBRD-only countries. The remaining 24 low-income and 47 middle-income countries, and Guyana, reporting to the Debtor Reporting System are either (a) eligible only for concessional lending from IDA and referred to as IDA-only countries; or (b) eligible for a mix of IBRD and IDA lending and referred to as "blend" countries. Together, IDA-only and IBRD-IDA blend countries are referred to as IDA-eligible countries. Figure B1.5.1 shows the distribution of the 119 low- and middle-income countries and Guyana included in *International Debt Report 2024* by income and lending groups. IDA countries receiving their IDA resources only on grant terms, which carry no repayments at all, are not part of the Debtor Reporting System. A comprehensive list of each country's income and lending classifications appears in the appendix of this report under "Country Groups."

(Box continues on next page)

> **Box 1.5** World Bank Income and Lending Classifications Used in *International Debt Report 2024 (continued)*
>
> **Figure B1.5.1** Number of Low- and Middle-Income Countries Covered in *International Debt Report 2024,* by FY2025 Income and Lending Group
>
>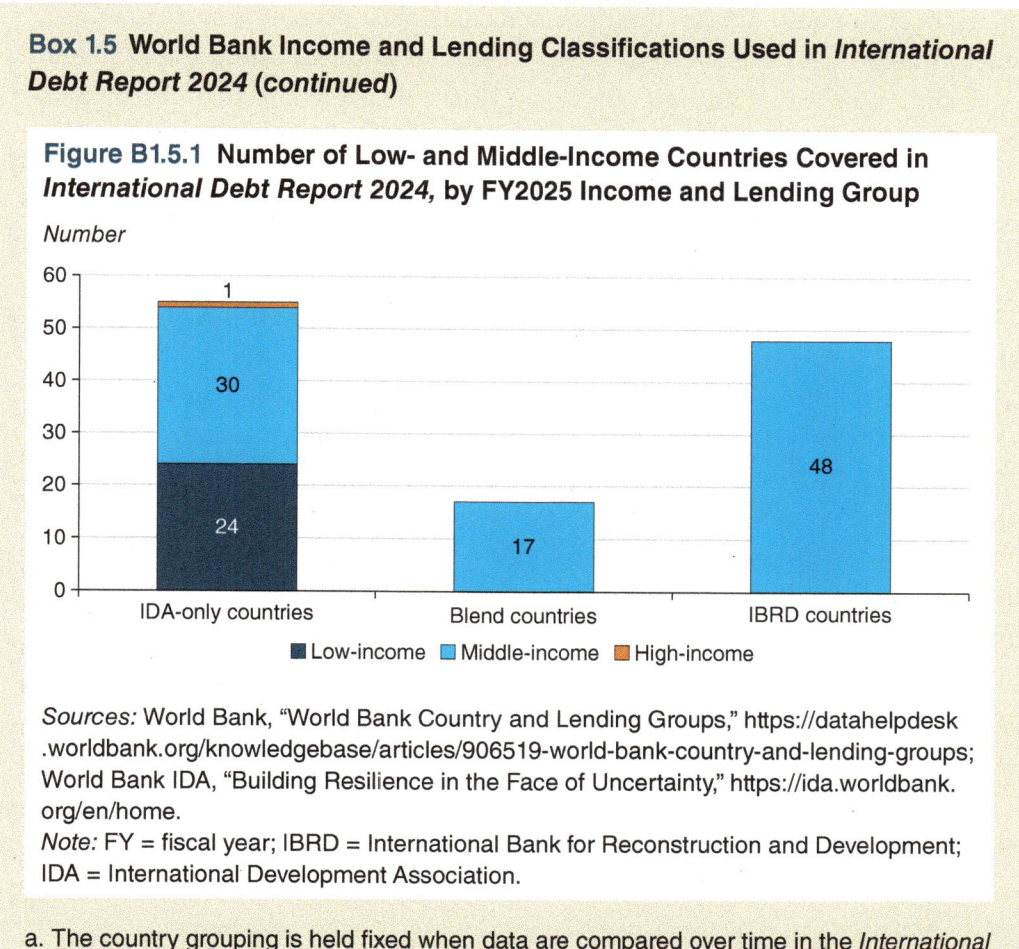
>
> *Sources:* World Bank, "World Bank Country and Lending Groups," https://datahelpdesk .worldbank.org/knowledgebase/articles/906519-world-bank-country-and-lending-groups; World Bank IDA, "Building Resilience in the Face of Uncertainty," https://ida.worldbank. org/en/home.
> *Note:* FY = fiscal year; IBRD = International Bank for Reconstruction and Development; IDA = International Development Association.
>
> a. The country grouping is held fixed when data are compared over time in the *International Debt Report.* For example, the aggregate for low-income countries from 2010 to 2023 consists of the same group of countries that are classified as low-income countries according to the latest World Bank income classification as of end-2023.
> b. For more information on the Atlas methodology, refer to World Bank, "The World Bank Atlas Method—Detailed Methodology," https://datahelpdesk.worldbank.org /knowledgebase/articles/378832-what-is-the-world-bank-atlas-method.

Unlike the wider IDA-eligible group, low-income countries experienced an improvement in their debt stock-to-export ratio, which decreased 2.8 percentage points to 203.2 percent in 2023. Export earnings for this group of countries increased 5.2 percent, to US$114.2 billion, outpacing the 3.8 precent increase to US$232.0 billion in debt stock. However, middle-income countries (excluding China) recorded a 5-percentage-point increase in their debt stock-to-export ratio, to 115 percent in 2023, exacerbated by steadiness in 2023 export earnings, which decreased slightly by 0.5 percent. For this group of countries, Samoa, the Kyrgyz Republic, and Tonga recorded the largest decreases in their debt stock-to-export ratios, whereas Senegal, Ukraine, and Mauritius recorded the largest increases in 2023. Refer to box 1.4 for a discussion of debt resolutions in LMICs.

Debt Servicing Burdens of LMICs, 2013–23

Total debt servicing costs (principal plus interest payments) of LMICs reached an all-time high of US$1.4 trillion in 2023. For LMICs excluding China, debt servicing costs climbed to a record of US$971.1 billion in 2023, an increase of 19.7 percent over the previous year and almost double the amounts seen a decade ago. In 2023, LMICs faced historically challenging debt service burdens due to high debt levels, interest rates that hit a two-decade high, and depreciation of local currencies against a strong US dollar. The tightening of monetary policy in the United States in 2022 affected exchange rate movements and drove an increase in the value of the US dollar relative to other currencies, which persisted in 2023 and made repayment of non–local currency debt more costly for LMICs as their local currencies depreciated.

The increase in total debt service payments for this group of countries is a direct outcome of the rapid accumulation of external debt over the past decade. Apart from a slight reduction in 2020 due to the suspension of debt service payments from Debt Service Suspension Initiative agreements, debt service burdens were on an increasing trajectory until 2023. Looking at these payments' composition shows that principal repayments rose 12.9 percent to US$698.9 billion in 2023 and interest payments rose by a significant 41.7 percent to US$272.3 billion over the same period, with each number reflecting an all-time high. Although borrowing countries can monitor and measure the principal repayment amounts of a debt instrument according to preestablished repayment schedules set in debt contract agreements since the inception of the liability, the interest payment amounts for debt contracted at variable interest rates are dependent and greatly affected by fluctuations in global interest rates (figure 1.7). The low-interest rate regime that prevailed until 2021 kept interest costs relatively low; however, as interest rates were aggressively increased in 2022, and further in 2023 to tame inflation, interest payments of variable-rate contracted debt also increased. Variable-rate loans account for 57 percent of the long-term external debt stock of LMICs (excluding China) and 40 percent of that of IDA-eligible countries.

Figure 1.7 **Variable Interest Rates and Interest Payments on Long-Term Debt of Low- and Middle-Income Countries (excluding China), by Creditor Type, 2020–23**

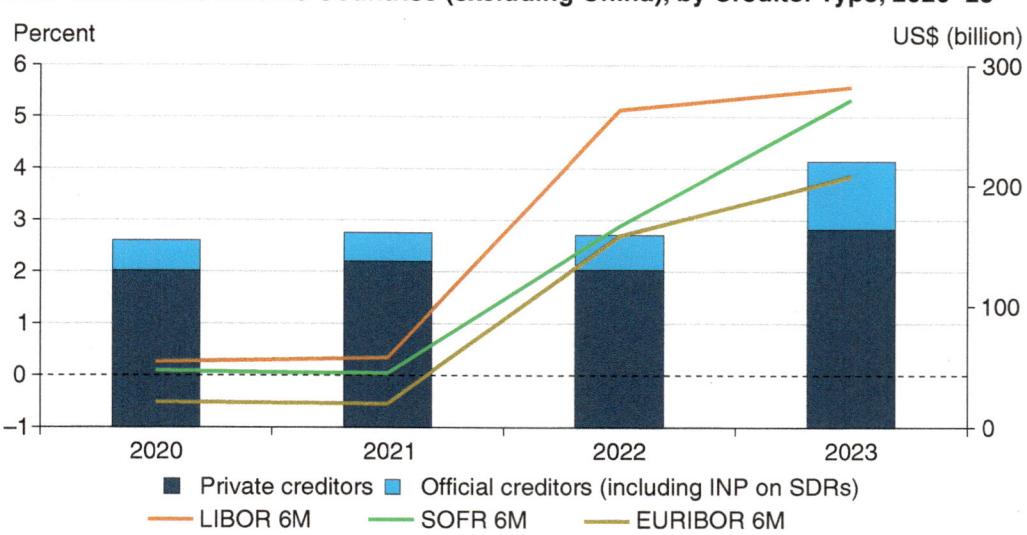

Source: World Bank International Debt Statistics database.
Note: EURIBOR 6M = 6-month Euro Interbank Offered Rate; INP = interest payment; LIBOR 6M = 6-month London Interbank Offered Rate; SDRs = special drawing rights; SOFR 6M = 6-month Secured Overnight Financing Rate.

High interest rates have affected not only the existing debt portfolio of LMICs but also new borrowing agreements, which are now being contracted at much higher rates. The lending terms of loans extended by official and private creditors in 2023 show a noticeable increase in average interest rate terms of new commitments offered by these two types of creditor groups (figure 1.8). The average interest rate of new commitments from official creditors increased 2.06 percentage points in 2023 to 4.09 percent. Historically, official creditors have extended loans that are more concessional in nature and have more generous terms than market loans, with lower interest rates and longer maturities. The average maturity of debt extended by official creditors has increased from 21 years in 2022 to 23 years in 2023, highlighting the concessional nature of these obligations. The average interest rate was much higher for lending extended by private creditors in 2023, increasing by 1.37 percentage points to 6.0 percent. Typically, the average terms extended by private creditors have higher interest rates and shorter maturities than those from official creditors because they offer a direct measure of the prevailing market financing conditions and risk pricing profiles. The average maturity of debt instruments offered from this creditor group also increased in 2023, from 10 to 13 years, though it remained 10 years shorter than the average maturity extended by official creditors.

Figure 1.8 Average Terms on New External Debt Commitments for Low- and Middle-Income Countries (excluding China), by Creditor Type, 2013–23

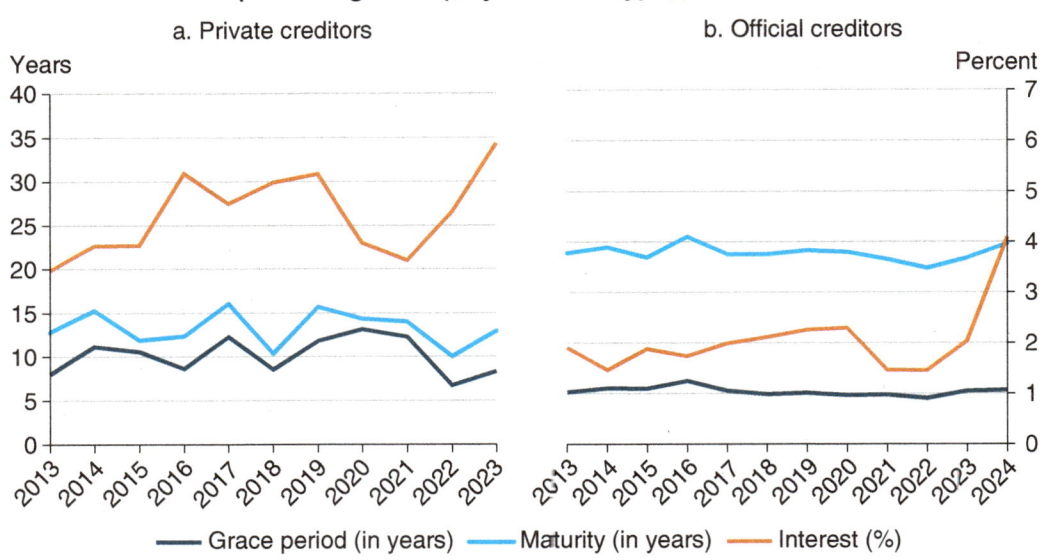

Source: World Bank International Debt Statistics database.

Interest payments on long-term PNG debt, expressed in nominal terms, increased 39.4 percent, to US$91.4 billion, and interest payments on long-term PPG debt increased 38.1 percent in 2023, to US$128.8 billion, for LMICs excluding China. These PPG payments include interest charges on allocations of IMF special drawing rights (SDRs; refer to box 1.6), which are presented on a gross basis according to the international definition of external debt, and do not net out the interest paid on holdings of the SDRs (that is, they do not subtract external assets in the form of debt instruments from gross external debt). The Debt Sustainability Assessment follows this methodology, and the distinction is important because the IMF SDR Department pays interest on holdings of SDRs and levies charges on the cumulative allocation of SDRs to IMF member countries at the same interest rate. Member countries whose holdings are below their cumulative holdings incur net charges. Excluding charges on allocations of SDRs, interest payments on long-term PPG debt of LMICs excluding China increased 34.0 percent to US$121.7 billion.

Excluding payments on allocations of SDRs, interest payments on PPG debt increased across all regions in 2023, reaching all-time highs in every region except Latin America and the Caribbean, whose interest payments were highest in 2019. This region recorded the highest volume of interest payments on PPG debt stock among all regions and saw a 29 percent increase in 2023, to US$46.3 billion, from the previous year (figure 1.9). Mexico and Brazil paid the highest PPG interest amounts in the region in 2023, at US$13.6 and US$9.7 billion, respectively. The South Asia region saw the biggest yearly increase in interest payments on PPG debt in 2023, rising 62 percent to US$12.5 billion. The increase was most noticeable in Bangladesh and India, whose interest payments increased by more than 90 percent in 2023; Pakistan made the second-largest interest payments in the region. Compared to a decade ago, the South Asia and Sub-Saharan Africa regions had the steepest increases, with interest payments increasing fourfold and threefold, respectively, in the 2013–23 period, a much faster pace than GNI and export revenue growth. LMICs' tightened fiscal space and high interest rates have put many countries in weak fiscal positions because of elevated payments.

> **Box 1.6 Allocation of the International Monetary Fund's Special Drawing Rights in 2023**
>
> In August 2021 the International Monetary Fund (IMF) made a general allocation of special drawing rights (SDRs) equivalent to US$650 billion. The newly created SDRs were credited to IMF members in proportion to their existing quotas in the Fund. The purpose was to help mitigate the economic crisis created by the COVID-19 pandemic and to meet the long-term need to supplement members' existing reserve assets in a manner that avoided economic stagnation and deflation as well as excess demand and inflation (IMF 2021b).
>
> SDR allocations do not change a country's net wealth but do create an increase in long-term debt liabilities and a corresponding increase in gross international reserves (holdings of SDRs). Both transactions are reflected in balance of payments statistics and international investment positions (IMF 2009). In government finance statistics, SDR allocations are recorded as a long-term debt liability within public sector gross debt, with a corresponding entry for SDR holdings as a part of the public sector's financial assets (IMF 2014). Following these guidelines, the International Debt Statistics database records SDR allocations as part of long-term gross external public debt and identifies them separately.
>
> SDR liabilities are not subject to debt limits in IMF programs because they do not fall within the definition of "debt" for program purposes under the Fund's Guidelines on Public Debt Conditionality in Fund Arrangements (IMF 2021a). SDR allocations are generally considered to have limited impact on debt sustainability, but that impact may depend on how they are used. New guidance issued in August 2021 on incorporating SDR allocations into debt sustainability analyses addresses this issue and aims to better reflect the use of SDRs and the impact on debt sustainability (IMF 2021a). In line with that guidance, the external debt stock figures in *International Debt Report 2024* (and related ratios to exports and gross national income) include SDR allocations. However, the measure of debt flows does not take SDR allocations into account.
>
> Total outstanding SDR allocations of the 119 low- and middle-income countries included in *International Debt Report 2024* were US$235.8 billion at end-2023,
>
> *(Box continues on next page)*

Box 1.6 Allocation of the International Monetary Fund's Special Drawing Rights in 2023 (*continued*)

equivalent on average to 3.7 percent of international reserves, but with sharp divergences at the regional level (figure B1.6.1).

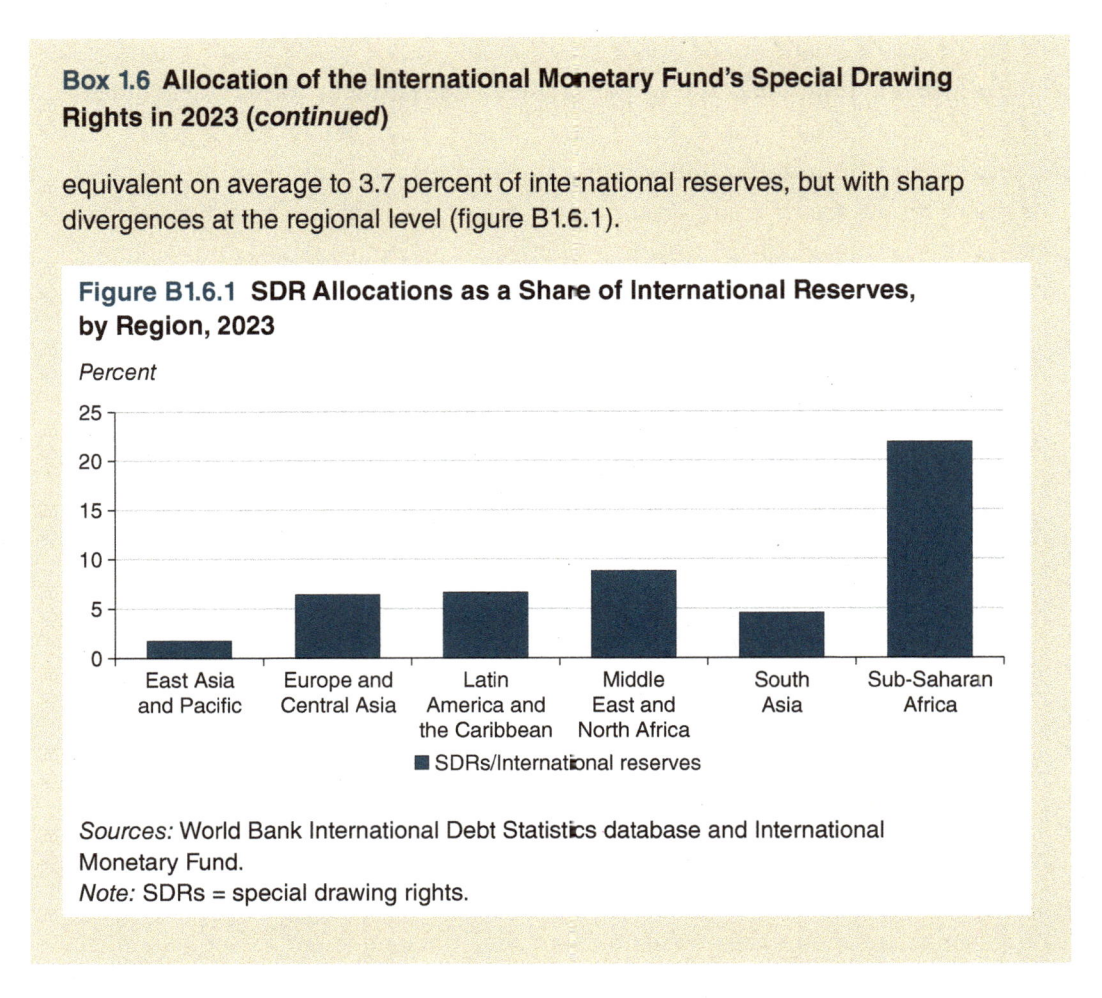

Figure B1.6.1 SDR Allocations as a Share of International Reserves, by Region, 2023

Percent

Sources: World Bank International Debt Statistics database and International Monetary Fund.
Note: SDRs = special drawing rights.

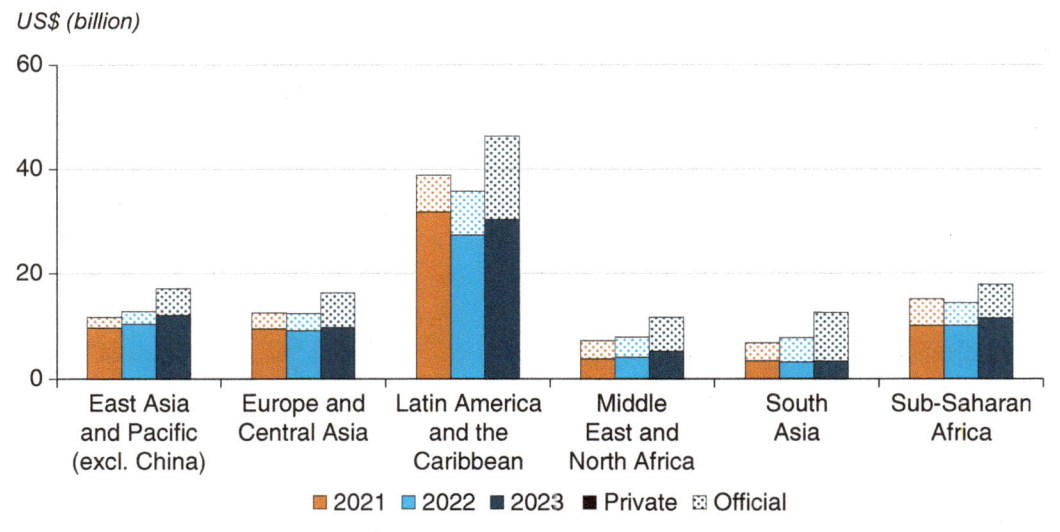

Figure 1.9 Interest Payments on Public and Publicly Guaranteed Debt of Low- and Middle-Income Countries, by Region and Creditor Type, 2013–23

US$ (billion)

Source: World Bank International Debt Statistics database.
Note: Excluding interest charges on special drawing right allocations.

For IDA-eligible countries, interest payments on total debt stock have tripled since 2013 to an all-time high of US$34.6 billion in 2023. Interest payments as a share of export earnings, a measure of the repayment capacity of a country, significantly increased by 1.6 percentage points in 2023 to 5.8 percent, equivalent to an increase last recorded in 2005. Mozambique (38.3 percent), Senegal (25.9 percent), Pakistan (13.6 percent), Kenya (12.8 percent), and Dominica (10.3 percent) had the highest ratios of interest payments on total debt to export earnings, a situation that has weakened their fiscal positions. Interest payments as a share of GNI also increased, but at a smaller pace, by 0.4 percentage point to 1.2 percent in 2023. When measured in terms of GNI, interest payments on total debt stock in 2023 were highest for Mozambique (19.6 percent), followed by Senegal (6.3 percent) and the Lao People's Democratic Republic (4.9 percent).

The composition of interest payments on external long-term debt stock, viewed from the borrower perspective, continued to shift in 2023, with the share of PNG interest payments increasing by 10 percentage points over the past two years to a 33 percent share in 2023 (to US$11.5 billion), and the PPG payments share decreasing by the same amount to a 54.6 percent share at US$18.9 billion (figure 1.10). Excluding charges on IMF credit and allocations of SDRs, interest

Figure 1.10 IDA-Eligible Countries' Interest Payments on External Debt, by Creditor Type, 2013–23

US$ (billion)

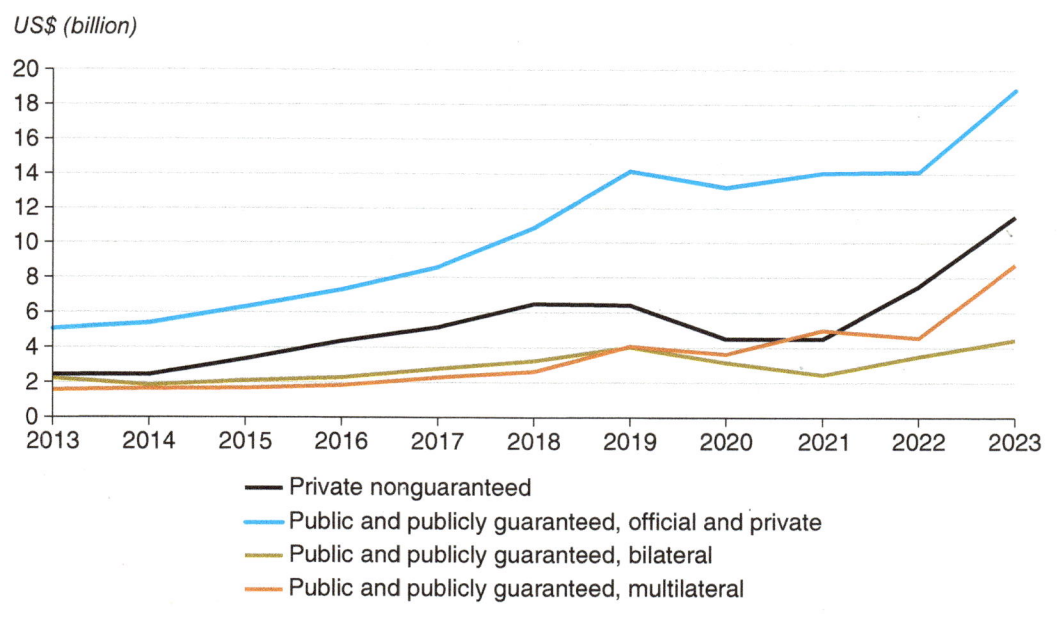

— Private nonguaranteed
— Public and publicly guaranteed, official and private
— Public and publicly guaranteed, bilateral
— Public and publicly guaranteed, multilateral

Source: World Bank International Debt Statistics database.
Note: IDA = International Development Association.

payments on PPG debt stock increased 23.7 percent in 2023 to US$16.4 billion. Apart from the increase in payments made in 2023, IDA-eligible countries also faced higher average interest rates on new external PPG debt contracted in 2023. These countries have historically relied on sustainable and highly concessional financing because of their limited resources. In 2023, the average maturities of the financing extended by their official and private creditors were 24 and 10 years, respectively, and did not noticeably deviate from the decade-long averages of 25 and 11 years (figure 1.11). However, IDA-eligible countries saw a shortening of the average grace period extended from private creditors to 4 and 3 years in 2022 and 2023, much shorter than the decade average of 6.5 years. This shortening indicates that the terms of these loans have become less favorable, because extended grace periods contribute to a loan's overall concessionality. The average grace period extended by official creditors remained unchanged at 6 years. The average interest rate extended by official creditors increased 1.27 percentage points in 2023, to 3.15 percent, and the average interest rate extended by private creditors increased by a sizeable 2.07 percentage points to 6.91 percent. The increase in average interest rates negatively affects the growth prospects and repayment ability of a group of countries already facing multiple vulnerabilities, with current rates above the recorded decade averages of 2 percent for credit extended by official creditors and 5 percent for credit extended by private creditors.

Figure 1.11 **Average Terms of Commitments of External Public and Publicly Guaranteed Debt to IDA-Eligible Countries, by Creditor Type, Average 2013–23**

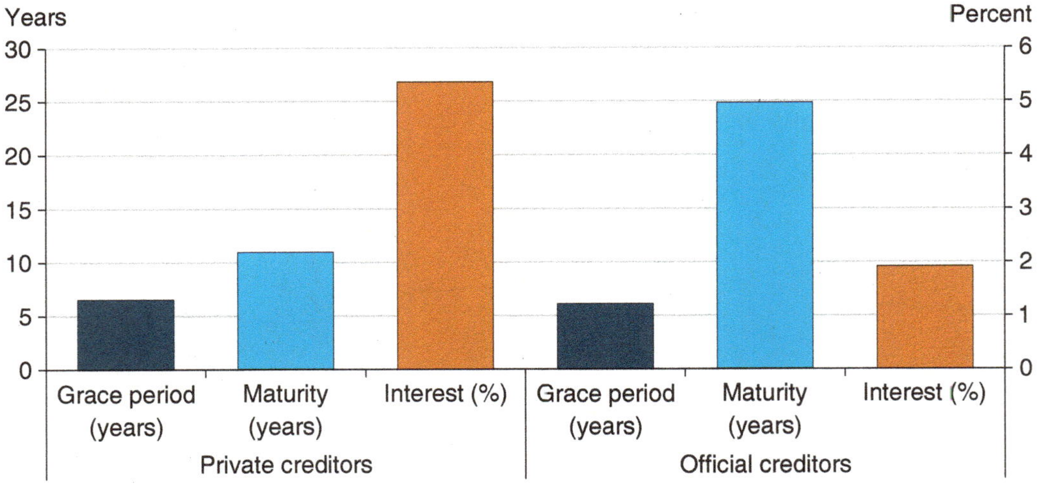

Source: World Bank International Debt Statistics database.
Note: IDA = International Development Association.

Trends in External Debt Flows, 2013–23

Net debt flows (disbursements minus principal repayments) to LMICs turned positive in 2023 to US$220.7 billion. The 2023 rebound reflected a more than fivefold increase over the 2022 level, but flows are still considerably lower than 2017–21 levels (figure 1.12). As LMICs continued to recover from the COVID-19 pandemic, the reversal in 2023 of net debt flows from negative to positive was driven largely by short-term debt, led by China's short-term debt inflows. Long-term debt flows benefited from a partial return of private creditor lending to PNG and PPG entities in LMICs.

The reversal of LMICs' net debt flows masks significant heterogeneity at the individual country, income, and regional levels. LMICs' debt inflows equaled US$220.7 billion in 2023, composed of US$71.1 billion in short-term and US$149.6 billion in long-term debt inflows. As a debtor group, these countries have inflows dominated by China's borrowing patterns, which recorded a reversal in short-term debt flows from a net outflow of US$181.0 billion in 2022 to a net inflow of US$22.2 billion in 2023, and persistent negative long-term net debt flows of US$40.6 billion. China's total net debt flows remained negative in 2023 at US$18.4 billion, despite recovering from the 2022 outflow lows of US$259.6 billion.

Figure 1.12 **Net Debt Inflows in Low- and Middle-Income Countries, by Maturity, 2013–23**

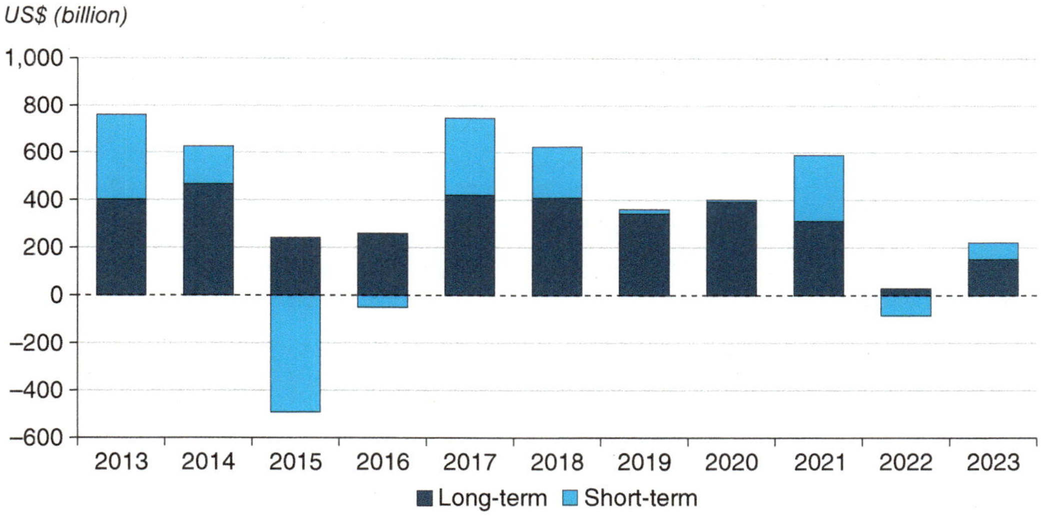

US$ (billion)

Source: World Bank International Debt Statistics database.

Excluding China, 4 of the top 10 LMIC borrowers recorded a reduction in their net debt flows in 2023. Thailand experienced net debt outflows in 2023 and a reversal from the 2022 inflows, at US$7.3 billion. Net debt inflows to Argentina and the Arab Republic of Egypt also fell sharply in 2023 but remained positive at US$916 million (US$9.7 billion in 2022) and US$5.1 billion (US$20.5 billion in 2022), respectively. Last, net debt inflows to Colombia decreased 12 percent to US$12.1 billion in 2023, the smallest decrease experienced by a top-10 borrower country. By contrast, the other 6 of the top 10 LMIC borrowers saw an increase in their net debt flows in 2023, with inflows to Ukraine increasing by more than fourfold the 2022 level, to US$28.3 billion, and those to India and Indonesia increasing by more than double to US$33.4 billion and US$13.1 billion, respectively. Inflows to Brazil and Mexico both increased by over 75 percent to US$30.6 billion and US$12.3 billion, respectively, while inflows to Türkiye increased by 25 percent to US$37.3 billion.

At the LMIC group level, when China is excluded, the rebound in total net debt inflows was even stronger, marking an increase of 16.3 percent, to US$239.1 billion, in 2023 when compared to the 7.6 percent decrease experienced in 2022. With China's exclusion, the driver of the increase and the maturity composition of the total net debt inflows change for the LMIC group. From a maturity standpoint, long-term net debt inflows increased 76.8 percent to US$190.2 billion, more than offsetting the fall in short-term net debt inflows, which decreased by half to US$48.9 billion in 2023. The increase in long-term debt inflows was heterogeneous because different creditor and debtor groups varied in their responses to the volatile international financial landscape. As a share, multilateral, commercial, and other private creditors' net debt inflows accounted for the biggest portion of long-term net debt inflows, each standing at 39 percent, whereas bilateral creditors and bondholders accounted for 7 percent and 15 percent, respectively.

Following the ongoing support provided at unprecedented levels since 2019, long-term net debt inflows from official creditors (composed of bilateral and multilateral creditors) remained positive but decreased by 6.6 percent to US$88.6 billion in 2023. Bilateral creditor net debt inflows increased 2.9 percent to US$13.7 billion, whereas net debt inflows from multilateral creditors decreased 8.1 percent to US$74.9 billion.

New disbursements from the two largest bilateral creditors lending to LMICs, China and Japan, slowed in 2023, decreasing by 2.1 and 11.3 percent, respectively, to US$10.7 billion and US$12.7 billion. Principal repayments to these two creditors also decreased: by 14.6 percent to US$13.2 billion paid to Chinese bilateral creditors and by 3.3 percent to US$6.0 billion paid to Japanese bilateral creditors. The decreases in both disbursements and principal payments caused net flows to Chinese bilateral creditors to improve but remain negative at US$2.5 billion in 2023, and net flows to Japanese bilateral creditors to decrease 17.3 percent to US$6.7 billion.

Net flows from the World Bank (IBRD and IDA lending), one of the two largest multilateral creditors lending to the LMICs group (excluding China), remained steady at US$28.2 billion, whereas net flows from the IMF turned negative, from an inflow of US$13.7 billion to an outflow of US$2.5 billion. For the World Bank, the 3.9 percent increase in new disbursements to US$46.7 billion offset a 12 percent increase in principal payments, which rose to US$18.4 billion. Net flows from the IMF turned negative in 2023 because of the 24.8 percent decrease in new disbursements to US$27.5 billion, and the 31.4 percent increase in principal repayments to US$30.0 billion. When Argentina, the dominant recipient and repayor of IMF funds since 2018, is excluded, net flows from the IMF still decreased by 64 percent but remained positive at US$2.6 billion. IMF repurchases for LMICs, excluding Argentina, more than doubled in 2023 to US$12.2 billion, with the top repurchases registered from Egypt, Ukraine, and Pakistan. IMF repurchases outpaced the increase in new lending, which rose 12.9 percent to US$14.8 billion in 2023, as new IMF lending has stabilized after the extraordinary support provided in 2020 during the aftermath of the COVID-19 pandemic.

Consequently, and irrespective of the classification type of the borrower entities, the increase in long-term net debt inflows can be attributed to the partial return of lending from private creditors, including bondholders, commercial banks, and other private creditors. After the reduced risk exposure displayed in 2022, private lending increased by almost eight times in 2023 to US$101.7 billion. Net debt flows from bondholders rebounded and turned positive to US$28.1 billion in 2023, and net debt inflows from commercial banks and other private creditors increased by 53 percent, to US$73.5 billion, indicating an increasing appetite among these creditors for LMIC debt.

Although the headline figures indicate an improvement in the confidence of private sector investors compared to 2022, the divergence in the components indicates only a partial rebound for private creditors lending to PPG entities, versus the PNG entities of LMIC economies (when China is excluded).

PPG borrowers' net debt flows to private creditors (composed of bondholders, commercial banks, and other private creditors) flipped from an outflow of US$7.1 billion in 2022 to an inflow of US$40.1 billion in 2023 (figure 1.13). The increase was completely attributable to the rise in net flows from bondholders, which turned positive in 2023 to US$42.1 billion, from an outflow of US$11.2 billion recorded in 2022. The reversal resulted from a combined

Figure 1.13 Long-Term External Debt Flows to Low- and Middle-Income Countries (excluding China), by Borrower Type, 2021–23

US$ (billion)

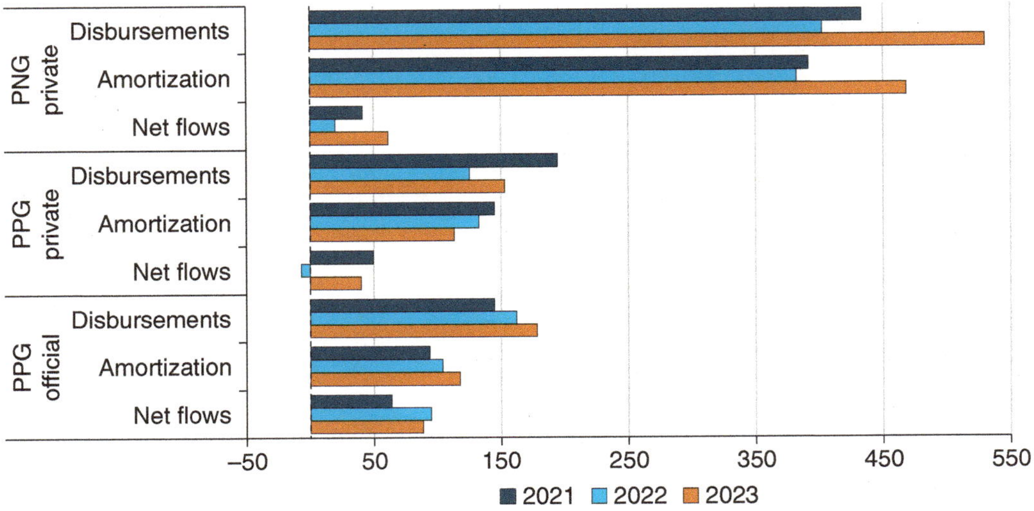

Source: World Bank International Debt Statistics database.
Note: PNG = private nonguaranteed; PPG = public and publicly guaranteed.

increase in new PPG bond issuances and a decrease in principal repayments to these creditors in 2023: new PPG bond issuances increased 42.7 percent to US$97.6 billion, whereas PPG bond repayments decreased 30.3 percent to US$55.5 billion. By contrast, net flows from commercial banks and other private creditors decreased 148 percent in 2023, turning from an inflow of US$4.1 billion in 2022 to an outflow of US$2.0 billion in 2023.

Brazil, Egypt, India, Indonesia, North Macedonia, and Türkiye were among the LMICs that issued new bonds in 2023 and set new milestones for their governments' commitments to sustainable policies. In 2023, Brazil debuted a US$2 billion sovereign sustainable bond, with its resources allocated evenly between environmental and social priorities. Egypt continued to diversify the type of debt instruments used in its portfolio and became the first country in the Middle East and North Africa region to issue a three-year Panda bond worth 3.5 billion yuan. Panda bonds are issued in the Chinese bond market by nonresidents of the economy and are denominated in Chinese renminbi. Egypt was the first country in the region to issue a green bond, in 2020, and to issue in Asia's capital markets. It accessed the Japanese bond market for a Samurai bond in 2022 worth 60 billion Japanese yen. In the Middle East and North Africa region, Morocco and Jordan also accessed the international bond market in 2023. Morocco issued a US$1.25 billion 5-year Eurobond and a US$1.25 billion 10.5-year Eurobond; Jordan issued a US$1.25 billion Eurobond in April 2023 and continued to tap international capital markets through the rest of the year.

In 2023, Indonesia issued its first sovereign blue bond in the Japanese capital market, worth 20.7 billion Japanese yen, in an effort to finance the protection and conservation of its blue economy and meet Sustainable Development Goals, and to diversify the instrument base used and widen the investor base. Türkiye also made its debut in 2023, issuing two of the country's first sovereign green bonds worth US$2.5 billion and US$715 million. The proceeds of the bonds will be used to support green infrastructure investment, boosting the commitment to sustainable financing and efforts to tackle climate challenges. In addition to issuing thematic bonds, LMICs have taken further steps to establish governance frameworks to support their sustainable finance strategy and objectives. The government of India established the sovereign green bond program with support from the World Bank's Sustainable Finance and Environmental, Social, Governance Advisory Services in the form of technical assistance and expertise to mobilize private capital (Hussain and Dill 2023). In July 2023, Thailand introduced Thailand Taxonomy, a classification system that adopts the traffic light approach to classify activities according to their environmental objectives. Refer to box 1.7 for a detailed discussion of debt-for-climate swap agreements, which represent another innovative financial instrument being used to support environmental sustainability.

Concurrently, PNG borrowers (excluding China) from private sector entities saw a threefold increase in net debt inflows in 2023, to US$61.5 billion. When compared to PPG borrowers, the contribution of the components was reversed: for PNG borrowers, the rise in net flows to private creditors was due to increased net flows from commercial banks and other private creditors, which increased 71.7 percent to US$75.5 billion, whereas net flows from bondholders increased in 2023 but remained negative for a second consecutive year, improving from an outflow of US$24.0 billion in 2022 to an outflow of US$14.0 billion in 2023 (figure 1.14) Despite the positive impact of a 25.1 percent decrease in principal repayments, to US$40.5 billion in 2023, net flows remained negative as new bond issuance from PNG bonds decreased 11.8 percent, to US$26.5 billion. The decrease in new issuance indicates that, although investor confidence in public sector entities improved in 2023 for this type of private creditor, the same was not the case for private sector borrowers that do not benefit from the guarantee of the public sector.

Figure 1.14 Bond Flows to Low- and Middle-Income Countries (excluding China), by Borrower Type, 2022–23

US$ (billion)

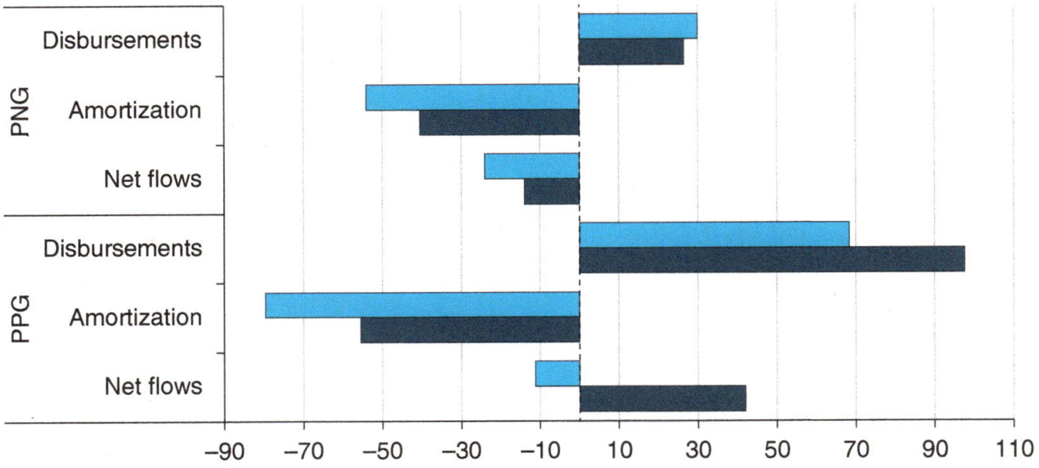

Source: World Bank International Debt Statistics database.
Note: PNG = private nonguaranteed; PPG = public and publicly guaranteed.

Box 1.7 Debt-for-Climate Swaps

Debt-for-climate swaps are motivated by two significant global issues: rising debt levels, particularly in low-income countries, and the increasing need to finance climate adaptation and conservation measures. Like debt-for-nature or debt-for-development swaps, a *debt-for-climate swap* is an agreement between a debtor government and its external creditors to replace (or swap) one category of sovereign external debt for other external liabilities or grants in return for a spending commitment over time toward a development goal—for example, nature preservation, environmental protection, marine conservation, and climate resilience infrastructure. Debt swaps can be classified into two categories, depending on the type of creditor of the debt being swapped: (a) bilateral debt swaps, which mean the official bilateral debt is written off or swapped in exchange for a commitment toward expenditures on specific nature or other development objectives, and (b) commercial debt (or buyback) swaps, which target debt held by private creditors. The latter may include bonds or commercial loans (IMF and World Bank 2024).

Debt-for-climate swaps offer several advantages. They can help countries manage their debt burdens, free up fiscal space, and support climate initiatives. In some cases, they can also contribute to improved credit ratings, such as Belize's 2021 debt swap that caused S&P Global Ratings to raise the country's sovereign credit rating from "Selective Default" to "B–." For creditors, these

(Box continues on next page)

Box 1.7 Debt-for-Climate Swaps (*continued*)

arrangements can reduce exposure while contributing to global public goods like climate action.

Debt-for-climate swaps also present challenges. Negotiations are often complex and lengthy, and implementing and monitoring the associated climate projects can place significant administrative burdens on debtor countries, particularly those with limited institutional capacity (Chamon et al. 2022). Additionally, the scale of debt relief provided through these swaps is often modest and may not sufficiently address broader debt burdens.

The first debt swap for environmental conservation occurred in Bolivia in 1987 in the context of the Brady operation. The deal, facilitated by the US-based nonprofit Conservation International, allowed Bolivia to repurchase US$650,000 of debt at an 85 percent discount to fund conservation efforts in the Beni Biosphere Reserve. In 1998, the US Congress enacted the Tropical Forest Conservation Act to enable 14 eligible countries to reduce the level of debt owed to US bilateral creditors in return for protecting tropical forests. In 2019, the act was expanded to become the Tropical Forest and Coral Reef Conservation Act. In 2023, Peru concluded a swap agreement under this act that will reduce its US bilateral debt by US$20 million. Other creditors that have concluded agreements to swap concessional bilateral claims include Canada, Germany, and Italy.

Despite the challenges associated with negotiating and implementing debt-for-climate swaps, these swaps are getting increased attention. Three recent debt-for-climate swaps—Belize in 2021 and Ecuador and Gabon in 2023—have a common structure that combines a discounted buyback of sovereign bonds, and a debt swap of obligations to bondholders for obligations to private creditors that financed the buyback. Belize's 2021 swap reduced its total debt stock by US$189 million, or 11.5 percent—funds that will be redirected to marine conservation. In 2023, Ecuador conducted the largest debt-for-climate swap to date in a buyback operation that repurchased US$1.6 billion of sovereign bonds for US$656 million, releasing close to US$1 billion for marine conservation around the Galápagos Islands. Later in 2023, Gabon executed the first debt-for-climate swap in continental Africa, in a buyback of US$500 million of sovereign bonds at a 10 percent discount to support similar marine conservation initiatives. Several other countries currently in negotiations for climate-related swaps include Cabo Verde, the Lao People's Democratic Republic, and Sri Lanka. The Arab Republic of Egypt recently announced that it is in the process of negotiating a swap agreement of concessional bilateral debt with China.

(Box continues on next page)

> **Box 1.7 Debt-for-Climate Swaps (*continued*)**
>
> The debt-for-climate operations described in this box are reflected in the Debtor Reporting System as (a) a reduction in debt stock owed to bondholders, equivalent to the face value of the bonds bought back, and (b) an increase in debt stock owed to private creditors equivalent to the discounted price paid to buy back the bonds. A disbursement of new financing from private creditors enables and offsets the payment made to bondholders. The reduction in debt stock owed to bondholders resulting from the difference between the face value of the bonds bought back and the discounted price paid is recorded as debt forgiveness.

Table 1.2 Net Debt Inflows to IDA-Eligible Countries, 2013–23

US$ (billion)

	2013	2014	2015	2016	2017	2018	2019	2020	2021	2022	2023
Net debt inflows	62.6	62.1	49.2	44.6	80.6	63.7	70.2	76.0	80.2	49.5	50.8
Long-term	55.9	61.7	49.2	45.4	61.7	67.9	57.2	76.8	64.2	45.1	60.1
Official creditors	19.2	25.4	26.6	24.0	30.7	36.2	40.5	54.4	35.9	38.4	44.6
Bilateral	12.1	14.8	12.7	11.7	14.5	19.9	16.6	13.6	14.2	7.7	11.0
Multilateral	7.1	10.6	13.9	12.3	16.2	16.3	23.9	40.8	21.7	30.7	33.6
World Bank	5.5	6.8	7.2	6.7	7.9	9.4	11.7	13.3	11.1	15.1	16.7
IMF	−2.2	−0.2	1.6	1.0	0.5	0.2	1.7	15.3	3.2	3.7	4.8
Private creditors	36.7	36.3	22.6	21.3	30.9	31.7	16.7	22.4	28.4	6.7	15.5
Bonds	5.5	15.6	7.2	4.2	13.8	13.4	7.2	3.4	15.2	−0.9	−0.4
Banks and other private	31.1	20.7	15.3	17.1	17.2	18.3	9.5	19.0	13.1	7.6	15.9
Short-term	6.7	0.4	0.0	−0.8	18.9	−4.2	13.0	−0.8	16.0	4.4	−9.3
Memorandum item											
Long-term PPG	28.8	40.5	37.2	29.3	46.9	54.0	49.8	64.0	53.4	36.0	46.1
Long-term PNG	27.1	21.2	11.9	16.1	14.7	13.9	7.4	12.8	10.8	9.1	13.9

Sources: World Bank International Debt Statistics database, International Monetary Fund, and Bank for International Settlements.
Note: World Bank includes IBRD and IDA; IMF includes use of credit only; IBRD = International Bank for Reconstruction and Development; IDA = International Development Association; IMF = International Monetary Fund; PNG = private nonguaranteed; PPG = public and publicly guaranteed.

For the group of countries eligible for IDA resources, total net debt flows increased 2.65 percent to US$50.8 billion in 2023 (table 1.2). The short-term debt flows turned negative for this group of countries in 2023, decreasing from an inflow of US$4.4 billion in 2022 to an outflow of US$9.3 billion. Long-term net debt flows compensated for the decrease in short-term flows, recording an increase of 33.2 percent to US$60.1 billion in 2023. Official creditors continued to boost their financing for this group of countries and recorded a combined 16.1 percent increase in net flows in 2023, resulting from a simultaneous increase of 42.3 percent to US$11.0 billion in net flows from bilateral creditors and a 9.4 percent increase to US$33.6 billion in net flows from multilateral creditors. New disbursements from bilateral creditors increased 17.4 percent to US$24.4 billion in 2023, outpacing the 2.6 percent increase in principal repayments to US$13.4 billion during the same year. New disbursements from multilateral creditors increased for a third year in a row in 2023, up 15.5 percent to US$48.9 billion, second in volume only to 2020 when multilaterals provided significant financial support during the COVID-19 pandemic to IDA-eligible countries. In 2023, principal repayments also increased 31.5 percent to US$15.3 billion. In the postpandemic era, multilateral creditors have tried to mitigate the liquidity reversal of other creditor groups and have significantly stepped up their financing for the poorest countries. In 2023, 60 percent of multilateral net flows went to IDA-eligible countries located in the Sub-Saharan Africa region and 28 percent to those in the South Asia region.

In 2023, net flows to private creditors bounced back, increasing more than twofold to US$15.5 billion. The rise was due to the increase in net flows to commercial banks and other private creditors, which doubled to US$15.9 billion in 2023. Of the net flows to commercial banks and other private creditors, 51 percent went to IDA-eligible countries in the Sub-Saharan Africa region and 40 percent to countries in the Europe and Central Asia region (figure 1.15). These flows were negative in the East Asia and Pacific region. Net flows to PPG bondholders and PNG bondholders improved slightly but remained negative for a second year in a row, at US$231.2 million and US$169.4 million, respectively. Lao PDR and Uzbekistan were among the few IDA-eligible countries tapping international capital markets in 2023. As they have done in the past, Lao PDR's public and private entities issued bonds denominated in Thai baht. Uzbekistan issued a US$660 million Eurobond and the country's first green sovereign Eurobond worth UBZ 4.25 trillion in 2023. Uzbek authorities stated that the proceeds of the issuances will finance environmentally focused projects related to water-saving technologies, sanitation initiatives, establishment of protective forests, and the expansion of railway and metro transportation systems (UNDP 2023).

Figure 1.15 Net Flows to IDA-Eligible Countries, by Region and Creditor Type, 2023

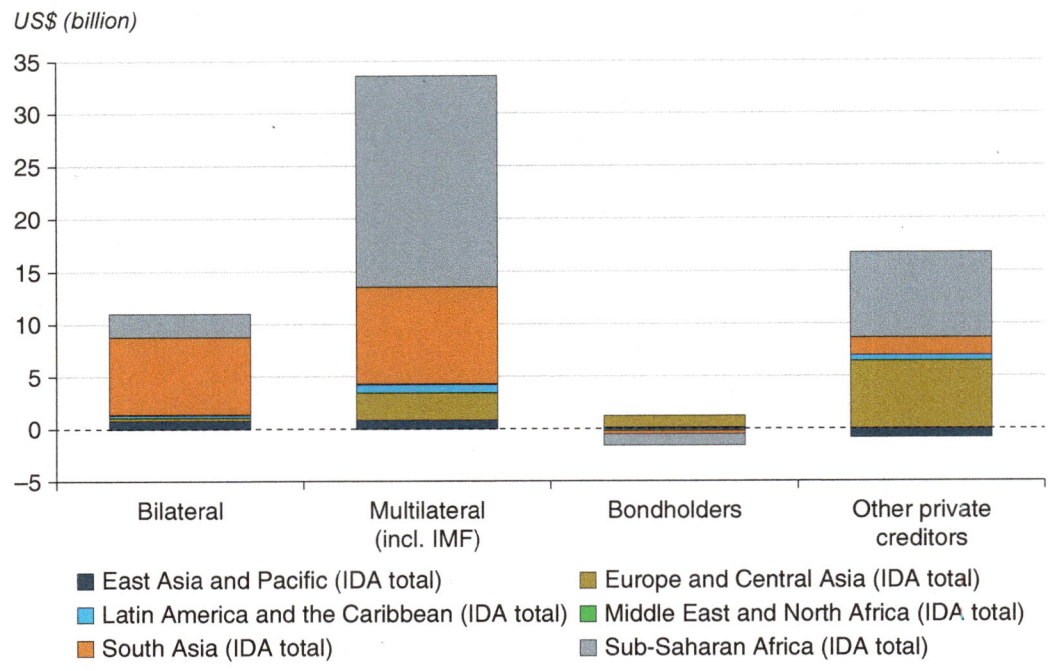

US$ (billion)

Legend:
- East Asia and Pacific (IDA total)
- Europe and Central Asia (IDA total)
- Latin America and the Caribbean (IDA total)
- Middle East and North Africa (IDA total)
- South Asia (IDA total)
- Sub-Saharan Africa (IDA total)

Source: World Bank International Debt Statistics database.
Note: IDA = International Development Association; IMF = International Monetary Fund.

Volatility in international financial markets extended beyond debt markets in 2023 and into equity financing and inflows of personal remittances, both of which are crucial to LMICs' economic growth and their progress toward the Sustainable Development Goals. Foreign direct investment (FDI) equity flows decreased for a second consecutive year after rebounding in 2021 from the pandemic (figure 1.16). China, the largest recipient of FDI equity flows, experienced an unprecedented drop in 2023, to US$71.7 billion, less than half the 2022 level. Just a decade ago, China's FDI inflows stood at US$265.4 billion, accounting for half of all FDI equity inflows to LMICs. Despite the volatility of this share over the last decade, it decreased drastically in the last two years, down to a 20 percent share of all FDI flows to LMICs in 2023, a low not seen since the early 1990s. Excluding China, FDI equity inflows to LMICs decreased 11.8 percent to US$287.7 billion in 2023, negatively affected by tighter monetary policy adopted by high-income countries, persistent uncertainty and risk aversion from international investors, and instability in international markets. The next three largest recipients of FDI equity flows—Brazil, Mexico, and India—also saw declines in their inflows in 2023, with the most sizable decline to inflows to India, down 45.8 percent to US$25.5 billion. Together with China, inflows to these four countries account for 51.2 percent of total FDI equity inflows to LMICs.

Figure 1.16 Net Equity Inflows and External Debt Flows to Low- and Middle-Income Countries, 2013–23

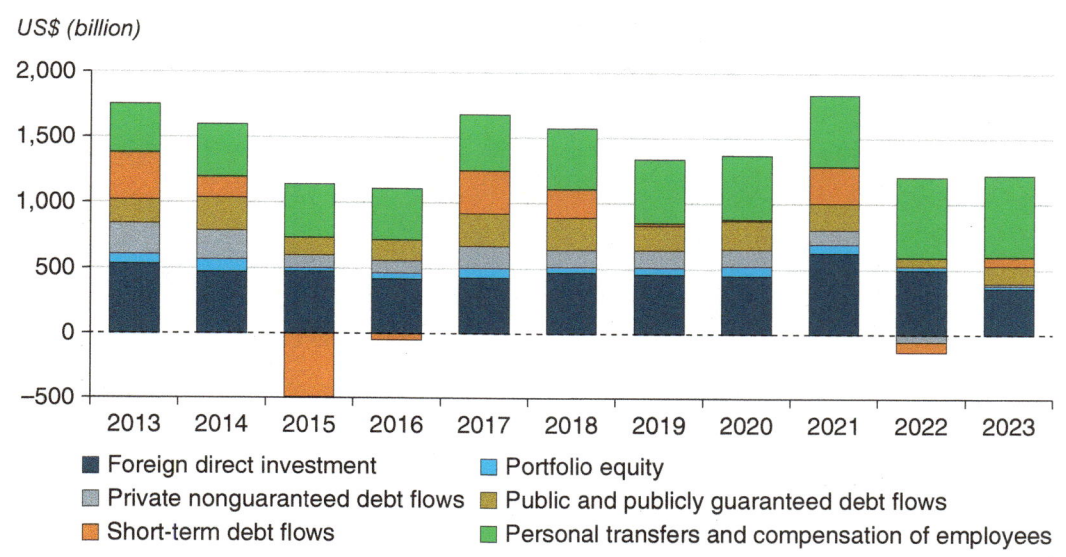

US$ (billion)

■ Foreign direct investment
■ Portfolio equity
■ Private nonguaranteed debt flows
■ Public and publicly guaranteed debt flows
■ Short-term debt flows
■ Personal transfers and compensation of employees

Sources: World Bank International Debt Statistics Database, International Monetary Fund, and UN Trade and Development.

Portfolio equity flows, which tend to be more volatile than FDI flows, also decreased in 2023, by 33.5 percent to US$19.5 billion. The decrease was attributable to an 80.6 percent drop in China's inflows, which stood at US$7.4 billion in 2023. China, historically also the top recipient of portfolio equity flows, accounted for a 38 percent share of LMICs' flows in 2023, dropping to second place. The top recipient of portfolio equity flows in 2023 was India, which registered inflows of US$21.4 billion, up from an outflow of US$16.6 billion registered in 2022. According to country reports, inflows into portfolio equity investment were primarily recorded in financial services, automobiles, capital goods, oil, gas and consumable fuels, and information technology sectors. Excluding the largest two recipients, China and India, portfolio equity flows for LMICs reversed from an inflow of US$7.4 billion in 2022 to an outflow of US$9.4 billion in 2023.

Inflows of personal remittances, composed of the sum of compensation of employees and personal transfers, remained stable in 2023, increasing by 1.1 percent to US$617.7 billion. The 2023 increase was much slower than in the prior two years when remittance growth averaged 11.7 percent, but in terms of volume these flows surpassed equity flows for the second year in a row. Labor markets stabilized in 2023, causing inflows of personal remittances to slow, following two years of high growth rates in 2021 and 2022 that were due to the recovery of job markets in source economies after the postpandemic reopening of economies. In terms of volume, the top five LMIC recipients of personal remittances in 2023 were India at US$119.5 billion, followed by Mexico (US$66.2 billion), the Philippines (US$39.1 billion), China (US$29.1 billion), and Pakistan (US$26.6 billion). When expressed as a percent of GNI, inflows of personal remittances represent a large share of external financing for the economies of some LMICs, with the top five being Tonga (above 40 percent of GNI), Lebanon (38.8 percent), Tajikistan (30.6 percent), Samoa (28.7 percent), and Honduras (28.1 percent).

Trends in Net Transfers on External Debt, 2013–23

The increase in interest payments has had a negative effect on net debt transfers, which measure the difference between what a country is receiving in new disbursements versus what it is paying to service its debt in interest and principal repayments. Positive net transfers occur when what is received in new disbursements exceeds debt service payments for the period; negative net transfers occur when interest and principal repayments exceed what is received in new disbursements. Following the onset of the COVID-19 pandemic, net debt transfers turned negative for the 2021–23 period in LMICs (excluding China), indicating that the amount that these countries have paid in interest and principal payments to service their debt obligations has exceeded what they have received in new disbursements. After collapsing in 2022 to an outflow of US$51.3 billion, net transfers on long-term debt for this group of countries experienced a 41.5 percent improvement in 2023 but remain negative at US$30.0 billion (figure 1.17). From a debt composition perspective, net transfers on long-term PNG debt have been negative since 2019, averaging an outflow of US$35.8 billion during the 2019–23 period; that is, total outflows on PNG long-term debt since 2019 accumulated to US$179 billion. By contrast, net transfers on long-term PPG debt (including the IMF) have been negative only for the past two years, with outflows of US$5.6 billion in 2022 and US$0.1 billion in 2023.

Figure 1.17 Long-Term Net Transfers on External Debt in Low-and Middle-Income Countries (excluding China), by Debtor Type, 2013–23

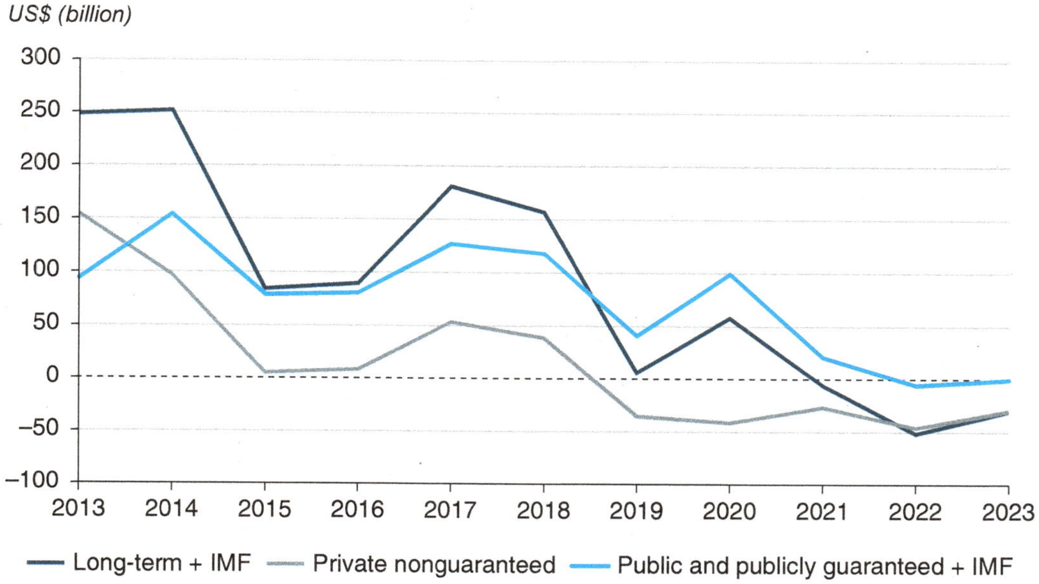

US$ (billion)

Legend: Long-term + IMF — Private nonguaranteed — Public and publicly guaranteed + IMF

Source: World Bank International Debt Statistics database.
Note: IMF = International Monetary Fund.

These negative aggregate figures mask a wide divergence between lending to public sector entities by official (bilateral and multilateral) creditors and private creditors (bondholders, commercial banks, and other private). Official multilateral creditors have been positive contributors to net transfers throughout the past decade, offering concessional financing at low interest rates and long maturities, and supporting countries through shocks that have negatively affected their economies since 2019. The African Development Bank, the African Export-Import Bank, the Asian Development Bank, the European Union, and the World Bank's IBRD and IDA lending arms were among the top 10 official multilateral lenders providing net positive transfers to LMICs (excluding China) in 2023. Net transfers from official bilateral creditors have also been positive during the last decade (except in 2019), dropping in 2023 to US$2.7 billion, 39 percent below net transfers of US$4.4 billion in 2022 (figure 1.18). Japan, India, and France led the bilateral creditors providing positive net transfers in 2023. Net transfers from China were negative, reflecting the sharp slowdown in net lending by China since the onset of the pandemic.

Figure 1.18 Long-Term Net Transfers on Public and Publicly Guaranteed External Debt in Low- and Middle-Income Countries (excluding China), by Creditor Type, 2013–23

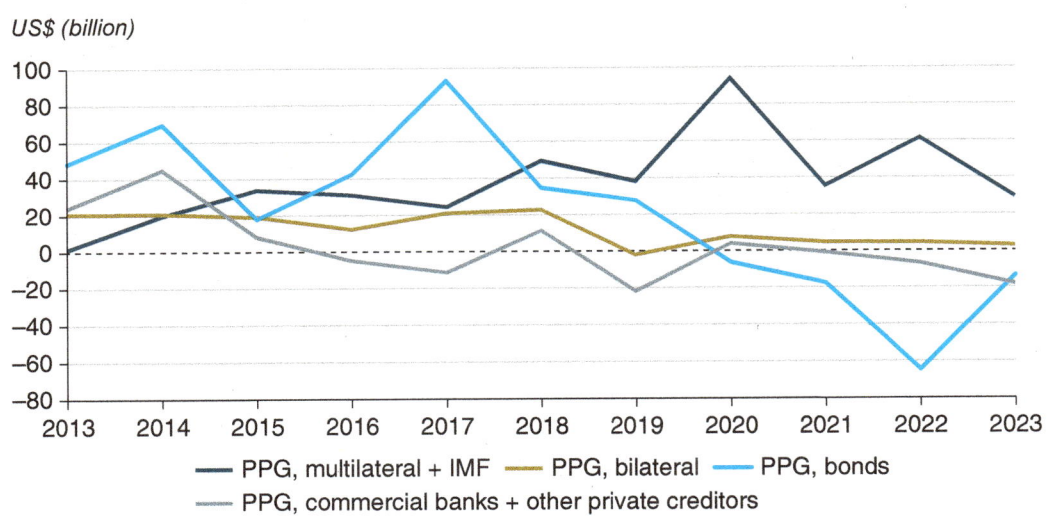

US$ (billion)

Legend: PPG, multilateral + IMF — PPG, bilateral — PPG, bonds — PPG, commercial banks + other private creditors

Source: World Bank International Debt Statistics database.
Note: IMF = International Monetary Fund; PPG = public and publicly guaranteed.

In contrast to net transfers from official creditors, net transfers from private creditors to public sector entities have been negative and have resulted instead in a withdrawal by this creditor base for the past three years. Net transfers on external debt owed to bondholders turned negative in 2020 and, despite a significant improvement, remained negative at US$13.8 billion in 2023. Higher interest payments and limited fiscal space have put immense pressure on governments to meet their obligations. In 2023, Ethiopia failed to make a US$33 million coupon payment on its sole Eurobond and formally went into default. Net transfers on external debt owed to commercial banks and other private creditors turned negative in 2021, with outflows almost tripling in 2023 to US$18.3 billion. As investor confidence is restored in LMICs, new disbursements from private creditors are expected to increase and positively affect net transfers for this group of countries. Although net transfers might not remain positive indefinitely, rapidly declining net transfers and prolonged periods of negative net transfers have become causes of concern for LMICs. The flows reversed when countries were facing multiple negative shocks and had limited fiscal space to support spending for vital resources, making sudden shifts in net transfers challenging to manage. Refer to box 1.8 for a discussion of the impact of debt servicing costs on government expenditures in key sectors of the economy.

Net transfers on long-term debt of IDA-eligible countries have remained positive over the past decade, to both public sector borrowers and nonguaranteed private sector entities. In general, IDA-eligible countries have limited capital market

Figure 1.19 Debt Flows on Public and Publicly Guaranteed Debt in IDA-Eligible Countries, by Creditor Type, 2021–23

US$ (billion)

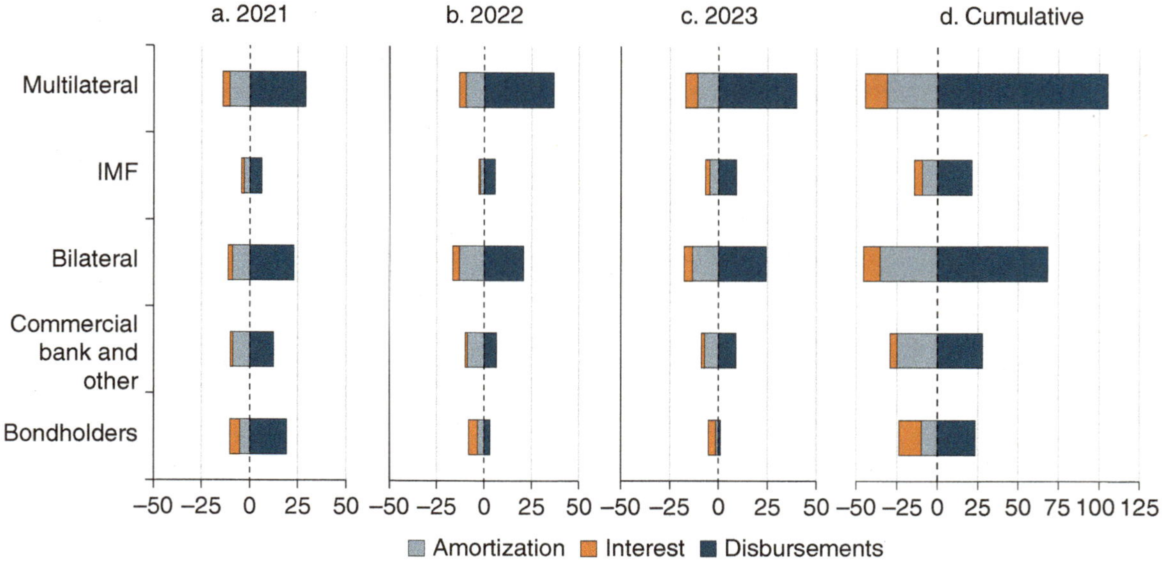

Source: World Bank International Debt Statistics database.
Note: IDA = International Development Association; IMF = International Monetary Fund.

access and thus do not rely heavily on PNG debt. Net transfers on PNG long-term debt increased by 48 percent in 2023, to a US$2.4 billion inflow. After falling 44.5 percent in 2022 and remaining positive, net transfers on PPG long-term debt increased 24.8 percent in 2023 to an inflow of US$27.3 billion (figure 1.19). For IDA-eligible countries, the PPG composition of net transfers between official and private creditors is also heterogeneous.

Net transfers on PPG debt of IDA-eligible countries owed to official creditors have remained positive over the last decade because of the resilient effect of new disbursements and lower exposure to interest rate fluctuations on obligations owed to multilateral creditors. IDA-eligible countries have been less affected by the global increase in interest rates, because these countries benefit from access to highly concessional loans from multilateral institutions, with low interest rates and long maturities. Furthermore, official creditors have been providing unprecedented levels of support to this group of countries in the form of new disbursements, which increased 16 percent in 2023 to US$73.3 billion (figure 1.20). Debt servicing costs also increased in 2023 for debt owed to this creditor group, but the combined effect through new disbursements and debt service payments has kept net transfers positive since 2007 for IDA-eligible countries. Whereas bilateral and multilateral creditor support has been a net positive for this group of countries, net transfers on PPG debt owed to private creditors turned negative in 2022 because of a retrenchment in new disbursements from private creditors, which decreased 69.1 percent to US$9.7 billion. New disbursements from private creditors improved in 2023 by 4.3 percent, to US$10.1 billion, but remain below the 2013–21 average of US$19.3 billion. Consequently, net transfers on PPG debt to private creditors improved in 2023 but remained negative at US$4.1 billion.

Figure 1.20 **Net Transfers on Public and Publicly Guaranteed Debt in IDA-Eligible Countries, by Creditor Type, 2021–23**

US$ (billion)

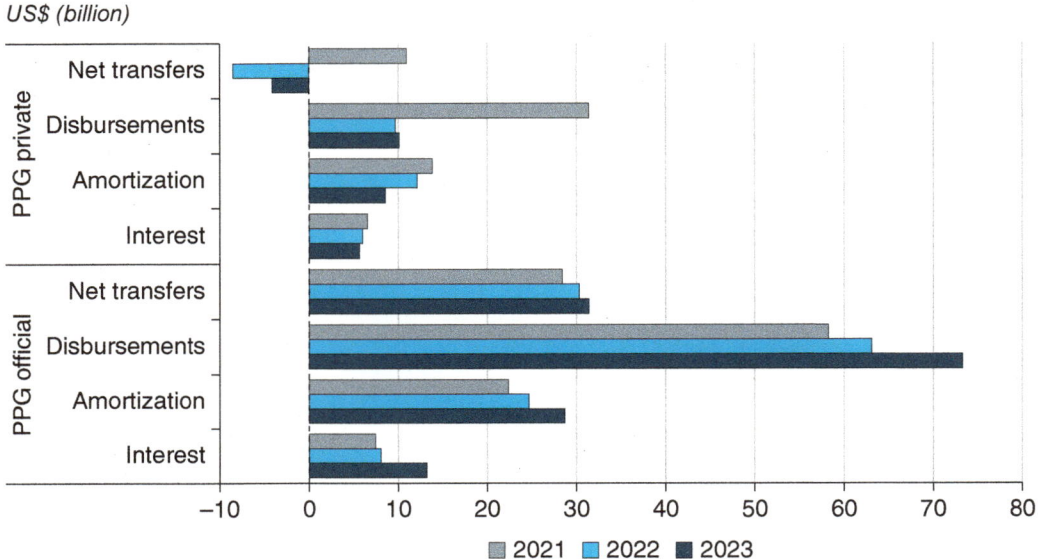

Source: World Bank International Debt Statistics database.
Note: IDA = International Development Association; PPG = public and publicly guaranteed.

Box 1.8 **Government Expenditures and External Debt Service in Developing Countries**

As developing countries' external debt obligations continue to grow, understanding the trends in how debt servicing relates to government spending in key sectors is crucial for sustainable development. To this end, the World Bank's Development Data Group conducted an analysis of the patterns between debt service and government expenditures in areas critical to economic and social development, including agriculture, environmental protection, education, and health.

The analysis examines the relationship between government spending and external debt service in developing countries from 2018 to 2023. It focuses on

(Box continues on next page)

Box 1.8 **Government Expenditures and External Debt Service in Developing Countries (*continued*)**

how external debt service, measured as a percentage of gross domestic product (GDP), is associated with government expenditure shares in these critical sectors. The analysis uses government expenditure data from the year before the debt service, reflecting how governments account for future debt obligations in their budgeting process. It covers 43 countries for agriculture-related expenditures, 34 countries for environmental protection, 105 countries for education, and 113 countries for health expenditures in the general government sector, with data sourced from the World Bank, the United Nations Food and Agriculture Organization, and the World Health Organization.

For agriculture-related expenditures, the analysis observed a nearly linear negative trend,[a] with a 1 percent increase in external debt service as a percentage of GDP in the following year associated with a 0.28 percent[b] decrease in the government expenditure share (0.18 percent–0.39 percent).[c] Similarly, environmental protection expenditure exhibits a smaller, yet still significant, negative relationship, with a 1 percent of GDP increase in external debt service linked to a 0.09 percent reduction in the expenditure share (0.03 percent–0.15 percent). Education expenditure follows a moderate U-curve pattern when external debt is below 1 percent of GDP. Beyond this level, the expenditure share drops sharply, and a 1 percent increase in external debt service of GDP is associated with a 0.50 percent (0.27 percent–0.74 percent) reduction in education expenditure share. By contrast, health expenditure did not present a clear trend with increased debt service. Although a U-curve is observed when external debt is below 1 percent of GDP, the expenditure share remains relatively stable beyond this point, possibly reflecting the rigidity of health budgets, particularly in response to pandemic-related needs, over this period. With covariates controlled, regression results suggest a negative but statistically insignificant association (p-value = 0.129).

For example, assuming a country with a US$100 billion GDP and US$20 billion in total government expenditure, if external debt service as a share of GDP were to increase by 1 percentage point, rising from 1 percent (US$1 billion) to 2 percent (US$2 billion), Development Data Group analysis observed that government spending on agriculture sectors may decrease by US$56 million (0.28 percent), environmental protection by US$18 million (0.09 percent), and education by US$100 million (0.50 percent) (figure B1.8.1). In sum, the analysis findings reveal a generally negative correlation between external debt service and government expenditure shares for agriculture, environmental protection, and education. This analysis does not imply causality and should be interpreted as observational trends. Note that external debt service does not account for debt rollovers, which may limit the capture of fiscal constraints. Further research would be needed to establish causal inference.

(Box continues on next page)

Box 1.8 Government Expenditures and External Debt Service in Developing Countries (*continued*)

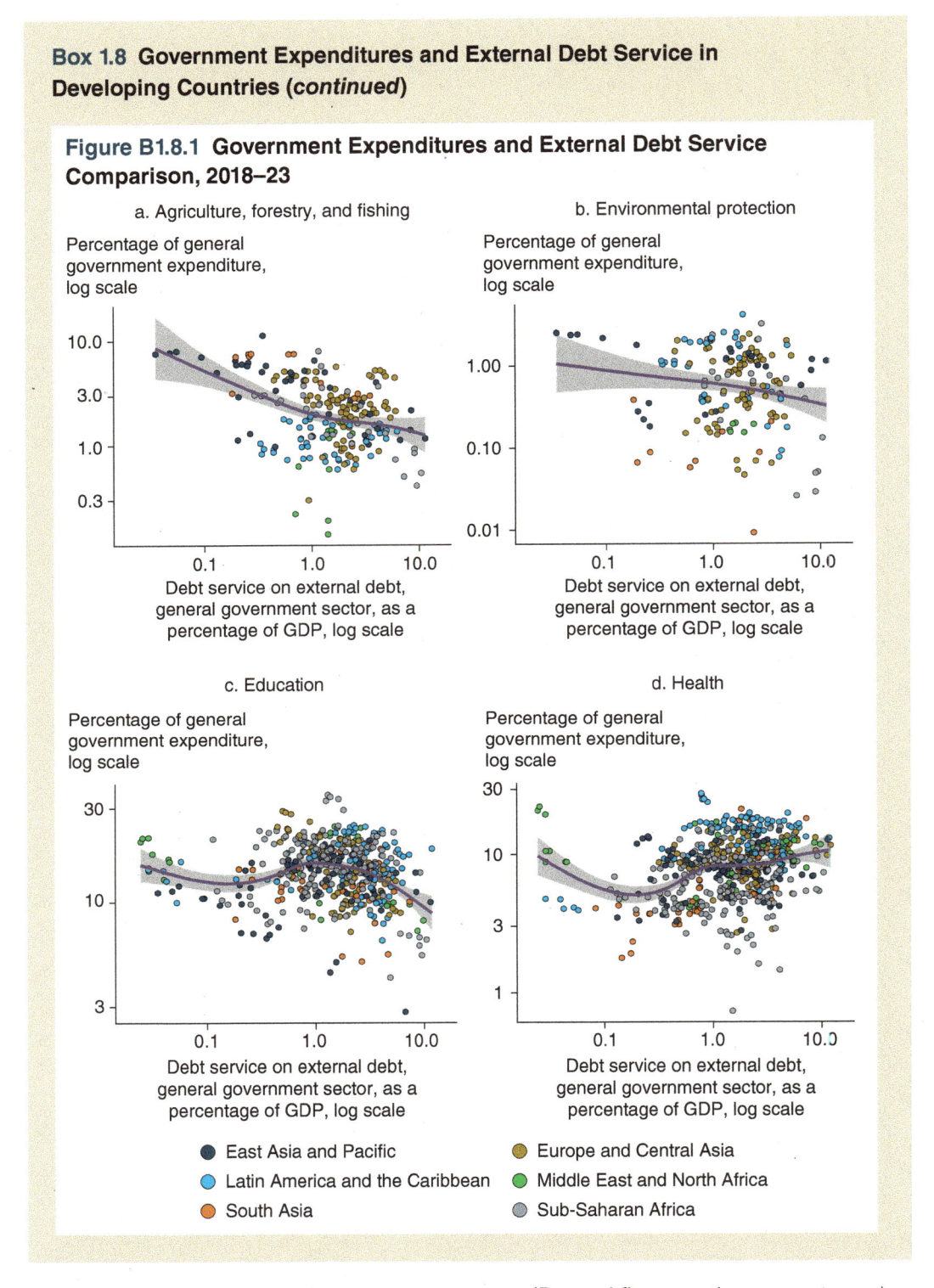

Figure B1.8.1 Government Expenditures and External Debt Service Comparison, 2018–23

(Box and figure continue on next page)

Box 1.8 Government Expenditures and External Debt Service in Developing Countries (*continued*)

Sources: World Bank International Debt Statistics and World Development Indicators databases, Food and Agriculture Organization, and World Health Organization.

Note: This figure shows the relationship between external debt service as a percentage of GDP and government expenditure shares in the previous year across four sectors: agriculture, environmental protection, education, and health. The analysis includes data from 2018 to 2023, covering a wide range of developing countries, with visual distinctions made by region. Axes are in log format. The trending line and confidence intervals are derived from the Generalized Additive Model with cubic spline assumption.

a. The observed trend reflects the relationship visualized in the figure, based on data from 2018 to 2023. The trend line and confidence intervals are derived from a semiparametric Generalized Additive Model.

b. Based on the General Linear Model, controlling for urban population as a percentage of total population, life expectancy at birth, and fixed effects on year, income classification, and region. The plotted curve represents a nonlinear relationship fitted with a Generalized Additive Model.

c. This is the 95 percent confidence interval range—that is, there is only a 5 percent chance the number is outside this range. A similar range is given here for government expenditure shares in all four sectors investigated.

Note

1. All mentions of LMIC debt and debt stock in the report refer to external debt, unless otherwise noted or where it is not clear. Refer to box 1.1 for a discussion of debt concepts, coverage, and the data sources used for this report.

References

Chamon, Marcos, Erik Klok, Vimal Thakoor, and Jeromin Zettelmeyer. 2022. "Debt-for-Climate Swaps: Analysis, Design, and Implementation." IMF Working Paper 2022/162, International Monetary Fund, Washington, DC. https://www.imf.org/en/Publications/WP/Issues/2022/08/11/Debt-for-Climate-Swaps-Analysis-Design-and-Implementation-522184.

Hussain, Farah Imrana, and Helene Dill. 2023. "India Incorporates Green Bonds into Its Climate Finance Strategy." *Development and a Changing Climate* (blog), June 12, 2023. https://blogs.worldbank.org/en/climatechange/india-incorporates-green-bonds-its-climate-finance-strategy.

IMF (International Monetary Fund). 2009. *Balance of Payments and International Investment Position Manual.* 6th edition. Washington, DC: IMF.

IMF (International Monetary Fund). 2014. *Government Finance Statistics Manual 2014.* Washington, DC: IMF.

IMF (International Monetary Fund). 2018. "Guidance Note on the Bank-Fund Debt Sustainability Framework for Low-Income Countries." IMF, Washington, DC. https://www.imf.org/en/Publications/Policy-Papers/Issues/2018/02/14/pp122617guidance-note-on-lic-dsf.

IMF (International Monetary Fund). 2020. *Update on the Joint IMF-WB Multipronged Approach to Address Debt Vulnerabilities*. Policy Paper No. 2020/066. Washington, DC: IMF. https://www.imf.org/en/Publications/Policy-Papers/Issues/2020/12/10/Update-on-the-Joint-IMF -WB-Multipronged-Approach-to-Address-Debt-Vulnerabilities-49946.

IMF (International Monetary Fund). 2021a. *Guidance Note for Fund Staff on the Treatment and Use of SDR Allocations*. Policy Paper No. 2021/059. Washington, DC: IMF. https://www.imf .org/en/Publications/Policy-Papers/Issues/2021/08/19/Guidance-Note-for-Fund-Staff-on-the -Treatment-and-Use-of-SDR-Allocations-464319.

IMF (International Monetary Fund). 2021b. "IMF Governors Approve a Historic US$650 Billion SDR Allocation of Special Drawing Rights." Press Release No. 21/235, August 2, 2021. https:// www.imf.org/en/News/Articles/2021/07/30/pr21235-imf-governors-approve-a-historic-us-650 -billion-sdr-allocation-of-special-drawing-rights.

IMF (International Monetary Fund). 2022. *Staff Guidance Note on the Sovereign Risk and Debt Sustainability Framework for Market Access Countries*. Policy Paper No. 2022/039. Washington, DC: IMF. https://www.imf.org/en/Publications/Policy-Papers/Issues/2022/08/08 /Staff-Guidance-Note-on-the-Sovereign-Risk-and-Debt-Sustainability-Framework-for -Market-521884.

IMF (International Monetary Fund). 2023. *Sri Lanka: First Review Under the Extended Arrangement Under the Extended Fund Facility, Requests for a Waiver of Nonobservance of Performance Criterion, Modification of Performance Criteria, Rephasing of Access, and Financing Assurances Review-Press Release; Staff Report; and Statement by the Executive Director for Sri Lanka*. Washington, DC: IMF. https://www.imf.org/en/Publications/CR /Issues/2023/12/12/Sri-Lanka-First-Review-Under-the-Extended-Arrangement-Under-the -Extended-Fund-Facility-542441.

IMF (International Monetary Fund). 2024. *Ghana: Second Review Under the Arrangement Under the Extended Credit Facility, Request for Modification of Performance Criteria, and Financing Assurances Review—Debt Sustainability Analysis*. Country Report No. 24/213. Washington, DC: IMF. https://www.imf.org/en/Publications/CR/Issues/2024/07/11/Ghana-Second-Review -under-the-Extended-Credit-Facility-Request-for-Modification-of-551740.

IMF (International Monetary Fund, Strategy, Policy, and Review Department) and World Bank. 2024. "Debt for Development Swaps: An Approach Framework." *Policy Papers* 2024: 038. https://doi.org/10.5089/9798400284625.007.

PBOC (People's Bank of China). 2024. "China Monetary Policy Report Q4 2023." Monetary Policy Analysis Group, PBOC, Beijing. http://www.pbc.gov.cn/en/3688229/3688353/3688356/475645 3/5330013/2024041610102997035.pdf.

UNDP (United Nations Development Programme). 2023. "Uzbekistan Issues First Ever Green Sovereign Eurobonds Worth 4.25 Trillion UZS on the London Stock Exchange." Press release, October 9, 2023. https://www.undp.org/uzbekistan/press-releases/uzbekistan-issues-first-ever -green-sovereign-eurobonds-worth-425-trillion-uzs-london-stock-exchange.

World Bank Group and IMF (International Monetary Fund). 2021. "World Bank Group and International Monetary Fund Support for Debt Relief under the Common Framework and Beyond." Document No. 2021-0002, World Bank Group and IMF, Washington, DC. https://www.devcommittee.org/content/dam/sites/devcommittee/doc/documents/mgr/DC2021 -0002%20Debt%20final.pdf.

2. The Macroeconomic and Debt Outlook for 2024 and Beyond

Introduction

Global growth is set to remain steady for the foreseeable future despite flaring geopolitical tensions and elevated uncertainty surrounding global trade policy. Global inflation is expected to moderate, allowing central banks to ease monetary policy to support economic activity. However, the outlook is still subdued for low- and middle-income countries (LMICs), and weaker for economies with low creditworthiness, constrained fiscal space, and heightened political and social unrest. Risks to the macroeconomic outlook in LMICs remain tilted to the downside, including an escalation of armed conflicts, further trade fragmentation, persistent global inflation and weaker global risk appetite, and slower-than-expected growth in major LMICs, especially China.

Although LMICs accumulated significant additional debt in 2023 and experienced the heavy debt service burden that goes with it, debt service costs are expected to moderate gradually because of the decline in global interest rates. However, the debt outlook for LMICs also has downside risks. The growing prominence of nontraditional creditors, in addition to the historical accumulation of debt owed to China, could make debt resolution more complex; and it is particularly critical in small states, which often have underdeveloped domestic financial markets. In addition, higher borrowing costs and increased debt service burdens could worsen fiscal challenges, amplified by tightening fiscal policy in LMICs.

Macroeconomic Outlook and Risks

Global gross domestic product growth is expected to stabilize in the short term, following several years of negative shocks. According to the World Bank's latest projections, global growth is projected to hold steady at 2.6 percent in 2024, before edging higher to 2.7 percent in 2025–26 (figure 2.1). In LMICs, growth is forecast to slow from 4.5 percent in 2023 to 4.2 percent in 2024 and remain broadly stable over 2025–26, mainly because of cyclical headwinds that are expected to slow growth in China over the near term. Excluding China, growth in LMICs is projected to increase from 3.7 percent in 2024 to 4.2 percent over the 2025–26 period. In countries eligible for support from the International Development

Figure 2.1 Percent Change in Gross Domestic Product, 2021–26

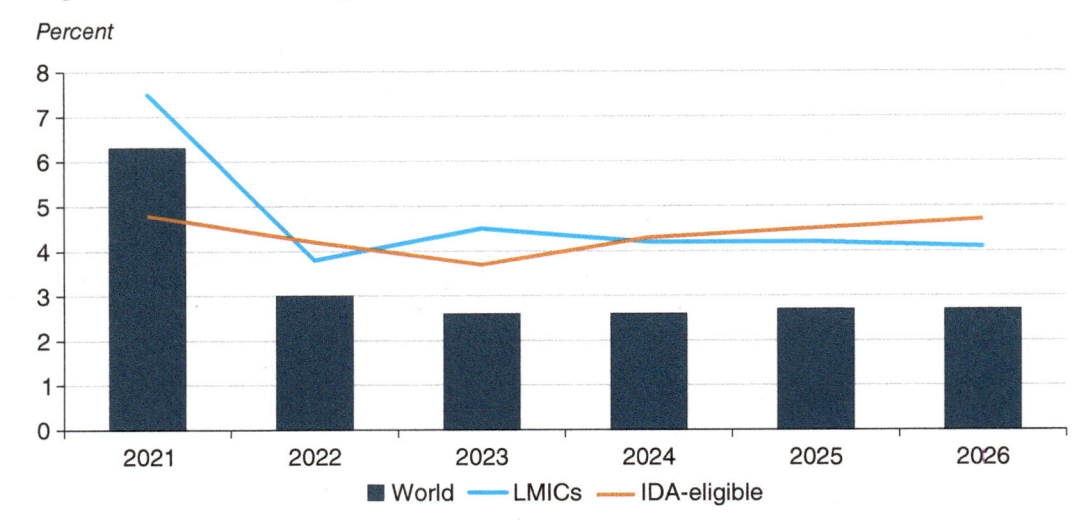

Percent

Source: World Bank 2024.
Note: Aggregate GDP growth rates are calculated as weighted averages, based on real GDP in constant 2010–19 prices, expressed in US dollars, as weights. Data for 2024 are estimates, and data for 2025–26 are forecasts. IDA = International Development Association; LMICs = low- and middle-income countries.

Association (IDA), an increase in activity among several commodity exporters, accompanied by expected stabilization in some fragile economies, will contribute to faster growth in 2024, at 4.3 percent, than in 2023, at 3.7 percent.

Although expected to remain steady, global growth remains weak compared to the decade that preceded the recent pandemic. The ongoing weakness reflects several factors, including the lagged effects of monetary tightening, resumed fiscal consolidation, and moderate consumption growth in the context of receding savings buffers and diminishing labor market tightness. Investment growth is expected to remain constrained in 2024, partly because of heightened policy uncertainty amid ongoing geopolitical tensions.

However, marginal improvement in the global economy is expected in 2025–26, supported by gradually subsiding inflation, declining policy rates, and firming trade growth. Global investment is projected to strengthen as monetary easing gains momentum. In contrast, although the differentials between interest rates and growth are expected to fall, fiscal consolidation efforts are anticipated to exert a mild drag on growth as many governments seek to rebuild fiscal buffers and address imbalances accumulated since the pandemic. In LMICs, less restrictive financing conditions and improving consumption growth are expected to gradually bolster growth, particularly when China is excluded. Still, the lingering effects of recent large shocks, including the pandemic and conflict events, will continue to put pressure on the recovery in LMICs.

Despite a small uptick, the outlook is expected to remain weak by historical standards, particularly in LMICs with low credit ratings. These economies often have limited access to capital markets amid domestic financial volatility. Growth prospects are also weak in economies experiencing highly constrained fiscal space, elevated debt levels, and heightened political and social unrest, including surges in conflict and violence. Overall, the recovery in LMICs is expected to be limited and uneven. Output levels in LMICs are expected to remain below prepandemic trajectories by more than 6 percent in 2026, revealing lasting economic scars and ongoing challenges from geopolitical tensions and trade policy uncertainty. The limited and uneven output recovery reflects unequal progress among LMIC efforts to close the per capita income gap with higher-income economies. Progress on closing the gap is expected to stall completely in LMICs when China and India are excluded. The level of per capita income in LMICs (not including China and India) relative to advanced economies is expected to be lower in 2024 than in 2019, extending the stagnation that started in the 2010s and putting poverty reduction progress at risk, especially in economies with fiscal and financial vulnerabilities. By the end of 2026, people in nearly 40 percent of LMICs with weak credit ratings are projected to be poorer than in 2019, but people will be poorer in only about 5 percent of LMICs with strong credit ratings. In addition, near-term per capita income growth in low-income countries (LICs) is expected to be slower than in middle-income countries (MICs), even after China is excluded (Kose and Ohnsorge 2024). The setback in income convergence toward MICs will make poverty reduction more challenging in LICs.

Risks to the outlook in LMICs remain tilted to the downside amid heightened uncertainty. Key downside risks include an escalation of conflicts or geopolitical tensions, further trade fragmentation, higher inflation and weaker risk appetite, and spillovers from slower-than-expected growth in China. The materialization of these risks could result in even weaker activity in LMICs.

- *The proliferation of armed conflicts and broader geopolitical risks have sharply increased in several LMICs, and further escalation could adversely affect economic activity.* The escalation of conflicts could stifle investment and economic activity because of the destruction of capital and increased political instability. It could also pose fiscal challenges through a decline in revenues and a surge in debt, and losses in human capital could compound long-term economic damage. If conflicts intensify, particularly in oil-exporting countries or regions, substantial disruptions to oil supply could lead to significant spikes in oil and other commodity prices, fueling inflationary pressures in LMICs. Heightened uncertainty surrounding conflicts could exacerbate geopolitical risks, dampening investment, reducing investor confidence, and increasing financial volatility, with negative spillovers to other LMICs.

- *Further trade fragmentation and trade policy uncertainty could slow activity in LMICs.* An increase in trade restriction measures has disrupted global supply chains, hampered technological diffusion, and undermined economic convergence, particularly in LMICs. In addition, elevated geopolitical tensions have segmented the global market into regional blocs and have reduced trade and investment flows between different blocs, leading to more complex and less efficient supply networks. Increased trade policy uncertainty could further weaken investor sentiment, slow business investment, and reduce productivity growth in LMICs. Growing public support for inward-looking policies, particularly accompanied by a divided political landscape, could also lead to greater protectionism, further hindering cross-border trade and investment in LMICs.

- *Higher global inflation and weaker risk appetite could lead to limited monetary easing and the slowdown of activity in LMICs.* If global inflation persists longer than anticipated, policy rate cuts could be postponed, leaving monetary conditions tighter than expected. This situation could lead to higher borrowing costs and lower real incomes, putting downward pressure on consumer spending in LMICs, where monetary authorities could slow monetary easing to avoid a surge in inflation from currency depreciation. The risk is particularly high in LMICs with weaker creditworthiness, because these economies could likely experience larger depreciation and capital outflows.

- *Adverse impacts of weaker-than-expected growth in China could spill over to other LMICs through different channels.* Despite the implementation of stimulus measures, economic activity in China could slow even further because of prolonged weakness in business sentiment and private investment, especially in the property sector, coupled with a faster decline in growth. These factors could disrupt the global trade recovery, particularly in commodity-exporting LMICs and tourism-dependent economies. Additionally, a sharper slowdown in China could reduce global risk appetite, tighten financial conditions, and disproportionately affect less creditworthy economies that rely on external financing.

Debt Outlook and Risks

Amid heightened downside risks, LMICs continued to accumulate debt in 2023. Total debt in LMICs increased by 2.4 percent in 2023 from the previous year, in current US dollar terms. Excluding China, the increase in total debt among LMICs was 3.8 percent in 2023. However, as national income grew faster than debt stocks, partly reflecting high inflation, the ratio of debt to gross national income (GNI) among LMICs marginally declined to 24.3 percent in 2023 from the previous year. In IDA-eligible countries, total debt stock increased by

4.8 percent in 2023. Consequently, the ratio of total debt stock to GNI increased by 1.9 percentage points because of slower income growth, partly stemming from the decline of activity in some major IDA-eligible countries. Among 68 IDA-eligible countries included in the list of LIC debt sustainability analyses as of the end of September 2024, 16 percent were in external debt distress and 35 percent were at high risk of distress.

The debt service burden has elevated in LMICs but is anticipated to moderate gradually. Debt service on total debt among LMICs increased to 3.7 percent of GNI in 2023—the same level seen during the 2020 pandemic-induced global recession. Excluding China, the cost of servicing total debt was 5.2 percent of GNI among LMICs. Heightened borrowing costs have contributed to the increase in the ratio. Interest payments on total debt rose by 0.3 percentage point to 1.1 percent of GNI in LMICs, the largest annual increase in the interest payment-to-GNI ratio of the past two decades (figure 2.2). Similarly, interest payments increased 0.4 percentage point in LMICs excluding China, also the largest annual increase over the same period. However, the debt service burden is projected to be mitigated in the near term, primarily because of the expected decline in global interest rates. In LMICs, interest payments on total debt over 2024–25 on a cumulative basis are expected to be 26 percent lower than over 2022–23. Consequently, total debt service, including principal repayments, over 2024–25 is anticipated to be 18 percent lower than over 2022–23. This decline in debt service burden will be mostly attributable to China, because the expected reduction in debt service in LMICs excluding China is 4 percent from 2022–23 to 2024–25.

Figure 2.2 Interest Payments on Total External Debt as a Share of GNI, 2013–23

Percent

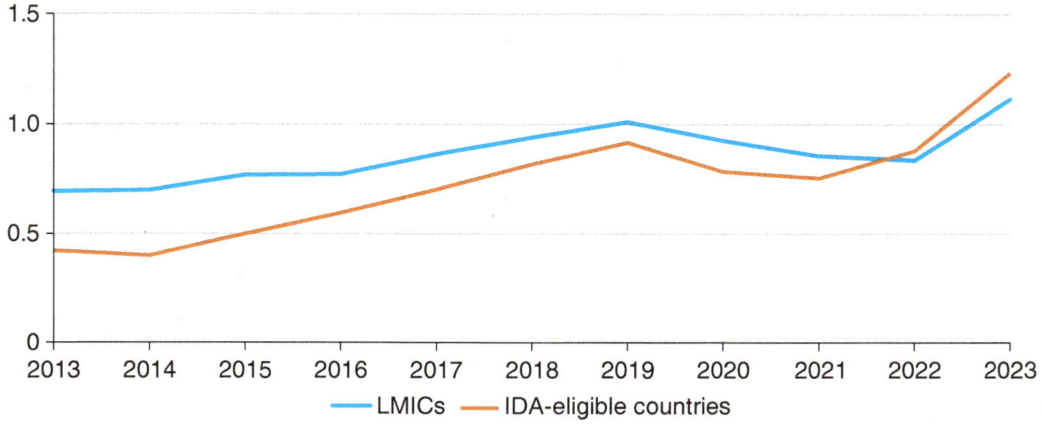

Source: World Bank International Debt Statistics database.
Note: GNI = gross national income; IDA = International Development Association; LMICs = low- and middle-income countries.

One particular risk to the debt outlook in LMICs is the increasing importance of nontraditional creditors, particularly commercial lenders, and the resulting shift in the composition of external creditors, both of which raise concerns about debt resolution and negotiation in LMICs and make them more complex. Lending from private sources tends to be made at market rates, and borrowing countries are therefore likely to be more exposed to refinancing risks, especially when borrowing costs increase. In addition, weaker-than-projected growth in China could adversely affect LMICs with heavy reliance on that country and limited access to the international market for financing.

Official creditors play a particularly prominent role in small states, where access to borrowing from domestic or foreign private sources is limited (World Bank 2024). In small states, heavy reliance on official borrowing could enable access to concessional terms. Still, it could also be partly the result of underdeveloped domestic financial systems, particularly in the smallest and poorest economies. The capacity to carry debt tends to be weaker in small states than in other LMICs, partly reflecting structural constraints on growth and susceptibility to external shocks, especially natural disasters.

Higher borrowing costs could lead to higher debt service burdens and larger fiscal policy challenges in LMICs. A persistence of global inflation and the potential delay in monetary policy easing that it would imply, particularly in high-income economies, could keep the cost of borrowing high in LMICs. Large, ongoing debt service burdens, especially in the public component of debt, accompanied by the expected fiscal tightening, could force some LMICs to spend less on other priorities, including social safety nets and public investment in physical and human capital. In LMICs with limited fiscal space, redirecting expenditure to the highest priorities and improving efficiency are critical to meeting spending needs. In addition, increasing vulnerability to currency movements could amplify debt service burdens, because LMICs continue to have a large share of public debt denominated in foreign currency (Kose et al. 2022). About 25 percent of public debt is in foreign currency in LMICs excluding China, and the share rises to more than 40 percent in LICs. A depreciation of LMIC currencies could lead to rising debt service costs, particularly in LMICs with heightened fiscal and financial vulnerabilities. In a growing number of LMICs, however, the portion of public debt held by domestic investors has increased. This situation could pose several challenges, including crowding out of private investment and, especially in LICs, opaque use of debt instruments and more complicated public debt portfolios (Saavedra, Francisco, and Rivetti 2024).

In IDA-eligible countries, the debt service burden is expected to remain large in the near term. Interest payments on total debt reached 1.2 percent of GNI in 2023, the highest since 2000. Although expected to decline gradually, the cost of servicing total debt will remain larger than in recent years, mainly because of an increase in principal repayments. In countries eligible for IDA support, government spending on interest payments increased to 20 percent of government revenues in 2023, an increase of 7 percentage points, on average, from the prepandemic decade. The elevated level of debt service will have implications for overall government expenditure, and it is particularly critical for IDA-eligible countries, which have faced significant development challenges and continue to have large financing needs. In IDA-eligible countries, especially economies with limited spending capacity, establishing robust fiscal frameworks by strengthening institutional arrangements and domestic governance could help rebuild fiscal buffers and improve policy outcomes, particularly over the longer term.

Vulnerabilities associated with elevated debt burdens could be mitigated through domestic revenue mobilization and prudent debt management in LMICs. Revenue collection in LMICs has been weaker than in high-income economies and is expected to remain limited in the short term. Weak revenue collection partly reflects less developed markets and limited institutional capacity, especially in IDA-eligible countries (figure 2.3). Countries could improve the collection mechanism by strengthening revenue administration and implementing tax reforms, including broadening tax bases and simplifying tax codes. In addition, improving debt transparency, notably in monitoring and reporting, could ensure the early detection of debt-related risks, particularly in countries at moderate or elevated risk of debt distress (refer to chapter 3 on the debt transparency agenda). Improvements in debt data collection practices, particularly in IDA-eligible countries, are also associated with a reduction in borrowing costs. Such positive impacts of transparency are greater in LMICs with better institutional quality and lower debt. Prudent management of public debt could also reduce the volatility of debt dynamics and mitigate the risk of sudden reversals in interest rate growth differentials.

Figure 2.3 Composition of Government Revenues as a Share of GDP, 2010s vs. 2020s

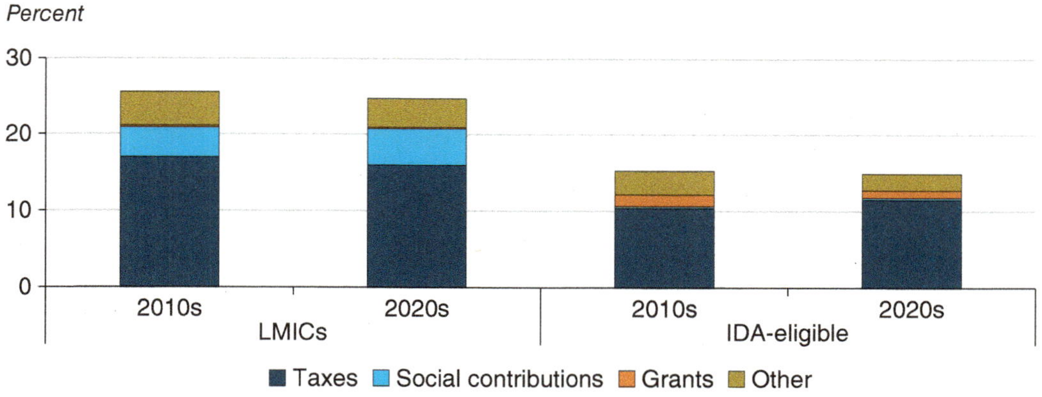

Percent

Sources: International Monetary Fund and World Bank.
Note: In some countries, data are for central governments. Data for 2020s cover 2020–22.
IDA = International Development Association; LMICs = low- and middle-income countries.

In sum, although global growth is expected to remain steady, supported by moderating inflation and lower global interest rates, LMICs still face multiple risks related to macroeconomic development and debt issues. If these risks materialize, the debt burden—already high because of years of debt accumulation—could be even heavier and the pressure this burden puts on spending for other priorities could increase. LMICs need to build robust fiscal frameworks and reinforce debt management to reduce debt-related vulnerabilities and keep debt dynamics under control.

References

Kose, M. Ayhan, Sergio Kurlat, Franziska Ohnsorge, and Naotaka Sugawara. 2022. "A Cross-Country Database of Fiscal Space." *Journal of International Money and Finance* 128: 102682. https://doi.org/10.1016/j.jimonfin.2022.102682.

Kose, M. Ayhan, and Franziska Ohnsorge, eds. 2024. *Falling Long-Term Growth Prospects: Trends, Expectations, and Policies*. Washington, DC: World Bank.

Saavedra, Pablo, Manuela Francisco, and Diego Rivetti. 2024. "Tackling the World's Hidden-Debt Problem." *Voices* (blog), March 29, 2024. https://blogs.worldbank.org/en/voices/tackling-the-world-s-hidden-debt-problem.

World Bank. 2024. *Global Economic Prospects, June 2024*. Washington, DC: World Bank.

3. The Debt Transparency Agenda: Moving It Forward

Introduction

Public debt disclosure and accountability are public goods, and comprehensive and transparent disclosure of public debt liabilities is vital to sustainable development. It facilitates new investment, reduces corruption, brings accountability, and helps prevent costly debt crises. Transparency is central to effective debt management by debtors and better risk assessment by creditors, as well as to responsible borrowing and lending practices.

A lack of transparency, by contrast, impedes borrowers' ability to manage debt, increases uncertainty, and raises borrowing costs. It also makes it more difficult to restructure unsustainable debt. Despite progress on transparency in recent decades, public disclosure of debt data by authorities in countries eligible for assistance from the International Development Association (IDA) is still limited, particularly in fragile countries.[1] As recently as 2020, less than half of these countries regularly published fully accessible public debt data on a government website.

Transparency has improved markedly over the past three years through the collaborative efforts of the governments of borrowing countries and creditors, supported by the international community and academia. Governments of borrowing countries and creditors have worked together to reconcile data discrepancies, expand data coverage, and improve the accuracy of debt data reported to the World Bank's Debtor Reporting System (DRS). The international community has worked to educate borrowing country governments on how to better service and reduce their debt as well as improve collection and reporting methods, and to promote information sharing to harmonize data, definitions, and standards. Academia and research institutions have provided additional research and intellectual input.

These collaborative efforts look to continue and even increase, with data-reconciliation exercises becoming annual events; and the World Bank and its development partners are committed to working ever more closely with governments on debt management and recording, with growing scrutiny from academia. As these four groups pursue this agenda, described in the sections that follow, debt transparency will continue to improve, with all the development benefits that result from it.

Borrower Countries

Borrowers bear the primary responsibility for debt transparency. Their goal is comprehensive and timely disclosure of public debt commitments, repayment terms, and transactions sufficiently granular to facilitate scrutiny of government borrowing and public accountability. Achieving this goal, however, requires both the willingness to disclose and the capacity to do so. Debt transparency is integral to debt management and its governance and accountability framework, both of which remain weak in many low- and middle-income countries (LMICs).

That said, progress toward greater debt transparency is encouraging. Since 2020, the number of LMICs that regularly publish debt bulletins has increased significantly. The World Bank Debt Reporting Heat Map, which was introduced in 2020 to measure debt transparency and accountability and is updated annually, tracks public debt disclosure for IDA-eligible borrowers.[2] It also charts accountability for public borrowing through publication of medium-term debt strategies, annual borrowing plans, and disclosure of data on guarantees and other contingent liabilities. The most recent 2023 Heat Map found that 51 countries, or 69 percent of IDA-eligible countries, regularly publish fully accessible public debt data on a government website (figure 3.1). This number represents a more than 20-percentage-point increase from 2020, when only 36 countries, or 47 percent, met the same criteria. Additionally, eight other countries had partially accessible public debt data in 2023; that is, information was available but was scattered across multiple documents or multiple websites. Countries in Sub-Saharan Africa drove the expansion in accessibility. In 2023, the Heat Map found that 79 percent of these countries have fully accessible public debt data, compared to 49 percent in 2020.

The increase in disclosure of public debt data is accompanied by a parallel expansion in data coverage. In 2023, 64 percent of IDA-eligible countries disclosed comprehensive public debt data covering domestic and external debt and guarantees, up from 43 percent in 2020. In Sub-Saharan Africa, 66.7 percent of countries disclosed comprehensive public debt data in 2023, compared to only 46 percent in 2020; in Latin America and the Caribbean, 63 percent of countries in 2023 met this goal, compared to 25 percent in 2020. Advances in disclosure of information on recently contracted external debt have been much more modest, however. In 2023, 36 percent of countries disclosed information on new external loans, a marginal 3-percentage-point increase from 2020, and only 18 percent provided information on the terms of loan contracts.

Figure 3.1 Public Debt Disclosure by IDA-Eligible Countries, Access and Coverage, 2020 vs. 2023

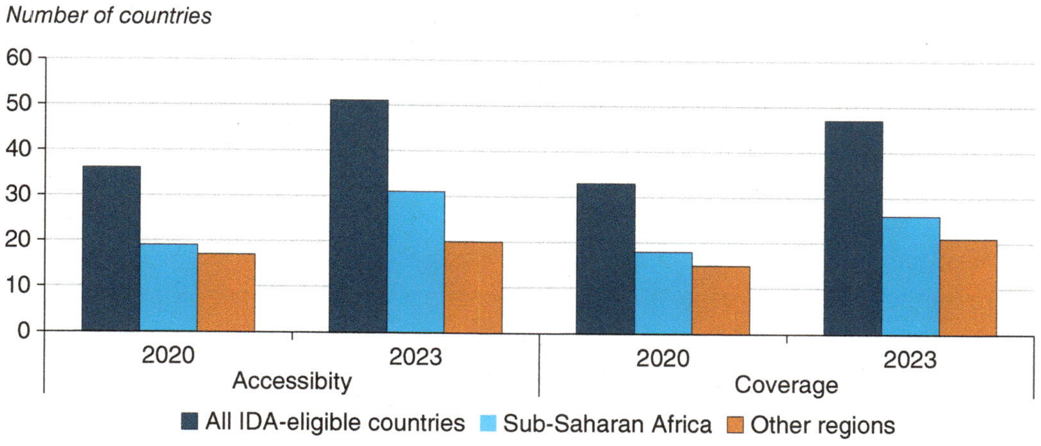

Number of countries

Source: World Bank Debt Reporting Heat Map, 2020 and 2023.
Note: IDA = International Development Association.

The IDA Sustainable Development Finance Policy, launched in July 2020, has been instrumental in increasing and institutionalizing the disclosure of public debt data. The policy aims to incentivize countries to adopt sustainable and transparent financing practices and deepen coordination between IDA and other creditors to promote information sharing and collective action by traditional and nontraditional creditors. The policy requires countries at moderate or elevated risk of debt distress to adopt performance and policy actions (PPAs) that address debt vulnerabilities and enhance transparency, promote fiscal sustainability, and strengthen debt management.[3] Since the policy became effective, a total of 576 PPAs were agreed through end-June 2024 by 55–60 countries each year.[4] Twenty-four percent of these PPAs related specifically to debt transparency with a focus on publication of comprehensive annual debt reports and/or quarterly debt bulletins.

In fiscal years 2023 and 2024, over 40 percent of countries had at least one PPA targeting improvements in debt transparency. Two-thirds of these PPAs concentrated on widening the scope of public debt reporting, often focusing on debt of state-owned enterprises (SOEs); one-third took actions to institutionalize debt publications through government orders or decrees. Debt transparency is integral to debt management, and PPAs to enhance debt management include actions designed to enable debt transparency, for example, legislative and institutional reforms and strengthening debt monitoring and recording. Technical assistance and advisory services from the World Bank and other development partners, and prior actions in development policy operations, support the implementation of PPAs.

Improvements in debt transparency at the national level have a direct impact on the timeliness of reports to the DRS and data published in the International Debt Statistics database (IDS). The DRS requires World Bank borrowers to provide an annual year-end loan-by-loan account of outstanding balance and transactions for all external public and publicly guaranteed debt. The first deadline for submission is end-March, with an extended deadline of end-June. For the latest 2023 reporting round, 50 percent of DRS reporters met the end-March 2024 deadline and 79 percent reported by end-April (figure 3.2). Only seven countries (5.9 percent), most of them in conflict situations, failed to report. By contrast, in the 2019 reporting round, 38 percent of countries met the March deadline, 18 percent missed the end-June deadline and 12 countries (10 percent) failed to report.

The accuracy and coverage of reporting to the DRS continued to improve in 2023. To disclose public debt data on a regular basis in debt reports and bulletins, national debt offices must implement effective mechanisms to record and validate public debt data. These mechanisms lead in turn to improvement in the coverage, accuracy, and timeliness of borrowers' reports to the DRS. Of note in 2023 was improvement in reporting by low-income countries and small states, which often have limited resources for debt management. These states include Burundi, the Central African Republic, the Democratic Republic of Congo, Dominica, The Gambia, St. Lucia, and Uganda. All these countries implemented at least one PPA focused on debt transparency. In other countries, expansion in the coverage and granularity of data the borrower discloses has been paralleled by steps to address stock-flow inconsistencies and omissions in DRS reports.

Figure 3.2 Reporting Timetable for Debtor Reporting System Countries, 2019–23

Percent

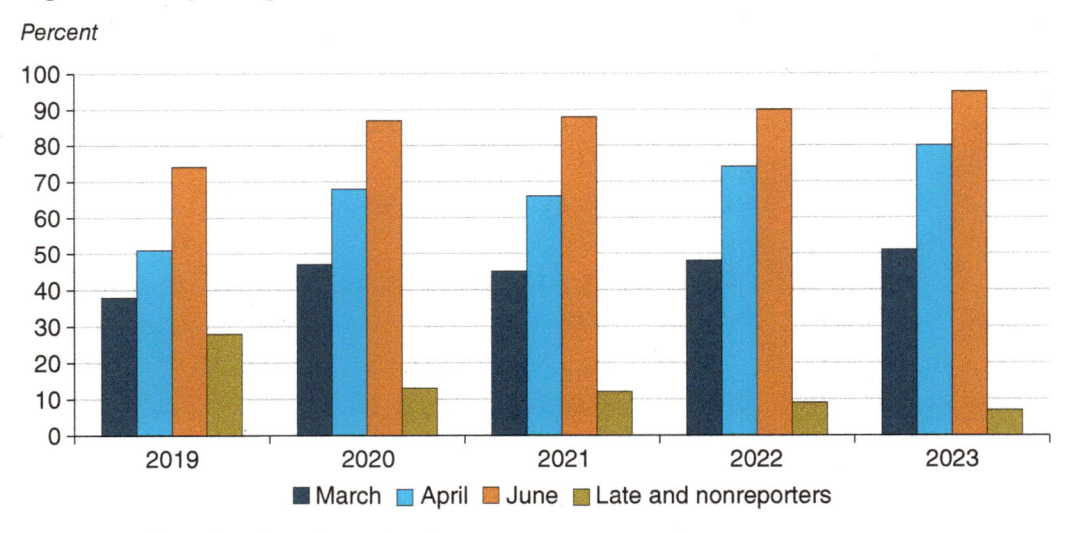

Source: World Bank Debtor Reporting System.

For example the Kyrgyz Republic has progressively expanded its annual debt report, established methodological guidelines by Ministerial Order, and broadened the 2023 annual debt report to include an analysis of government debt, the creditor and currency breakdown, and information on government guarantees, on-lent debt, and repayment arrears on the on-lent debt.

Advances in debt management systems and technology are making it easier for countries to manage public debt portfolios. The public debt management systems developed by Commonwealth Secretariat (ComSec) and the UN Trade and Development (UNCTAD) offer an integrated tool to record, analyze, and report public debt. The systems have the capacity to manage the domestic and external public debt liabilities of sovereign and subnational borrowers, and both conventional and complex financial products, loans, and securities offered by a wide range of creditors. About 80 percent of DRS reporters use the ComSec or UNCTAD systems, and both systems enable automated validation of data entries, facilitate reconciliation of borrower and creditor records, and allow for straight-through electronic reporting to the DRS. The holistic design features of these systems facilitate accurate and timely reporting both by countries like Eswatini and The Gambia, which recently transitioned to ComSec Meridian and borrow primarily from official creditors, and by market-based International Bank for Reconstruction and Development borrowers like the Arab Republic of Egypt and India, which both have large and very complex debt portfolios.

Gaps in the DRS on borrowing by SOEs are gradually being closed. An increased number of PPAs focus on extending national debt office legislative authority to monitor borrowing by SOEs. For example, Grenada amended the Fiscal Responsibility Act to broaden the coverage of public debt to include the debt of SOEs and main statutory bodies, as well as any explicit contingent liabilities related to public-private partnerships.[5] Actions like these lay the groundwork for implementation of reporting systems that capture loan-level information on SOEs' obligations, which not only strengthens debt sustainability analyses but also enables borrowers to meet DRS reporting requirements. In the interim, PPAs that require disclosure of information on the debt liabilities of SOEs help to quantify potential gaps in DRS data and facilitate the Debt Statistics Team dialogue with national compilers to close the gaps.

The World Bank is also doing all it can to enhance reporting on nonguaranteed external borrowing by private sector entities. For this category of debt, the DRS requires aggregate data with a breakdown by type of creditor, including foreign parents and affiliates. The liabilities reported to the DRS are rigorously reconciled for consistency with data reported to the International Monetary Fund (IMF) Balance of Payments and International Investment Position and the joint IMF-World Bank Quarterly External Debt Statistics. The World Bank Debt Statistics Team is also working closely with central banks like the Bank of Mexico to identify ways to ensure that systems for reporting and recording private nonguaranteed debt capture the debt liabilities associated with foreign direct investment.

Creditor Countries

Creditors also have a vital role to play in debt transparency. The most effective and foolproof way to validate the accuracy of debt data and close data gaps is systematic reconciliation of debtor and creditor records. This reconciliation requires an ongoing commitment to data sharing by creditors, however, as well as timely and transparent disclosure of loan-specific information on lending activities. The Group of Twenty (G-20) bilateral creditors have committed to a range of good transparency-related lending practices, and most of the Group of Seven (G-7) countries publish detailed information on national websites. No international reporting system exists that requires regular, standardized reporting, however, and many G-20 bilateral creditors do not disclose the amounts and terms of lending to LMICs. The International Institute of Finance has taken a leadership role in promoting transparency for private creditors and has developed a set of disclosure principles and guidelines. These efforts contributed to the Organisation for Economic Co-operation and Development's decision to create a public debt data repository for low-income countries. Thus far, however, buy-in by private creditors has been marginal and only a handful of loans have been reported to the repository.

The data sharing initiative between G-20 bilateral creditors and the World Bank is a crucial step toward advancing debt transparency and harmonizing debtor and creditor data. The initiative, launched in 2022, aims to eliminate inaccuracies and data gaps through a loan-level reconciliation of information reported to the DRS by IDA-eligible countries with the comparable claims of G-20 bilateral creditors. This reconciliation is particularly relevant for these countries, where monitoring and reporting on public debt may still be limited despite the considerable progress made by these borrowers to strengthen their debt management capacity over the past decade.

Eighteen of the 22 permanent members of the Paris Club participated in the first data sharing exercise. The group comprised all G-7 countries and 11 other permanent members (Australia, Brazil, Denmark, Finland, Israel, the Republic of Korea, the Netherlands, Norway, Spain, Sweden, and Switzerland). The reconciliation centered on public sector debt owed to official bilateral creditors—that is, sovereign governments and public institutions in which the government has a 50 percent or greater share. Creditors provided loan-by-loan information in a standardized format on loan amounts and terms and end-2021 debt stocks and flows (disbursements and debt service payments) for 77 LMICs. These data were reconciled with comparable end-2021 data reported to the DRS.

Preliminary findings of the data sharing exercise, presented at the G-7 meeting in Hiroshima, Japan, in May 2023, were encouraging. About 80 percent of the 3,655 individual loans recorded by creditors, accounting for 90 percent of US$63 billion in creditor claims, matched a counterpart in the DRS. In a second round of reconciliation of the end-2021 data, the World Bank made a detailed assessment of differences in methodology, accounting, and compilation practices between DRS norms and each creditor. It also identified the reasons that the amounts reported by borrowers to the DRS were sometimes higher than creditor claims. Aside from some double counting, the primary reason for overstatement of borrowers' obligations was a lag in recording debt forgiveness in the context of the Heavily Indebted Poor Countries Initiative or bilateral debt conversion mechanisms.[6] To remedy this problem, the World Bank's Debt Statistics Team addressed reporting issues and discrepancies on the borrower side through dialogue with national debt offices. The two-pronged approach reduced the overall margin of error between the creditor and debtor data sets to about 2 percent.

The data sharing initiative of the World Bank and G-20 bilateral creditors is an ongoing process designed to ensure that debtor and creditor records remain harmonized. The second round, reconciliation of 2022 and 2023 data, is currently under way for creditors participating in the first round. This time around the process should be far less time consuming because it starts from a solid foundation. Other G-20 bilateral creditors have signaled an intent to share data, and current participants are encouraging them to engage. The World Bank also advocates the importance of data sharing and promotes the value of these comparison exercises in various forums to galvanize buy-in from creditors that have not yet shared data. The aim is for data sharing and reconciliation of debtor and creditor data to become established practices for all G-20 countries and other official creditors.

In recent years the academic community has taken a keener interest in debt held by LMICs, particularly in light of rising debt levels among these borrowers as well as a marked increase in bilateral loans extended to them, particularly by China. Major academic research has been conducted by universities and research institutions, including but not limited to the AidData Lab at William & Mary University in Virginia, the China Africa Research Initiative at the Johns Hopkins

University School of Advanced International Studies in Washington, DC, Germany's Kiel Institute for the World Economy, and the Peterson Institute for International Economics in Washington, DC. For example, the China Africa Research Initiative researches Chinese lending to Africa and publishes a global debt relief dashboard, AidData has created a database on China's external lending, and the Kiel Institute publishes research on lending to African countries.

The World Bank welcomes this academic research into LMIC debt, though the findings can differ significantly from World Bank debt data reported to the DRS and published in the *International Debt Report*. These discrepancies often result from comparisons of data sets that differ in coverage and use different definitions, and so can be misleading. For example, the report by AidData that accompanied the release in 2021 of its extensive database on China's external lending (Malik et al. 2021) found that lending by China to LMICs between 2000 and 2017 totaled US$676 billion, significantly higher than the US$310 billion reported to the World Bank and recorded in IDS.[7] Although this discrepancy suggested that the World Bank was not capturing all of China's lending, a like-for-like comparison of loans made by China during the period paints a very different picture (refer to box 3.1 for further discussion of China's lending). AidData recorded loans from 165 countries, 45 of which do not report loans to the Bank because they are not World Bank borrowers, including countries like República Bolivariana de Venezuela, one of China's largest debtors.[8] For the 120 LMICs common to AidData and DRS databases, the DRS recorded US$309 billion in loan commitments from China to public and publicly guaranteed borrowers in 2000–17. For the same period, AidData reported China's lending to borrowers categorized as "sovereign" (broadly equivalent to the DRS public and publicly guaranteed debt) as US$257 billion, 17 percent lower than the DRS total (Malik et al. 2021, table A-27).

A loan-by-loan comparison by the World Bank of the DRS and the AidData database identified misalignment of country and sector coverage as the key driver of AidData's findings. The comparison was based on public and publicly guaranteed loan commitments reported to the DRS from 2000 to 2017 and the comparable loan commitments recorded in the AidData database. In addition to the 45 countries included in AidData's total that were not World Bank borrowers and therefore not required to report to the DRS, AidData included borrowing by private entities and special purpose vehicles, which it categorized as a contingent liability of the sovereign. The DRS treats such borrowing as a direct obligation of the private sector; more important, such data are reported to the DRS in aggregate,[9] which makes it impossible to compare lending by any individual creditor (such as China). AidData also deviated from international standards and definitions, notably regarding the separation of domestic and external debt, and also had a small amount of double counting (for example, attribution to a borrower of lending from one Chinese entity to another). As noted earlier, the gaps in reporting to the DRS were small in relation to the overall volume of China's lending and occurred primarily in countries with limited debt management capacity.

Box 3.1 How China Lends

Research findings are an important input to understanding emergent trends in borrowing and lending practices in low- and middle-income countries, and they also challenge the World Bank to assess the coverage and accuracy of the data it disseminates. Research findings often highlight shortcomings in disclosure and reporting to the Debtor Reporting System (DRS) that need to be addressed, though not in every case.

A research paper published in March 2021 by several academic and international organizations, titled "How China Lends: A Rare Look into 100 Debt Contracts with Foreign Governments," found that Chinese loan contracts contained unusual confidentiality clauses that bar borrowers from revealing the terms or even the existence of the loan (Gelpern et al. 2021). The paper argued that these clauses contribute to the problem of "hidden debt." The loan contracts on which the research findings were based were drawn from the database compiled by the AidData Lab at the College of William & Mary, Virginia (refer to the main text of the chapter for more on AidData).

All creditors, including commercial banks, hedge funds, suppliers, and export credit agencies, seek a measure of influence over debtors to maximize their prospects of repayment by any legal, economic, and political means available to them (for example, Gelpern 2004, 2007; Schumacher, Trebesch, and Enderlein 2021). The research paper found that many of the terms and conditions in the loan contracts it reviewed exhibited a difference in degree, not in kind, from those used by other official bilateral lenders and commercial lenders. However, it identified several unique provisions in China's contracts, such as broad borrower confidentiality undertakings, the promise to exclude Chinese lenders from Paris Club and other collective restructuring initiatives, and expansive cross-defaults clauses designed to bolster China's position in the borrowing country. It also found that many of the contracts contained or referred to borrowers' promises not to disclose their terms—or, in some cases, even the fact of the contract's existence.

Any confidentiality clause that specifically requires secrecy actively undermines debt transparency. Lenders and borrowers should restrict confidentiality requirements that seek to keep borrowing secret by invoking a nondisclosure

(Box continues on next page)

Box 3.1 How China Lends (*continued*)

clause (recognizing, however, that in specific instances, such as national security laws, disclosure by a borrower or lender may be exempted). Moreover, a borrower that agrees to keep loan information secret risks being in breach of undertakings made in favor of other lenders, being noncompliant with periodic reporting and information-sharing undertakings, and likely impeding the compilation of accurate debt sustainability assessments. Undisclosed or hidden debt may also hamper the borrower's ability to obtain new financing or restructure its debt should the need arise. Despite the stringent confidentiality clauses identified by the research paper in loan contracts between China and low- and middle-income countries, these clauses do not appear to prevent the countries from publishing detailed information on borrowing from China. For example, Angola's bond prospectus, Kenya's online loan registry, and Nigeria's Debt Management Office statements all provide detailed information on loans contracted with China. Moreover, as the paper noted, Cameroon publishes all project-related loan contracts with external creditors. Similarly, the clauses have not prevented borrowers from reporting loan amounts and terms to the DRS.

Most of the 100 loan contracts referenced in the research paper had already been reported to the DRS by the borrower in the year the loan was contracted and are in the DRS database. Four of the contracts are term facility agreements—that is, formal expressions of interest to lend but not binding commitments. Of the 96 loan contracts, 90 were reported to the DRS and 23 (or 25 percent) were with Cameroon. Regarding the six other contracts in the sample, two were to high-income countries (Antigua and Barbuda and Uruguay) that are not included in this publication or the International Debt Statistics database. Two others, a short-term debt instrument and a loan to a special purpose vehicle, fall under categories of debt reported in aggregate to the DRS. Only two loan contracts were missing from the DRS, one to a local government and another to a state-owned enterprise. Both omissions arose from shortcomings in monitoring and reporting mechanisms; follow-up by the World Bank Debt Statistics Team with national debt offices closed this small reporting gap.

The International Community

In addition to the extensive data set reconciliation work done by the G-7 and G-20, described earlier, multilateral institutions—particularly the World Bank—continue to promote more accurate and comprehensive debt data reporting, set and enforce international standards and definitions, and provide ongoing information, education, and guidance on data collection, analytics, and debt management.

LMICs disclose external debt at both the national level and collectively through the World Bank's DRS. Regular, quarterly, and annual reporting to the DRS in a prescribed format is a mandatory requirement for World Bank (both IDA and International Bank for Reconstruction and Development) borrowers. The World Bank has long regarded data drawn from the DRS as a global public good and has published these data for over 50 years: IDS constitutes the only long-series, cross-country comparable data for debt of LMICs. The World Bank Debt Statistics Team strives to ensure the accuracy and comprehensiveness of IDS. To this end, it routinely reconciles data reported to the DRS with data published in national bulletins and reported to the joint IMF–World Bank Quarterly External Debt Statistics, Quarterly Public Sector Debt, and IMF's Balance of Payments and International Investment Position. It also draws on the Organisation for Economic Co-operation and Development's Creditor Reporting System, online data made available by official creditors or presented in annual reports, and market sources of information compiled by private entities like AidData, the China Africa Research Initiative, and Dealogic.

The World Bank is transparent about gaps in the data disseminated in IDS. Country notes that accompany every release of the database signal data limitations to users, including instances when estimated data series or specific reporting issues may compromise the validity of data. These issues most often relate to nonguaranteed borrowing by SOEs. The DRS's comprehensive definition of public debt includes the debt of all SOEs in which the government owns a majority share, regardless of whether it benefits from a sovereign guarantee. Many borrowers have a narrower definition, however, and the resulting omission of SOE debt reflects the legal framework and the mandate of the public debt office more than any unwillingness to disclose.

The expectation is that greater debt transparency will bring clarity, but divergent figures for borrowers' liabilities or creditors' loans are common. They raise doubts about data accuracy, underrecording, or deliberate nondisclosure and hidden debt. Although such factors are not uncommon, the existence of two different numbers that purport to measure the same thing does not necessarily indicate that one is wrong. A major reason for such discrepancies is the divergence in standards, definitions, and statistical and accounting norms. These differences present a minefield for users trying to compare data, and in extreme cases have led to discrepancies as large as 30 percent of gross domestic product across sources with the same expected coverage (Rivetti 2021). Issues as simple as the separation of domestic and external debt on a currency basis can result in a lower number for external debt stock in national bulletins than in IDS, which uses the international residency criterion. Conversely, information in IDS on a creditor's lending will likely be lower than the creditor record because the World Bank figure is a subset that excludes loans to nonguaranteed private sector borrowers (which are reported to the DRS in aggregate) and to non–World Bank borrowers. Differences in instrument and sectoral coverage and accounting and compilation conventions all compound reconciliation across data sets.

International standards and definitions are the bedrock of viable comparisons across countries and data sets. In collaboration with the Bank for International Settlement, IMF, and the Organisation for Economic Co-operation and Development, the World Bank plays a central role in setting international standards and definitions for measurement and compilation of public debt statistics. Raising LMICs' awareness of the importance of adherence to these standards when reporting to the DRS, as well as the advantages of incorporating them into national debt reporting practices, is an ongoing activity for the World Bank's Debt Statistics Team. The team provides technical support to national compilers and is a regular participant in workshops and seminars on this topic sponsored by the IMF and other development partners, notably ComSec and UNCTAD.

The new World Bank Group Academy offers various courses to help member countries improve data collection, management, and analytics. Among the academy's offerings is a series of courses designed to provide comprehensive insights into debt statistics. At the launch in June 2024, in Perugia, Italy, the World Bank's Development Data Group presented a new course, "Making Debt Data Transparent and Sustainable amidst Debt Distress." The course provided guidance and instruction to help borrowing countries avoid having to choose between servicing their debt and investing in the health, education, and welfare of their citizens, as well as guidance for reducing debt, increasing transparency, and facilitating swifter restructurings.

The Development Data Group also engages in ongoing efforts to improve its methodologies on debt reporting and collection, and continues to update and improve manuals and other information it makes available on these topics to member countries.

In conclusion, LMICs currently disclose far more information on the size and composition of their public debt portfolios than they did five years ago. Although achieving the overarching goals of the debt transparency agenda still has a long way to go, the actions required are well documented and agreed upon by borrowers, creditors, and international partners, with increasing confidence that these goals can be met. For the World Bank, closing data gaps and reconciling borrower and creditor records to ensure the accuracy of the data it disseminates is a constant priority. Looking forward, additional efforts include a redesign of the

DRS to align with changes in countries' borrowing patterns and creditor lending instruments, and transitioning to a cloud-based, state-of-the-art data platform that will facilitate borrower reporting to the DRS and streamline user access to IDS. A new and exciting part of this project aims to expand the DRS to domestic public debt, which has become an increasingly important component of LMICs' public debt portfolios.

Notes

1. Countries with gross national income per capital below US$1,335 in 2024 are eligible for support from the IDA.
2. For more on the Debt Reporting Heat Map, refer to https://www.worldbank.org/en/topic/debt /brief/debt-transparency-report/2023.
3. Countries that do not satisfactorily implement their PPAs on time will have 10 or 20 percent of their annual Country Allocations set aside depending on their debt risk, and face restrictions in their access to frontloading and reallocations.
4. Approved PPAs each fiscal year include carryover PPAs that were not satisfactorily implemented the previous fiscal year.
5. Refer to World Bank, "IDA's Sustainable Development Finance Policy (SDFP) Approved FY24 Performance and Policy Actions (PPAs)," https://thedocs.worldbank.org/en/doc/a32f9de56a5e 1d56f130a1df492dc804-0410012024/original/SDFP-Approved-FY24-PPAs.pdf or https://ida .worldbank.org/en/financing/debt/sustainable-development-finance-policy.
6. The World Bank, IMF, and other creditors launched the Heavily Indebted Poor Countries Initiative in 1996 to ensure that the world's poorest countries are not overwhelmed by unsustainable debt burdens. The program reduces the debt of countries that meet strict criteria.
7. "The AidData database is compiled from official sources, such as grant and loan agreements published in government registers and gazettes, official records extracted from the aid and debt information management systems of host countries, annual reports published by Chinese state-owned banks, Chinese Embassy and Ministry of Commerce websites, reports published by parliamentary oversight institutions in host countries, and our own direct correspondence with finance ministry officials in developing countries" (Malik et al. 2021, 6).
8. Differences for data sets that include countries that do not report to the DRS cannot be reconciled because of one-sided information.
9. For borrowing by a private sector entity, the World Bank DRS requirement for loan-by-loan information applies only in cases in which a loan is guaranteed by the sovereign or other public sector entity.

References

Gelpern, Anna. 2004. "Building a Better Seating Chart for Sovereign Restructurings." *Emory Law Journal* 53: 1115–58.

Gelpern, Anna. 2007. "Odious, Not Debt." *Law and Contemporary Problems* 70 (3): 81–114.

Gelpern, Anna, Sebastian Horn, Scott Morris, Brad Parks, and Christoph Trebesch. 2021. "How China Lends: A Rare Look into 100 Debt Contracts with Foreign Governments." Peterson Institute for International Economics, Kiel Institute for the World Economy, Center for Global Development, and AidData at William & Mary. https://www.aiddata.org/publications/how -china-lends.

Malik, Ammar A., Bradley Parks, Brooke Russell, Joyce Jiahui Lin, Katherine Walsh, Kyra Solomon, Sheng Zhang, Thai-Binh Elston, and Seth Goodman. 2021. *Banking on the Belt and Road: Insights from a New Global Dataset of 13,427 Chinese Development Projects.* Williamsburg, VA: AidData at William & Mary.

Rivetti, Diego. 2021. *Debt Transparency in Developing Economies.* Washington, DC: World Bank.

Schumacher, Julian, Christoph Trebesch, and Hendrik Enderlein. 2021. "Sovereign Defaults in Court." ECB Working Paper No. 2135, European Central Bank. https://www.ecb.europa.eu/pub/pdf/scpwps/ecb.wp2135.en.pdf.

PART 2
Aggregate and Country Tables

ALL LOW- AND MIDDLE-INCOME COUNTRIES

(US$ billion, unless otherwise indicated)

Snapshot	2023
Total external debt stocks	**8,837**
External debt stocks as % of:	
Exports	96
GNI	24
Debt service as % of:	
Exports	15
GNI	4
Net financial flows, debt and equity	600
Net debt inflows	221
Net equity inflows	379
GNI	**36,294**
Population (million)	**6,494**

Figure 2 Average terms on new debt commitments from official and private creditors

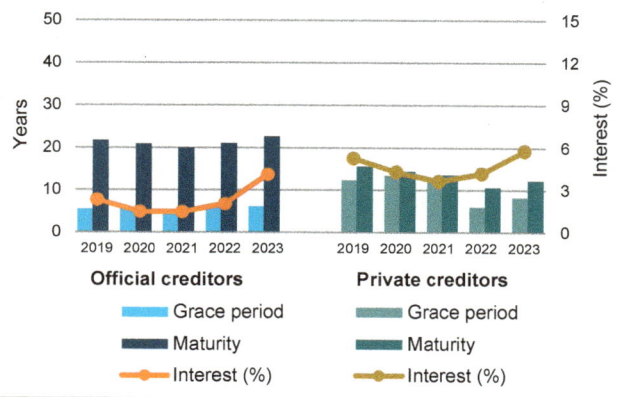

Official creditors
- Grace period
- Maturity
- Interest (%)

Private creditors
- Grace period
- Maturity
- Interest (%)

Figure 1 Public and publicly guaranteed debt, by creditor and creditor type in 2023, including IMF credit

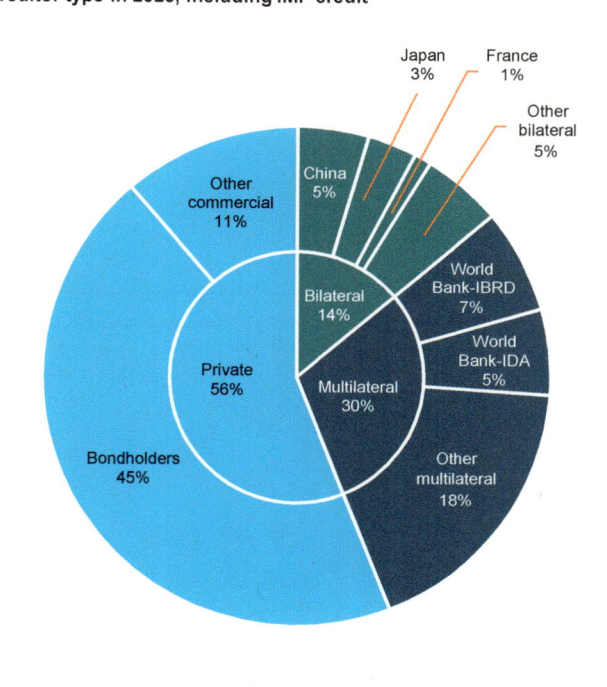

Summary External Debt Data	2010	2019	2020	2021	2022	2023
Total external debt stocks	**3,865**	**7,754**	**8,173**	**8,819**	**8,631**	**8,837**
Long-term external debt stocks	**2,646**	**5,543**	**5,896**	**6,091**	**5,984**	**6,113**
Public and publicly guaranteed debt from:	*1,395*	*2,950*	*3,185*	*3,328*	*3,317*	*3,450*
Official creditors	811	1,169	1,283	1,312	1,350	1,440
Multilateral	461	692	775	808	857	941
of which: World Bank	235	340	376	389	407	437
Bilateral	350	477	508	504	492	499
Private creditors	583	1,781	1,902	2,016	1,968	2,010
Bondholders	435	1,433	1,550	1,632	1,573	1,602
Commercial banks and others	148	348	352	384	395	408
Private nonguaranteed debt from:	*1,251*	*2,593*	*2,711*	*2,762*	*2,667*	*2,663*
Bondholders	207	544	648	666	590	539
Commercial banks and others	1,044	2,049	2,063	2,096	2,078	2,125
Use of IMF credit and SDR allocations	**125**	**162**	**215**	**388**	**382**	**383**
IMF credit	49	94	145	142	148	147
SDR allocations	76	68	71	246	234	236
Short-term external debt stocks	**1,094**	**2,048**	**2,062**	**2,341**	**2,264**	**2,341**
Disbursements, long-term	**577**	**1,134**	**1,140**	**1,156**	**937**	**1,073**
Public and publicly guaranteed sector	235	417	458	462	336	367
Private sector not guaranteed	342	717	682	694	601	706
Principal repayments, long-term	**315**	**813**	**793**	**845**	**922**	**921**
Public and publicly guaranteed sector	105	228	240	260	266	232
Private sector not guaranteed	210	585	553	585	655	689
Interest payments, long-term	**85**	**211**	**183**	**203**	**199**	**255**
Public and publicly guaranteed sector	45	115	99	105	107	137
Private sector not guaranteed	41	96	84	98	92	119

EAST ASIA AND PACIFIC

(US$ billion, unless otherwise indicated)

Snapshot	2023
Total external debt stocks	**3,393**
External debt stocks as % of:	
Exports	68
GNI	16
Debt service as % of:	
Exports	11
GNI	3
Net financial flows, debt and equity	**122**
Net debt inflows	-4
Net equity inflows	127
GNI	**20,563**
Population (million)	**2,073**

Figure 2 Average terms on new debt commitments from official and private creditors

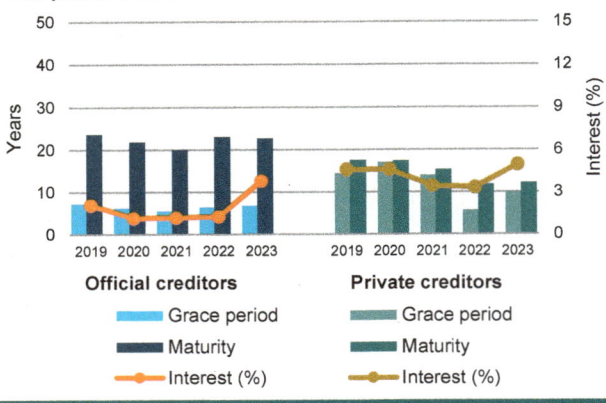

Official creditors
- Grace period
- Maturity
- Interest (%)

Private creditors
- Grace period
- Maturity
- Interest (%)

Figure 1 Public and publicly guaranteed debt, by creditor and creditor type in 2023, including IMF credit

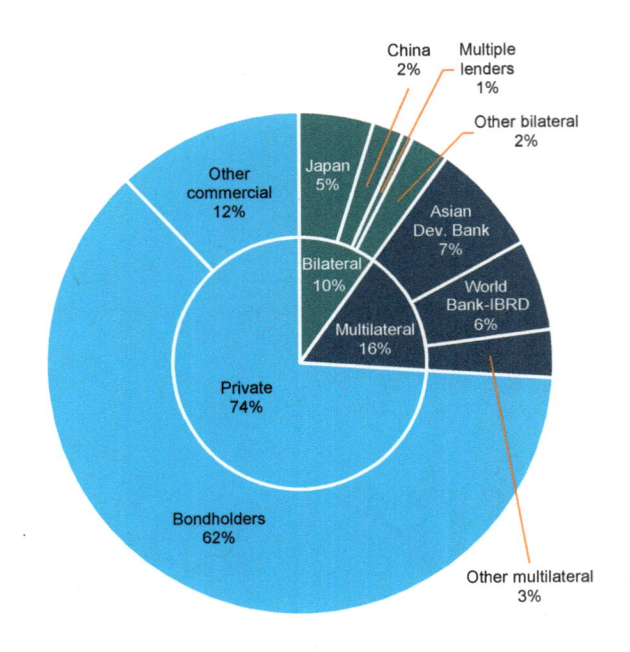

Summary External Debt Data	2010	2019	2020	2021	2022	2023
Total external debt stocks	**1,193**	**2,992**	**3,265**	**3,697**	**3,415**	**3,393**
Long-term external debt stocks	559	1,625	1,853	2,007	1,896	1,851
Public and publicly guaranteed debt from:	*319*	*735*	*839*	*918*	*886*	*900*
Official creditors	217	216	236	235	229	233
Multilateral	87	116	130	135	138	144
of which: World Bank	47	62	66	68	69	71
Bilateral	130	99	106	100	91	89
Private creditors	102	519	603	683	657	667
Bondholders	73	450	534	597	560	559
Commercial banks and others	29	69	68	86	96	108
Private nonguaranteed debt from:	*240*	*890*	*1,014*	*1,089*	*1,010*	*951*
Bondholders	20	276	371	393	352	311
Commercial banks and others	220	614	643	696	657	640
Use of IMF credit and SDR allocations	18	17	18	75	72	72
IMF credit	0	0	1	1	1	1
SDR allocations	18	16	17	74	70	71
Short-term external debt stocks	616	1,351	1,393	1,615	1,447	1,469
Disbursements, long-term	**117**	**513**	**501**	**511**	**376**	**342**
Public and publicly guaranteed sector	48	130	151	166	83	78
Private sector not guaranteed	69	383	350	345	293	264
Principal repayments, long-term	**65**	**314**	**283**	**335**	**449**	**371**
Public and publicly guaranteed sector	29	44	60	70	96	61
Private sector not guaranteed	36	270	222	265	354	310
Interest payments, long-term	**16**	**58**	**53**	**64**	**66**	**77**
Public and publicly guaranteed sector	9	23	23	29	33	40
Private sector not guaranteed	7	35	30	35	33	37

EUROPE AND CENTRAL ASIA

(US$ billion, unless otherwise indicated)

Snapshot	2023
Total external debt stocks	**1,122**
External debt stocks as % of:	
Exports	140
GNI	55
Debt service as % of:	
Exports	21
GNI	8
Net financial flows, debt and equity	**124**
Net debt inflows	87
Net equity inflows	37
GNI	**2,054**
Population (million)	**247**

Figure 2 Average terms on new debt commitments from official and private creditors

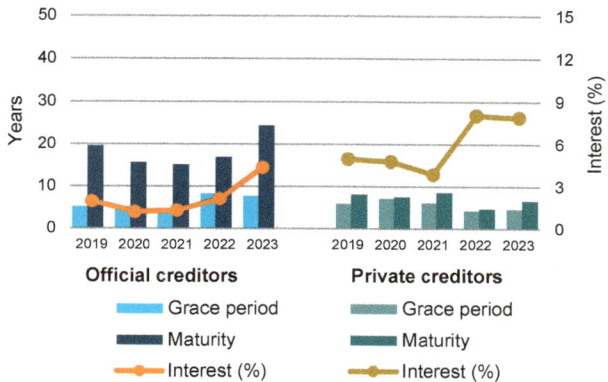

Figure 1 Public and publicly guaranteed debt, by creditor and creditor type in 2023, including IMF credit

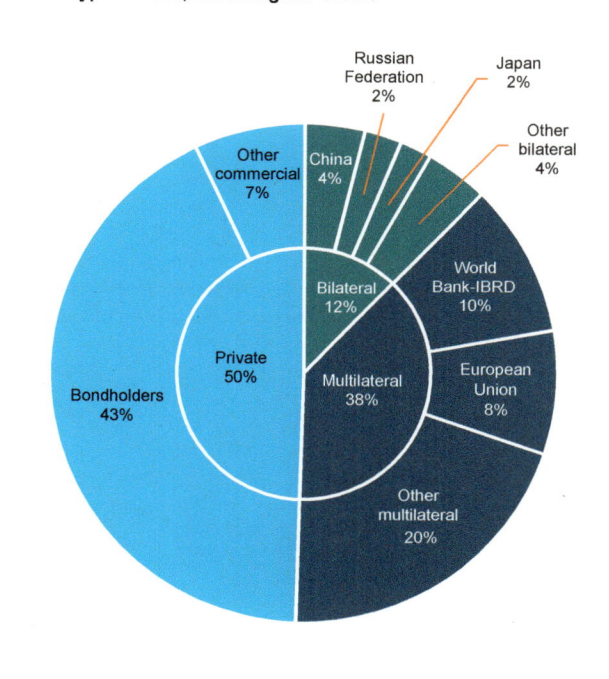

Summary External Debt Data	2010	2019	2020	2021	2022	2023
Total external debt stocks	**697**	**914**	**965**	**988**	**1,029**	**1,122**
Long-term external debt stocks	**508**	**740**	**768**	**767**	**772**	**829**
Public and publicly guaranteed debt from:	*170*	*301*	*327*	*338*	*356*	*397*
Official creditors	85	138	146	146	163	193
Multilateral	57	87	95	96	110	141
of which: World Bank	29	39	41	41	44	51
Bilateral	28	51	51	50	53	52
Private creditors	85	163	181	192	193	205
Bondholders	58	143	158	167	167	175
Commercial banks and others	27	20	23	25	26	29
Private nonguaranteed debt from:	*338*	*439*	*441*	*429*	*416*	*432*
Bondholders	32	52	52	51	42	41
Commercial banks and others	306	387	389	378	374	390
Use of IMF credit and SDR allocations	**36**	**18**	**22**	**37**	**37**	**39**
IMF credit	28	11	15	14	15	17
SDR allocations	8	7	7	23	22	22
Short-term external debt stocks	**153**	**156**	**175**	**184**	**220**	**254**
Disbursements, long-term	**147**	**136**	**148**	**129**	**141**	**176**
Public and publicly guaranteed sector	34	42	48	51	53	68
Private sector not guaranteed	114	94	99	78	88	108
Principal repayments, long-term	**113**	**128**	**129**	**116**	**121**	**121**
Public and publicly guaranteed sector	10	29	30	31	27	30
Private sector not guaranteed	103	100	99	86	94	91
Interest payments, long-term	**19**	**25**	**25**	**25**	**25**	**32**
Public and publicly guaranteed sector	6	12	12	12	12	15
Private sector not guaranteed	13	13	13	12	13	17

(US$ billion, unless otherwise indicated)

Snapshot	2023
Total external debt stocks	**2,054**
External debt stocks as % of:	
Exports	134
GNI	36
Debt service as % of:	
Exports	27
GNI	7
Net financial flows, debt and equity	190
Net debt inflows	67
Net equity inflows	123
GNI	**5,727**
Population (million)	**590**

Figure 1 Public and publicly guaranteed debt, by creditor and creditor type in 2023, including IMF credit

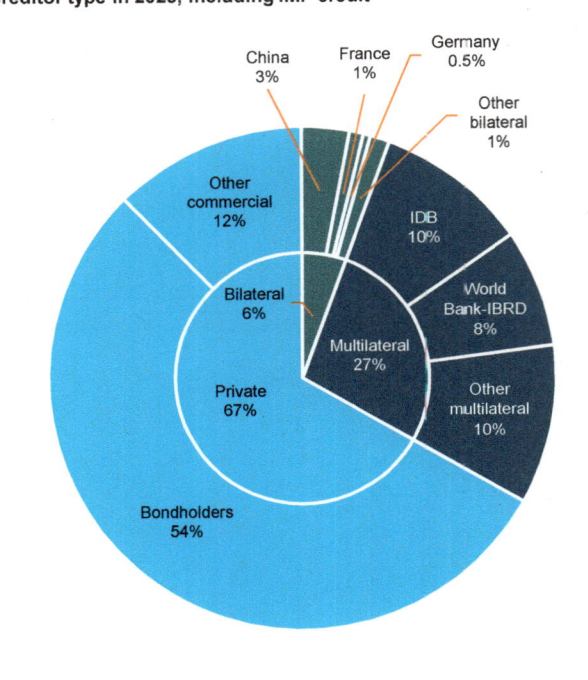

Figure 2 Average terms on new debt commitments from official and private creditors

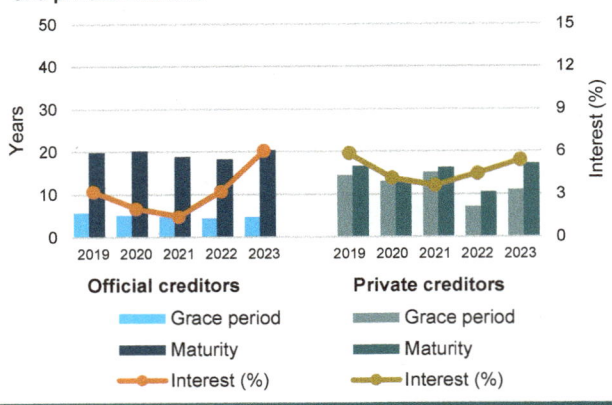

Official creditors / Private creditors

- Grace period (Official) / Grace period (Private)
- Maturity (Official) / Maturity (Private)
- Interest (%) (Official) / Interest (%) (Private)

Summary External Debt Data	2010	2019	2020	2021	2022	2023
Total external debt stocks	**1,013**	**1,927**	**1,927**	**1,973**	**1,995**	**2,054**
Long-term external debt stocks	**842**	**1,621**	**1,650**	**1,644**	**1,653**	**1,690**
Public and publicly guaranteed debt from:	*426*	*877*	*909*	*917*	*918*	*941*
Official creditors	158	228	244	256	266	275
Multilateral	121	168	183	195	208	219
of which: World Bank	48	60	67	71	77	79
Bilateral	36	60	61	60	57	56
Private creditors	268	649	665	661	652	666
Bondholders	227	517	539	532	522	543
Commercial banks and others	41	132	125	129	130	123
Private nonguaranteed debt from:	*416*	*745*	*740*	*728*	*736*	*749*
Bondholders	133	184	187	178	151	145
Commercial banks and others	283	561	553	550	585	604
Use of IMF credit and SDR allocations	**19**	**62**	**78**	**113**	**116**	**112**
IMF credit	2	47	62	57	63	58
SDR allocations	17	15	16	56	54	54
Short-term external debt stocks	**151**	**243**	**199**	**216**	**225**	**252**
Disbursements, long-term	**190**	**251**	**285**	**295**	**241**	**336**
Public and publicly guaranteed sector	83	101	132	96	84	90
Private sector not guaranteed	108	150	153	198	157	246
Principal repayments, long-term	**83**	**238**	**226**	**245**	**195**	**291**
Public and publicly guaranteed sector	39	91	73	78	59	63
Private sector not guaranteed	44	147	153	168	136	227
Interest payments, long-term	**35**	**79**	**63**	**72**	**59**	**79**
Public and publicly guaranteed sector	19	50	37	37	34	42
Private sector not guaranteed	15	29	26	34	25	36

MIDDLE EAST AND NORTH AFRICA

(US$ billion, unless otherwise indicated)

Snapshot	2023
Total external debt stocks	**443**
External debt stocks as % of:	
Exports	91
GNI	28
Debt service as % of:	
Exports	10
GNI	3
Net financial flows, debt and equity	**17**
Net debt inflows	7
Net equity inflows	10
GNI	**1,560**
Population (million)	**419**

Figure 1 Public and publicly guaranteed debt, by creditor and creditor type in 2023, including IMF credit

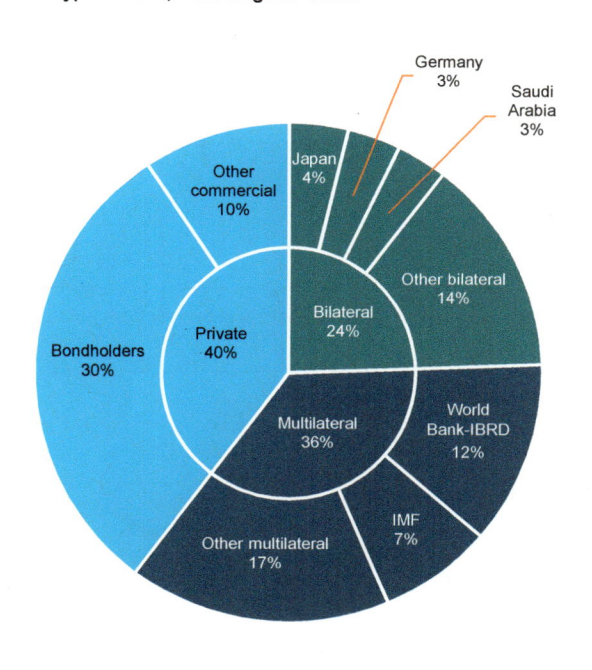

Figure 2 Average terms on new debt commitments from official and private creditors

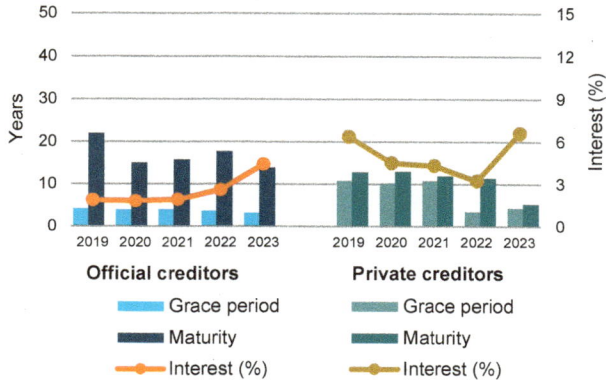

Summary External Debt Data	2010	2019	2020	2021	2022	2023
Total external debt stocks	**211**	**370**	**399**	**422**	**432**	**443**
Long-term external debt stocks	**161**	**290**	**302**	**300**	**292**	**304**
Public and publicly guaranteed debt from:	*130*	*237*	*259*	*262*	*257*	*270*
Official creditors	92	138	151	147	147	155
Multilateral	37	66	76	77	79	84
of which: World Bank	13	30	33	34	35	36
Bilateral	54	73	75	70	68	71
Private creditors	39	99	108	115	110	115
Bondholders	27	79	86	91	84	88
Commercial banks and others	12	19	21	23	25	27
Private nonguaranteed debt from:	*31*	*52*	*43*	*39*	*35*	*33*
Bondholders	1	1	1	1	1	0
Commercial banks and others	30	52	43	38	34	33
Use of IMF credit and SDR allocations	**11**	**26**	**36**	**52**	**48**	**46**
IMF credit	1	17	27	26	24	21
SDR allocations	10	9	9	26	24	25
Short-term external debt stocks	**38**	**55**	**61**	**70**	**92**	**93**
Disbursements, long-term	**23**	**40**	**36**	**38**	**26**	**34**
Public and publicly guaranteed sector	14	31	34	35	25	32
Private sector not guaranteed	9	9	2	3	1	3
Principal repayments, long-term	**18**	**27**	**29**	**32**	**28**	**24**
Public and publicly guaranteed sector	11	15	17	25	23	19
Private sector not guaranteed	8	12	12	7	4	5
Interest payments, long-term	**5**	**10**	**7**	**7**	**8**	**12**
Public and publicly guaranteed sector	5	9	6	7	7	10
Private sector not guaranteed	1	1	1	1	1	1

SOUTH ASIA

(US$ billion, unless otherwise indicated)

Snapshot	2023
Total external debt stocks	**961**
External debt stocks as % of:	
Exports	103
GNI	22
Debt service as % of:	
Exports	12
GNI	2
Net financial flows, debt and equity	95
Net debt inflows	44
Net equity inflows	51
GNI	**4,432**
Population (million)	**1,939**

Figure 2 Average terms on new debt commitments from official and private creditors

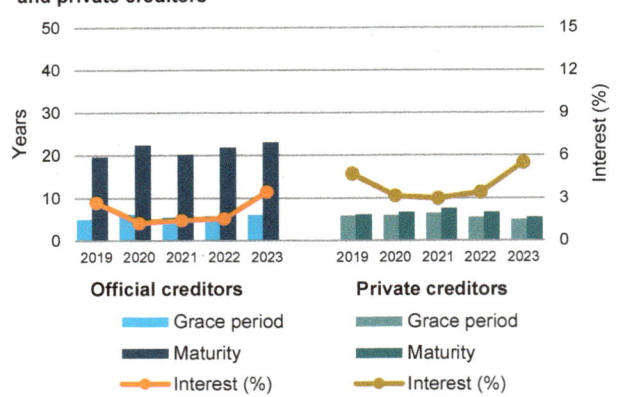

Official creditors
- Grace period
- Maturity
- Interest (%)

Private creditors
- Grace period
- Maturity
- Interest (%)

Figure 1 Public and publicly guaranteed debt, by creditor and creditor type in 2023, including IMF credit

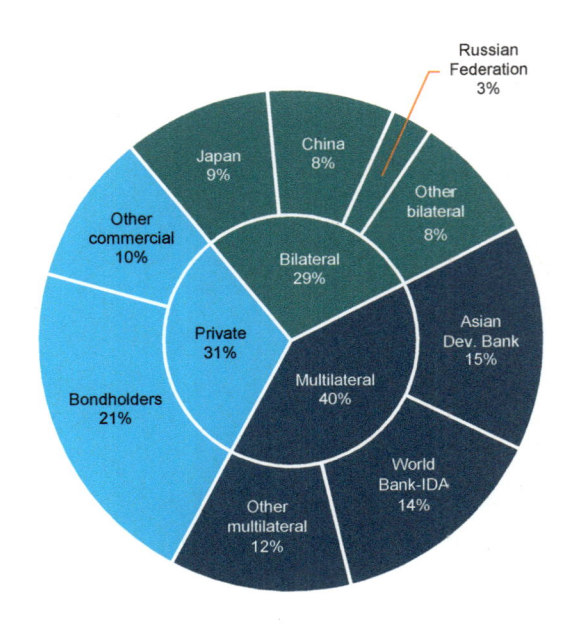

Summary External Debt Data	2010	2019	2020	2021	2022	2023
Total external debt stocks	**410**	**804**	**831**	**913**	**919**	**961**
Long-term external debt stocks	323	652	680	719	713	761
Public and publicly guaranteed debt from:	*189*	*367*	*387*	*418*	*419*	*441*
Official creditors	156	227	257	273	281	300
Multilateral	101	130	146	154	161	173
of which: World Bank	64	75	82	84	83	89
Bilateral	56	97	111	119	120	127
Private creditors	33	140	130	145	138	140
Bondholders	18	104	93	99	95	97
Commercial banks and others	15	36	37	46	43	44
Private nonguaranteed debt from:	*134*	*285*	*293*	*302*	*295*	*321*
Bondholders	13	19	27	33	34	32
Commercial banks and others	120	266	266	269	261	289
Use of IMF credit and SDR allocations	20	17	20	42	41	42
IMF credit	11	9	11	10	10	12
SDR allocations	9	8	9	32	30	30
Short-term external debt stocks	67	135	131	152	165	158
Disbursements, long-term	**52**	**106**	**98**	**101**	**74**	**119**
Public and publicly guaranteed sector	31	51	49	64	44	53
Private sector not guaranteed	22	54	50	38	30	66
Principal repayments, long-term	**24**	**52**	**78**	**56**	**68**	**68**
Public and publicly guaranteed sector	9	26	36	27	30	29
Private sector not guaranteed	15	26	42	29	37	39
Interest payments, long-term	**6**	**18**	**16**	**17**	**20**	**30**
Public and publicly guaranteed sector	3	8	6	7	8	12
Private sector not guaranteed	4	10	10	10	13	18

SUB-SAHARAN AFRICA

(US$ billion, unless otherwise indicated)

Snapshot	2023
Total external debt stocks	**864**
External debt stocks as % of:	
Exports	170
GNI	44
Debt service as % of:	
Exports	16
GNI	4
Net financial flows, debt and equity	51
Net debt inflows	21
Net equity inflows	31
GNI	**1,955**
Population (million)	**1,226**

Figure 2 Average terms on new debt commitments from official and private creditors

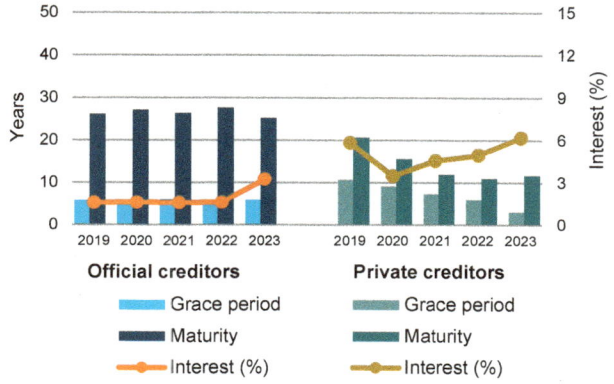

Official creditors
- Grace period
- Maturity
- Interest (%)

Private creditors
- Grace period
- Maturity
- Interest (%)

Figure 1 Public and publicly guaranteed debt, by creditor and creditor type in 2023, including IMF credit

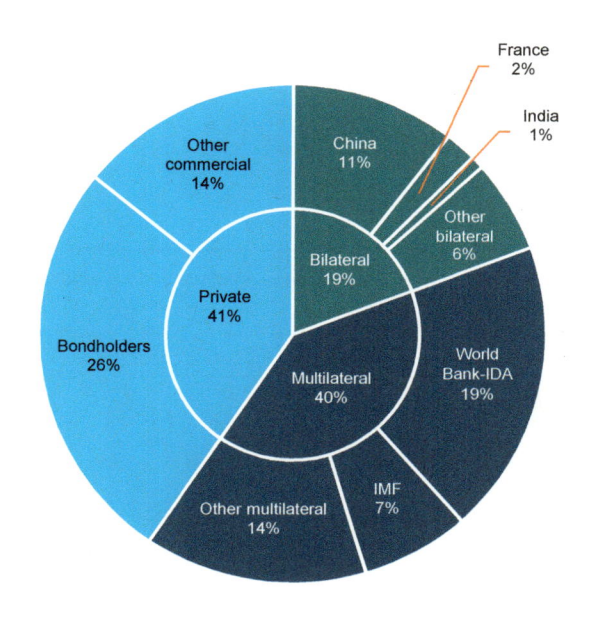

Summary External Debt Data	2010	2019	2020	2021	2022	2023
Total external debt stocks	**341**	**747**	**787**	**826**	**841**	**864**
Long-term external debt stocks	**253**	**615**	**643**	**653**	**658**	**678**
Public and publicly guaranteed debt from:	*160*	*433*	*464*	*476*	*482*	*501*
Official creditors	104	222	248	256	264	284
Multilateral	59	125	144	151	161	181
of which: World Bank	34	74	86	91	99	112
Bilateral	45	97	104	105	103	104
Private creditors	57	211	216	220	218	217
Bondholders	32	139	139	146	143	140
Commercial banks and others	24	72	77	74	75	77
Private nonguaranteed debt from:	*93*	*182*	*179*	*176*	*176*	*177*
Bondholders	9	12	10	11	10	9
Commercial banks and others	84	170	169	166	166	168
Use of IMF credit and SDR allocations	**19**	**23**	**41**	**69**	**68**	**71**
IMF credit	6	11	29	33	34	37
SDR allocations	14	12	13	35	34	34
Short-term external debt stocks	**69**	**108**	**102**	**104**	**115**	**115**
Disbursements, long-term	**47**	**90**	**72**	**82**	**78**	**66**
Public and publicly guaranteed sector	26	62	44	51	47	47
Private sector not guaranteed	21	28	28	31	32	20
Principal repayments, long-term	**12**	**54**	**49**	**61**	**60**	**47**
Public and publicly guaranteed sector	7	24	24	30	31	29
Private sector not guaranteed	5	30	25	31	29	17
Interest payments, long-term	**4**	**22**	**19**	**18**	**21**	**26**
Public and publicly guaranteed sector	3	15	15	14	14	17
Private sector not guaranteed	1	7	5	5	7	9

AFGHANISTAN

(US$ million, unless otherwise indicated)

Snapshot	2023
Total external debt stocks	**3,428**
External debt stocks as % of:	
Exports	..
GNI	..
Debt service as % of:	
Exports	..
GNI	..
Net financial flows, debt and equity	-6
Net debt inflows	-6
Net equity inflows	..
GNI	..
Population (million)	**42**

Figure 2 Average terms on new debt commitments from official and private creditors

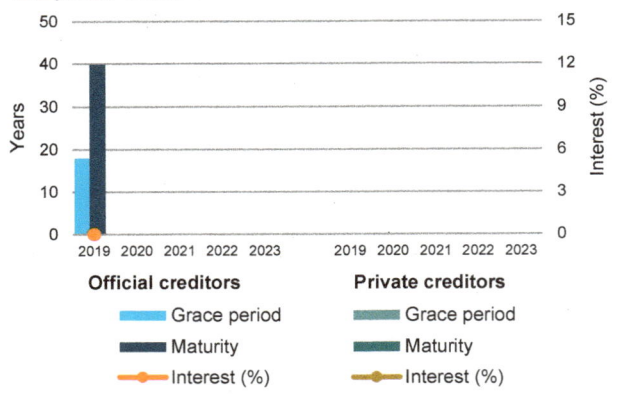

Official creditors
- Grace period
- Maturity
- Interest (%)

Private creditors
- Grace period
- Maturity
- Interest (%)

Figure 1 Public and publicly guaranteed debt, by creditor and creditor type in 2023, including IMF credit

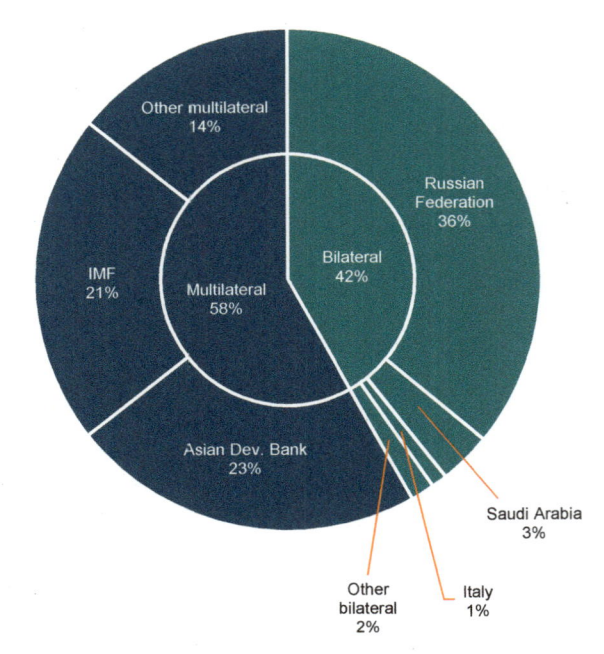

Summary External Debt Data	2010	2019	2020	2021	2022	2023
Total external debt stocks	**2,436**	**2,662**	**3,040**	**3,556**	**3,393**	**3,428**
Long-term external debt stocks	**1,976**	**1,965**	**1,976**	**1,926**	**1,877**	**1,874**
Public and publicly guaranteed debt from:	*1,976*	*1,944*	*1,958*	*1,908*	*1,859*	*1,857*
Official creditors	1,976	1,944	1,958	1,908	1,859	1,857
Multilateral	1,016	955	968	919	872	869
of which: World Bank	406	338	344	329	303	297
Bilateral	959	989	991	989	987	988
Private creditors	0	..	..	..	..	..
Bondholders	..	..	..	..	..	..
Commercial banks and others	0	..	..	..	..	..
Private nonguaranteed debt from:	..	*21*	*18*	*18*	*18*	*18*
Bondholders	..	..	..	..	..	..
Commercial banks and others	..	21	18	18	18	18
Use of IMF credit and SDR allocations	**355**	**277**	**629**	**1,185**	**1,122**	**1,127**
IMF credit	116	62	405	534	502	502
SDR allocations	239	215	224	652	620	625
Short-term external debt stocks	**105**	**420**	**435**	**445**	**394**	**427**
Disbursements, long-term	**76**	**29**	**0**	**..**	**..**	**0**
Public and publicly guaranteed sector	76	29	0	..	..	0
Private sector not guaranteed	..	..	..	..	..	..
Principal repayments, long-term	**1**	**31**	**26**	**14**	**9**	**10**
Public and publicly guaranteed sector	1	25	22	14	9	10
Private sector not guaranteed	..	6	5	..	..	..
Interest payments, long-term	**8**	**9**	**8**	**5**	**3**	**3**
Public and publicly guaranteed sector	8	7	7	5	3	3
Private sector not guaranteed	..	1	1	..	..	..

ALBANIA

(US$ million, unless otherwise indicated)

Snapshot	2023
Total external debt stocks	11,364
External debt stocks as % of:	
Exports	114
GNI	50
Debt service as % of:	
Exports	8
GNI	4
Net financial flows, debt and equity	2,420
Net debt inflows	762
Net equity inflows	1,658
GNI	22,675
Population (million)	3

Figure 1 Public and publicly guaranteed debt, by creditor and creditor type in 2023, including IMF credit

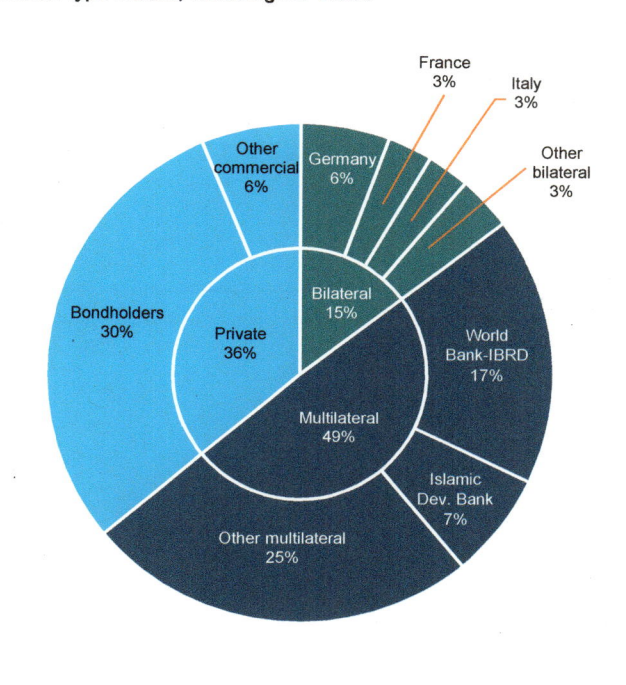

Figure 2 Average terms on new debt commitments from official and private creditors

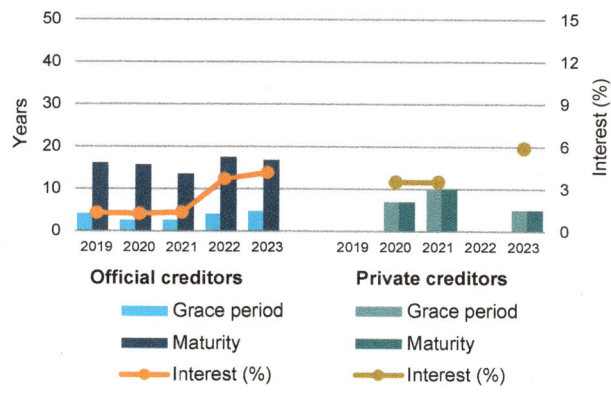

Summary External Debt Data	2010	2019	2020	2021	2022	2023
Total external debt stocks	**5,437**	**9,274**	**10,477**	**11,055**	**10,420**	**11,364**
Long-term external debt stocks	**4,564**	**7,976**	**8,886**	**9,094**	**8,505**	**9,586**
Public and publicly guaranteed debt from:	*3,210*	*4,160*	*4,896*	*5,303*	*4,859*	*5,553*
Official creditors	2,175	3,004	3,254	3,411	3,327	3,451
Multilateral	1,521	2,338	2,547	2,638	2,537	2,590
of which: World Bank	875	1,330	1,418	1,409	1,310	1,400
Bilateral	654	666	708	773	790	861
Private creditors	1,035	1,156	1,642	1,892	1,533	2,103
Bondholders	477	642	1,116	1,441	1,142	1,733
Commercial banks and others	558	514	526	451	391	369
Private nonguaranteed debt from:	*1,354*	*3,816*	*3,990*	*3,792*	*3,646*	*4,032*
Bondholders	69	306	284	267	248	254
Commercial banks and others	1,285	3,510	3,706	3,525	3,397	3,778
Use of IMF credit and SDR allocations	**129**	**448**	**627**	**734**	**632**	**525**
IMF credit	58	383	560	482	393	283
SDR allocations	72	64	67	252	240	241
Short-term external debt stocks	**743**	**850**	**964**	**1,226**	**1,283**	**1,254**
Disbursements, long-term	**866**	**457**	**1,162**	**1,532**	**604**	**1,442**
Public and publicly guaranteed sector	631	207	880	1,234	318	921
Private sector not guaranteed	235	250	283	298	286	521
Principal repayments, long-term	**250**	**472**	**948**	**693**	**499**	**539**
Public and publicly guaranteed sector	174	263	537	369	283	311
Private sector not guaranteed	76	209	410	323	216	228
Interest payments, long-term	**110**	**112**	**146**	**116**	**126**	**170**
Public and publicly guaranteed sector	66	95	96	101	101	146
Private sector not guaranteed	44	17	50	15	25	24

ALGERIA

(US$ million, unless otherwise indicated)

Snapshot	2023
Total external debt stocks	**7,315**
External debt stocks as % of:	
Exports	12
GNI	3
Debt service as % of:	
Exports	1
GNI	0
Net financial flows, debt and equity	1,287
Net debt inflows	133
Net equity inflows	1,154
GNI	**236,496**
Population (million)	**46**

Figure 2 Average terms on new debt commitments from official and private creditors

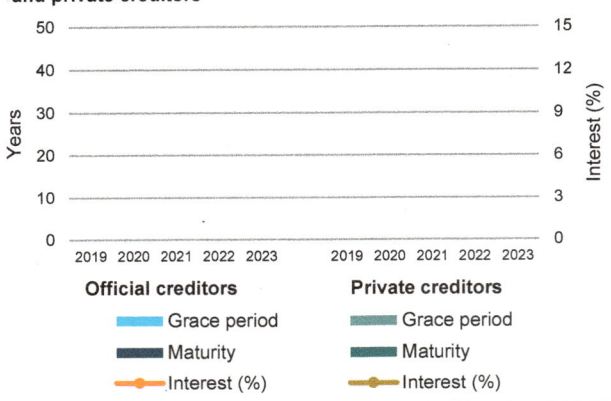

Official creditors
- Grace period
- Maturity
- Interest (%)

Private creditors
- Grace period
- Maturity
- Interest (%)

Figure 1 Public and publicly guaranteed debt, by creditor and creditor type in 2023, including IMF credit

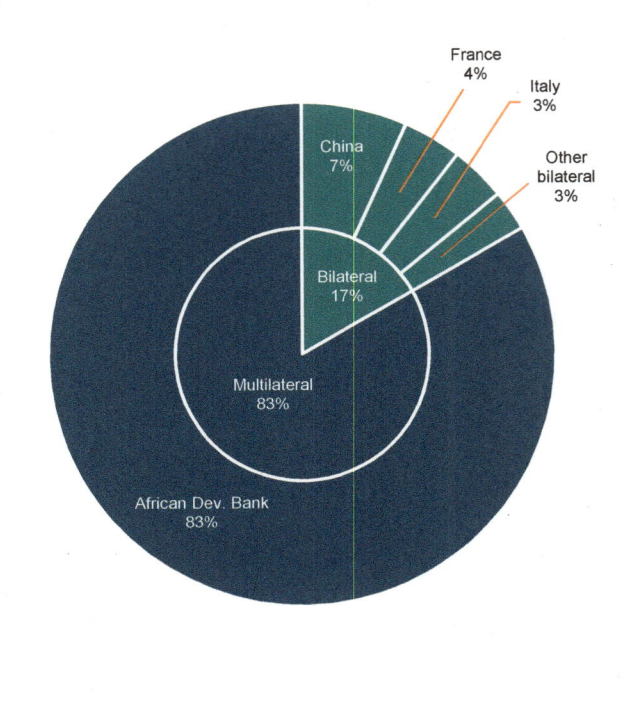

Summary External Debt Data	2010	2019	2020	2021	2022	2023
Total external debt stocks	**7,253**	**5,492**	**5,178**	**7,379**	**7,129**	**7,315**
Long-term external debt stocks	**3,630**	**1,571**	**1,669**	**1,476**	**1,291**	**1,275**
Public and publicly guaranteed debt from:	*2,662*	*1,398*	*1,436*	*1,240*	*1,056*	*993*
Official creditors	1,986	1,393	1,433	1,239	1,056	993
Multilateral	10	1,007	1,095	984	860	826
of which: World Bank	9	..	..	..	..	..
Bilateral	1,976	386	338	256	195	166
Private creditors	676	6	3	1	0	0
Bondholders	..	..	..	..	..	..
Commercial banks and others	676	6	3	1	0	..
Private nonguaranteed debt from:	*968*	*173*	*232*	*236*	*235*	*282*
Bondholders	..	..	..	..	..	..
Commercial banks and others	968	173	232	236	235	282
Use of IMF credit and SDR allocations	**1,845**	**1,657**	**1,726**	**4,306**	**4,095**	**4,128**
IMF credit	0	0	0	0	0	0
SDR allocations	1,845	1,657	1,726	4,306	4,095	4,128
Short-term external debt stocks	**1,778**	**2,264**	**1,784**	**1,597**	**1,744**	**1,913**
Disbursements, long-term	**42**	**33**	**98**	**70**	**53**	**137**
Public and publicly guaranteed sector	40	0	0	0	0	0
Private sector not guaranteed	2	33	98	70	53	137
Principal repayments, long-term	**557**	**118**	**119**	**147**	**147**	**172**
Public and publicly guaranteed sector	324	93	77	101	107	98
Private sector not guaranteed	234	25	41	46	39	74
Interest payments, long-term	**95**	**25**	**23**	**22**	**18**	**17**
Public and publicly guaranteed sector	64	23	22	22	18	17
Private sector not guaranteed	31	2	1	1	..	..

Note: Figure 2 shows no data values because the country did not have new commitments from 2019 to 2023.

ANGOLA

(US$ million, unless otherwise indicated)

Snapshot	2023
Total external debt stocks	**57,032**
External debt stocks as % of:	
Exports	152
GNI	74
Debt service as % of:	
Exports	33
GNI	16
Net financial flows, debt and equity	**-5,128**
Net debt inflows	-3,649
Net equity inflows	-1,480
GNI	**77,036**
Population (million)	**37**

Figure 2 Average terms on new debt commitments from official and private creditors

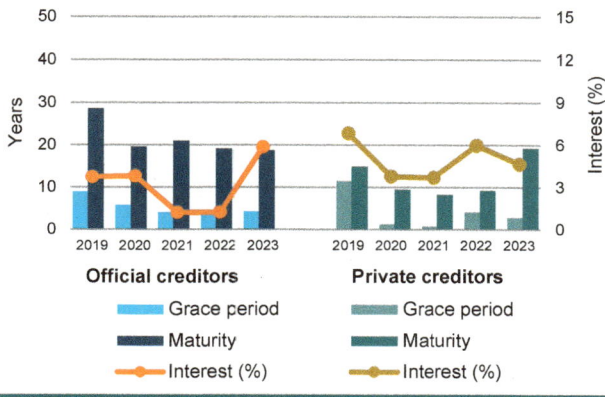

Official creditors
- Grace period
- Maturity
- Interest (%)

Private creditors
- Grace period
- Maturity
- Interest (%)

Figure 1 Public and publicly guaranteed debt, by creditor and creditor type in 2023, including IMF credit

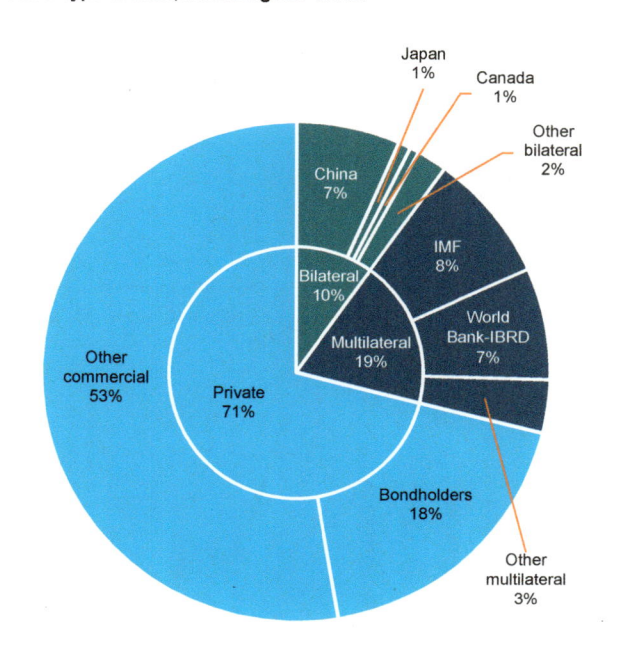

Summary External Debt Data	2010	2019	2020	2021	2022	2023
Total external debt stocks	**26,796**	**62,292**	**65,405**	**66,020**	**60,446**	**57,032**
Long-term external debt stocks	**20,926**	**57,848**	**57,062**	**55,508**	**50,669**	**46,652**
Public and publicly guaranteed debt from:	*15,662*	*47,597*	*47,384*	*46,646*	*48,157*	*45,215*
Official creditors	4,746	9,643	9,925	10,551	10,517	10,089
Multilateral	445	2,847	3,069	3,857	4,559	5,216
of which: World Bank	378	1,636	1,746	2,481	3,235	3,885
Bilateral	4,301	6,796	6,856	6,694	5,958	4,872
Private creditors	10,916	37,954	37,459	36,095	37,640	35,127
Bondholders	..	8,000	8,000	8,000	9,114	9,114
Commercial banks and others	10,916	29,954	29,459	28,095	28,525	26,012
Private nonguaranteed debt from:	*5,264*	*10,251*	*9,679*	*8,862*	*2,513*	*1,436*
Bondholders	..	..	..	..	..	..
Commercial banks and others	5,264	10,251	9,679	8,862	2,513	1,436
Use of IMF credit and SDR allocations	**1,302**	**1,861**	**2,992**	**5,872**	**5,584**	**5,449**
IMF credit	882	1,484	2,599	4,497	4,277	4,131
SDR allocations	420	378	393	1,375	1,307	1,318
Short-term external debt stocks	**4,568**	**2,583**	**5,351**	**4,639**	**4,193**	**4,931**
Disbursements, long-term	**6,714**	**8,105**	**3,966**	**6,194**	**7,945**	**3,820**
Public and publicly guaranteed sector	4,082	8,105	3,966	6,194	7,945	3,820
Private sector not guaranteed	2,632	..	..	..	..	..
Principal repayments, long-term	**2,639**	**7,803**	**5,129**	**7,611**	**12,520**	**8,028**
Public and publicly guaranteed sector	2,113	7,546	4,557	6,795	6,170	6,951
Private sector not guaranteed	526	257	572	816	6,350	1,077
Interest payments, long-term	**257**	**2,820**	**2,571**	**2,234**	**2,526**	**3,756**
Public and publicly guaranteed sector	177	2,480	2,408	2,128	2,477	3,675
Private sector not guaranteed	80	340	163	106	48	81

ARGENTINA

(US$ million, unless otherwise indicated)

Snapshot	2023
Total external debt stocks	**266,167**
External debt stocks as % of:	
Exports	298
GNI	42
Debt service as % of:	
Exports	51
GNI	7
Net financial flows, debt and equity	9,645
Net debt inflows	916
Net equity inflows	8,729
GNI	**626,338**
Population (million)	**47**

Figure 1 Public and publicly guaranteed debt, by creditor and creditor type in 2023, including IMF credit

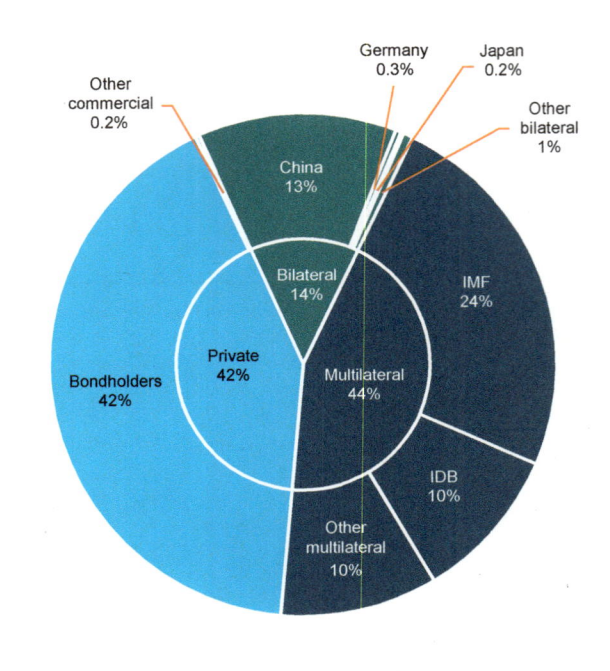

Figure 2 Average terms on new debt commitments from official and private creditors

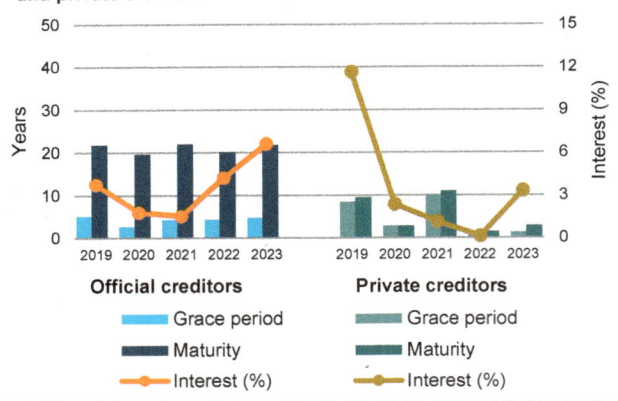

Summary External Debt Data	2010	2019	2020	2021	2022	2023
Total external debt stocks	**126,642**	**299,354**	**275,475**	**266,760**	**266,900**	**266,167**
Long-term external debt stocks	**107,119**	**185,414**	**183,994**	**174,731**	**164,954**	**163,605**
Public and publicly guaranteed debt from:	*69,184*	*139,989*	*137,952*	*135,204*	*127,936*	*126,390*
Official creditors	22,874	47,783	50,177	51,865	53,706	56,420
Multilateral	17,016	23,879	25,301	27,107	29,787	33,292
of which: World Bank	5,349	7,128	7,721	8,517	9,205	9,889
Bilateral	5,859	23,904	24,875	24,758	23,919	23,128
Private creditors	46,310	92,206	87,775	83,339	74,230	69,970
Bondholders	44,344	91,240	86,537	82,219	73,775	69,561
Commercial banks and others	1,966	966	1,238	1,119	455	408
Private nonguaranteed debt from:	*37,934*	*45,425*	*46,042*	*39,527*	*37,018*	*37,216*
Bondholders	7,855	15,378	15,742	15,354	13,617	12,322
Commercial banks and others	30,080	30,047	30,300	24,173	23,401	24,893
Use of IMF credit and SDR allocations	**3,111**	**46,924**	**48,874**	**48,055**	**52,290**	**47,612**
IMF credit	0	44,131	45,964	40,953	45,536	40,804
SDR allocations	3,111	2,793	2,909	7,103	6,754	6,809
Short-term external debt stocks	**16,413**	**67,016**	**42,607**	**43,974**	**49,657**	**54,950**
Disbursements, long-term	**6,923**	**25,171**	**24,403**	**16,702**	**9,030**	**16,501**
Public and publicly guaranteed sector	2,623	11,559	13,573	5,442	7,069	7,828
Private sector not guaranteed	4,300	13,612	10,830	11,260	1,961	8,673
Principal repayments, long-term	**11,690**	**30,072**	**21,686**	**17,860**	**11,653**	**15,434**
Public and publicly guaranteed sector	6,035	19,526	8,200	4,473	7,676	6,477
Private sector not guaranteed	5,655	10,546	13,485	13,388	3,977	8,957
Interest payments, long-term	**3,789**	**11,498**	**5,608**	**4,152**	**3,067**	**6,056**
Public and publicly guaranteed sector	2,700	8,883	2,484	1,290	1,929	3,594
Private sector not guaranteed	1,089	2,615	3,124	2,863	1,137	2,462

ARMENIA

(US$ million, unless otherwise indicated)

Snapshot	2023
Total external debt stocks	**15,839**
External debt stocks as % of:	
Exports	105
GNI	67
Debt service as % of:	
Exports	18
GNI	12
Net financial flows, debt and equity	**50**
Net debt inflows	-137
Net equity inflows	187
GNI	**23,567**
Population (million)	**3**

Figure 1 Public and publicly guaranteed debt, by creditor and creditor type in 2023, including IMF credit

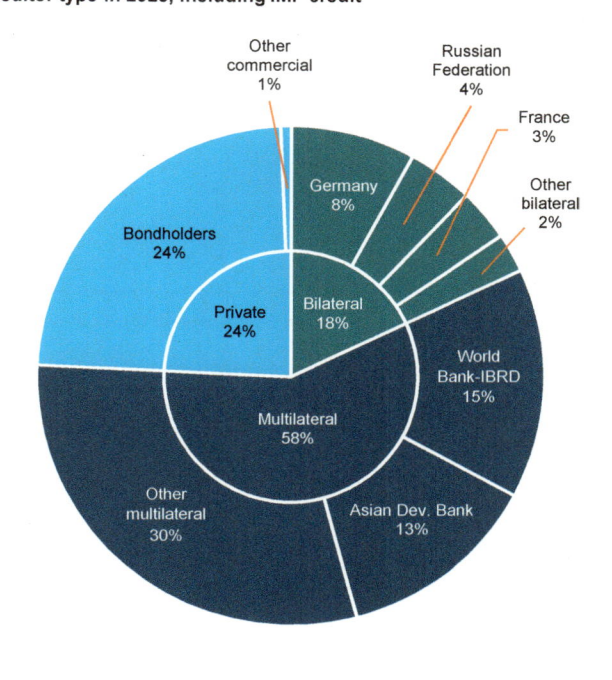

Figure 2 Average terms on new debt commitments from official and private creditors

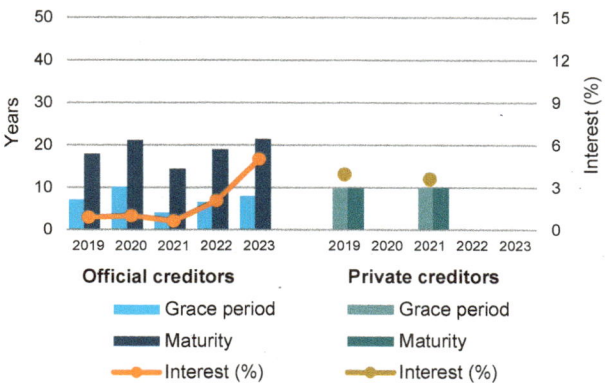

Summary External Debt Data	2010	2019	2020	2021	2022	2023
Total external debt stocks	**6,307**	**11,884**	**13,062**	**14,040**	**15,931**	**15,839**
Long-term external debt stocks	**4,775**	**9,915**	**10,813**	**11,781**	**11,931**	**12,062**
Public and publicly guaranteed debt from:	*2,560*	*5,652*	*5,616*	*6,246*	*6,320*	*6,241*
Official creditors	2,556	4,496	4,555	4,460	4,539	4,633
Multilateral	1,513	3,352	3,401	3,334	3,297	3,438
of which: World Bank	1,267	1,824	1,830	1,763	1,659	1,717
Bilateral	1,042	1,144	1,154	1,125	1,242	1,195
Private creditors	4	1,156	1,061	1,786	1,780	1,608
Bondholders	..	1,098	1,000	1,733	1,733	1,563
Commercial banks and others	4	59	61	53	47	45
Private nonguaranteed debt from:	*2,216*	*4,262*	*5,197*	*5,535*	*5,612*	*5,821*
Bondholders	..	..	300	300	300	300
Commercial banks and others	2,216	4,262	4,897	5,235	5,312	5,521
Use of IMF credit and SDR allocations	**876**	**375**	**646**	**735**	**758**	**670**
IMF credit	741	253	519	439	476	386
SDR allocations	136	122	127	296	281	284
Short-term external debt stocks	**656**	**1,595**	**1,603**	**1,524**	**3,242**	**3,107**
Disbursements, long-term	**1,734**	**2,377**	**2,136**	**2,552**	**1,681**	**1,979**
Public and publicly guaranteed sector	198	867	129	1,092	471	355
Private sector not guaranteed	1,536	1,510	2,007	1,460	1,210	1,624
Principal repayments, long-term	**857**	**1,586**	**1,386**	**1,368**	**1,388**	**1,887**
Public and publicly guaranteed sector	24	568	313	246	256	473
Private sector not guaranteed	833	1,018	1,073	1,122	1,132	1,414
Interest payments, long-term	**60**	**362**	**443**	**446**	**417**	**560**
Public and publicly guaranteed sector	35	189	167	145	162	238
Private sector not guaranteed	25	174	276	302	256	322

AZERBAIJAN

(US$ million, unless otherwise indicated)

Snapshot	2023
Total external debt stocks	**14,533**
External debt stocks as % of:	
Exports	39
GNI	21
Debt service as % of:	
Exports	5
GNI	3
Net financial flows, debt and equity	**-549**
Net debt inflows	-800
Net equity inflows	252
GNI	**69,157**
Population (million)	**10**

Figure 2 Average terms on new debt commitments from official and private creditors

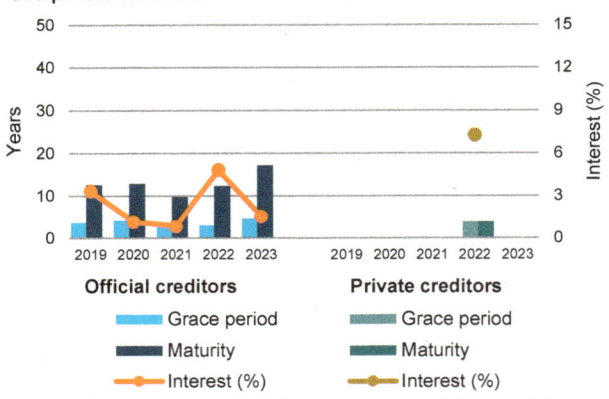

Official creditors
- Grace period
- Maturity
- Interest (%)

Private creditors
- Grace period
- Maturity
- Interest (%)

Figure 1 Public and publicly guaranteed debt, by creditor and creditor type in 2023, including IMF credit

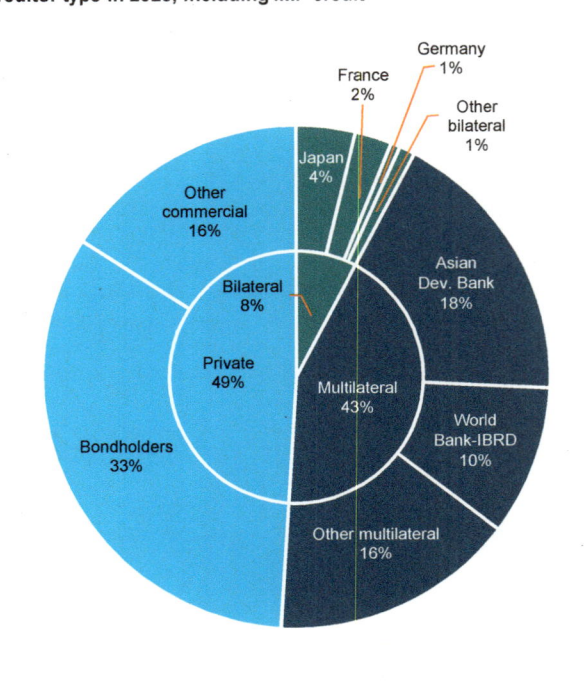

Summary External Debt Data	2010	2019	2020	2021	2022	2023
Total external debt stocks	**7,286**	**16,539**	**16,478**	**15,648**	**15,277**	**14,533**
Long-term external debt stocks	6,004	15,710	15,805	14,908	14,067	13,211
Public and publicly guaranteed debt from:	*3,846*	*14,675*	*14,667*	*13,623*	*12,911*	*12,233*
Official creditors	2,661	7,822	7,838	7,266	6,657	6,238
Multilateral	1,738	6,566	6,484	6,084	5,641	5,294
of which: World Bank	1,063	2,395	2,098	1,681	1,487	1,333
Bilateral	922	1,256	1,354	1,182	1,016	944
Private creditors	1,186	6,853	6,829	6,358	6,254	5,994
Bondholders	..	3,750	3,750	3,750	4,050	4,050
Commercial banks and others	1,186	3,103	3,079	2,608	2,204	1,944
Private nonguaranteed debt from:	*2,158*	*1,035*	*1,138*	*1,284*	*1,156*	*978*
Bondholders	..	..	500	500	500	500
Commercial banks and others	2,158	1,035	638	784	656	478
Use of IMF credit and SDR allocations	282	212	221	740	704	710
IMF credit	46	0	0	0	0	0
SDR allocations	237	212	221	740	704	710
Short-term external debt stocks	999	617	452	0	506	612
Disbursements, long-term	**2,643**	**1,412**	**1,080**	**1,094**	**513**	**174**
Public and publicly guaranteed sector	729	1,408	553	653	503	155
Private sector not guaranteed	1,914	4	527	442	11	19
Principal repayments, long-term	**306**	**1,463**	**1,298**	**1,703**	**1,104**	**1,080**
Public and publicly guaranteed sector	234	1,016	866	1,408	969	880
Private sector not guaranteed	72	447	432	296	135	200
Interest payments, long-term	**78**	**585**	**554**	**443**	**497**	**693**
Public and publicly guaranteed sector	65	519	496	403	448	635
Private sector not guaranteed	13	66	58	41	49	58

BANGLADESH

(US$ million, unless otherwise indicated)

Snapshot	2023
Total external debt stocks	**101,447**
External debt stocks as % of:	
Exports	171
GNI	22
Debt service as % of:	
Exports	13
GNI	2
Net financial flows, debt and equity	5,978
Net debt inflows	4,905
Net equity inflows	1,072
GNI	**454,873**
Population (million)	**173**

Figure 2 Average terms on new debt commitments from official and private creditors

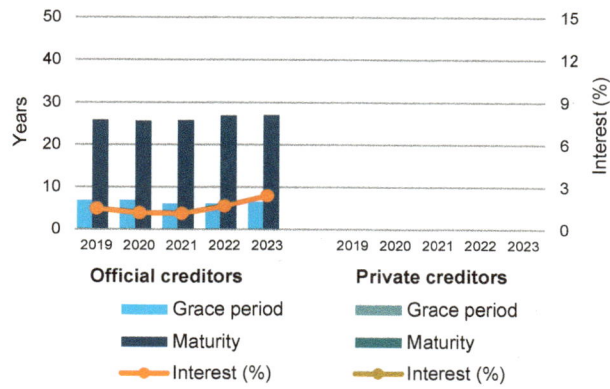

Official creditors
- Grace period
- Maturity
- Interest (%)

Private creditors
- Grace period
- Maturity
- Interest (%)

Figure 1 Public and publicly guaranteed debt, by creditor and creditor type in 2023, including IMF credit

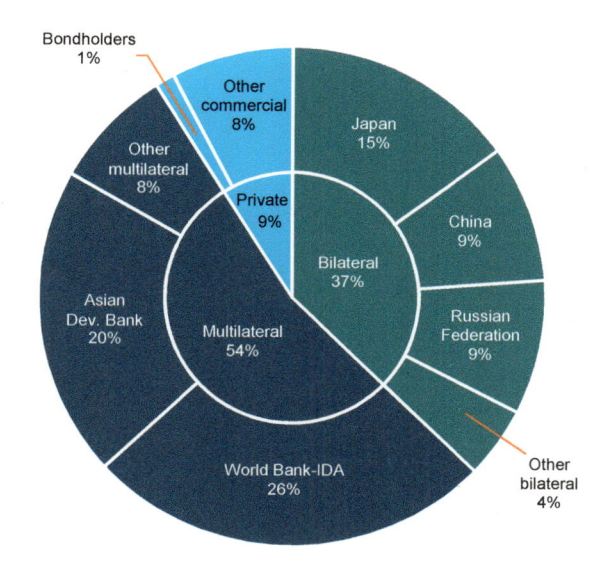

Summary External Debt Data	2010	2019	2020	2021	2022	2023
Total external debt stocks	26,572	62,468	73,551	91,478	97,020	101,447
Long-term external debt stocks	22,222	51,317	60,455	70,088	75,509	83,284
Public and publicly guaranteed debt from:	*21,146*	*46,417*	*54,830*	*62,473*	*67,617*	*74,131*
Official creditors	21,129	41,599	49,518	54,880	60,391	67,245
Multilateral	18,463	27,732	31,181	33,382	35,101	39,021
of which: World Bank	10,653	15,788	17,572	17,832	18,226	19,772
Bilateral	2,666	13,866	18,337	21,498	25,291	28,224
Private creditors	16	4,818	5,313	7,594	7,226	6,886
Bondholders	..	1,569	1,736	1,675	1,266	952
Commercial banks and others	16	3,249	3,577	5,919	5,959	5,934
Private nonguaranteed debt from:	*1,076*	*4,901*	*5,625*	*7,615*	*7,892*	*9,153*
Bondholders	..	..	..	..	..	..
Commercial banks and others	1,076	4,901	5,625	7,615	7,892	9,153
Use of IMF credit and SDR allocations	**1,403**	**1,414**	**2,109**	**3,301**	**2,981**	**3,932**
IMF credit	617	708	1,374	1,156	941	1,876
SDR allocations	786	706	735	2,145	2,040	2,056
Short-term external debt stocks	**2,947**	**9,737**	**10,986**	**18,088**	**18,530**	**14,231**
Disbursements, long-term	**1,355**	**9,321**	**10,220**	**13,975**	**13,384**	**12,842**
Public and publicly guaranteed sector	968	6,208	7,931	9,564	10,549	9,869
Private sector not guaranteed	388	3,113	2,289	4,410	2,835	2,973
Principal repayments, long-term	**821**	**4,681**	**2,871**	**4,401**	**5,141**	**4,560**
Public and publicly guaranteed sector	724	1,250	1,307	1,981	2,583	2,847
Private sector not guaranteed	97	3,431	1,565	2,420	2,558	1,713
Interest payments, long-term	**203**	**809**	**863**	**900**	**1,037**	**1,721**
Public and publicly guaranteed sector	195	657	707	798	819	1,578
Private sector not guaranteed	8	152	155	102	218	143

BELARUS

(US$ million, unless otherwise indicated)

Snapshot	2023
Total external debt stocks	**36,705**
External debt stocks as % of:	
Exports	75
GNI	53
Debt service as % of:	
Exports	16
GNI	11
Net financial flows, debt and equity	**-893**
Net debt inflows	-2,793
Net equity inflows	1,900
GNI	**69,257**
Population (million)	**9**

Figure 2 Average terms on new debt commitments from official and private creditors

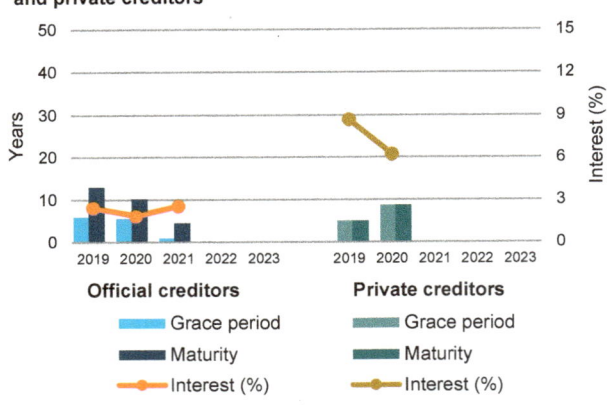

Official creditors
- ▆ Grace period
- ▆ Maturity
- ━ Interest (%)

Private creditors
- ▆ Grace period
- ▆ Maturity
- ━ Interest (%)

Figure 1 Public and publicly guaranteed debt, by creditor and creditor type in 2023, including IMF credit

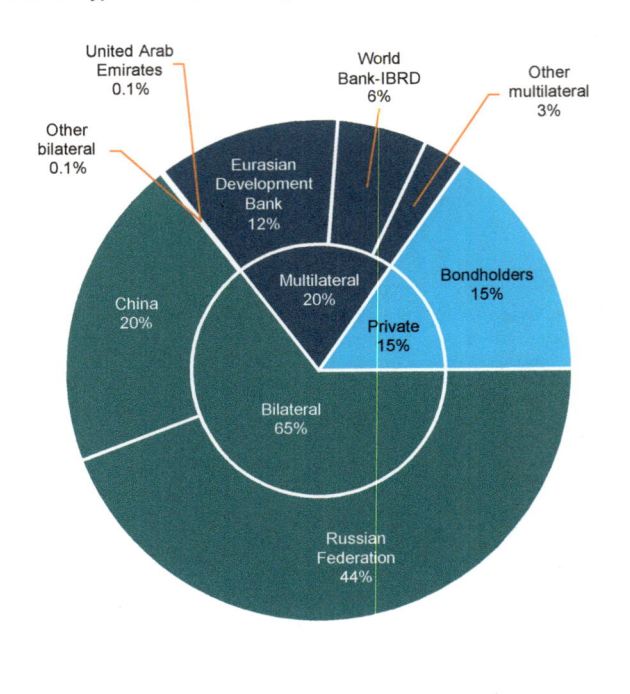

Summary External Debt Data	2010	2019	2020	2021	2022	2023
Total external debt stocks	**28,412**	**40,734**	**41,792**	**41,654**	**39,859**	**36,705**
Long-term external debt stocks	**12,486**	**30,026**	**31,180**	**29,859**	**28,355**	**24,953**
Public and publicly guaranteed debt from:	*8,014*	*19,511*	*20,270*	*19,979*	*19,208*	*17,500*
Official creditors	5,729	16,595	16,710	16,437	15,803	14,823
Multilateral	295	3,480	3,595	3,678	3,620	3,519
of which: World Bank	291	948	955	1,002	993	1,005
Bilateral	5,434	13,115	13,115	12,759	12,183	11,304
Private creditors	2,286	2,916	3,560	3,543	3,405	2,678
Bondholders	1,019	2,162	3,521	3,519	3,392	2,673
Commercial banks and others	1,266	755	39	23	13	5
Private nonguaranteed debt from:	*4,471*	*10,514*	*10,910*	*9,880*	*9,147*	*7,452*
Bondholders	..	..	368	367	371	356
Commercial banks and others	4,471	10,514	10,542	9,512	8,776	7,097
Use of IMF credit and SDR allocations	**4,063**	**510**	**531**	**1,430**	**1,360**	**1,371**
IMF credit	3,495	0	0	0	0	0
SDR allocations	568	510	531	1,430	1,360	1,371
Short-term external debt stocks	**11,864**	**10,199**	**10,082**	**10,365**	**10,144**	**10,381**
Disbursements, long-term	**3,810**	**4,106**	**4,099**	**1,691**	**3,767**	**2,611**
Public and publicly guaranteed sector	2,679	1,996	3,533	1,691	1,935	1,921
Private sector not guaranteed	1,132	2,111	566	..	1,832	690
Principal repayments, long-term	**1,265**	**2,900**	**2,881**	**2,968**	**5,226**	**5,641**
Public and publicly guaranteed sector	463	2,563	2,712	1,938	2,658	3,272
Private sector not guaranteed	802	338	169	1,030	2,568	2,369
Interest payments, long-term	**208**	**1,307**	**1,282**	**1,240**	**1,356**	**1,579**
Public and publicly guaranteed sector	128	1,015	892	853	906	1,162
Private sector not guaranteed	80	292	391	387	451	417

BELIZE

(US$ million, unless otherwise indicated)

Snapshot	2023
Total external debt stocks	**1,510**
External debt stocks as % of:	
Exports	102
GNI	48
Debt service as % of:	
Exports	8
GNI	4
Net financial flows, debt and equity	**57**
Net debt inflows	40
Net equity inflows	16
GNI	**3,170**
Population (thousand)	**411**

Figure 1 Public and publicly guaranteed debt, by creditor and creditor type in 2023, including IMF credit

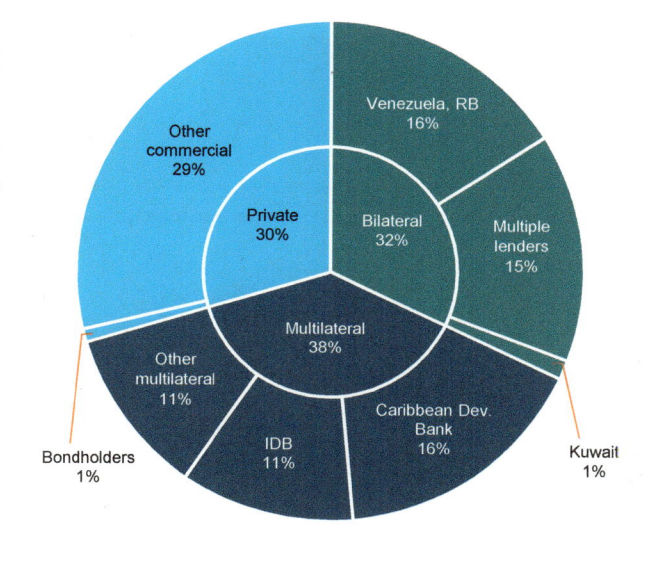

Figure 2 Average terms on new debt commitments from official and private creditors

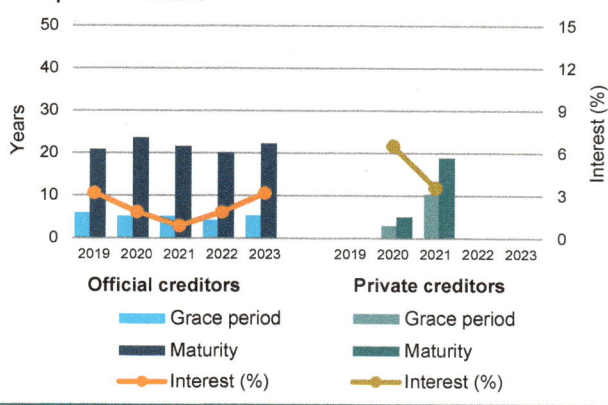

Official creditors / Private creditors

Grace period — Grace period
Maturity — Maturity
Interest (%) — Interest (%)

Summary External Debt Data	2010	2019	2020	2021	2022	2023
Total external debt stocks	**1,304**	**1,377**	**1,527**	**1,452**	**1,468**	**1,510**
Long-term external debt stocks	**1,262**	**1,348**	**1,494**	**1,381**	**1,400**	**1,440**
Public and publicly guaranteed debt from:	*1,019*	*1,285*	*1,410*	*1,278*	*1,302*	*1,347*
Official creditors	425	734	823	874	898	949
Multilateral	254	368	430	487	509	518
of which: World Bank	13	19	28	38	36	36
Bilateral	171	366	392	387	389	431
Private creditors	594	552	587	404	404	398
Bondholders	21	527	563	17	17	12
Commercial banks and others	573	25	24	387	387	387
Private nonguaranteed debt from:	*243*	*63*	*84*	*103*	*98*	*93*
Bondholders	..	..	..	..	..	..
Commercial banks and others	243	63	84	103	98	93
Use of IMF credit and SDR allocations	**35**	**25**	**26**	**61**	**58**	**58**
IMF credit	7	0	0	0	0	0
SDR allocations	28	25	26	61	58	58
Short-term external debt stocks	**7**	**4**	**8**	**10**	**10**	**12**
Disbursements, long-term	**39**	**79**	**154**	**482**	**66**	**101**
Public and publicly guaranteed sector	32	70	148	458	66	101
Private sector not guaranteed	7	9	7	24	..	0
Principal repayments, long-term	**69**	**50**	**45**	**599**	**43**	**61**
Public and publicly guaranteed sector	49	44	43	597	41	56
Private sector not guaranteed	20	6	2	2	2	4
Interest payments, long-term	**58**	**54**	**34**	**19**	**33**	**51**
Public and publicly guaranteed sector	47	50	32	17	31	50
Private sector not guaranteed	11	4	2	3	2	1

BENIN

(US$ million, unless otherwise indicated)

Snapshot	2023
Total external debt stocks	**12,483**
External debt stocks as % of:	
Exports	279
GNI	64
Debt service as % of:	
Exports	21
GNI	5
Net financial flows, debt and equity	1,987
Net debt inflows	1,553
Net equity inflows	434
GNI	**19,550**
Population (million)	**14**

Figure 1 Public and publicly guaranteed debt, by creditor and creditor type in 2023, including IMF credit

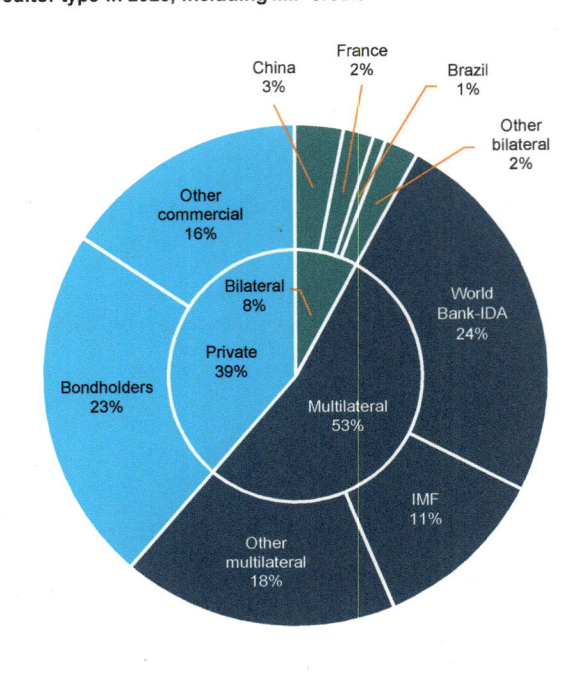

Figure 2 Average terms on new debt commitments from official and private creditors

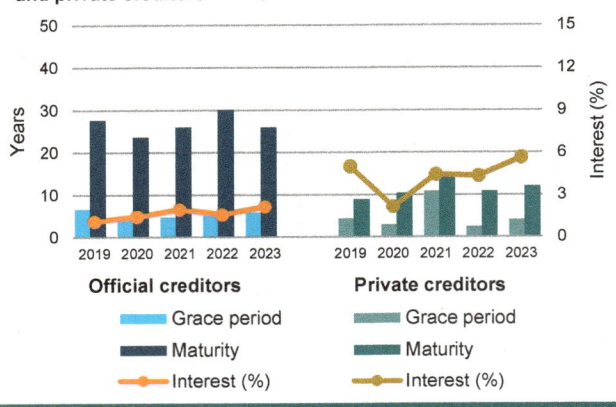

Official creditors
- Grace period
- Maturity
- Interest (%)

Private creditors
- Grace period
- Maturity
- Interest (%)

Summary External Debt Data	2010	2019	2020	2021	2022	2023
Total external debt stocks	**2,284**	**6,949**	**8,420**	**10,080**	**10,737**	**12,483**
Long-term external debt stocks	**1,481**	**5,360**	**6,432**	**7,882**	**8,277**	**9,458**
Public and publicly guaranteed debt from:	*1,112*	*3,603*	*4,414*	*5,786*	*5,990*	*7,172*
Official creditors	1,112	2,539	3,155	3,284	3,563	4,050
Multilateral	937	2,100	2,627	2,675	2,895	3,401
of which: World Bank	383	1,082	1,309	1,369	1,555	1,977
Bilateral	175	439	528	609	668	649
Private creditors	..	1,064	1,259	2,501	2,427	3,122
Bondholders	..	557	614	1,898	1,788	1,852
Commercial banks and others	..	508	646	603	639	1,270
Private nonguaranteed debt from:	*368*	*1,757*	*2,018*	*2,097*	*2,287*	*2,287*
Bondholders	..	..	..	..	..	..
Commercial banks and others	368	1,757	2,018	2,097	2,287	2,287
Use of IMF credit and SDR allocations	**146**	**267**	**563**	**699**	**944**	**1,142**
IMF credit	55	185	477	450	707	903
SDR allocations	91	82	85	249	237	239
Short-term external debt stocks	**658**	**1,322**	**1,425**	**1,498**	**1,516**	**1,882**
Disbursements, long-term	**218**	**934**	**891**	**2,369**	**986**	**1,599**
Public and publicly guaranteed sector	175	850	631	2,290	796	1,599
Private sector not guaranteed	43	83	261	79	190	..
Principal repayments, long-term	**26**	**113**	**99**	**623**	**292**	**602**
Public and publicly guaranteed sector	26	113	99	623	292	602
Private sector not guaranteed	..	..	..	..	..	..
Interest payments, long-term	**13**	**78**	**112**	**116**	**172**	**196**
Public and publicly guaranteed sector	13	77	111	105	163	190
Private sector not guaranteed	0	1	1	10	9	6

BHUTAN

(US$ million, unless otherwise indicated)

Snapshot	2023
Total external debt stocks	**3,269**
External debt stocks as % of:	
Exports	384
GNI	..
Debt service as % of:	
Exports	16
GNI	..
Net financial flows, debt and equity	117
Net debt inflows	115
Net equity inflows	2
GNI	..
Population (thousand)	**787.4**

Figure 2 Average terms on new debt commitments from official and private creditors

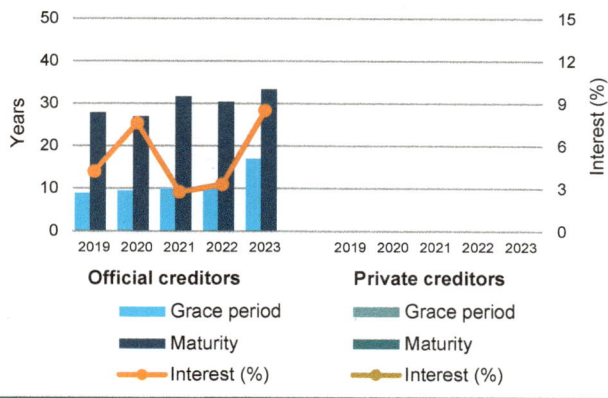

Official creditors
- Grace period
- Maturity
- Interest (%)

Private creditors
- Grace period
- Maturity
- Interest (%)

Figure 1 Public and publicly guaranteed debt, by creditor and creditor type in 2023, including IMF credit

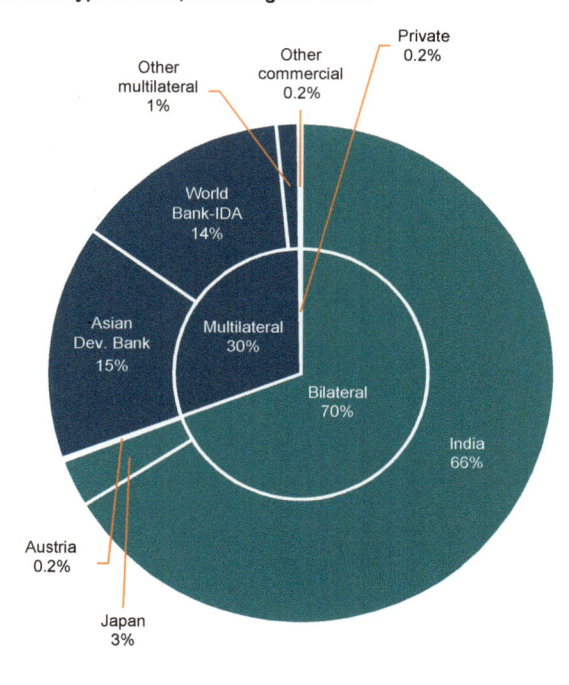

Summary External Debt Data	2010	2019	2020	2021	2022	2023
Total external debt stocks	**935**	**2,804**	**3,237**	**3,269**	**3,160**	**3,269**
Long-term external debt stocks	**919**	**2,768**	**3,227**	**3,230**	**3,121**	**3,234**
Public and publicly guaranteed debt from:	*919*	*2,716*	*3,185*	*3,186*	*3,077*	*3,190*
Official creditors	899	2,692	3,164	3,171	3,066	3,184
Multilateral	330	646	789	829	905	967
of which: World Bank	112	271	337	353	390	438
Bilateral	568	2,046	2,374	2,341	2,161	2,216
Private creditors	21	24	22	16	10	7
Bondholders	..	..	..	..	..	..
Commercial banks and others	21	24	22	16	10	7
Private nonguaranteed debt from:	..	*51*	*41*	*44*	*44*	*44*
Bondholders	..	..	..	..	..	..
Commercial banks and others	..	51	41	44	44	44
Use of IMF credit and SDR allocations	**9**	**8**	**9**	**36**	**34**	**34**
IMF credit	0	0	0	0	0	0
SDR allocations	9	8	9	36	34	34
Short-term external debt stocks	**6**	**28**	**1**	**3**	**6**	**1**
Disbursements, long-term	**178**	**198**	**508**	**138**	**215**	**194**
Public and publicly guaranteed sector	178	198	508	135	215	194
Private sector not guaranteed	..	1	..	3	..	..
Principal repayments, long-term	**47**	**28**	**37**	**73**	**71**	**74**
Public and publicly guaranteed sector	47	24	27	73	71	74
Private sector not guaranteed	..	5	10	..	..	..
Interest payments, long-term	**41**	**39**	**34**	**59**	**60**	**63**
Public and publicly guaranteed sector	41	37	33	57	58	61
Private sector not guaranteed	..	1	1	2	2	2

BOLIVIA

(US$ million, unless otherwise indicated)

Snapshot	2023
Total external debt stocks	**16,307**
External debt stocks as % of:	
Exports	136
GNI	36
Debt service as % of:	
Exports	14
GNI	4
Net financial flows, debt and equity	**711**
Net debt inflows	346
Net equity inflows	365
GNI	**44,844**
Population (million)	**12**

Figure 1 Public and publicly guaranteed debt, by creditor and creditor type in 2023, including IMF credit

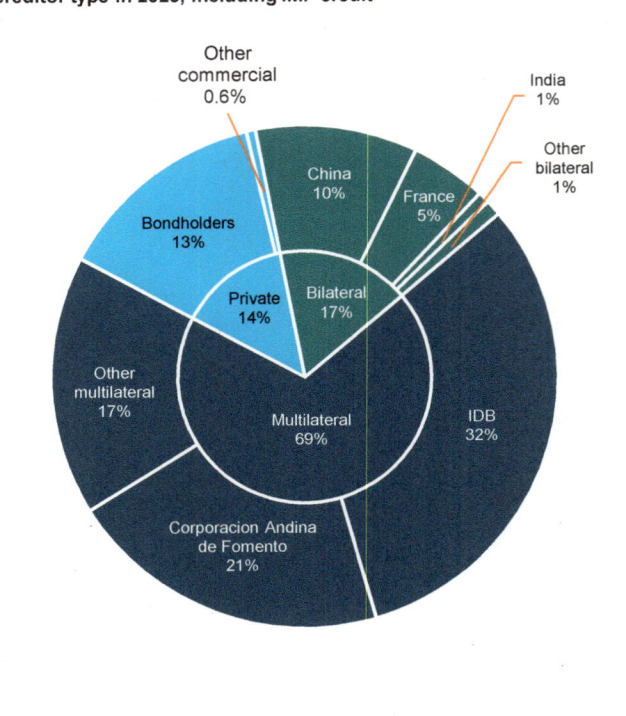

Figure 2 Average terms on new debt commitments from official and private creditors

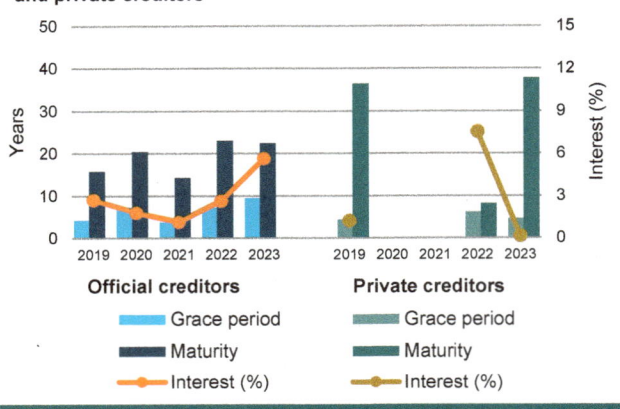

Official creditors
- Grace period
- Maturity
- Interest (%)

Private creditors
- Grace period
- Maturity
- Interest (%)

Summary External Debt Data	2010	2019	2020	2021	2022	2023
Total external debt stocks	**5,777**	**14,301**	**15,420**	**16,026**	**15,930**	**16,307**
Long-term external debt stocks	5,187	13,437	14,260	14,714	14,775	14,985
Public and publicly guaranteed debt from:	*2,830*	*11,000*	*11,877*	*12,773*	*13,372*	*13,660*
Official creditors	2,806	8,959	9,818	10,673	11,253	11,732
Multilateral	2,285	7,467	8,248	8,669	9,136	9,418
of which: World Bank	355	927	1,300	1,416	1,445	1,535
Bilateral	521	1,492	1,569	2,003	2,118	2,314
Private creditors	24	2,041	2,060	2,100	2,118	1,928
Bondholders	..	2,000	2,000	2,000	2,033	1,850
Commercial banks and others	24	41	60	100	85	78
Private nonguaranteed debt from:	*2,358*	*2,437*	*2,383*	*1,942*	*1,403*	*1,325*
Bondholders	..	..	..	..	..	..
Commercial banks and others	2,358	2,437	2,383	1,942	1,403	1,325
Use of IMF credit and SDR allocations	253	227	582	552	525	529
IMF credit	0	0	346	0	0	0
SDR allocations	253	227	236	552	525	529
Short-term external debt stocks	336	637	577	759	631	793
Disbursements, long-term	**548**	**1,741**	**1,445**	**1,456**	**2,123**	**1,125**
Public and publicly guaranteed sector	518	1,514	1,244	1,456	2,123	1,125
Private sector not guaranteed	30	227	201	..	..	..
Principal repayments, long-term	**569**	**658**	**764**	**936**	**1,959**	**941**
Public and publicly guaranteed sector	247	412	458	495	1,420	863
Private sector not guaranteed	322	246	306	441	539	78
Interest payments, long-term	**76**	**400**	**391**	**332**	**410**	**714**
Public and publicly guaranteed sector	54	371	363	307	389	630
Private sector not guaranteed	22	28	29	26	21	84

BOSNIA AND HERZEGOVINA

(US$ million, unless otherwise indicated)

Snapshot	2023
Total external debt stocks	**14,010**
External debt stocks as % of:	
Exports	108
GNI	52
Debt service as % of:	
Exports	13
GNI	6
Net financial flows, debt and equity	1,149
Net debt inflows	478
Net equity inflows	671
GNI	**26,986**
Population (million)	**3**

Figure 2 Average terms on new debt commitments from official and private creditors

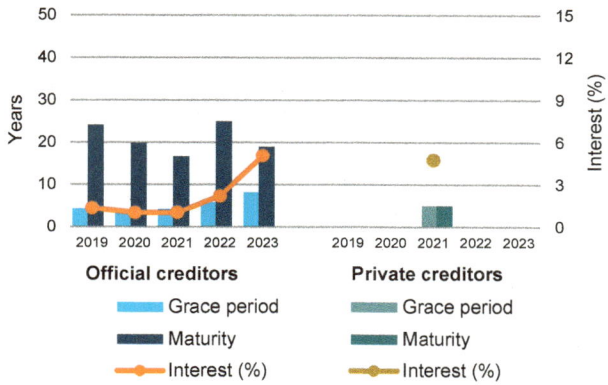

Figure 1 Public and publicly guaranteed debt, by creditor and creditor type in 2023, including IMF credit

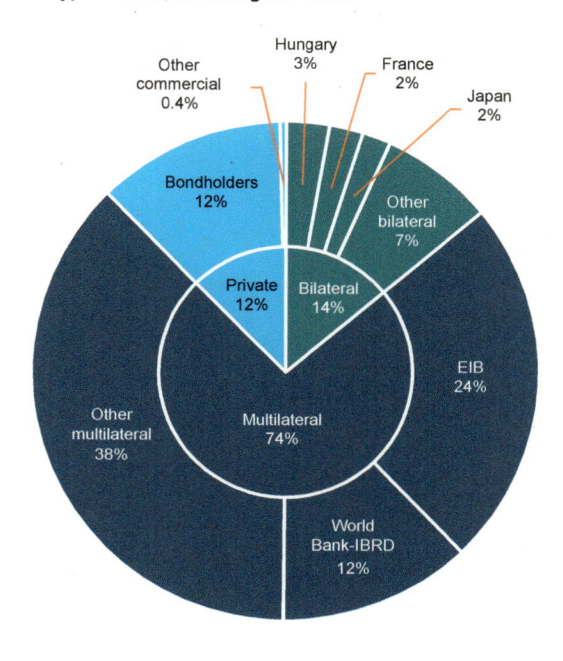

Summary External Debt Data	2010	2019	2020	2021	2022	2023
Total external debt stocks	**14,357**	**12,789**	**14,075**	**13,826**	**13,386**	**14,010**
Long-term external debt stocks	**12,439**	**9,582**	**10,499**	**10,106**	**9,714**	**10,189**
Public and publicly guaranteed debt from:	*3,801*	*4,901*	*5,200*	*5,548*	*5,126*	*5,126*
Official creditors	3,323	4,615	4,922	4,642	4,280	4,443
Multilateral	2,483	3,762	4,017	3,845	3,590	3,674
of which: World Bank	1,626	1,584	1,670	1,586	1,423	1,319
Bilateral	840	853	904	797	690	769
Private creditors	478	286	278	905	845	683
Bondholders	273	231	229	868	818	661
Commercial banks and others	204	55	50	37	28	22
Private nonguaranteed debt from:	*8,638*	*4,681*	*5,299*	*4,558*	*4,589*	*5,063*
Bondholders	..	..	..	..	..	..
Commercial banks and others	8,638	4,681	5,299	4,558	4,589	5,063
Use of IMF credit and SDR allocations	**769**	**398**	**796**	**1,115**	**1,039**	**930**
IMF credit	521	175	565	534	487	373
SDR allocations	248	222	232	581	552	557
Short-term external debt stocks	**1,149**	**2,810**	**2,779**	**2,605**	**2,632**	**2,891**
Disbursements, long-term	**566**	**807**	**1,242**	**1,516**	**524**	**1,337**
Public and publicly guaranteed sector	441	409	393	1,259	269	564
Private sector not guaranteed	125	398	849	257	255	773
Principal repayments, long-term	**375**	**763**	**525**	**1,305**	**612**	**1,001**
Public and publicly guaranteed sector	147	388	402	428	388	703
Private sector not guaranteed	227	375	123	877	224	299
Interest payments, long-term	**177**	**107**	**102**	**131**	**238**	**333**
Public and publicly guaranteed sector	56	81	83	80	85	148
Private sector not guaranteed	121	27	19	51	153	185

BOTSWANA

(US$ million, unless otherwise indicated)

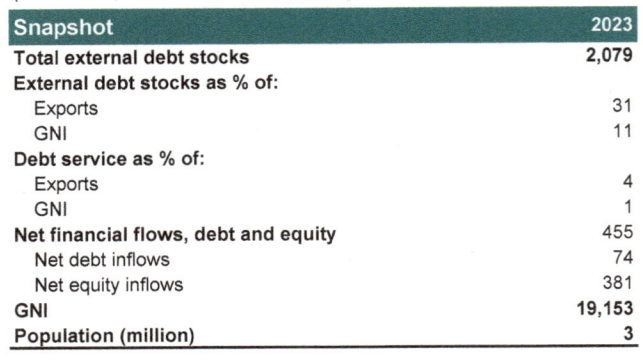

Snapshot	2023
Total external debt stocks	**2,079**
External debt stocks as % of:	
Exports	31
GNI	11
Debt service as % of:	
Exports	4
GNI	1
Net financial flows, debt and equity	455
Net debt inflows	74
Net equity inflows	381
GNI	**19,153**
Population (million)	**3**

Figure 2 Average terms on new debt commitments from official and private creditors

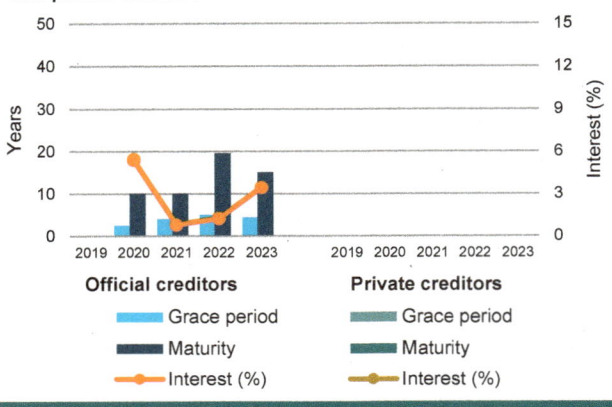

Figure 1 Public and publicly guaranteed debt, by creditor and creditor type in 2023, including IMF credit

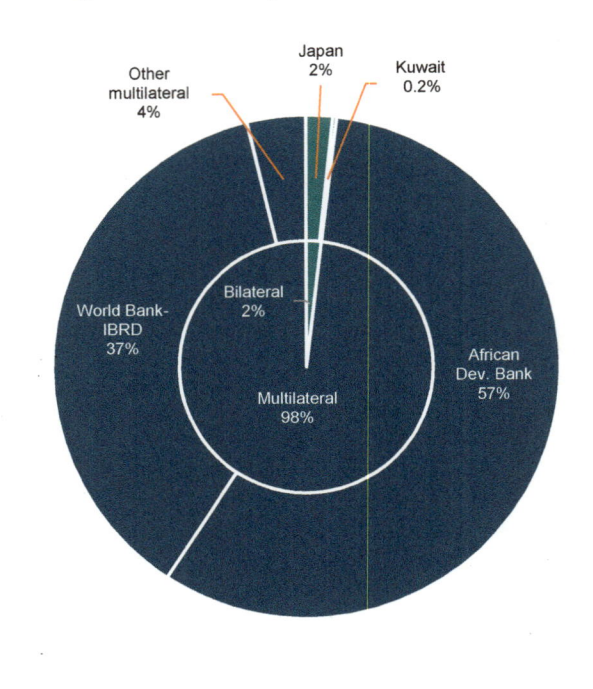

Summary External Debt Data	2010	2019	2020	2021	2022	2023
Total external debt stocks	**1,807**	**1,564**	**1,603**	**1,997**	**2,003**	**2,079**
Long-term external debt stocks	**1,358**	**1,346**	**1,303**	**1,497**	**1,563**	**1,458**
Public and publicly guaranteed debt from:	*1,358*	*1,333*	*1,284*	*1,482*	*1,558*	*1,458*
Official creditors	1,357	1,333	1,284	1,482	1,558	1,458
Multilateral	1,219	1,285	1,240	1,447	1,529	1,429
of which: World Bank	11	172	194	470	521	540
Bilateral	138	48	44	36	29	28
Private creditors	1	0	..	..	..	..
Bondholders	..	..	..	..	..	..
Commercial banks and others	1	0	..	..	..	..
Private nonguaranteed debt from:	*..*	*12*	*19*	*14*	*4*	*0*
Bondholders	..	..	..	..	..	..
Commercial banks and others	..	12	19	14	4	0
Use of IMF credit and SDR allocations	**88**	**79**	**83**	**345**	**328**	**331**
IMF credit	0	0	0	0	0	0
SDR allocations	88	79	83	345	328	331
Short-term external debt stocks	**360**	**139**	**218**	**156**	**112**	**290**
Disbursements, long-term	**17**	**55**	**96**	**348**	**221**	**46**
Public and publicly guaranteed sector	17	33	80	341	221	46
Private sector not guaranteed	..	22	16	7	..	..
Principal repayments, long-term	**58**	**152**	**147**	**145**	**149**	**150**
Public and publicly guaranteed sector	58	141	138	135	140	146
Private sector not guaranteed	..	10	10	10	9	4
Interest payments, long-term	**18**	**40**	**32**	**15**	**20**	**69**
Public and publicly guaranteed sector	18	40	31	14	20	69
Private sector not guaranteed	..	1	1	0	0	0

BRAZIL

(US$ million, unless otherwise indicated)

Snapshot	2023
Total external debt stocks	**607,115**
External debt stocks as % of:	
Exports	144
GNI	29
Debt service as % of:	
Exports	54
GNI	11
Net financial flows, debt and equity	84,558
Net debt inflows	30,558
Net equity inflows	54,000
GNI	**2,110,557**
Population (million)	**216**

Figure 1 Public and publicly guaranteed debt, by creditor and creditor type in 2023, including IMF credit

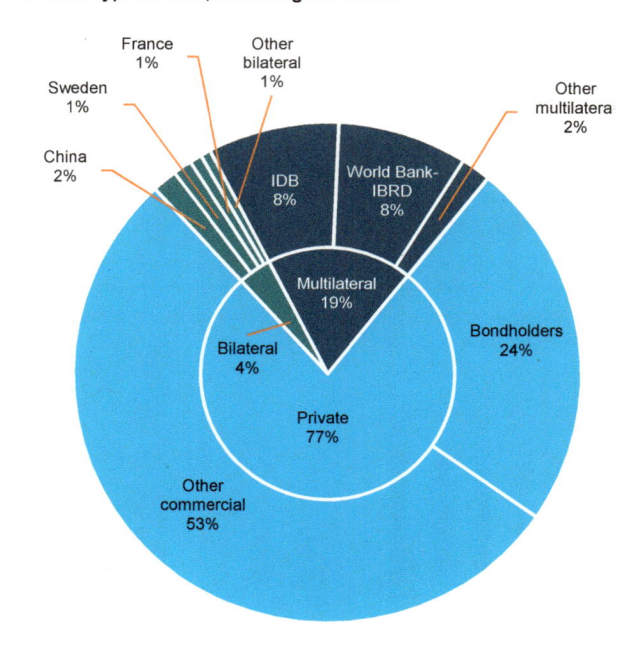

Figure 2 Average terms on new debt commitments from official and private creditors

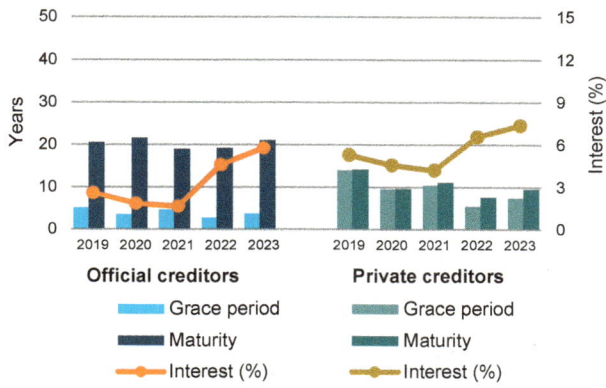

Summary External Debt Data	2010	2019	2020	2021	2022	2023
Total external debt stocks	**352,364**	**568,709**	**549,326**	**571,531**	**579,468**	**607,115**
Long-term external debt stocks	**282,426**	**485,537**	**476,185**	**473,925**	**493,770**	**508,551**
Public and publicly guaranteed debt from:	*97,486*	*193,800*	*194,329*	*194,186*	*190,558*	*190,754*
Official creditors	41,553	43,216	44,000	44,844	43,976	45,093
Multilateral	29,980	33,266	33,715	35,500	35,874	37,104
of which: World Bank	13,523	16,253	15,682	15,419	16,061	15,579
Bilateral	11,573	9,950	10,285	9,344	8,102	7,989
Private creditors	55,933	150,584	150,329	149,342	146,581	145,660
Bondholders	46,806	45,004	49,385	46,520	43,098	44,888
Commercial banks and others	9,127	105,580	100,943	102,822	103,483	100,772
Private nonguaranteed debt from:	*184,940*	*291,737*	*281,856*	*279,739*	*303,212*	*317,797*
Bondholders	83,032	37,553	35,903	31,375	27,194	30,054
Commercial banks and others	101,908	254,184	245,953	248,364	276,018	287,744
Use of IMF credit and SDR allocations	**4,446**	**3,992**	**4,158**	**18,853**	**17,927**	**18,073**
IMF credit	0	0	0	0	0	0
SDR allocations	4,446	3,992	4,158	18,853	17,927	18,073
Short-term external debt stocks	**65,492**	**79,179**	**68,983**	**78,753**	**67,772**	**80,492**
Disbursements, long-term	**85,379**	**114,564**	**126,735**	**156,033**	**133,895**	**214,244**
Public and publicly guaranteed sector	19,957	23,884	39,465	16,625	23,584	20,077
Private sector not guaranteed	65,422	90,680	87,270	139,408	110,310	194,168
Principal repayments, long-term	**32,026**	**123,463**	**109,833**	**132,313**	**106,220**	**196,406**
Public and publicly guaranteed sector	9,628	30,505	23,170	20,388	22,917	21,845
Private sector not guaranteed	22,398	92,958	86,663	111,924	83,303	174,562
Interest payments, long-term	**13,157**	**25,702**	**19,055**	**28,690**	**17,783**	**24,547**
Public and publicly guaranteed sector	5,172	11,385	7,764	8,520	7,980	9,664
Private sector not guaranteed	7,985	14,317	11,292	20,169	9,803	14,884

BURKINA FASO

(US$ million, unless otherwise indicated)

Snapshot	2023
Total external debt stocks	**10,397**
External debt stocks as % of:	
Exports	172
GNI	53
Debt service as % of:	
Exports	14
GNI	4
Net financial flows, debt and equity	**517**
Net debt inflows	432
Net equity inflows	85
GNI	**19,485**
Population (million)	**23**

Figure 1 Public and publicly guaranteed debt, by creditor and creditor type in 2023, including IMF credit

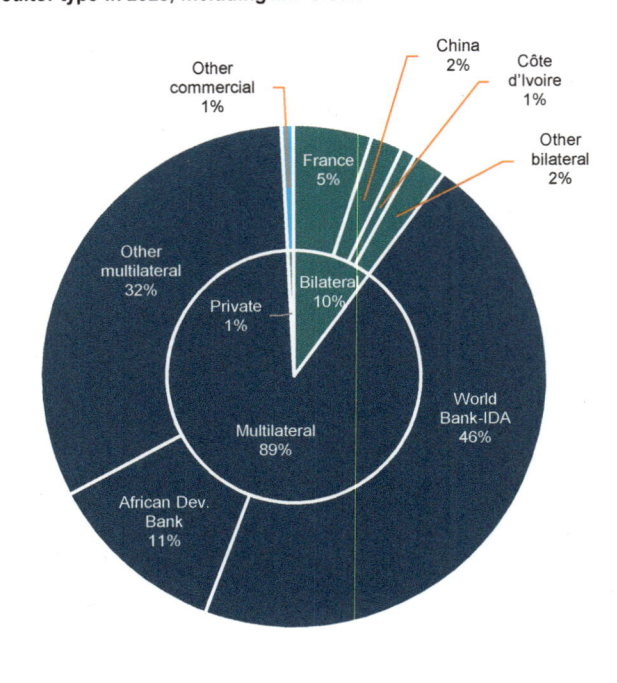

Figure 2 Average terms on new debt commitments from official and private creditors

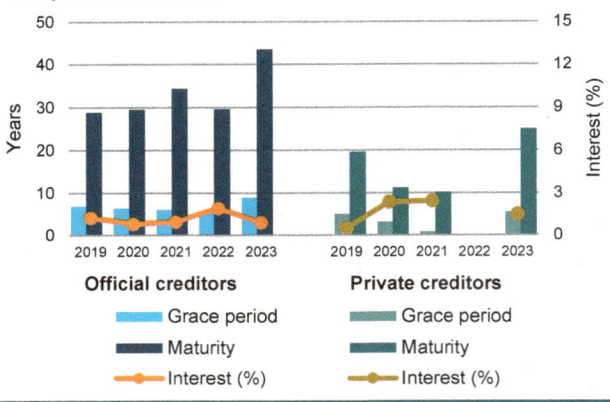

Summary External Debt Data	2010	2019	2020	2021	2022	2023
Total external debt stocks	**4,808**	**9,159**	**9,761**	**10,296**	**9,851**	**10,397**
Long-term external debt stocks	4,590	8,850	9,295	9,710	9,317	9,765
Public and publicly guaranteed debt from:	*1,968*	*3,374*	*4,024*	*4,328*	*4,385*	*4,900*
Official creditors	1,927	3,362	4,013	4,317	4,376	4,860
Multilateral	1,619	3,011	3,551	3,836	3,891	4,323
of which: World Bank	776	1,673	2,014	2,146	2,187	2,417
Bilateral	308	351	463	481	485	537
Private creditors	41	12	10	11	9	40
Bondholders	..	..	..	..	..	..
Commercial banks and others	41	12	10	11	9	40
Private nonguaranteed debt from:	*2,622*	*5,475*	*5,271*	*5,382*	*4,932*	*4,865*
Bondholders	..	..	..	..	..	..
Commercial banks and others	2,622	5,475	5,271	5,382	4,932	4,865
Use of IMF credit and SDR allocations	**217**	**310**	**466**	**586**	**534**	**632**
IMF credit	129	230	383	344	304	400
SDR allocations	89	80	83	242	230	232
Short-term external debt stocks	**0**	**0**	**0**	**0**	**0**	**0**
Disbursements, long-term	**1,393**	**463**	**2,084**	**1,045**	**820**	**827**
Public and publicly guaranteed sector	287	463	524	624	424	573
Private sector not guaranteed	1,106	..	1,560	421	396	254
Principal repayments, long-term	**293**	**1,934**	**1,865**	**413**	**984**	**488**
Public and publicly guaranteed sector	31	98	100	102	138	167
Private sector not guaranteed	262	1,836	1,764	310	846	321
Interest payments, long-term	**149**	**348**	**274**	**55**	**64**	**344**
Public and publicly guaranteed sector	18	32	36	41	46	63
Private sector not guaranteed	131	316	238	14	18	281

BURUNDI

(US$ million, unless otherwise indicated)

Snapshot	2023
Total external debt stocks	**1,043**
External debt stocks as % of:	
Exports	255
GNI	39
Debt service as % of:	
Exports	11
GNI	2
Net financial flows, debt and equity	121
Net debt inflows	82
Net equity inflows	39
GNI	**2,648**
Population (million)	**13**

Figure 1 **Public and publicly guaranteed debt, by creditor and creditor type in 2023, including IMF credit**

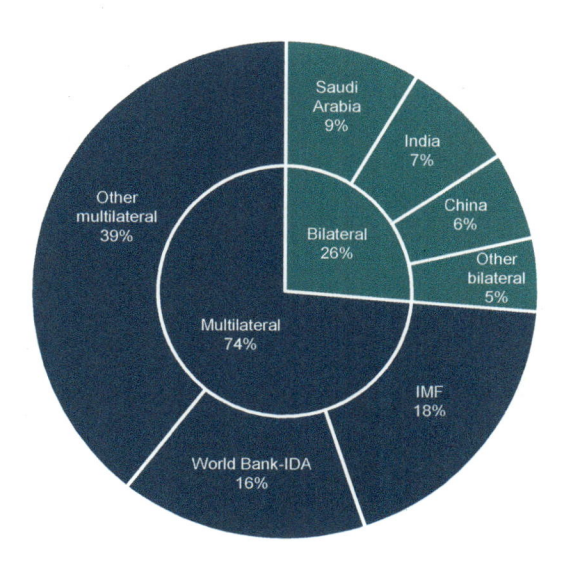

Figure 2 **Average terms on new debt commitments from official and private creditors**

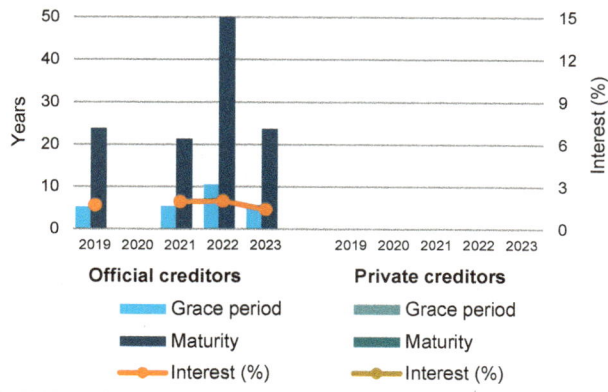

Summary External Debt Data	2010	2019	2020	2021	2022	2023
Total external debt stocks	**621**	**629**	**665**	**976**	**955**	**1,043**
Long-term external debt stocks	**382**	**479**	**532**	**576**	**578**	**607**
Public and publicly guaranteed debt from:	*382*	*479*	*532*	*576*	*578*	*607*
Official creditors	382	479	532	576	578	607
Multilateral	325	347	361	390	388	411
of which: World Bank	163	138	140	132	122	118
Bilateral	57	133	171	186	191	196
Private creditors	..	..	..	..	..	..
Bondholders	..	..	..	..	..	..
Commercial banks and others	..	..	..	..	..	..
Private nonguaranteed debt from:	..	..	..	..	..	..
Bondholders	..	..	..	..	..	..
Commercial banks and others	..	..	..	..	..	..
Use of IMF credit and SDR allocations	**223**	**149**	**132**	**400**	**376**	**435**
IMF credit	110	47	26	90	82	138
SDR allocations	114	102	106	310	295	297
Short-term external debt stocks	**16**	**0**	**0**	**0**	**0**	**0**
Disbursements, long-term	**32**	**69**	**50**	**62**	**40**	**49**
Public and publicly guaranteed sector	32	69	50	62	40	49
Private sector not guaranteed	..	..	..	..	..	..
Principal repayments, long-term	**2**	**16**	**10**	**13**	**20**	**22**
Public and publicly guaranteed sector	2	16	10	13	20	22
Private sector not guaranteed	..	..	..	..	..	..
Interest payments, long-term	**1**	**4**	**4**	**6**	**5**	**5**
Public and publicly guaranteed sector	1	4	4	6	5	5
Private sector not guaranteed	..	..	..	..	..	..

CABO VERDE

(US$ million, unless otherwise indicated)

Snapshot	2023
Total external debt stocks	**2,451**
External debt stocks as % of:	
Exports	243
GNI	95
Debt service as % of:	
Exports	16
GNI	6
Net financial flows, debt and equity	166
Net debt inflows	7
Net equity inflows	159
GNI	**2,577**
Population (thousand)	**598.7**

Figure 1 Public and publicly guaranteed debt, by creditor and creditor type in 2023, including IMF credit

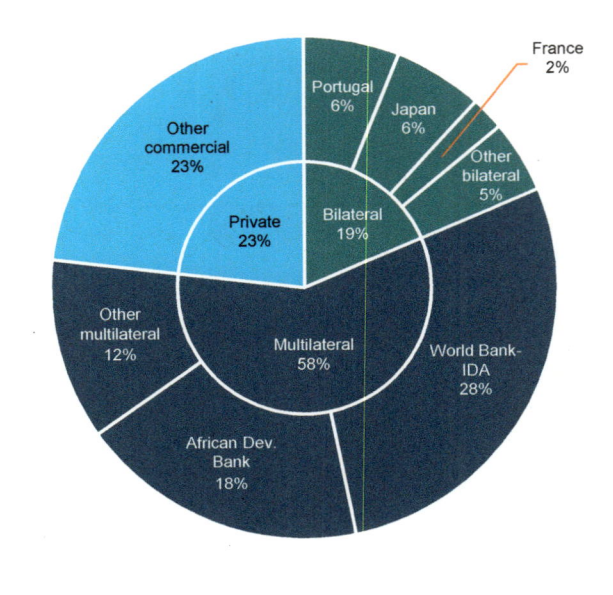

Figure 2 Average terms on new debt commitments from official and private creditors

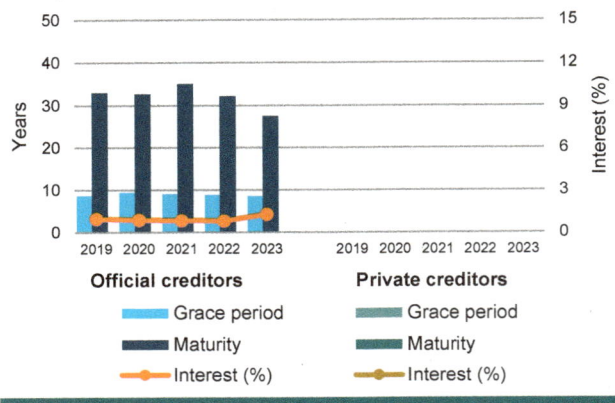

Summary External Debt Data	2010	2019	2020	2021	2022	2023
Total external debt stocks	**885**	**2,148**	**2,423**	**2,456**	**2,411**	**2,451**
Long-term external debt stocks	**862**	**1,810**	**2,025**	**1,982**	**1,920**	**1,934**
Public and publicly guaranteed debt from:	*862*	*1,810*	*2,025*	*1,982*	*1,920*	*1,934*
Official creditors	778	1,303	1,467	1,467	1,445	1,470
Multilateral	598	882	1,014	1,041	1,050	1,096
of which: World Bank	303	406	482	523	547	601
Bilateral	181	420	453	426	395	374
Private creditors	84	507	558	515	475	464
Bondholders	..	..	..	..	..	..
Commercial banks and others	84	507	558	515	475	464
Private nonguaranteed debt from:	..	..	..	..	..	..
Bondholders	..	..	..	..	..	..
Commercial banks and others	..	..	..	..	..	..
Use of IMF credit and SDR allocations	**23**	**13**	**47**	**78**	**89**	**111**
IMF credit	9	0	34	33	47	68
SDR allocations	14	13	13	45	42	43
Short-term external debt stocks	**0**	**325**	**350**	**396**	**401**	**407**
Disbursements, long-term	**203**	**118**	**124**	**115**	**127**	**85**
Public and publicly guaranteed sector	203	118	124	115	127	85
Private sector not guaranteed	..	..	..	..	..	..
Principal repayments, long-term	**25**	**41**	**43**	**44**	**77**	**105**
Public and publicly guaranteed sector	25	41	43	44	77	105
Private sector not guaranteed	..	..	..	..	..	..
Interest payments, long-term	**8**	**19**	**17**	**11**	**20**	**30**
Public and publicly guaranteed sector	8	19	17	11	20	30
Private sector not guaranteed	..	..	..	..	..	..

CAMBODIA

(US$ million, unless otherwise indicated)

Snapshot	2023
Total external debt stocks	**22,534**
External debt stocks as % of:	
Exports	80
GNI	73
Debt service as % of:	
Exports	9
GNI	8
Net financial flows, debt and equity	4,081
Net debt inflows	122
Net equity inflows	3,959
GNI	**30,819**
Population (million)	**17**

Figure 1 Public and publicly guaranteed debt, by creditor and creditor type in 2023, including IMF credit

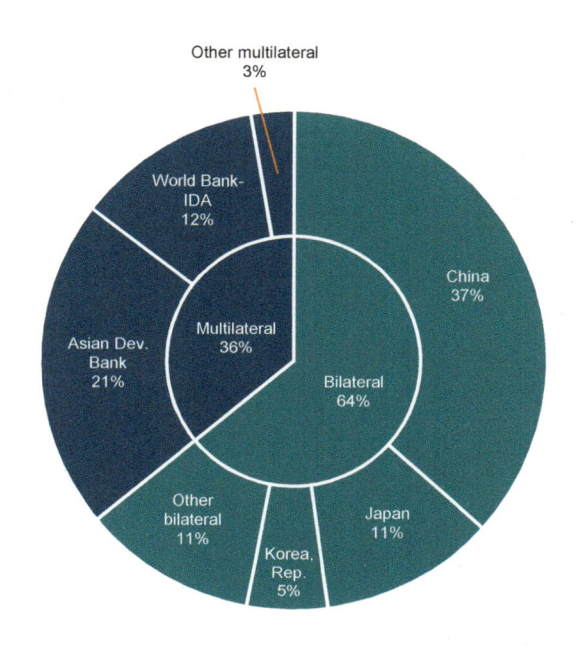

Figure 2 Average terms on new debt commitments from official and private creditors

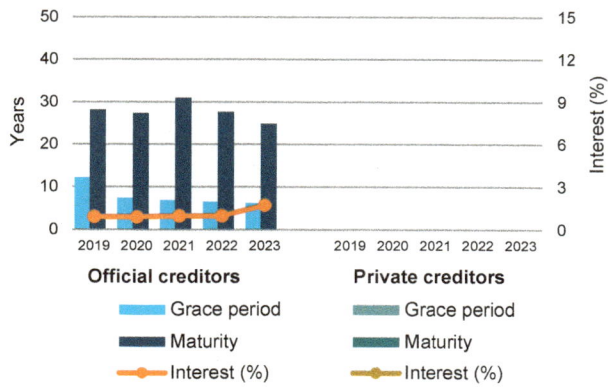

Summary External Debt Data	2010	2019	2020	2021	2022	2023
Total external debt stocks	**4,010**	**15,363**	**17,594**	**20,050**	**22,474**	**22,534**
Long-term external debt stocks	**3,502**	**11,834**	**13,691**	**15,261**	**17,529**	**17,824**
Public and publicly guaranteed debt from:	*3,060*	*7,582*	*8,789*	*9,481*	*10,067*	*11,098*
Official creditors	3,060	7,582	8,789	9,481	10,067	11,098
Multilateral	1,529	2,123	2,717	2,874	3,232	3,988
of which: World Bank	565	585	685	727	936	1,315
Bilateral	1,531	5,459	6,073	6,608	6,835	7,111
Private creditors	..	..	..	..	..	..
Bondholders	..	..	..	..	..	..
Commercial banks and others	..	..	..	..	..	..
Private nonguaranteed debt from:	*442*	*4,252*	*4,902*	*5,779*	*7,462*	*6,725*
Bondholders	..	300	650	550	550	550
Commercial banks and others	442	3,952	4,252	5,229	6,912	6,175
Use of IMF credit and SDR allocations	**129**	**116**	**121**	**352**	**335**	**338**
IMF credit	0	0	0	0	0	0
SDR allocations	129	116	121	352	335	338
Short-term external debt stocks	**379**	**3,413**	**3,782**	**4,437**	**4,610**	**4,372**
Disbursements, long-term	**596**	**2,070**	**2,945**	**3,687**	**4,778**	**2,317**
Public and publicly guaranteed sector	348	828	1,215	1,155	1,352	1,476
Private sector not guaranteed	248	1,242	1,729	2,532	3,426	841
Principal repayments, long-term	**33**	**1,263**	**1,344**	**1,946**	**2,095**	**1,958**
Public and publicly guaranteed sector	33	218	264	291	352	379
Private sector not guaranteed	..	1,045	1,079	1,654	1,743	1,578
Interest payments, long-term	**27**	**139**	**150**	**171**	**186**	**212**
Public and publicly guaranteed sector	26	93	95	103	113	118
Private sector not guaranteed	1	47	55	67	74	94

CAMEROON

(US$ million, unless otherwise indicated)

Snapshot	2023
Total external debt stocks	**15,299**
External debt stocks as % of:	
Exports	171
GNI	33
Debt service as % of:	
Exports	19
GNI	4
Net financial flows, debt and equity	764
Net debt inflows	-35
Net equity inflows	799
GNI	**46,953**
Population (million)	**29**

Figure 2 Average terms on new debt commitments from official and private creditors

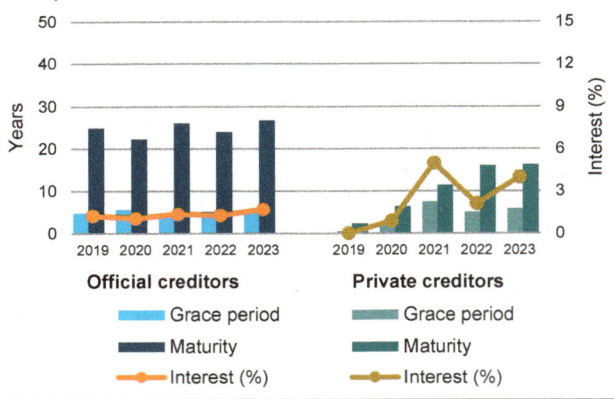

Official creditors
- Grace period
- Maturity
- Interest (%)

Private creditors
- Grace period
- Maturity
- Interest (%)

Figure 1 Public and publicly guaranteed debt, by creditor and creditor type in 2023, including IMF credit

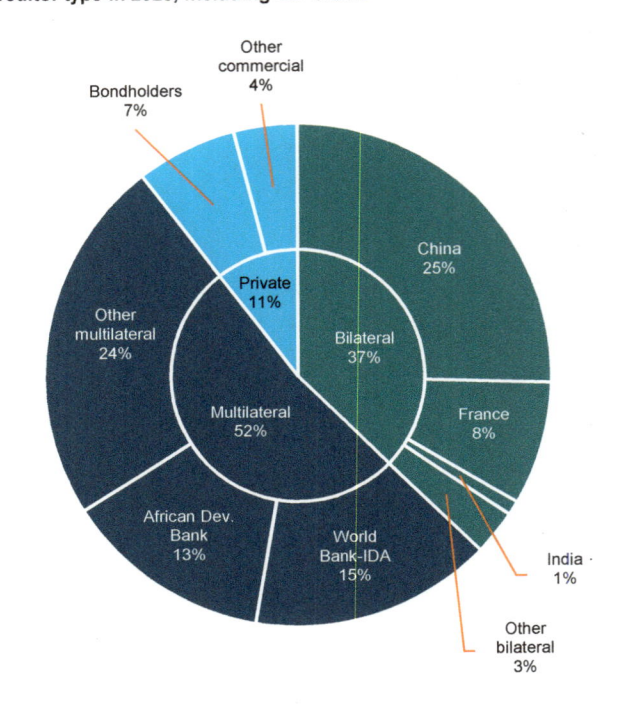

Summary External Debt Data	2010	2019	2020	2021	2022	2023
Total external debt stocks	**3,190**	**12,929**	**14,723**	**15,377**	**15,110**	**15,299**
Long-term external debt stocks	**2,737**	**11,791**	**13,086**	**12,950**	**12,357**	**12,386**
Public and publicly guaranteed debt from:	*2,160*	*10,388*	*11,391*	*12,379*	*11,853*	*12,025*
Official creditors	2,143	8,929	9,949	10,290	10,419	10,613
Multilateral	787	3,746	4,318	4,718	5,040	5,588
of which: World Bank	374	1,733	1,915	2,068	2,234	2,543
Bilateral	1,356	5,184	5,631	5,572	5,379	5,025
Private creditors	17	1,459	1,442	2,089	1,434	1,412
Bondholders	..	750	750	1,526	891	870
Commercial banks and others	17	709	692	563	543	543
Private nonguaranteed debt from:	*577*	*1,403*	*1,695*	*571*	*504*	*360*
Bondholders	..	..	..	..	..	..
Commercial banks and others	577	1,403	1,695	571	504	360
Use of IMF credit and SDR allocations	**445**	**760**	**1,269**	**1,777**	**1,874**	**2,055**
IMF credit	172	515	1,014	1,159	1,286	1,463
SDR allocations	273	245	255	618	588	593
Short-term external debt stocks	**9**	**377**	**368**	**650**	**879**	**858**
Disbursements, long-term	**278**	**2,588**	**1,724**	**1,851**	**1,346**	**935**
Public and publicly guaranteed sector	278	1,752	1,091	1,851	1,304	924
Private sector not guaranteed	..	837	633	0	42	11
Principal repayments, long-term	**160**	**759**	**964**	**1,648**	**1,474**	**1,116**
Public and publicly guaranteed sector	122	433	623	523	1,366	947
Private sector not guaranteed	38	325	341	1,125	109	169
Interest payments, long-term	**42**	**342**	**343**	**283**	**280**	**473**
Public and publicly guaranteed sector	27	230	330	276	275	468
Private sector not guaranteed	15	112	13	8	4	5

CENTRAL AFRICAN REPUBLIC

(US$ million, unless otherwise indicated)

Snapshot	2023
Total external debt stocks	**1,021**
External debt stocks as % of:	
Exports	259
GNI	38
Debt service as % of:	
Exports	10
GNI	1
Net financial flows, debt and equity	67
Net debt inflows	28
Net equity inflows	39
GNI	**2,707**
Population (million)	**6**

Figure 2 Average terms on new debt commitments from official and private creditors

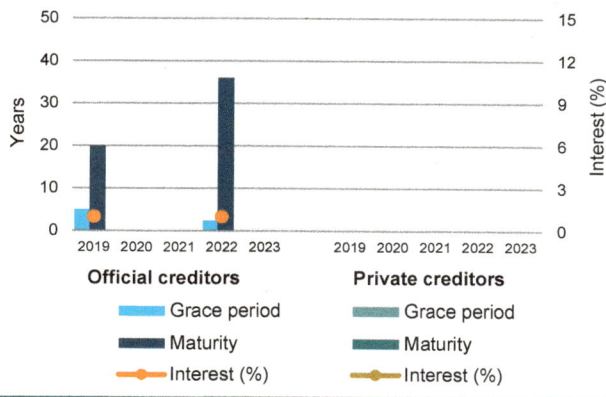

Figure 1 Public and publicly guaranteed debt, by creditor and creditor type in 2023, including IMF credit

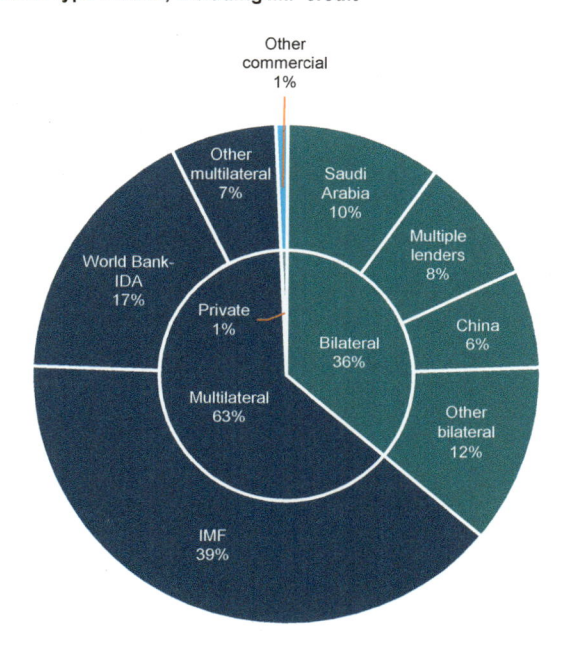

Summary External Debt Data	2010	2019	2020	2021	2022	2023
Total external debt stocks	634	850	901	1,120	1,015	1,021
Long-term external debt stocks	376	421	412	439	430	443
Public and publicly guaranteed debt from:	376	421	412	439	430	443
Official creditors	337	395	407	431	424	437
Multilateral	43	154	177	177	172	174
of which: World Bank	14	107	130	133	126	124
Bilateral	294	241	230	254	252	264
Private creditors	39	26	5	7	6	5
Bondholders	..	..	..	..	..	..
Commercial banks and others	39	26	5	7	6	5
Private nonguaranteed debt from:	..	..	..	..	..	..
Bondholders	..	..	..	..	..	..
Commercial banks and others	..	..	..	..	..	..
Use of IMF credit and SDR allocations	173	296	355	518	483	504
IMF credit	90	223	279	294	270	289
SDR allocations	82	74	77	224	213	215
Short-term external debt stocks	86	132	133	163	102	74
Disbursements, long-term	35	22	26	33	8	16
Public and publicly guaranteed sector	35	22	26	33	8	16
Private sector not guaranteed	..	..	..	..	..	..
Principal repayments, long-term	2	15	3	6	5	5
Public and publicly guaranteed sector	2	15	3	6	5	5
Private sector not guaranteed	..	..	..	..	..	..
Interest payments, long-term	1	2	1	1	2	2
Public and publicly guaranteed sector	1	2	1	1	2	2
Private sector not guaranteed	..	..	..	..	..	..

CHAD

(US$ million, unless otherwise indicated)

Snapshot	2023
Total external debt stocks	**3,214**
External debt stocks as % of:	
Exports	61
GNI	25
Debt service as % of:	
Exports	8
GNI	3
Net financial flows, debt and equity	**779**
Net debt inflows	-134
Net equity inflows	913
GNI	**12,957**
Population (million)	**18**

Figure 2 **Average terms on new debt commitments from official and private creditors**

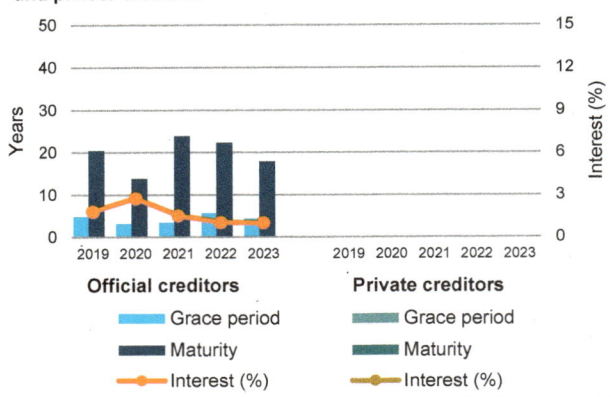

Official creditors
- ▢ Grace period
- ▪ Maturity
- ─●─ Interest (%)

Private creditors
- ▢ Grace period
- ▪ Maturity
- ─●─ Interest (%)

Figure 1 Public and publicly guaranteed debt, by creditor and creditor type in 2023, including IMF credit

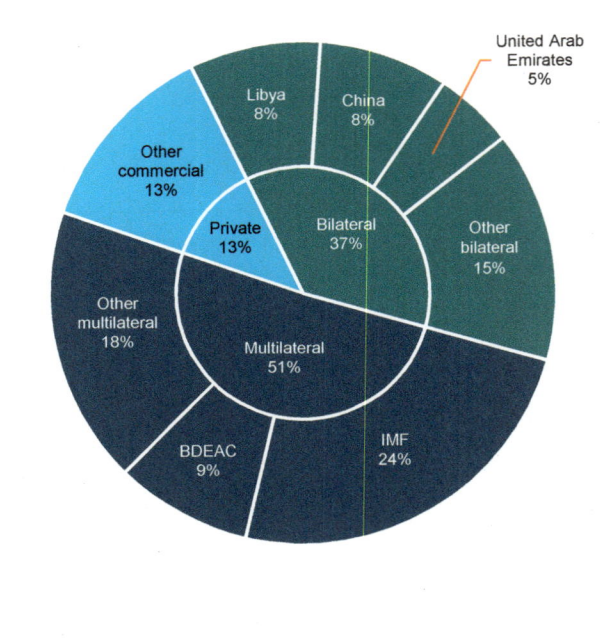

Summary External Debt Data	2010	2019	2020	2021	2022	2023
Total external debt stocks	**2,158**	**3,216**	**3,487**	**3,586**	**3,320**	**3,214**
Long-term external debt stocks	2,049	2,720	2,778	2,639	2,290	2,215
Public and publicly guaranteed debt from:	*2,049*	*2,720*	*2,778*	*2,639*	*2,290*	*2,215*
Official creditors	2,032	1,562	1,702	1,711	1,662	1,849
Multilateral	1,529	660	712	757	715	779
of which: World Bank	865	176	180	169	155	151
Bilateral	504	902	990	954	947	1,070
Private creditors	17	1,158	1,076	929	628	366
Bondholders	..	..	..	..	..	..
Commercial banks and others	17	1,158	1,076	929	628	366
Private nonguaranteed debt from:	..	..	..	..	..	..
Bondholders	..	..	..	..	..	..
Commercial banks and others	..	..	..	..	..	..
Use of IMF credit and SDR allocations	99	470	678	914	996	964
IMF credit	17	396	601	651	746	712
SDR allocations	83	74	77	263	250	252
Short-term external debt stocks	9	27	31	32	34	35
Disbursements, long-term	**366**	**49**	**123**	**174**	**62**	**222**
Public and publicly guaranteed sector	366	49	123	174	62	222
Private sector not guaranteed	..	..	..	..	..	..
Principal repayments, long-term	**45**	**74**	**135**	**270**	**344**	**316**
Public and publicly guaranteed sector	45	74	135	270	344	316
Private sector not guaranteed	..	..	..	..	..	..
Interest payments, long-term	**17**	**59**	**50**	**49**	**49**	**51**
Public and publicly guaranteed sector	17	59	50	49	49	51
Private sector not guaranteed	..	..	..	..	..	..

CHINA

(US$ million, unless otherwise indicated)

Snapshot	2023
Total external debt stocks	**2,420,211**
External debt stocks as % of:	
Exports	65
GNI	14
Debt service as % of:	
Exports	10
GNI	2
Net financial flows, debt and equity	60,700
Net debt inflows	-18,407
Net equity inflows	79,106
GNI	**17,663,712**
Population (million)	**1,411**

Figure 2 Average terms on new debt commitments from official and private creditors

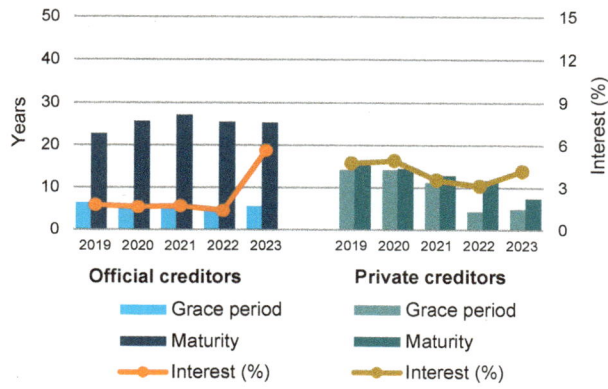

Figure 1 Public and publicly guaranteed debt, by creditor and creditor type in 2023, including IMF credit

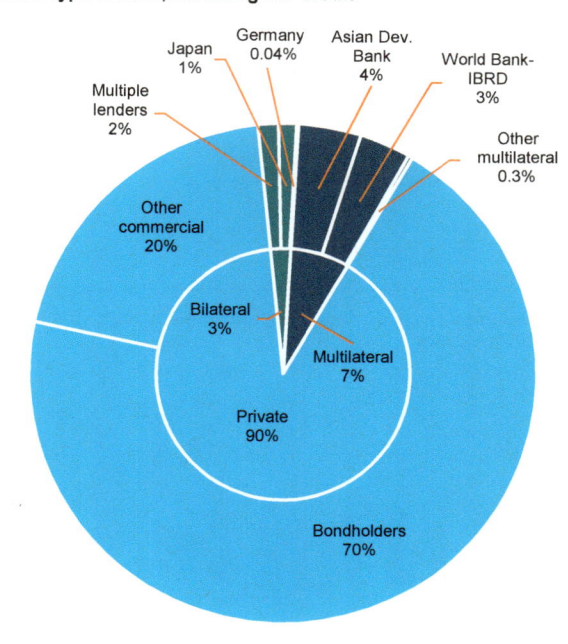

Summary External Debt Data	2010	2019	2020	2021	2022	2023
Total external debt stocks	742,737	2,114,162	2,326,233	2,724,354	2,448,050	2,420,211
Long-term external debt stocks	219,650	899,184	1,079,933	1,227,455	1,134,675	1,084,231
Public and publicly guaranteed debt from:	102,275	318,064	391,682	475,167	464,366	467,996
Official creditors	75,476	53,840	52,994	51,622	48,897	47,246
Multilateral	35,527	35,427	36,007	36,424	35,840	35,189
of which: World Bank	22,135	16,271	16,236	16,585	16,067	15,447
Bilateral	39,949	18,412	16,987	15,198	13,057	12,057
Private creditors	26,799	264,225	338,688	423,545	415,469	420,750
Bondholders	12,398	214,523	288,234	352,395	332,378	326,995
Commercial banks and others	14,401	49,701	50,454	71,150	83,091	93,756
Private nonguaranteed debt from:	117,375	581,120	688,252	752,287	670,309	616,235
Bondholders	5,561	234,623	323,512	340,314	300,804	268,008
Commercial banks and others	111,814	346,497	364,739	411,974	369,505	348,227
Use of IMF credit and SDR allocations	10,764	9,665	10,067	50,674	48,185	48,577
IMF credit	0	0	0	0	0	0
SDR allocations	10,764	9,665	10,067	50,674	48,185	48,577
Short-term external debt stocks	512,323	1,205,312	1,236,232	1,446,225	1,265,190	1,287,403
Disbursements, long-term	39,167	338,220	361,370	383,267	246,626	211,402
Public and publicly guaranteed sector	12,421	79,493	95,258	123,006	48,183	35,543
Private sector not guaranteed	26,746	258,727	266,112	260,262	198,443	175,860
Principal repayments, long-term	18,782	180,617	181,917	226,388	325,205	252,022
Public and publicly guaranteed sector	11,978	20,632	25,312	33,310	52,419	31,405
Private sector not guaranteed	6,803	159,985	156,605	193,078	272,786	220,618
Interest payments, long-term	5,484	35,730	31,593	46,492	46,523	49,845
Public and publicly guaranteed sector	1,819	8,670	8,506	17,050	20,444	22,766
Private sector not guaranteed	3,665	27,059	23,087	29,442	26,079	27,078

COLOMBIA

(US$ million, unless otherwise indicated)

Snapshot	2023
Total external debt stocks	**197,505**
External debt stocks as % of:	
Exports	256
GNI	55
Debt service as % of:	
Exports	37
GNI	8
Net financial flows, debt and equity	26,378
Net debt inflows	12,134
Net equity inflows	14,244
GNI	**361,334**
Population (million)	**52**

Figure 1 Public and publicly guaranteed debt, by creditor and creditor type in 2023, including IMF credit

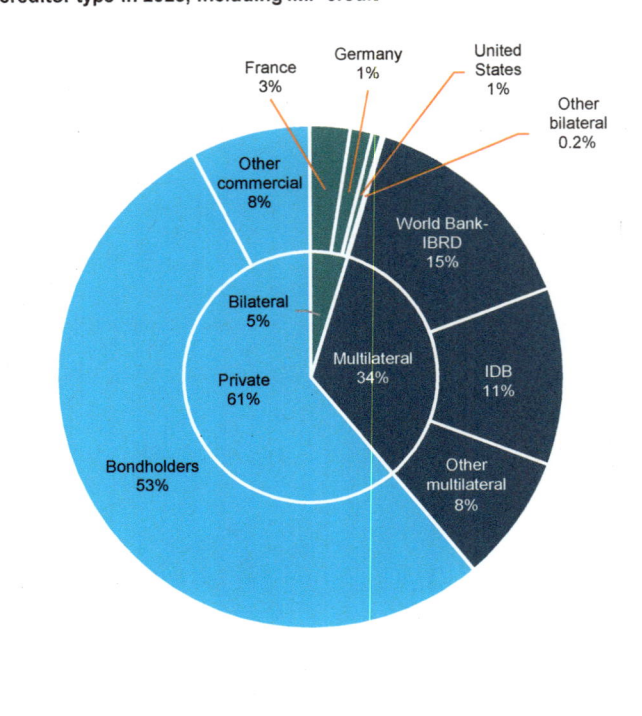

Figure 2 Average terms on new debt commitments from official and private creditors

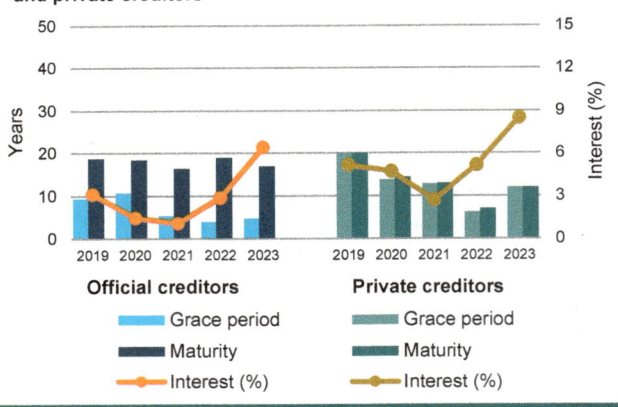

Official creditors
- Grace period
- Maturity
- Interest (%)

Private creditors
- Grace period
- Maturity
- Interest (%)

Summary External Debt Data	2010	2019	2020	2021	2022	2023
Total external debt stocks	**64,432**	**138,985**	**155,773**	**172,155**	**184,403**	**197,505**
Long-term external debt stocks	55,383	122,328	135,409	147,272	156,458	168,933
Public and publicly guaranteed debt from:	*37,058*	*75,170*	*85,599*	*93,979*	*97,650*	*103,450*
Official creditors	16,483	28,024	31,368	33,780	35,905	37,223
Multilateral	15,898	22,690	25,539	28,047	30,163	32,038
of which: World Bank	7,504	10,582	11,989	13,515	15,122	15,797
Bilateral	585	5,334	5,829	5,733	5,742	5,185
Private creditors	20,574	47,146	54,231	60,199	61,745	66,227
Bondholders	17,965	41,868	48,536	52,916	52,448	57,982
Commercial banks and others	2,609	5,278	5,695	7,283	9,297	8,245
Private nonguaranteed debt from:	*18,325*	*47,159*	*49,810*	*53,294*	*58,808*	*65,483*
Bondholders	3,329	10,481	8,954	9,604	8,249	7,140
Commercial banks and others	14,996	36,677	40,856	43,689	50,558	58,344
Use of IMF credit and SDR allocations	1,137	1,021	6,464	9,024	8,581	8,651
IMF credit	0	0	5,401	5,248	4,991	5,031
SDR allocations	1,137	1,021	1,063	3,776	3,590	3,620
Short-term external debt stocks	7,912	15,635	13,900	15,858	19,364	19,921
Disbursements, long-term	**12,970**	**17,189**	**27,645**	**31,053**	**30,004**	**30,509**
Public and publicly guaranteed sector	3,629	5,037	13,525	18,768	9,698	13,573
Private sector not guaranteed	9,340	12,153	14,120	12,286	20,306	16,936
Principal repayments, long-term	**6,566**	**12,078**	**15,060**	**18,335**	**19,717**	**18,931**
Public and publicly guaranteed sector	2,318	4,670	3,591	9,533	4,925	8,671
Private sector not guaranteed	4,248	7,408	11,469	8,802	14,792	10,261
Interest payments, long-term	**2,839**	**6,391**	**5,991**	**6,226**	**6,442**	**8,328**
Public and publicly guaranteed sector	2,121	3,792	3,478	3,808	3,881	4,910
Private sector not guaranteed	717	2,600	2,513	2,418	2,561	3,417

COMOROS

(US$ million, unless otherwise indicated)

Snapshot	2023
Total external debt stocks	**409.3**
External debt stocks as % of:	
Exports	251.3
GNI	30.2
Debt service as % of:	
Exports	11.6
GNI	1.4
Net financial flows, debt and equity	25.9
Net debt inflows	20.9
Net equity inflows	5.0
GNI	**1,355.2**
Population (thousand)	**852**

Figure 1 Public and publicly guaranteed debt, by creditor and creditor type in 2023, including IMF credit

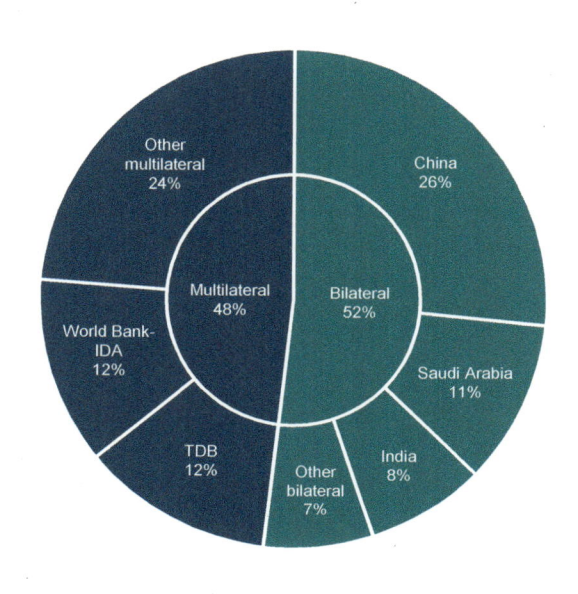

Figure 2 Average terms on new debt commitments from official and private creditors

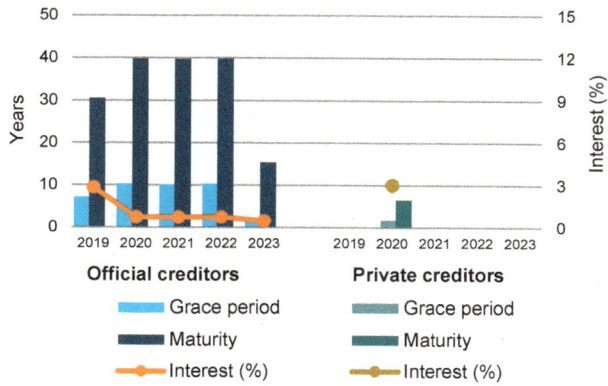

Summary External Debt Data	2010	2019	2020	2021	2022	2023
Total external debt stocks	**278.4**	**283.1**	**319.7**	**371.6**	**388.8**	**409.3**
Long-term external debt stocks	**248.5**	**250.5**	**275.9**	**306.9**	**329.9**	**348.1**
Public and publicly guaranteed debt from:	*248.5*	*250.5*	*275.9*	*306.9*	*329.9*	*348.1*
Official creditors	248.5	250.5	275.9	306.9	329.9	348.1
Multilateral	201.6	91.9	99.8	113.3	132.0	153.9
of which: World Bank	115.5	12.3	16.7	21.8	33.1	45.4
Bilateral	46.9	158.6	176.2	193.6	197.9	194.2
Private creditors	..	..	0.0	0.0	0.0	0.0
Bondholders	..	..	..	..	..	..
Commercial banks and others	..	..	0.0	0.0	0.0	0.0
Private nonguaranteed debt from:	..	..	..	..	..	..
Bondholders	..	..	..	..	..	..
Commercial banks and others	..	..	..	..	..	..
Use of IMF credit and SDR allocations	**25.4**	**30.7**	**41.9**	**62.9**	**57.3**	**60.8**
IMF credit	12.3	19.0	29.7	27.1	23.3	26.5
SDR allocations	13.1	11.8	12.2	35.8	34.0	34.3
Short-term external debt stocks	**4.4**	**1.9**	**1.8**	**1.8**	**1.6**	**0.5**
Disbursements, long-term	**0.0**	**14.5**	**18.7**	**33.8**	**38.9**	**24.3**
Public and publicly guaranteed sector	0.0	14.5	18.7	33.8	38.9	24.3
Private sector not guaranteed	..	..	..	..	..	..
Principal repayments, long-term	**3.1**	**4.7**	**4.6**	**1.1**	**1.2**	**6.4**
Public and publicly guaranteed sector	3.1	4.7	4.6	1.1	1.2	6.4
Private sector not guaranteed	..	..	..	..	..	..
Interest payments, long-term	**1.1**	**0.6**	**3.3**	**0.5**	**0.5**	**4.1**
Public and publicly guaranteed sector	1.1	0.6	3.3	0.5	0.5	4.1
Private sector not guaranteed	..	..	..	..	..	..

CONGO, DEMOCRATIC REPUBLIC OF

(US$ million, unless otherwise indicated)

Snapshot	2023
Total external debt stocks	**11,067**
External debt stocks as % of:	
Exports	37
GNI	17
Debt service as % of:	
Exports	2
GNI	1
Net financial flows, debt and equity	3,156
Net debt inflows	1,287
Net equity inflows	1,869
GNI	**64,288**
Population (million)	**102**

Figure 1 Public and publicly guaranteed debt, by creditor and creditor type in 2023, including IMF credit

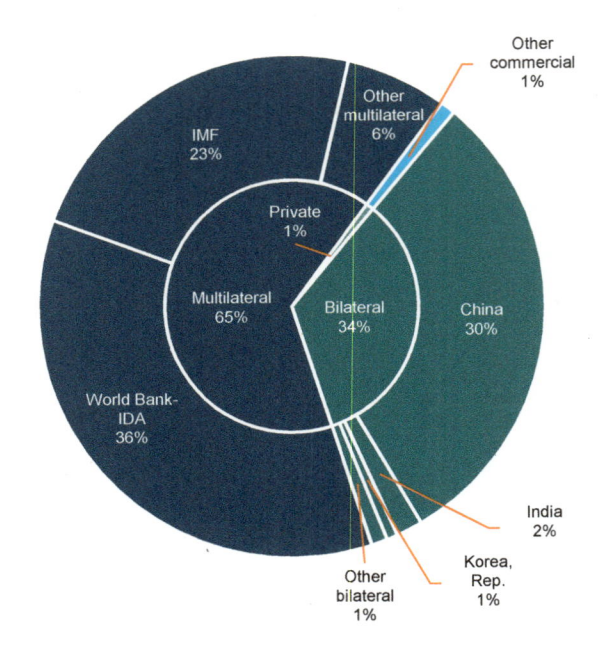

Figure 2 Average terms on new debt commitments from official and private creditors

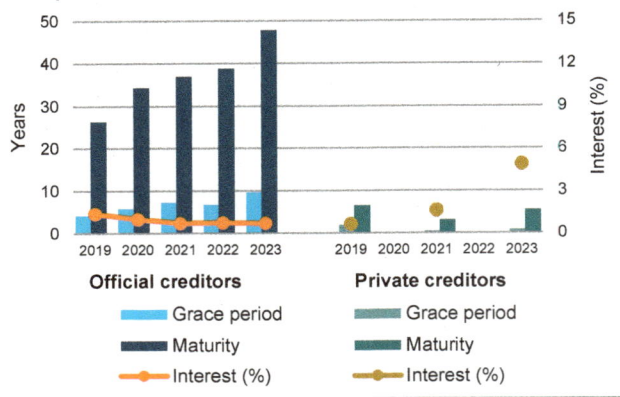

Summary External Debt Data	2010	2019	2020	2021	2022	2023
Total external debt stocks	**6,127**	**6,503**	**7,103**	**9,168**	**9,714**	**11,067**
Long-term external debt stocks	**4,583**	**4,992**	**5,230**	**5,396**	**5,567**	**6,468**
Public and publicly guaranteed debt from:	*4,583*	*4,992*	*5,230*	*5,396*	*5,567*	*6,468*
Official creditors	4,505	4,889	5,133	5,296	5,490	6,388
Multilateral	2,585	2,128	2,290	2,448	2,689	3,542
of which: World Bank	849	1,288	1,521	1,772	2,125	2,997
Bilateral	1,920	2,761	2,843	2,848	2,802	2,846
Private creditors	77	102	97	99	76	80
Bondholders	..	..	..	..	..	..
Commercial banks and others	77	102	97	99	76	80
Private nonguaranteed debt from:						
Bondholders	..	..	..	..	..	..
Commercial banks and others	..	..	..	..	..	..
Use of IMF credit and SDR allocations	**1,110**	**1,130**	**1,511**	**3,317**	**3,560**	**3,997**
IMF credit	323	423	775	1,172	1,520	1,941
SDR allocations	787	706	736	2,145	2,040	2,056
Short-term external debt stocks	**435**	**382**	**362**	**455**	**588**	**602**
Disbursements, long-term	**178**	**440**	**300**	**484**	**590**	**1,156**
Public and publicly guaranteed sector	178	440	300	484	590	1,156
Private sector not guaranteed	..	..	..	..	..	..
Principal repayments, long-term	**89**	**196**	**161**	**257**	**298**	**262**
Public and publicly guaranteed sector	89	196	161	257	298	262
Private sector not guaranteed	..	..	..	..	..	..
Interest payments, long-term	**124**	**773**	**59**	**54**	**49**	**137**
Public and publicly guaranteed sector	124	773	59	54	49	137
Private sector not guaranteed	..	..	..	..	..	..

CONGO, REPUBLIC OF

(US$ million, unless otherwise indicated)

Snapshot	2023
Total external debt stocks	**7,779**
External debt stocks as % of:	
Exports	81
GNI	54
Debt service as % of:	
Exports	8
GNI	5
Net financial flows, debt and equity	480
Net debt inflows	-147
Net equity inflows	626
GNI	**14,486**
Population (million)	**6**

Figure 2 Average terms on new debt commitments from official and private creditors

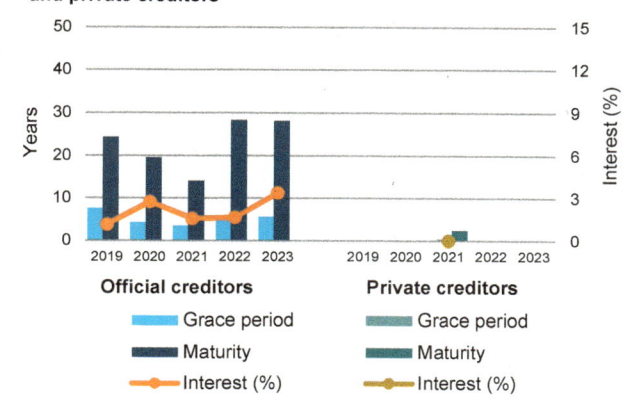

Official creditors
- Grace period
- Maturity
- Interest (%)

Private creditors
- Grace period
- Maturity
- Interest (%)

Figure 1 Public and publicly guaranteed debt, by creditor and creditor type in 2023, including IMF credit

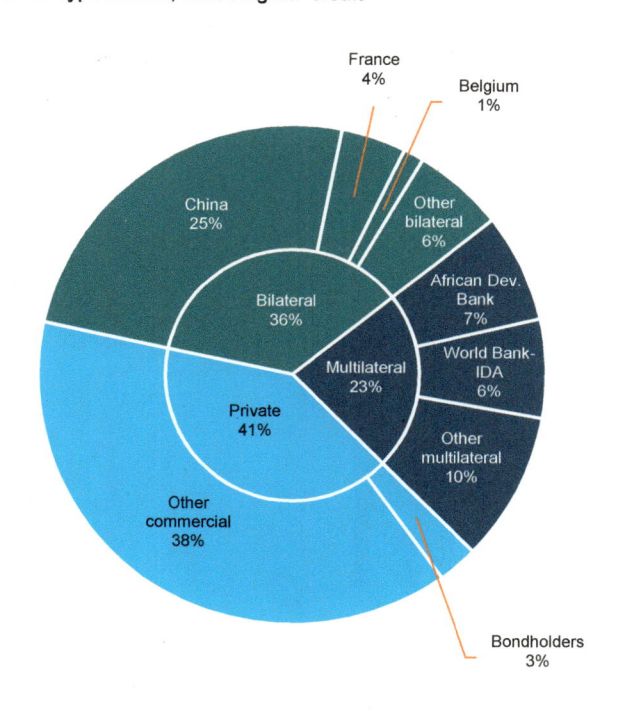

Summary External Debt Data	2010	2019	2020	2021	2022	2023
Total external debt stocks	**2,796**	**8,397**	**8,224**	**8,254**	**7,862**	**7,779**
Long-term external debt stocks	**2,450**	**8,006**	**7,778**	**7,590**	**7,141**	**6,875**
Public and publicly guaranteed debt from:	*2,450*	*8,006*	*7,772*	*7,581*	*7,131*	*6,865*
Official creditors	1,023	4,101	4,081	4,061	3,922	3,891
Multilateral	182	869	985	1,022	1,108	1,279
of which: World Bank	84	243	342	413	543	629
Bilateral	842	3,232	3,096	3,039	2,815	2,612
Private creditors	1,426	3,905	3,691	3,521	3,209	2,974
Bondholders	454	295	268	241	213	186
Commercial banks and others	973	3,610	3,423	3,280	2,995	2,788
Private nonguaranteed debt from:	..	..	*6*	*9*	*10*	*11*
Bondholders	..	..	..	..	..	..
Commercial banks and others	..	..	6	9	10	11
Use of IMF credit and SDR allocations	**150**	**157**	**162**	**374**	**528**	**706**
IMF credit	27	47	48	45	216	391
SDR allocations	123	110	115	329	313	315
Short-term external debt stocks	**197**	**234**	**284**	**290**	**193**	**197**
Disbursements, long-term	**882**	**639**	**189**	**204**	**317**	**330**
Public and publicly guaranteed sector	882	639	183	198	313	328
Private sector not guaranteed	..	..	6	5	3	2
Principal repayments, long-term	**95**	**418**	**542**	**322**	**718**	**631**
Public and publicly guaranteed sector	95	418	542	320	716	629
Private sector not guaranteed	..	..	..	2	2	2
Interest payments, long-term	**24**	**80**	**94**	**69**	**153**	**126**
Public and publicly guaranteed sector	24	80	93	68	152	125
Private sector not guaranteed	..	..	0	1	1	1

COSTA RICA

(US$ million, unless otherwise indicated)

Snapshot	2023
Total external debt stocks	**39,025**
External debt stocks as % of:	
Exports	113
GNI	49
Debt service as % of:	
Exports	15
GNI	6
Net financial flows, debt and equity	4,976
Net debt inflows	602
Net equity inflows	4,374
GNI	**79,835**
Population (million)	**5**

Figure 1 Public and publicly guaranteed debt, by creditor and creditor type in 2023, including IMF credit

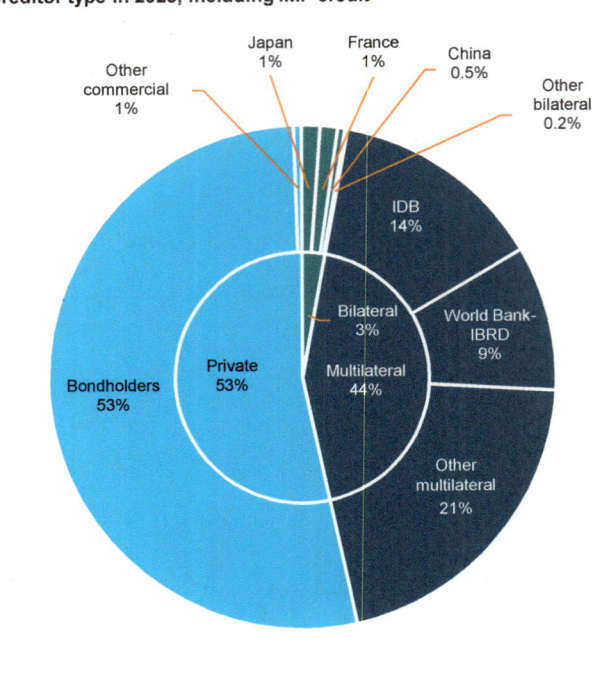

Figure 2 Average terms on new debt commitments from official and private creditors

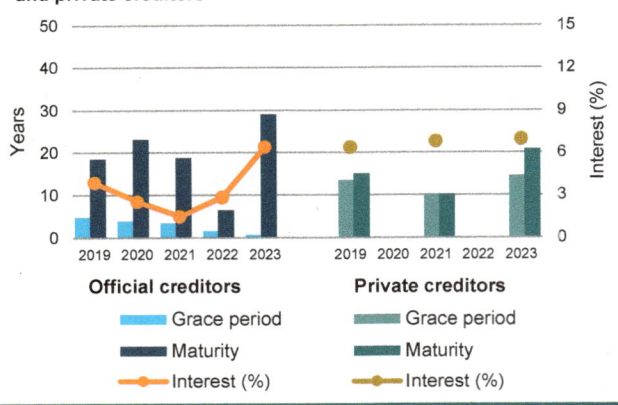

Summary External Debt Data	2010	2019	2020	2021	2022	2023
Total external debt stocks	**8,154**	**29,802**	**30,831**	**33,662**	**38,683**	**39,025**
Long-term external debt stocks	**5,482**	**26,830**	**26,132**	**27,458**	**29,864**	**31,378**
Public and publicly guaranteed debt from:	*3,822*	*13,393*	*12,138*	*12,260*	*13,725*	*15,083*
Official creditors	2,196	4,911	4,509	4,969	6,618	6,202
Multilateral	1,767	4,443	4,045	4,528	6,154	5,715
of which: World Bank	570	955	1,021	1,292	1,562	1,550
Bilateral	430	467	463	441	464	487
Private creditors	1,626	8,482	7,629	7,291	7,107	8,881
Bondholders	1,310	7,600	6,983	6,800	6,800	8,800
Commercial banks and others	316	882	647	491	307	81
Private nonguaranteed debt from:	*1,660*	*13,437*	*13,994*	*15,198*	*16,139*	*16,295*
Bondholders	..	2,100	2,100	1,250	1,250	700
Commercial banks and others	1,660	11,337	11,894	13,948	14,889	15,595
Use of IMF credit and SDR allocations	**241**	**216**	**757**	**1,520**	**1,995**	**2,226**
IMF credit	0	0	532	806	1,315	1,541
SDR allocations	241	216	225	715	680	685
Short-term external debt stocks	**2,431**	**2,755**	**3,942**	**4,683**	**6,824**	**5,422**
Disbursements, long-term	**1,455**	**3,570**	**1,927**	**3,223**	**2,964**	**4,411**
Public and publicly guaranteed sector	928	2,487	552	1,079	2,022	3,305
Private sector not guaranteed	528	1,083	1,375	2,144	942	1,106
Principal repayments, long-term	**617**	**1,959**	**2,650**	**1,859**	**549**	**2,620**
Public and publicly guaranteed sector	342	1,073	1,811	919	549	1,670
Private sector not guaranteed	275	886	839	939	..	950
Interest payments, long-term	**313**	**1,123**	**589**	**870**	**1,602**	**1,953**
Public and publicly guaranteed sector	213	674	313	578	610	866
Private sector not guaranteed	100	448	276	292	992	1,087

CÔTE D'IVOIRE

(US$ million, unless otherwise indicated)

Snapshot	2023
Total external debt stocks	**36,548**
External debt stocks as % of:	
Exports	203
GNI	48
Debt service as % of:	
Exports	20
GNI	5
Net financial flows, debt and equity	5,744
Net debt inflows	3,991
Net equity inflows	1,753
GNI	**75,606**
Population (million)	**29**

Figure 2 Average terms on new debt commitments from official and private creditors

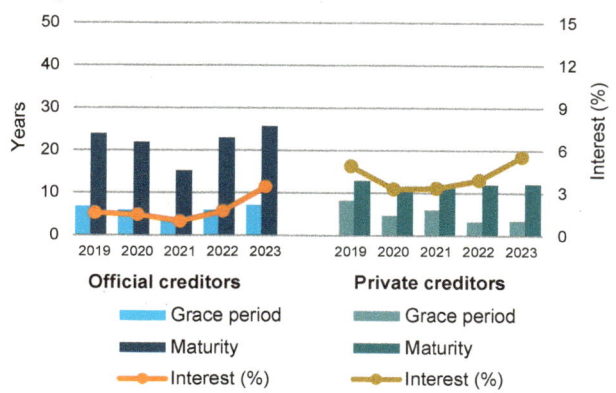

Figure 1 Public and publicly guaranteed debt, by creditor and creditor type in 2023, including IMF credit

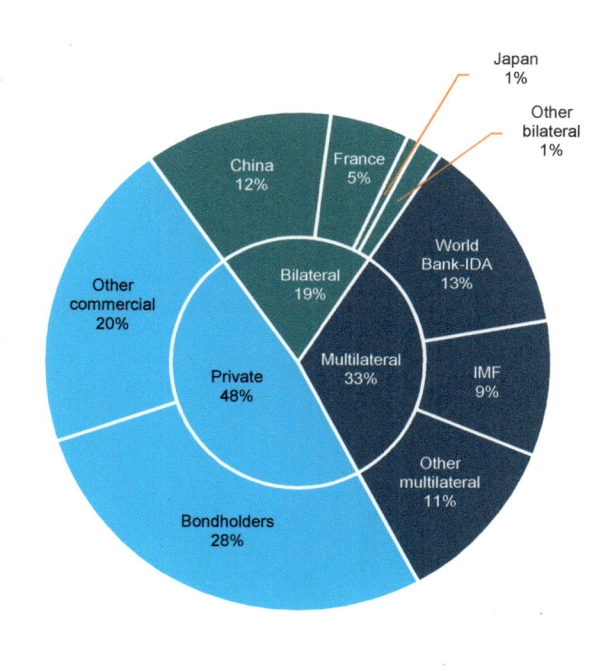

Summary External Debt Data	2010	2019	2020	2021	2022	2023
Total external debt stocks	**11,703**	**19,831**	**25,107**	**29,768**	**31,787**	**36,548**
Long-term external debt stocks	**10,431**	**17,027**	**21,003**	**23,933**	**26,798**	**29,562**
Public and publicly guaranteed debt from:	*9,413*	*15,748*	*20,013*	*23,184*	*26,275*	*29,169*
Official creditors	9,301	5,972	7,962	10,078	11,522	13,607
Multilateral	2,373	2,609	4,009	4,754	5,847	7,497
of which: World Bank	1,763	1,204	1,882	2,488	3,117	4,189
Bilateral	6,928	3,363	3,952	5,324	5,676	6,110
Private creditors	112	9,776	12,051	13,106	14,752	15,562
Bondholders	0	7,589	8,532	9,010	8,592	8,747
Commercial banks and others	112	2,187	3,519	4,097	6,161	6,815
Private nonguaranteed debt from:	*1,018*	*1,279*	*991*	*749*	*524*	*393*
Bondholders	..	..	..	..	..	..
Commercial banks and others	1,018	1,279	991	749	524	393
Use of IMF credit and SDR allocations	**861**	**1,915**	**3,047**	**3,647**	**3,303**	**4,002**
IMF credit	383	1,485	2,600	2,339	2,060	2,749
SDR allocations	479	430	448	1,308	1,243	1,253
Short-term external debt stocks	**411**	**890**	**1,056**	**2,188**	**1,686**	**2,984**
Disbursements, long-term	**599**	**5,083**	**4,307**	**4,989**	**5,167**	**3,932**
Public and publicly guaranteed sector	244	4,511	4,307	4,989	5,167	3,932
Private sector not guaranteed	355	572	..	..	..	0
Principal repayments, long-term	**623**	**2,247**	**1,565**	**803**	**1,247**	**1,907**
Public and publicly guaranteed sector	438	1,946	1,226	603	1,050	1,765
Private sector not guaranteed	185	302	340	200	197	142
Interest payments, long-term	**114**	**556**	**701**	**700**	**614**	**1,036**
Public and publicly guaranteed sector	58	518	671	683	602	1,010
Private sector not guaranteed	56	38	29	17	12	26

DJIBOUTI

(US$ million, unless otherwise indicated)

Snapshot	2023
Total external debt stocks	**3,429**
External debt stocks as % of:	
Exports	59
GNI	86
Debt service as % of:	
Exports	2
GNI	3
Net financial flows, debt and equity	353
Net debt inflows	216
Net equity inflows	137
GNI	**4,007**
Population (million)	**1**

Figure 2 Average terms on new debt commitments from official and private creditors

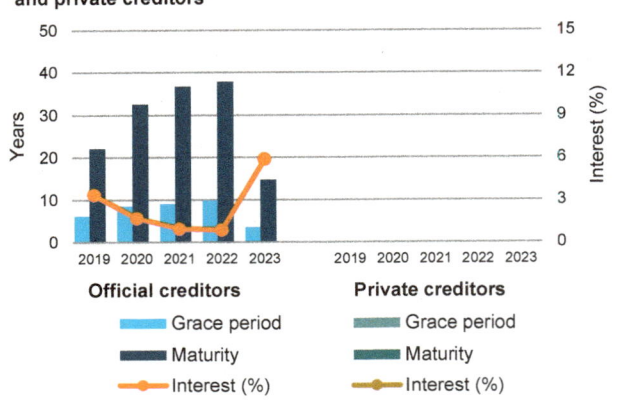

Figure 1 Public and publicly guaranteed debt, by creditor and creditor type in 2023, including IMF credit

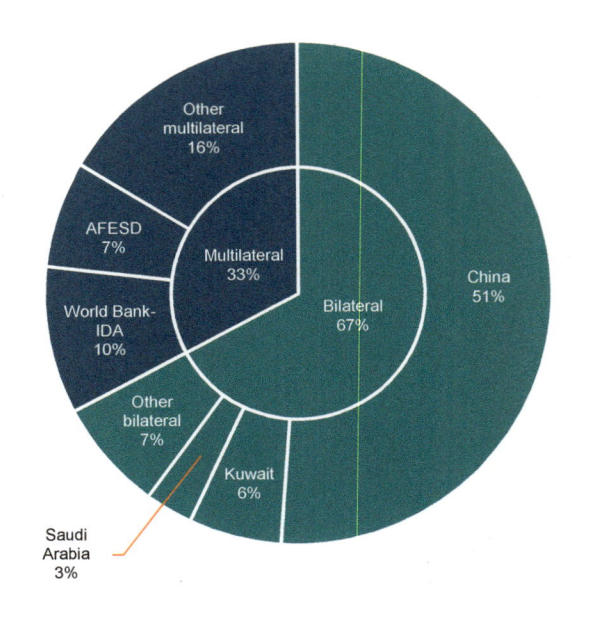

Summary External Debt Data	2010	2019	2020	2021	2022	2023
Total external debt stocks	**769**	**2,553**	**2,900**	**3,207**	**3,170**	**3,429**
Long-term external debt stocks	**612**	**2,146**	**2,575**	**2,427**	**2,439**	**2,846**
Public and publicly guaranteed debt from:	*612*	*2,146*	*2,354*	*2,407*	*2,409*	*2,836*
Official creditors	595	2,146	2,354	2,407	2,409	2,836
Multilateral	406	611	660	692	708	898
of which: World Bank	155	161	191	215	230	274
Bilateral	189	1,534	1,694	1,715	1,701	1,938
Private creditors	16	..	..	..	..	..
Bondholders	..	..	..	..	..	..
Commercial banks and others	16	..	..	..	..	..
Private nonguaranteed debt from:	..	..	*221*	*21*	*30*	*10*
Bondholders	..	..	219	20	20	0
Commercial banks and others	..	..	2	1	10	10
Use of IMF credit and SDR allocations	**35**	**32**	**72**	**109**	**103**	**104**
IMF credit	12	11	51	45	42	43
SDR allocations	23	21	22	64	61	61
Short-term external debt stocks	**122**	**375**	**253**	**670**	**628**	**478**
Disbursements, long-term	**35**	**136**	**435**	**86**	**75**	**306**
Public and publicly guaranteed sector	35	136	214	86	66	306
Private sector not guaranteed	..	..	221	..	9	..
Principal repayments, long-term	**22**	**35**	**28**	**30**	**33**	**45**
Public and publicly guaranteed sector	22	35	28	28	33	25
Private sector not guaranteed	..	..	..	1	..	20
Interest payments, long-term	**8**	**29**	**34**	**21**	**21**	**26**
Public and publicly guaranteed sector	8	29	25	20	19	24
Private sector not guaranteed	..	..	8	1	1	1

DOMINICA

(US$ million, unless otherwise indicated)

Snapshot	2023
Total external debt stocks	**598.1**
External debt stocks as % of:	
Exports	309.4
GNI	91.2
Debt service as % of:	
Exports	24.4
GNI	7.2
Net financial flows, debt and equity	22.4
Net debt inflows	-1.5
Net equity inflows	23.9
GNI	**655.8**
Population (thousand)	**73.0**

Figure 2 Average terms on new debt commitments from official and private creditors

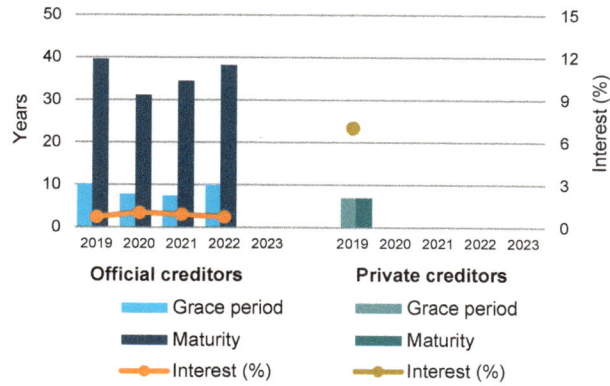

Official creditors
- ■ Grace period
- ■ Maturity
- ━━ Interest (%)

Private creditors
- ■ Grace period
- ■ Maturity
- ━━ Interest (%)

Figure 1 Public and publicly guaranteed debt, by creditor and creditor type in 2023, including IMF credit

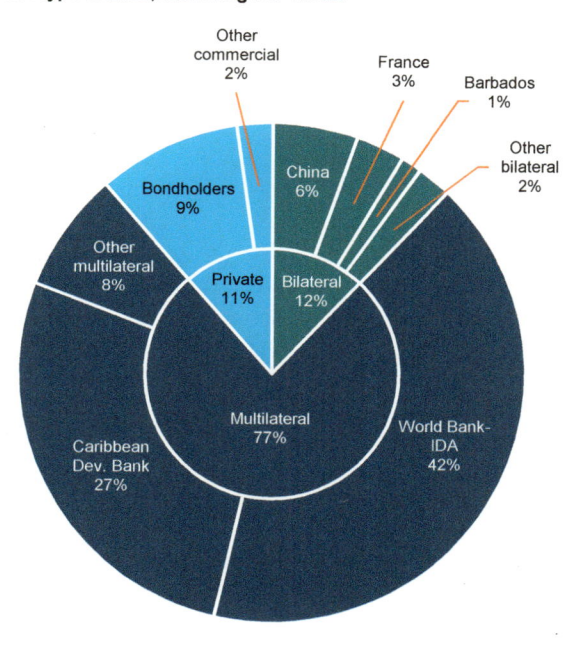

Summary External Debt Data	2010	2019	2020	2021	2022	2023
Total external debt stocks	**271.4**	**460.2**	**480.9**	**510.0**	**598.8**	**598.1**
Long-term external debt stocks	**235.6**	**268.2**	**302.6**	**335.5**	**356.7**	**378.6**
Public and publicly guaranteed debt from:	*235.6*	*250.7*	*279.4*	*314.8*	*339.0*	*364.0*
Official creditors	172.4	190.7	225.6	263.8	292.0	320.4
Multilateral	117.0	122.1	159.6	197.1	236.4	274.3
of which: World Bank	27.8	35.6	51.4	88.2	121.4	158.2
Bilateral	55.4	68.6	66.0	66.6	55.5	46.1
Private creditors	63.2	60.0	53.8	51.0	47.0	43.6
Bondholders	57.1	45.0	40.2	39.0	36.4	34.9
Commercial banks and others	6.0	15.0	13.5	12.1	10.6	8.7
Private nonguaranteed debt from:	..	*17.6*	*23.3*	*20.7*	*17.8*	*14.6*
Bondholders	..	..	..	..	..	..
Commercial banks and others	..	17.6	23.3	20.7	17.8	14.6
Use of IMF credit and SDR allocations	**30.2**	**20.8**	**35.8**	**48.0**	**43.7**	**42.4**
IMF credit	18.2	9.9	24.5	21.6	18.6	17.1
SDR allocations	12.1	10.8	11.3	26.4	25.1	25.3
Short-term external debt stocks	**5.5**	**171.2**	**142.5**	**126.5**	**198.4**	**177.1**
Disbursements, long-term	**29.7**	**22.4**	**45.0**	**47.7**	**50.8**	**47.0**
Public and publicly guaranteed sector	29.7	22.4	39.3	47.7	50.8	47.0
Private sector not guaranteed	..	..	5.7	..	..	..
Principal repayments, long-term	**9.8**	**22.5**	**20.4**	**14.4**	**23.4**	**25.6**
Public and publicly guaranteed sector	9.8	18.5	20.4	11.9	20.5	22.4
Private sector not guaranteed	..	3.9	..	2.6	2.9	3.2
Interest payments, long-term	**5.4**	**7.0**	**7.1**	**6.9**	**8.8**	**8.9**
Public and publicly guaranteed sector	5.4	6.6	6.6	6.4	8.2	8.3
Private sector not guaranteed	..	0.4	0.4	0.4	0.5	0.6

DOMINICAN REPUBLIC

(US$ million, unless otherwise indicated)

Snapshot	2023
Total external debt stocks	**52,257**
External debt stocks as % of:	
Exports	192
GNI	45
Debt service as % of:	
Exports	19
GNI	4
Net financial flows, debt and equity	8,569
Net debt inflows	4,024
Net equity inflows	4,545
GNI	**116,007**
Population (million)	**11**

Figure 1 Public and publicly guaranteed debt, by creditor and creditor type in 2023, including IMF credit

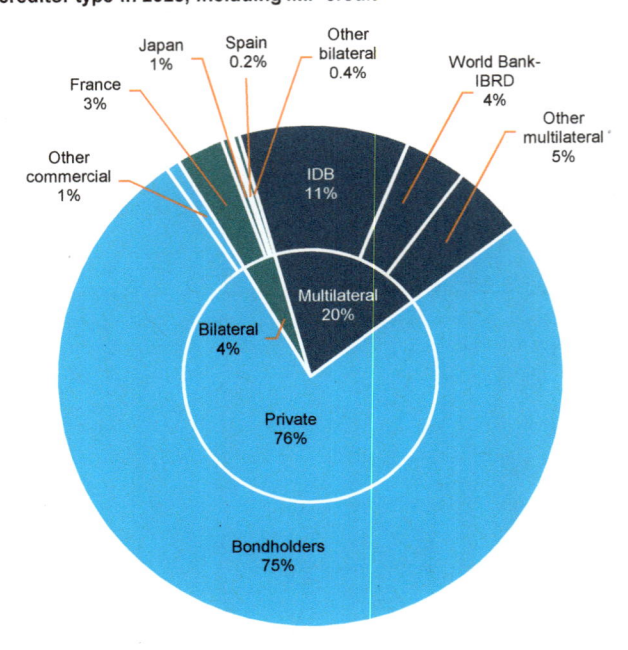

Figure 2 Average terms on new debt commitments from official and private creditors

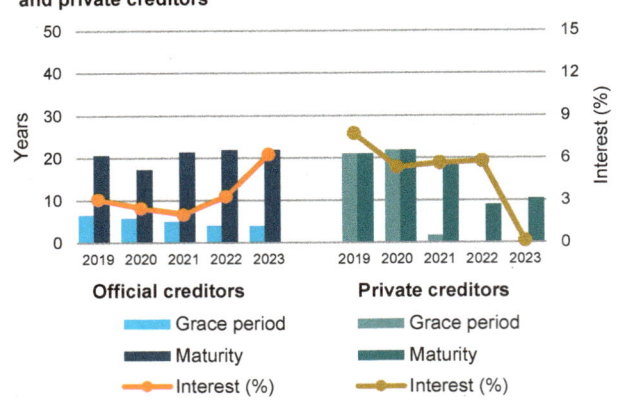

Summary External Debt Data	2010	2019	2020	2021	2022	2023
Total external debt stocks	**13,499**	**35,096**	**40,560**	**43,885**	**48,243**	**52,257**
Long-term external debt stocks	**10,283**	**32,292**	**37,400**	**39,973**	**43,553**	**46,917**
Public and publicly guaranteed debt from:	*9,441*	*23,006*	*29,856*	*32,507*	*35,559*	*38,277*
Official creditors	6,343	6,068	7,089	7,134	7,491	8,673
Multilateral	3,079	5,086	5,900	5,779	6,042	7,053
of which: World Bank	872	939	1,183	1,185	1,174	1,528
Bilateral	3,264	982	1,189	1,356	1,448	1,620
Private creditors	3,098	16,938	22,767	25,372	28,069	29,604
Bondholders	1,134	16,229	22,158	24,893	27,671	29,266
Commercial banks and others	1,964	709	609	479	398	338
Private nonguaranteed debt from:	*843*	*9,285*	*7,544*	*7,467*	*7,994*	*8,640*
Bondholders	843	1,395	707	1,007	1,007	1,007
Commercial banks and others	0	7,890	6,837	6,460	6,987	7,633
Use of IMF credit and SDR allocations	**1,461**	**289**	**988**	**1,601**	**1,522**	**1,374**
IMF credit	1,139	0	688	668	635	480
SDR allocations	322	289	301	933	887	894
Short-term external debt stocks	**1,754**	**2,515**	**2,172**	**2,311**	**3,168**	**3,965**
Disbursements, long-term	**2,111**	**2,459**	**9,769**	**3,510**	**4,981**	**5,420**
Public and publicly guaranteed sector	2,111	2,395	9,769	3,210	4,352	4,735
Private sector not guaranteed	..	64	..	300	629	685
Principal repayments, long-term	**799**	**1,867**	**4,531**	**926**	**1,413**	**2,033**
Public and publicly guaranteed sector	798	679	2,789	549	1,311	1,994
Private sector not guaranteed	0	1,188	1,742	377	102	39
Interest payments, long-term	**444**	**1,744**	**1,662**	**1,870**	**2,086**	**2,623**
Public and publicly guaranteed sector	336	1,295	1,415	1,668	1,851	2,190
Private sector not guaranteed	108	449	247	203	235	433

ECUADOR

(US$ million, unless otherwise indicated)

Snapshot	2023
Total external debt stocks	**60,564**
External debt stocks as % of:	
Exports	173
GNI	52
Debt service as % of:	
Exports	19
GNI	6
Net financial flows, debt and equity	**1,703**
Net debt inflows	1,175
Net equity inflows	528
GNI	**116,176**
Population (million)	**18**

Figure 2 Average terms on new debt commitments from official and private creditors

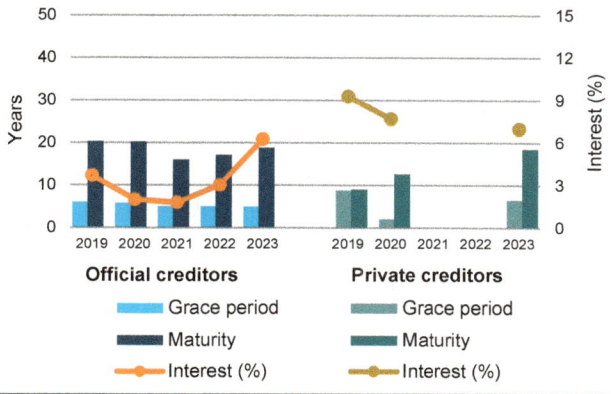

Figure 1 Public and publicly guaranteed debt, by creditor and creditor type in 2023, including IMF credit

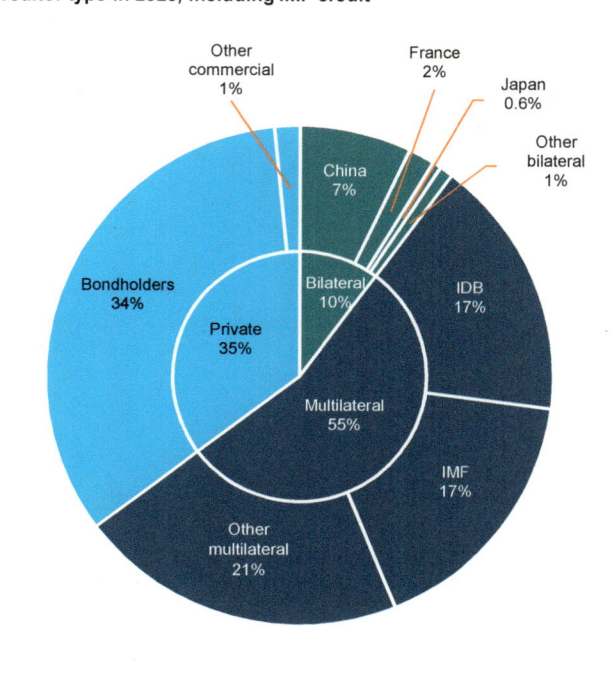

Summary External Debt Data	2010	2019	2020	2021	2022	2023
Total external debt stocks	**15,389**	**51,909**	**56,397**	**58,116**	**60,684**	**60,564**
Long-term external debt stocks	**13,881**	**48,862**	**48,488**	**48,680**	**49,373**	**49,591**
Public and publicly guaranteed debt from:	*8,800*	*38,404*	*37,785*	*38,753*	*39,483*	*39,658*
Official creditors	7,559	18,132	19,646	20,996	21,874	22,876
Multilateral	5,207	11,085	13,258	14,813	16,614	18,021
of which: World Bank	456	1,251	2,596	2,897	4,353	5,240
Bilateral	2,352	7,047	6,388	6,183	5,260	4,855
Private creditors	1,241	20,272	18,139	17,757	17,609	16,782
Bondholders	1,082	18,307	17,694	17,494	17,440	16,008
Commercial banks and others	159	1,965	445	263	169	774
Private nonguaranteed debt from:	*5,082*	*10,458*	*10,703*	*9,928*	*9,890*	*9,933*
Bondholders	..	..	..	..	..	..
Commercial banks and others	5,082	10,458	10,703	9,928	9,890	9,933
Use of IMF credit and SDR allocations	**444**	**2,114**	**6,781**	**8,183**	**9,387**	**9,233**
IMF credit	0	1,716	6,365	6,843	8,113	7,949
SDR allocations	444	399	415	1,340	1,274	1,284
Short-term external debt stocks	**1,064**	**933**	**1,128**	**1,253**	**1,923**	**1,740**
Disbursements, long-term	**2,977**	**12,286**	**7,629**	**4,650**	**4,150**	**5,353**
Public and publicly guaranteed sector	2,307	6,877	3,649	2,735	2,690	3,295
Private sector not guaranteed	670	5,409	3,981	1,916	1,460	2,058
Principal repayments, long-term	**1,259**	**6,505**	**7,548**	**4,441**	**3,378**	**3,765**
Public and publicly guaranteed sector	636	3,917	3,813	1,750	1,881	1,750
Private sector not guaranteed	623	2,588	3,735	2,691	1,498	2,016
Interest payments, long-term	**470**	**2,792**	**1,517**	**1,858**	**1,629**	**2,018**
Public and publicly guaranteed sector	332	2,385	1,173	1,360	1,353	1,603
Private sector not guaranteed	139	407	344	497	276	416

EGYPT, ARAB REPUBLIC OF

(US$ million, unless otherwise indicated)

Snapshot	2023
Total external debt stocks	**168,062**
External debt stocks as % of:	
Exports	239
GNI	44
Debt service as % of:	
Exports	30
GNI	6
Net financial flows, debt and equity	**14,683**
Net debt inflows	5,095
Net equity inflows	9,588
GNI	**378,608**
Population (million)	**113**

Figure 1 Public and publicly guaranteed debt, by creditor and creditor type in 2023, including IMF credit

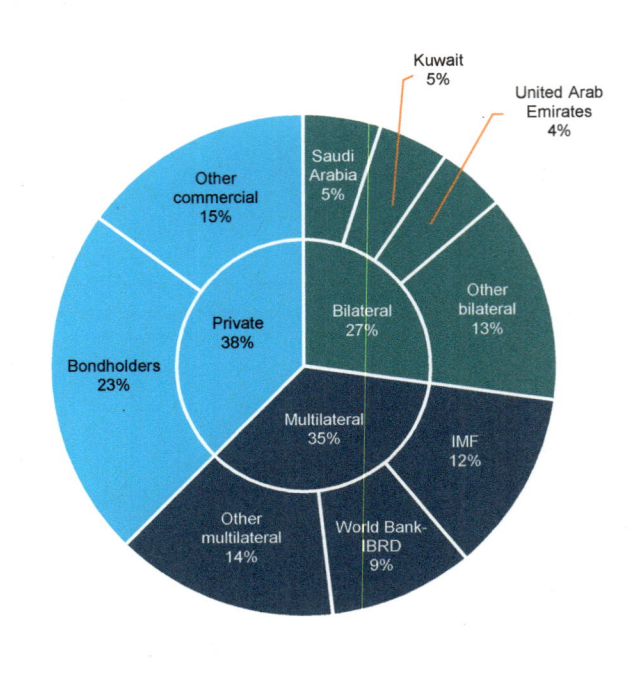

Figure 2 Average terms on new debt commitments from official and private creditors

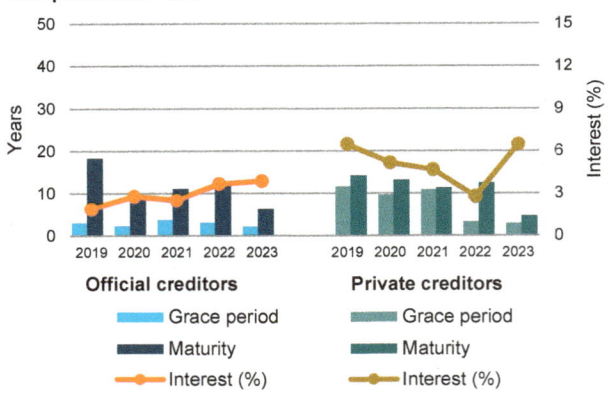

Summary External Debt Data	2010	2019	2020	2021	2022	2023
Total external debt stocks	**36,804**	**114,910**	**132,539**	**145,998**	**163,092**	**168,062**
Long-term external debt stocks	**32,271**	**90,496**	**100,218**	**109,475**	**111,093**	**119,260**
Public and publicly guaranteed debt from:	*32,218*	*90,136*	*99,816*	*108,692*	*110,194*	*117,380*
Official creditors	28,033	57,944	62,977	62,687	64,050	67,856
Multilateral	9,293	21,569	26,322	28,442	29,967	31,963
of which: World Bank	3,881	11,250	11,993	12,037	12,318	12,314
Bilateral	18,741	36,375	36,655	34,244	34,083	35,894
Private creditors	4,184	32,192	36,838	46,005	46,144	49,524
Bondholders	3,333	22,677	25,905	31,457	29,080	29,798
Commercial banks and others	851	9,515	10,933	14,548	17,064	19,727
Private nonguaranteed debt from:	*54*	*360*	*402*	*784*	*899*	*1,879*
Bondholders	..	..	..	100	100	100
Commercial banks and others	54	360	402	684	799	1,779
Use of IMF credit and SDR allocations	**1,384**	**13,130**	**20,362**	**23,681**	**21,753**	**19,319**
IMF credit	0	11,888	19,068	19,691	17,959	15,494
SDR allocations	1,384	1,242	1,294	3,990	3,794	3,825
Short-term external debt stocks	**3,149**	**11,284**	**11,959**	**12,842**	**30,246**	**29,483**
Disbursements, long-term	**3,625**	**15,686**	**17,824**	**25,481**	**14,561**	**17,780**
Public and publicly guaranteed sector	3,620	15,616	17,631	24,771	14,355	16,493
Private sector not guaranteed	5	71	193	710	206	1,287
Principal repayments, long-term	**2,164**	**4,878**	**8,216**	**13,283**	**10,696**	**9,326**
Public and publicly guaranteed sector	2,139	4,722	8,065	13,054	10,505	9,019
Private sector not guaranteed	25	156	151	229	191	307
Interest payments, long-term	**770**	**3,406**	**3,389**	**3,702**	**4,192**	**6,272**
Public and publicly guaranteed sector	769	3,388	3,378	3,623	4,153	6,166
Private sector not guaranteed	1	19	12	79	39	106

EL SALVADOR

(US$ million, unless otherwise indicated)

Snapshot	2023
Total external debt stocks	**22,742**
External debt stocks as % of:	
Exports	205
GNI	71
Debt service as % of:	
Exports	83
GNI	29
Net financial flows, debt and equity	1,292
Net debt inflows	823
Net equity inflows	469
GNI	**31,874**
Population (million)	**6**

Figure 2 Average terms on new debt commitments from official and private creditors

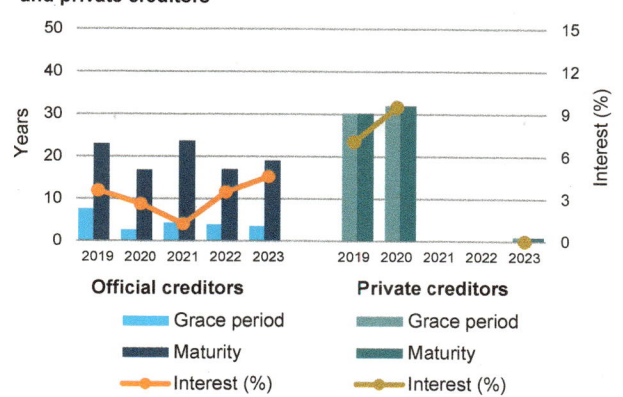

Official creditors — Grace period, Maturity, Interest (%)
Private creditors — Grace period, Maturity, Interest (%)

Figure 1 Public and publicly guaranteed debt, by creditor and creditor type in 2023, including IMF credit

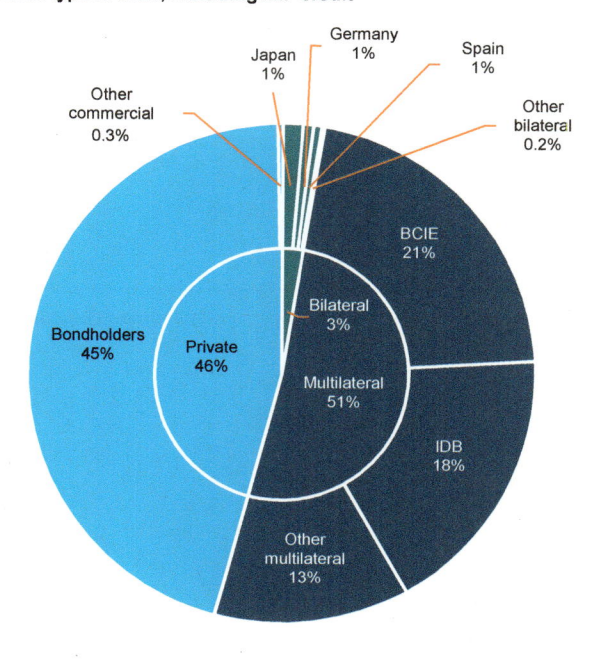

Summary External Debt Data	2010	2019	2020	2021	2022	2023
Total external debt stocks	**11,496**	**17,369**	**18,485**	**20,342**	**21,309**	**22,742**
Long-term external debt stocks	**10,408**	**14,910**	**15,965**	**17,068**	**17,974**	**18,951**
Public and publicly guaranteed debt from:	*6,839*	*9,826*	*10,797*	*11,560*	*12,004*	*12,510*
Official creditors	4,211	4,397	4,539	5,335	5,551	6 651
Multilateral	3,549	4,049	4,158	4,987	5,234	6 308
of which: World Bank	922	831	786	768	879	875
Bilateral	661	348	382	348	317	343
Private creditors	2,628	5,429	6,258	6,225	6,452	5,859
Bondholders	2,596	5,392	6,223	6,194	6,424	5,820
Commercial banks and others	32	37	35	31	28	39
Private nonguaranteed debt from:	*3,569*	*5,083*	*5,167*	*5,508*	*5,970*	*6,442*
Bondholders	..	12	0	0	20	20
Commercial banks and others	3,569	5,071	5,167	5,508	5,950	6,422
Use of IMF credit and SDR allocations	**252**	**227**	**650**	**1,016**	**967**	**878**
IMF credit	0	0	414	402	382	289
SDR allocations	252	227	236	615	584	589
Short-term external debt stocks	**836**	**2,232**	**1,871**	**2,258**	**2,369**	**2,912**
Disbursements, long-term	**1,455**	**5,283**	**5,297**	**5,683**	**2,135**	**8,036**
Public and publicly guaranteed sector	1,107	1,419	1,379	1,232	667	1,607
Private sector not guaranteed	348	3,865	3,918	4,451	1,467	6,429
Principal repayments, long-term	**605**	**4,873**	**4,205**	**4,524**	**2,062**	**7,661**
Public and publicly guaranteed sector	456	1,179	421	413	1,046	1,100
Private sector not guaranteed	149	3,694	3,785	4,111	1,015	6,561
Interest payments, long-term	**495**	**684**	**927**	**1,241**	**1,187**	**1,207**
Public and publicly guaranteed sector	380	684	625	696	737	806
Private sector not guaranteed	115	..	302	545	450	402

ERITREA

Snapshot	2023
Total external debt stocks	**712.8**
External debt stocks as % of:	
Exports	..
GNI	..
Debt service as % of:	
Exports	..
GNI	..
Net financial flows, debt and equity	-8.2
Net debt inflows	-10.3
Net equity inflows	2.1
GNI	..
Population (million)	**3.7**

Figure 1 Public and publicly guaranteed debt, by creditor and creditor type in 2023, including IMF credit

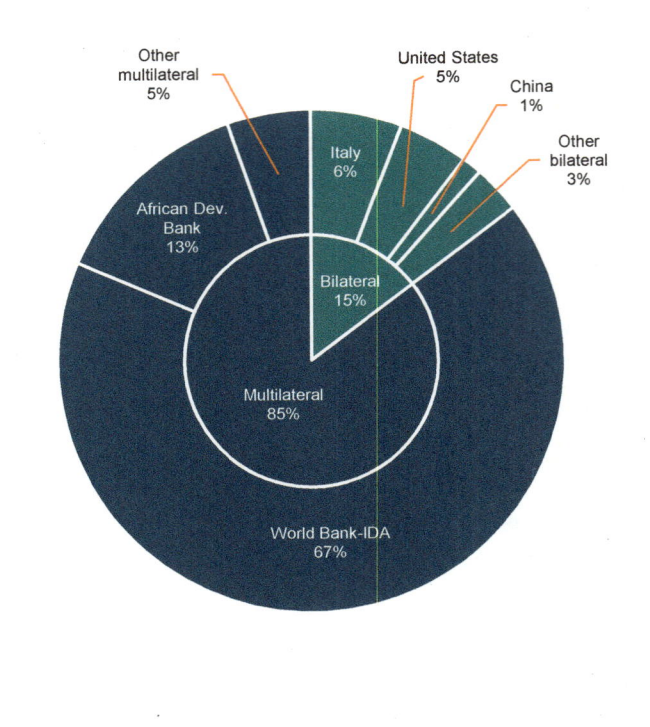

Figure 2 Average terms on new debt commitments from official and private creditors

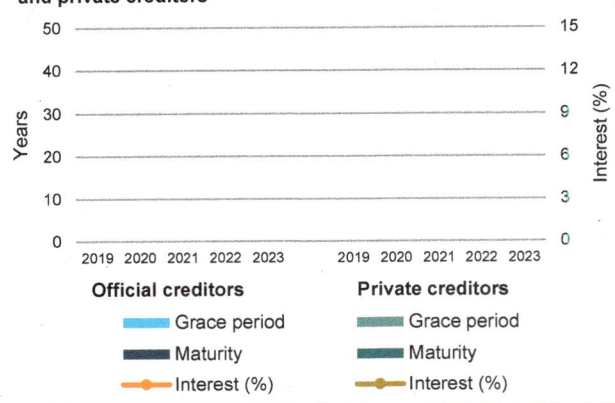

Summary External Debt Data	2010	2019	2020	2021	2022	2023
Total external debt stocks	**1,037.3**	**771.7**	**789.7**	**761.8**	**715.3**	**712.8**
Long-term external debt stocks	**998.4**	**718.1**	**730.5**	**680.4**	**634.6**	**628.3**
Public and publicly guaranteed debt from:	*998.4*	*718.1*	*730.5*	*680.4*	*634.6*	*628.3*
Official creditors	998.4	718.1	730.5	680.4	634.6	628.3
Multilateral	651.4	567.1	587.8	565.4	533.2	535.9
of which: World Bank	467.9	432.0	449.9	437.2	415.7	419.3
Bilateral	347.1	151.0	142.8	115.0	101.5	92.3
Private creditors	..	..	..	..	..	..
Bondholders	..	..	..	..	..	..
Commercial banks and others	..	..	..	..	..	..
Private nonguaranteed debt from:	..	..	..	..	..	..
Bondholders	..	..	..	..	..	..
Commercial banks and others	..	..	..	..	..	..
Use of IMF credit and SDR allocations	**23.3**	**21.0**	**21.8**	**42.5**	**40.5**	**40.8**
IMF credit	0.0	0.0	0.0	0.0	0.0	0.0
SDR allocations	23.3	21.0	21.8	42.5	40.5	40.8
Short-term external debt stocks	**15.5**	**32.7**	**37.3**	**38.9**	**40.2**	**43.7**
Disbursements, long-term	**8.6**	**4.2**	**2.8**	**0.9**	**0.8**	**4.2**
Public and publicly guaranteed sector	8.6	4.2	2.8	0.9	0.8	4.2
Private sector not guaranteed	..	..	..	..	..	..
Principal repayments, long-term	**16.9**	**18.4**	**17.8**	**18.4**	**14.8**	**14.5**
Public and publicly guaranteed sector	16.9	18.4	17.8	18.4	14.8	14.5
Private sector not guaranteed	..	..	..	..	..	..
Interest payments, long-term	**10.0**	**2.6**	**2.4**	**2.2**	**1.8**	**1.4**
Public and publicly guaranteed sector	10.0	2.6	2.4	2.2	1.8	1.4
Private sector not guaranteed	..	..	..	..	..	..

Note: Figure 2 shows no data values because the country did not have new commitments from 2019 to 2023.

ESWATINI

(US$ million, unless otherwise indicated)

Snapshot	2023
Total external debt stocks	**1,241**
External debt stocks as % of:	
Exports	54
GNI	29
Debt service as % of:	
Exports	7
GNI	4
Net financial flows, debt and equity	**77**
Net debt inflows	-5
Net equity inflows	82
GNI	**4,289**
Population (million)	**1**

Figure 2 Average terms on new debt commitments from official and private creditors

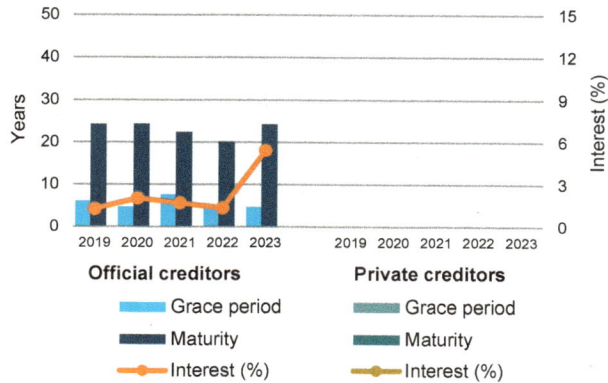

Official creditors
- Grace period
- Maturity
- Interest (%)

Private creditors
- Grace period
- Maturity
- Interest (%)

Figure 1 Public and publicly guaranteed debt, by creditor and creditor type in 2023, including IMF credit

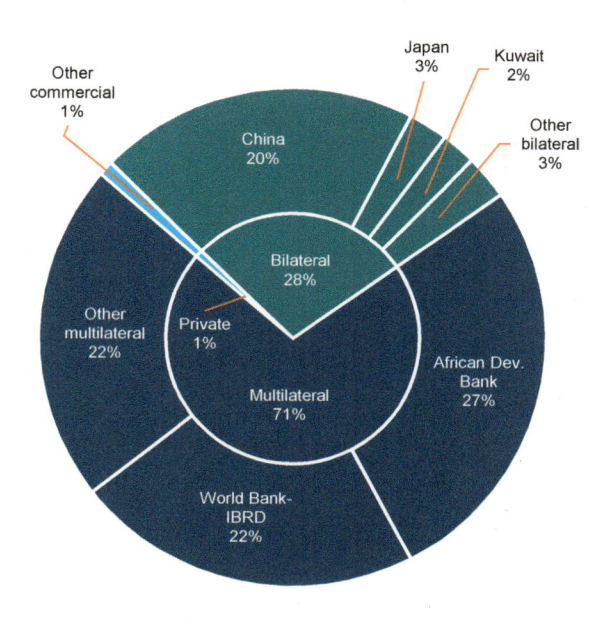

Summary External Debt Data	2010	2019	2020	2021	2022	2023
Total external debt stocks	**1,016**	**834**	**957**	**1,179**	**1,248**	**1,241**
Long-term external debt stocks	**733**	**747**	**748**	**857**	**967**	**926**
Public and publicly guaranteed debt from:	*431*	*540*	*584*	*620*	*758*	*773*
Official creditors	390	529	574	611	749	765
Multilateral	239	245	274	341	497	523
of which: World Bank	5	36	43	87	175	192
Bilateral	152	285	300	270	252	242
Private creditors	41	11	10	9	9	8
Bondholders	..	..	..	..	..	..
Commercial banks and others	41	11	10	9	9	8
Private nonguaranteed debt from:	*302*	*207*	*164*	*237*	*209*	*153*
Bondholders	..	..	..	..	..	..
Commercial banks and others	302	207	164	237	209	153
Use of IMF credit and SDR allocations	**74**	**67**	**183**	**283**	**269**	**258**
IMF credit	0	0	113	110	104	92
SDR allocations	74	67	70	173	164	166
Short-term external debt stocks	**208**	**20**	**26**	**40**	**12**	**57**
Disbursements, long-term	**320**	**92**	**78**	**170**	**192**	**55**
Public and publicly guaranteed sector	18	71	78	97	192	55
Private sector not guaranteed	302	21	..	73	..	..
Principal repayments, long-term	**34**	**31**	**82**	**49**	**64**	**92**
Public and publicly guaranteed sector	34	31	39	49	36	36
Private sector not guaranteed	..	..	43	..	27	57
Interest payments, long-term	**17**	**22**	**20**	**15**	**17**	**48**
Public and publicly guaranteed sector	17	22	20	15	17	39
Private sector not guaranteed	..	..	..	..	..	9

ETHIOPIA

(US$ million, unless otherwise indicated)

Snapshot	2023
Total external debt stocks	**33,290**
External debt stocks as % of:	
Exports	304
GNI	20
Debt service as % of:	
Exports	14
GNI	1
Net financial flows, debt and equity	5,796
Net debt inflows	2,533
Net equity inflows	3,263
GNI	**163,284**
Population (million)	**127**

Figure 1 Public and publicly guaranteed debt, by creditor and creditor type in 2023, including IMF credit

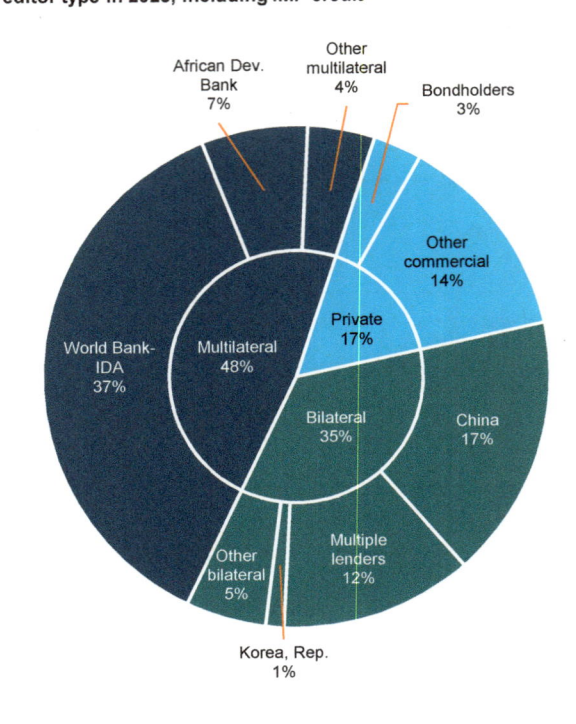

Figure 2 Average terms on new debt commitments from official and private creditors

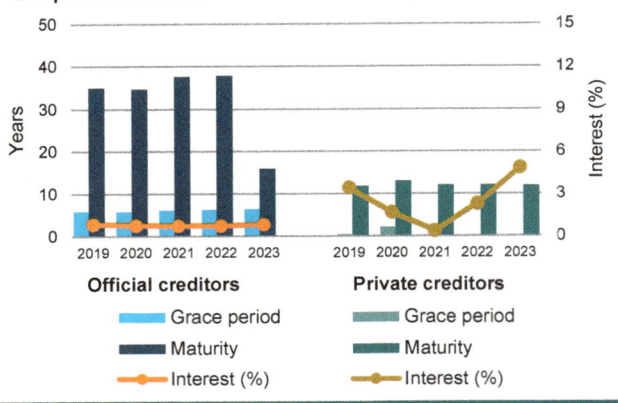

Summary External Debt Data	2010	2019	2020	2021	2022	2023
Total external debt stocks	**7,287**	**30,377**	**32,364**	**32,000**	**30,637**	**33,290**
Long-term external debt stocks	**6,500**	**29,577**	**31,016**	**30,152**	**29,047**	**31,914**
Public and publicly guaranteed debt from:	*6,500*	*29,577*	*31,016*	*30,152*	*29,047*	*31,914*
Official creditors	4,613	22,619	24,505	24,225	23,798	26,530
Multilateral	2,812	12,200	14,024	14,194	14,244	14,991
of which: World Bank	1,804	9,354	10,991	11,170	11,211	11,984
Bilateral	1,800	10,419	10,482	10,031	9,554	11,539
Private creditors	1,887	6,958	6,511	5,927	5,249	5,384
Bondholders	..	1,000	1,000	1,000	1,000	1,000
Commercial banks and others	1,887	5,958	5,511	4,927	4,249	4,384
Private nonguaranteed debt from:	..	..	..	..	..	..
Bondholders	..	..	..	..	..	..
Commercial banks and others	..	..	..	..	..	..
Use of IMF credit and SDR allocations	**485**	**318**	**940**	**1,317**	**1,252**	**1,161**
IMF credit	288	141	755	734	698	603
SDR allocations	197	177	184	582	554	558
Short-term external debt stocks	**302**	**482**	**408**	**531**	**338**	**215**
Disbursements, long-term	**1,763**	**2,363**	**2,194**	**1,082**	**1,132**	**3,824**
Public and publicly guaranteed sector	1,763	2,363	2,194	1,082	1,132	3,824
Private sector not guaranteed	..	..	..	..	..	..
Principal repayments, long-term	**129**	**1,431**	**1,371**	**1,544**	**1,519**	**1,035**
Public and publicly guaranteed sector	129	1,431	1,371	1,544	1,519	1,035
Private sector not guaranteed	..	..	..	..	..	..
Interest payments, long-term	**46**	**720**	**620**	**460**	**460**	**379**
Public and publicly guaranteed sector	46	720	620	460	460	379
Private sector not guaranteed	..	..	..	..	..	..

FIJI

(US$ million, unless otherwise indicated)

Snapshot	2023
Total external debt stocks	**3,348**
External debt stocks as % of:	
Exports	105
GNI	65
Debt service as % of:	
Exports	7
GNI	4
Net financial flows, debt and equity	**481**
Net debt inflows	372
Net equity inflows	110
GNI	**5,113**
Population (thousand)	**936**

Figure 2 Average terms on new debt commitments from official and private creditors

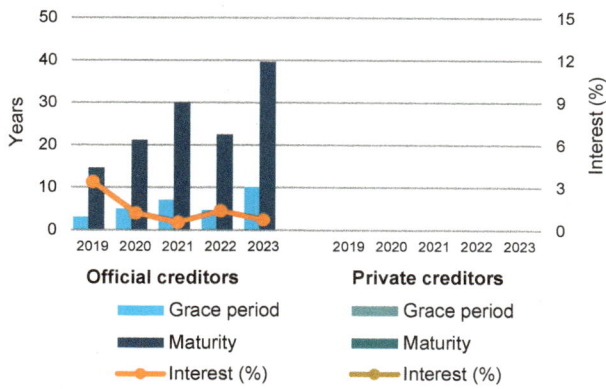

Figure 1 Public and publicly guaranteed debt, by creditor and creditor type in 2023, including IMF credit

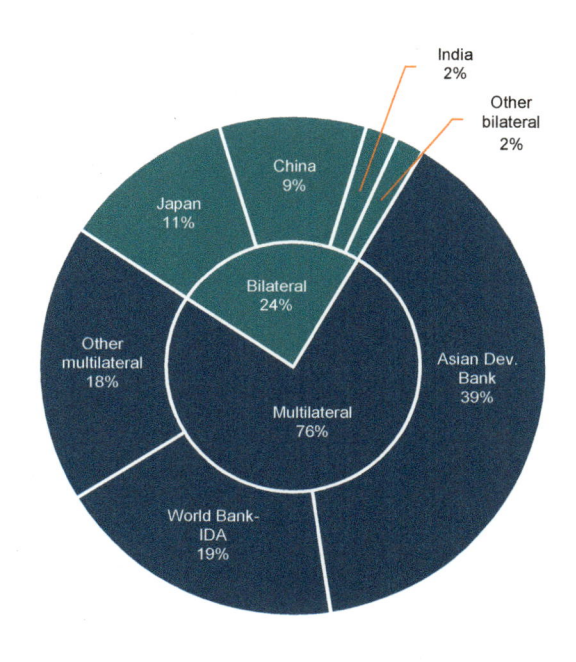

Summary External Debt Data	2010	2019	2020	2021	2022	2023
Total external debt stocks	**1,107**	**1,832**	**2,047**	**2,498**	**2,988**	**3,348**
Long-term external debt stocks	**926**	**1,365**	**1,628**	**1,905**	**2,265**	**2,338**
Public and publicly guaranteed debt from:	*426*	*714*	*904*	*1,213*	*1,603*	*1,595*
Official creditors	276	514	904	1,213	1,603	1,595
Multilateral	113	263	638	828	1,203	1,207
of which: World Bank	..	76	142	326	468	479
Bilateral	162	251	265	384	400	388
Private creditors	150	200	0	..	..	..
Bondholders	150	200	0	..	..	..
Commercial banks and others	..	..	..	..	..	..
Private nonguaranteed debt from:	*500*	*651*	*724*	*692*	*662*	*743*
Bondholders	..	..	..	..	..	..
Commercial banks and others	500	651	724	692	662	743
Use of IMF credit and SDR allocations	**103**	**93**	**97**	**226**	**215**	**217**
IMF credit	0	0	0	0	0	0
SDR allocations	103	93	97	226	215	217
Short-term external debt stocks	**78**	**374**	**323**	**367**	**509**	**794**
Disbursements, long-term	**50**	**153**	**433**	**399**	**511**	**153**
Public and publicly guaranteed sector	38	17	403	326	481	72
Private sector not guaranteed	13	136	30	73	30	81
Principal repayments, long-term	**36**	**59**	**250**	**120**	**105**	**66**
Public and publicly guaranteed sector	9	38	231	15	44	66
Private sector not guaranteed	27	21	19	106	60	..
Interest payments, long-term	**23**	**151**	**24**	**9**	**62**	**94**
Public and publicly guaranteed sector	15	146	24	9	59	75
Private sector not guaranteed	7	5	0	0	3	19

GABON

(US$ million, unless otherwise indicated)

Snapshot	2023
Total external debt stocks	**7,588**
External debt stocks as % of:	
Exports	..
GNI	41
Debt service as % of:	
Exports	..
GNI	6
Net financial flows, debt and equity	1,120
Net debt inflows	-31
Net equity inflows	1,151
GNI	**18,421**
Population (million)	**2**

Figure 1 Public and publicly guaranteed debt, by creditor and creditor type in 2023, including IMF credit

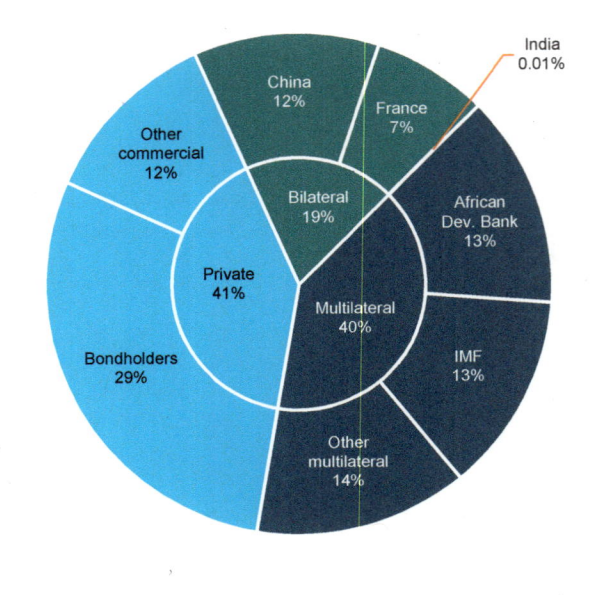

Figure 2 Average terms on new debt commitments from official and private creditors

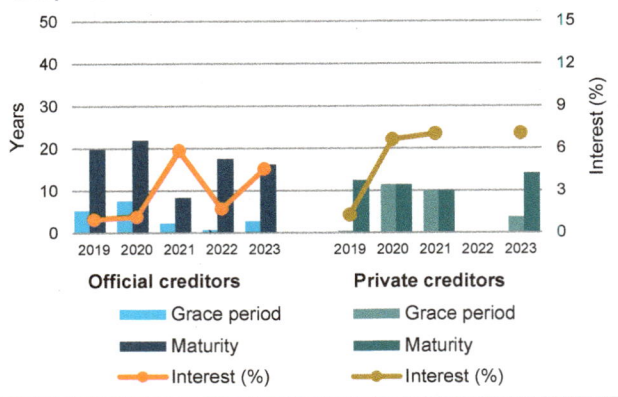

Summary External Debt Data	2010	2019	2020	2021	2022	2023
Total external debt stocks	**2,915**	**7,291**	**7,730**	**7,834**	**7,997**	**7,588**
Long-term external debt stocks	**2,519**	**6,210**	**6,592**	**6,389**	**6,193**	**6,090**
Public and publicly guaranteed debt from:	*2,519*	*6,210*	*6,592*	*6,389*	*6,193*	*6,090*
Official creditors	1,122	3,451	3,650	3,405	3,311	3,251
Multilateral	466	1,920	2,082	1,936	1,910	1,906
of which: World Bank	22	581	680	654	649	660
Bilateral	656	1,531	1,568	1,469	1,401	1,345
Private creditors	1,397	2,759	2,942	2,984	2,882	2,839
Bondholders	879	2,186	2,436	2,573	2,549	2,024
Commercial banks and others	518	573	506	411	333	815
Private nonguaranteed debt from:	..	..	..	..	..	..
Bondholders	..	..	..	..	..	..
Commercial banks and others	..	..	..	..	..	..
Use of IMF credit and SDR allocations	**226**	**722**	**1,063**	**1,427**	**1,480**	**1,374**
IMF credit	0	519	851	932	1,009	899
SDR allocations	226	203	211	495	471	475
Short-term external debt stocks	**170**	**360**	**76**	**17**	**324**	**124**
Disbursements, long-term	**509**	**602**	**1,273**	**905**	**293**	**715**
Public and publicly guaranteed sector	509	602	1,273	905	293	715
Private sector not guaranteed	..	..	..	..	..	..
Principal repayments, long-term	**313**	**424**	**1,135**	**909**	**313**	**403**
Public and publicly guaranteed sector	313	424	1,135	909	313	403
Private sector not guaranteed	..	..	..	..	..	..
Interest payments, long-term	**137**	**252**	**274**	**217**	**188**	**567**
Public and publicly guaranteed sector	137	252	274	217	188	567
Private sector not guaranteed	..	..	..	..	..	..

GAMBIA, THE

(US$ million, unless otherwise indicated)

Snapshot	2023
Total external debt stocks	**1,325**
External debt stocks as % of:	
Exports	199
GNI	57
Debt service as % of:	
Exports	8
GNI	2
Net financial flows, debt and equity	**345**
Net debt inflows	137
Net equity inflows	208
GNI	**2,309**
Population (million)	**3**

Figure 1 Public and publicly guaranteed debt, by creditor and creditor type in 2023, including IMF credit

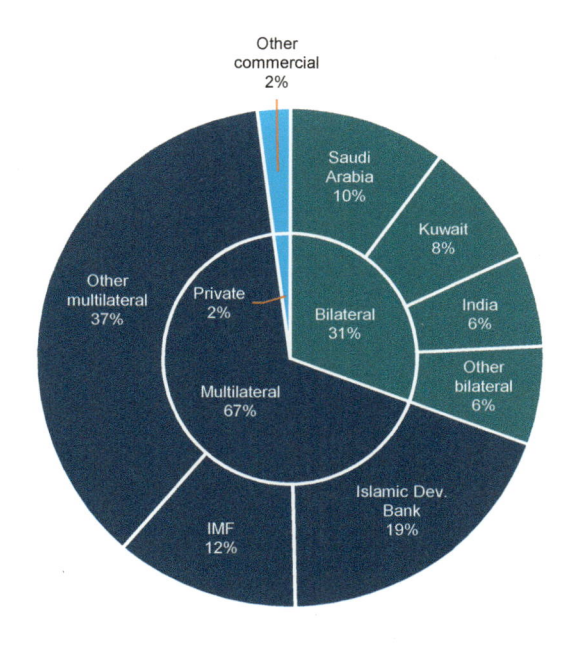

Figure 2 Average terms on new debt commitments from official and private creditors

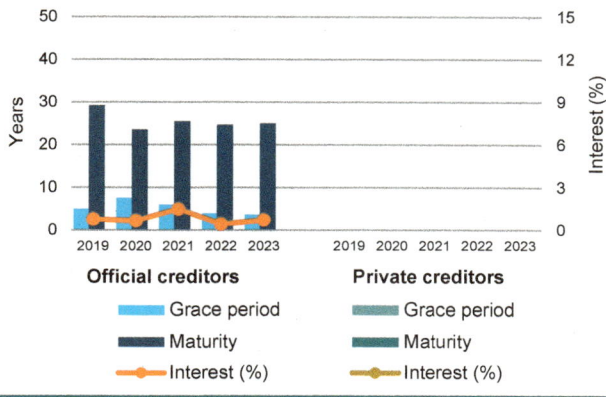

Summary External Debt Data	2010	2019	2020	2021	2022	2023
Total external debt stocks	**544**	**852**	**964**	**1,113**	**1,180**	**1,325**
Long-term external debt stocks	**422**	**749**	**832**	**847**	**891**	**983**
Public and publicly guaranteed debt from:	*422*	*749*	*832*	*847*	*891*	*983*
Official creditors	416	707	796	816	864	959
Multilateral	296	477	530	533	551	619
of which: World Bank	65	118	128	131	126	128
Bilateral	120	230	266	283	313	340
Private creditors	6	42	36	31	27	24
Bondholders	..	..	..	..	..	..
Commercial banks and others	6	42	36	31	27	24
Private nonguaranteed debt from:	..	..	..	..	..	..
Bondholders	..	..	..	..	..	..
Commercial banks and others	..	..	..	..	..	..
Use of IMF credit and SDR allocations	**77**	**77**	**103**	**228**	**248**	**251**
IMF credit	31	36	61	103	129	131
SDR allocations	46	41	43	125	119	120
Short-term external debt stocks	**45**	**26**	**29**	**38**	**40**	**91**
Disbursements, long-term	**43**	**107**	**92**	**50**	**89**	**115**
Public and publicly guaranteed sector	43	107	92	50	89	115
Private sector not guaranteed	..	..	..	..	..	..
Principal repayments, long-term	**18**	**32**	**26**	**26**	**26**	**30**
Public and publicly guaranteed sector	18	32	26	26	26	30
Private sector not guaranteed	..	..	..	..	..	..
Interest payments, long-term	**7**	**8**	**8**	**11**	**9**	**10**
Public and publicly guaranteed sector	7	8	8	11	9	10
Private sector not guaranteed	..	..	..	..	..	..

GEORGIA

(US$ million, unless otherwise indicated)

Snapshot	2023
Total external debt stocks	**24,468**
External debt stocks as % of:	
Exports	143
GNI	86
Debt service as % of:	
Exports	21
GNI	12
Net financial flows, debt and equity	2,802
Net debt inflows	348
Net equity inflows	2,455
GNI	**28,505**
Population (million)	**4**

Figure 1 Public and publicly guaranteed debt, by creditor and creditor type in 2023, including IMF credit

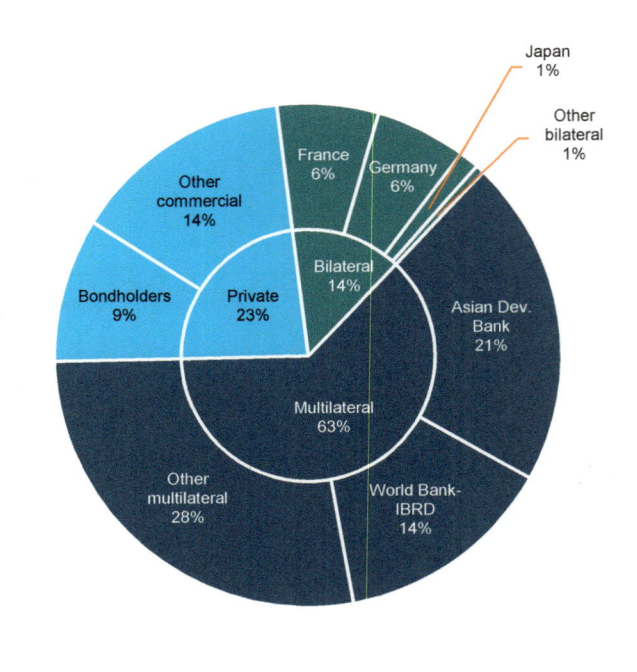

Figure 2 Average terms on new debt commitments from official and private creditors

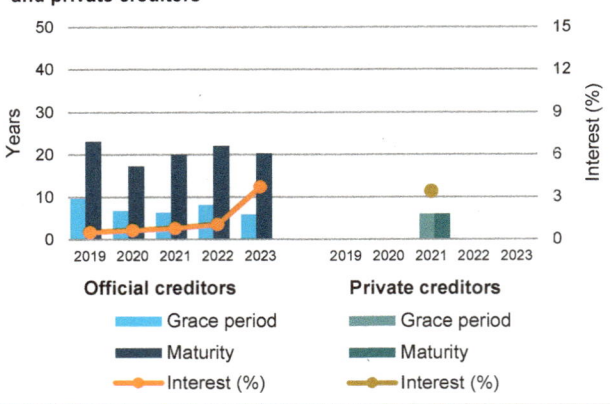

Summary External Debt Data	2010	2019	2020	2021	2022	2023
Total external debt stocks	**8,790**	**18,758**	**20,090**	**22,054**	**23,982**	**24,468**
Long-term external debt stocks	**6,418**	**16,034**	**16,975**	**18,524**	**19,089**	**19,238**
Public and publicly guaranteed debt from:	*3,274*	*6,994*	*7,968*	*9,082*	*9,723*	*10,264*
Official creditors	2,448	4,881	6,332	6,944	7,149	7,727
Multilateral	1,802	3,935	4,801	5,378	5,627	6,197
of which: World Bank	1,359	1,879	2,054	2,043	2,009	2,125
Bilateral	645	946	1,531	1,567	1,522	1,530
Private creditors	827	2,113	1,635	2,138	2,575	2,537
Bondholders	750	1,250	750	1,000	1,000	1,000
Commercial banks and others	77	863	885	1,138	1,575	1,537
Private nonguaranteed debt from:	*3,143*	*9,040*	*9,007*	*9,442*	*9,366*	*8,975*
Bondholders	..	3,320	3,372	3,535	3,381	2,641
Commercial banks and others	3,143	5,720	5,635	5,907	5,985	6,333
Use of IMF credit and SDR allocations	**1,272**	**448**	**792**	**1,158**	**1,084**	**1,063**
IMF credit	1,050	249	585	674	624	599
SDR allocations	222	199	207	484	460	464
Short-term external debt stocks	**1,101**	**2,276**	**2,322**	**2,372**	**3,809**	**4,167**
Disbursements, long-term	**1,026**	**2,984**	**2,508**	**3,792**	**2,908**	**2,426**
Public and publicly guaranteed sector	651	617	1,452	2,543	846	823
Private sector not guaranteed	375	2,367	1,056	1,249	2,062	1,603
Principal repayments, long-term	**510**	**1,669**	**1,820**	**2,002**	**2,466**	**2,406**
Public and publicly guaranteed sector	169	324	799	1,079	364	429
Private sector not guaranteed	342	1,345	1,022	923	2,102	1,977
Interest payments, long-term	**247**	**676**	**587**	**655**	**693**	**844**
Public and publicly guaranteed sector	87	185	135	100	131	260
Private sector not guaranteed	160	491	452	554	562	584

GHANA

(US$ million, unless otherwise indicated)

Snapshot	2023
Total external debt stocks	**43,742**
External debt stocks as % of:	
Exports	168
GNI	58
Debt service as % of:	
Exports	5
GNI	2
Net financial flows, debt and equity	841
Net debt inflows	-389
Net equity inflows	1,230
GNI	**75,420**
Population (million)	**34**

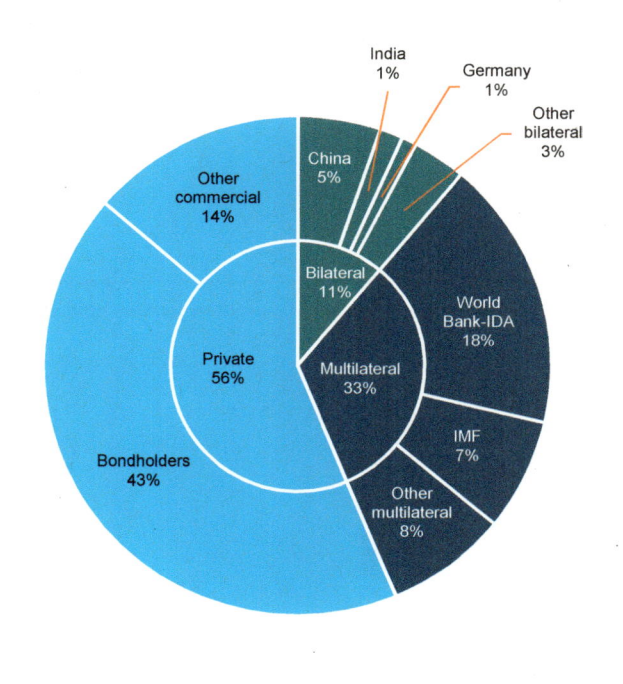

Figure 1 Public and publicly guaranteed debt, by creditor and creditor type in 2023, including IMF credit

Figure 2 Average terms on new debt commitments from official and private creditors

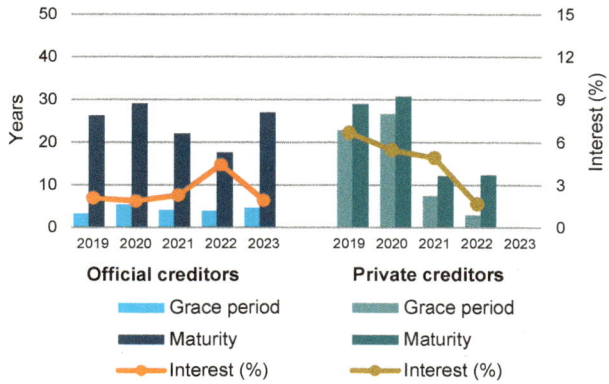

	Official creditors	Private creditors
Grace period	Grace period	
Maturity	Maturity	
Interest (%)	Interest (%)	

Summary External Debt Data	2010	2019	2020	2021	2022	2023
Total external debt stocks	17,985	32,595	40,594	43,805	42,672	43,742
Long-term external debt stocks	14,956	26,379	32,809	35,252	34,895	36,354
Public and publicly guaranteed debt from:	*5,399*	*19,601*	*22,915*	*26,647*	*27,650*	*28,538*
Official creditors	4,270	8,837	9,366	9,754	10,566	11,204
Multilateral	2,749	5,513	6,080	6,306	7,142	7,783
of which: World Bank	1,868	3,989	4,477	4,663	4,747	5,393
Bilateral	1,521	3,324	3,287	3,448	3,424	3,421
Private creditors	1,130	10,764	13,548	16,892	17,084	17,334
Bondholders	..	7,695	10,215	13,120	13,104	13,104
Commercial banks and others	1,130	3,069	3,333	3,772	3,980	4,230
Private nonguaranteed debt from:	*9,556*	*6,778*	*9,894*	*8,605*	*7,245*	*7,815*
Bondholders	0	874	1,161	1,103	1,103	1,103
Commercial banks and others	9,556	5,904	8,733	7,502	6,142	6,712
Use of IMF credit and SDR allocations	937	1,576	2,612	3,411	3,124	3,630
IMF credit	392	1,086	2,102	1,926	1,711	2,206
SDR allocations	545	489	510	1,485	1,412	1,424
Short-term external debt stocks	2,092	4,641	5,173	5,142	4,653	3,758
Disbursements, long-term	4,582	4,403	7,534	5,892	3,219	1,560
Public and publicly guaranteed sector	1,321	3,990	4,417	5,892	2,435	990
Private sector not guaranteed	3,261	414	3,117	..	783	570
Principal repayments, long-term	171	8,410	1,538	2,692	3,106	386
Public and publicly guaranteed sector	171	1,373	1,538	1,754	963	386
Private sector not guaranteed	0	7,037	..	938	2,143	..
Interest payments, long-term	243	1,032	1,029	1,293	1,279	599
Public and publicly guaranteed sector	96	853	915	1,196	989	151
Private sector not guaranteed	147	178	114	97	290	448

GRENADA

(US$ million, unless otherwise indicated)

Snapshot	2023
Total external debt stocks	**727.1**
External debt stocks as % of:	
Exports	78.1
GNI	58.8
Debt service as % of:	
Exports	5.9
GNI	4.5
Net financial flows, debt and equity	187.2
Net debt inflows	25.4
Net equity inflows	161.8
GNI	**1,237.4**
Population (thousand)	**126.2**

Figure 2 Average terms on new debt commitments from official and private creditors

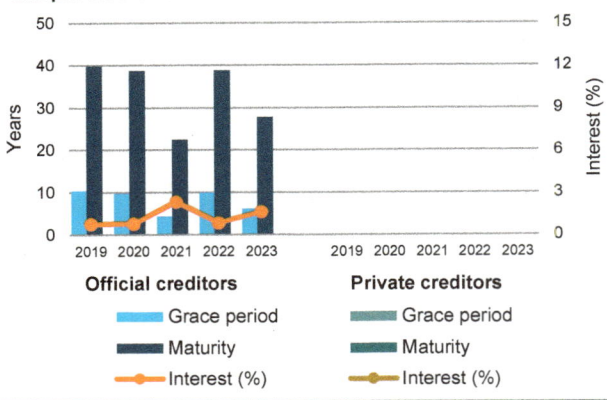

Official creditors
- Grace period
- Maturity
- Interest (%)

Private creditors
- Grace period
- Maturity
- Interest (%)

Figure 1 Public and publicly guaranteed debt, by creditor and creditor type in 2023, including IMF credit

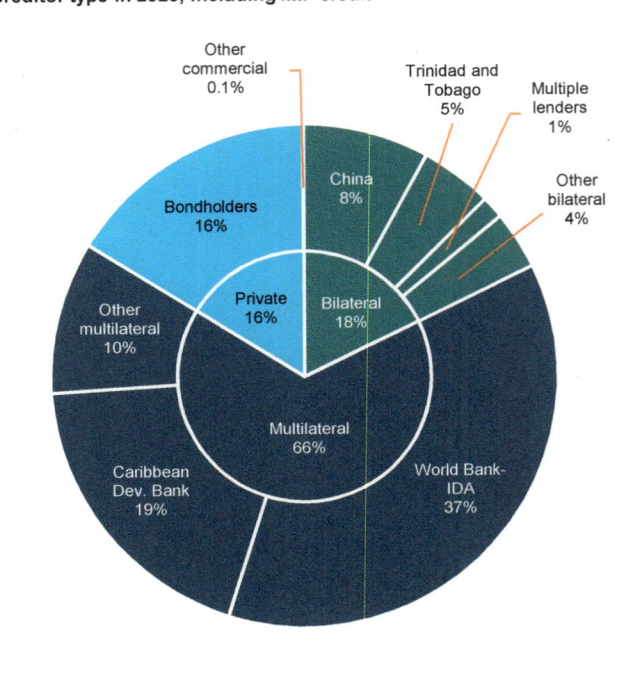

Summary External Debt Data	2010	2019	2020	2021	2022	2023
Total external debt stocks	**560.6**	**545.9**	**681.6**	**753.3**	**699.8**	**727.1**
Long-term external debt stocks	**476.7**	**496.5**	**520.7**	**556.4**	**565.8**	**605.7**
Public and publicly guaranteed debt from:	*476.7*	*496.5*	*520.7*	*556.4*	*565.8*	*605.7*
Official creditors	278.2	359.7	391.9	433.4	453.8	503.0
Multilateral	187.8	279.7	315.3	339.1	362.7	389.8
of which: World Bank	58.2	131.4	161.4	187.0	211.6	248.9
Bilateral	90.4	80.1	76.6	94.3	91.1	113.3
Private creditors	198.5	136.7	128.8	123.0	112.0	102.7
Bondholders	193.2	136.4	128.5	122.7	111.7	102.4
Commercial banks and others	5.3	0.3	0.3	0.3	0.3	0.3
Private nonguaranteed debt from:	..	..	..	..	..	..
Bondholders	..	..	..	..	..	..
Commercial banks and others	..	..	..	..	..	..
Use of IMF credit and SDR allocations	**46.3**	**35.6**	**58.8**	**76.6**	**69.3**	**66.1**
IMF credit	29.1	20.2	42.7	38.9	33.6	30.1
SDR allocations	17.2	15.4	16.1	37.6	35.8	36.1
Short-term external debt stocks	**37.6**	**13.8**	**102.2**	**120.3**	**64.7**	**55.3**
Disbursements, long-term	**21.1**	**12.0**	**44.9**	**65.8**	**48.5**	**70.4**
Public and publicly guaranteed sector	21.1	12.0	44.9	65.8	48.5	70.4
Private sector not guaranteed	..	..	..	..	..	..
Principal repayments, long-term	**15.1**	**34.2**	**28.7**	**30.8**	**31.6**	**31.5**
Public and publicly guaranteed sector	15.1	34.2	28.7	30.8	31.6	31.5
Private sector not guaranteed	..	..	..	..	..	..
Interest payments, long-term	**10.5**	**17.5**	**16.1**	**15.7**	**15.3**	**16.0**
Public and publicly guaranteed sector	10.5	17.5	16.1	15.7	15.3	16.0
Private sector not guaranteed	..	..	..	..	..	..

GUATEMALA

(US$ million, unless otherwise indicated)

Snapshot	2023
Total external debt stocks	**25,365**
External debt stocks as % of:	
Exports	132
GNI	25
Debt service as % of:	
Exports	9
GNI	2
Net financial flows, debt and equity	**2,631**
Net debt inflows	1,075
Net equity inflows	1,556
GNI	**100,246**
Population (million)	**18**

Figure 1 Public and publicly guaranteed debt, by creditor and creditor type in 2023, including IMF credit

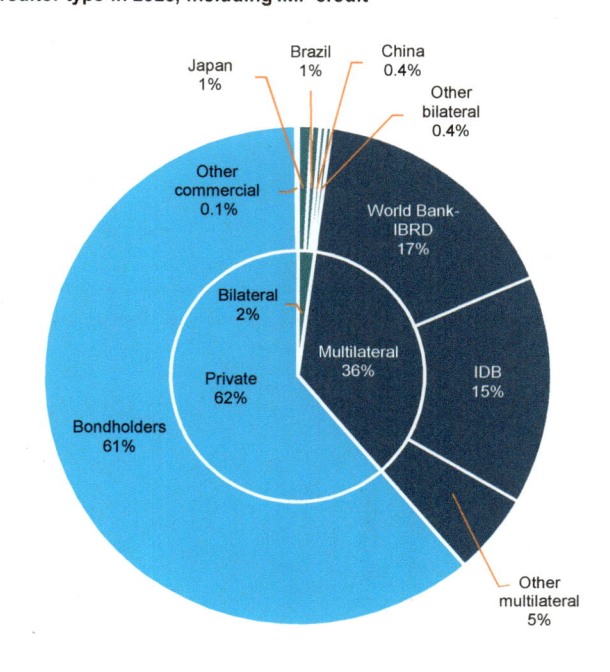

Figure 2 Average terms on new debt commitments from official and private creditors

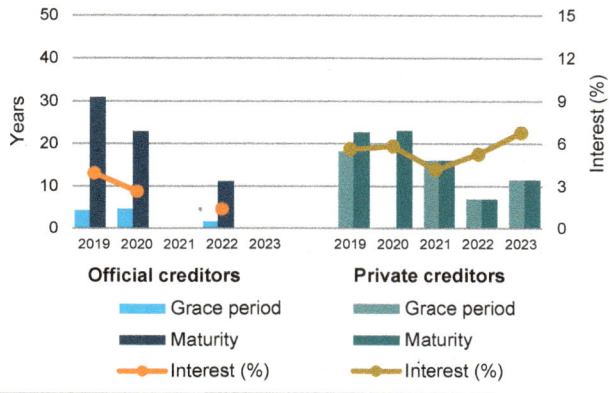

Official creditors
- Grace period
- Maturity
- Interest (%)

Private creditors
- Grace period
- Maturity
- Interest (%)

Summary External Debt Data	2010	2019	2020	2021	2022	2023
Total external debt stocks	**15,043**	**24,596**	**24,357**	**26,313**	**25,269**	**25,365**
Long-term external debt stocks	**13,149**	**22,980**	**22,681**	**24,094**	**24,153**	**24,462**
Public and publicly guaranteed debt from:	*5,559*	*9,343*	*10,561*	*11,210*	*11,201*	*12,554*
Official creditors	4,600	5,188	5,209	4,861	5,052	4,841
Multilateral	4,241	4,686	4,820	4,509	4,754	4,573
of which: World Bank	1,372	1,641	1,758	1,689	2,114	2,061
Bilateral	359	502	389	352	298	268
Private creditors	959	4,155	5,353	6,349	6,149	7,713
Bondholders	955	4,130	5,330	6,330	6,130	7,695
Commercial banks and others	4	25	23	19	19	18
Private nonguaranteed debt from:	*7,589*	*13,637*	*12,119*	*12,884*	*12,952*	*11,908*
Bondholders	5	1,500	700	1,700	3,700	3,700
Commercial banks and others	7,584	12,137	11,419	11,184	9,252	8,208
Use of IMF credit and SDR allocations	**309**	**278**	**289**	**856**	**814**	**821**
IMF credit	0	0	0	0	0	0
SDR allocations	309	278	289	856	814	821
Short-term external debt stocks	**1,585**	**1,338**	**1,388**	**1,364**	**302**	**82**
Disbursements, long-term	**1,472**	**1,581**	**1,957**	**2,092**	**3,146**	**1,717**
Public and publicly guaranteed sector	881	1,312	1,745	1,061	1,096	1,717
Private sector not guaranteed	592	270	212	1,030	2,050	..
Principal repayments, long-term	**949**	**994**	**2,269**	**659**	**3,063**	**422**
Public and publicly guaranteed sector	264	394	539	393	1,081	359
Private sector not guaranteed	685	599	1,730	266	1,981	64
Interest payments, long-term	**636**	**999**	**1,195**	**1,013**	**1,053**	**1,298**
Public and publicly guaranteed sector	284	408	490	466	484	599
Private sector not guaranteed	352	591	705	547	570	699

GUINEA

(US$ million, unless otherwise indicated)

Snapshot	2023
Total external debt stocks	**5,164**
External debt stocks as % of:	
Exports	43
GNI	25
Debt service as % of:	
Exports	3
GNI	1
Net financial flows, debt and equity	**233**
Net debt inflows	236
Net equity inflows	-3
GNI	**21,019**
Population (million)	**14**

Figure 1 Public and publicly guaranteed debt, by creditor and creditor type in 2023, including IMF credit

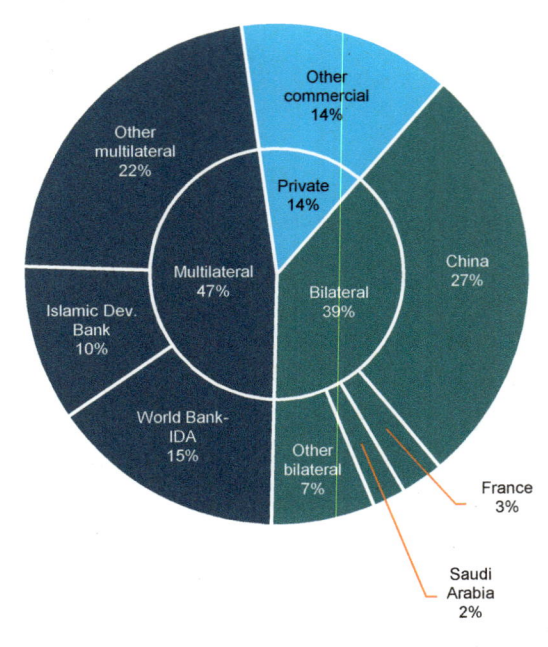

Figure 2 Average terms on new debt commitments from official and private creditors

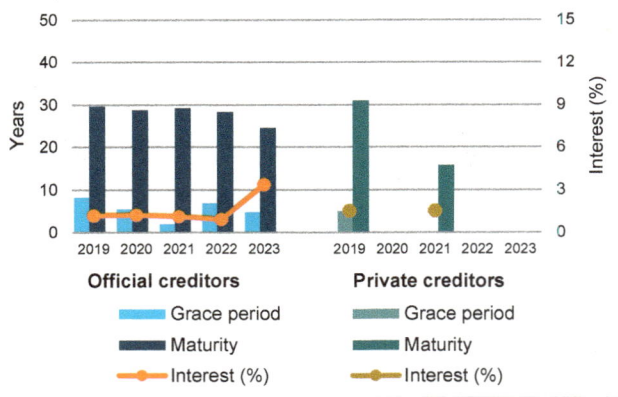

Summary External Debt Data	2010	2019	2020	2021	2022	2023
Total external debt stocks	**3,239**	**3,540**	**4,117**	**4,642**	**4,904**	**5,164**
Long-term external debt stocks	**2,926**	**2,872**	**3,306**	**3,540**	**3,773**	**4,021**
Public and publicly guaranteed debt from:	*2,926*	*2,872*	*3,306*	*3,540*	*3,668*	*3,931*
Official creditors	2,900	2,804	3,077	3,256	3,270	3,338
Multilateral	1,875	1,031	1,242	1,409	1,461	1,637
of which: World Bank	1,248	471	572	621	616	655
Bilateral	1,025	1,772	1,836	1,847	1,809	1,701
Private creditors	26	69	229	284	397	593
Bondholders	..	..	..	..	..	..
Commercial banks and others	26	69	229	284	397	593
Private nonguaranteed debt from:	..	..	..	..	*105*	*90*
Bondholders	..	..	..	..	..	..
Commercial banks and others	..	..	..	..	105	90
Use of IMF credit and SDR allocations	**205**	**481**	**668**	**886**	**884**	**845**
IMF credit	48	339	520	455	475	432
SDR allocations	158	142	148	431	410	413
Short-term external debt stocks	**108**	**186**	**143**	**217**	**247**	**298**
Disbursements, long-term	**36**	**999**	**371**	**343**	**433**	**387**
Public and publicly guaranteed sector	36	999	371	343	328	387
Private sector not guaranteed	..	..	..	..	105	..
Principal repayments, long-term	**48**	**70**	**37**	**50**	**106**	**151**
Public and publicly guaranteed sector	48	70	37	50	106	136
Private sector not guaranteed	..	..	..	..	..	15
Interest payments, long-term	**21**	**30**	**41**	**52**	**58**	**74**
Public and publicly guaranteed sector	21	30	41	52	58	69
Private sector not guaranteed	..	..	..	..	0	4

GUINEA-BISSAU

(US$ million, unless otherwise indicated)

Snapshot	2023
Total external debt stocks	**1,128**
External debt stocks as % of:	
Exports	408
GNI	57
Debt service as % of:	
Exports	21
GNI	3
Net financial flows, debt and equity	**67**
Net debt inflows	44
Net equity inflows	24
GNI	**1,994**
Population (million)	**2**

Figure 1 Public and publicly guaranteed debt, by creditor and creditor type in 2023, including IMF credit

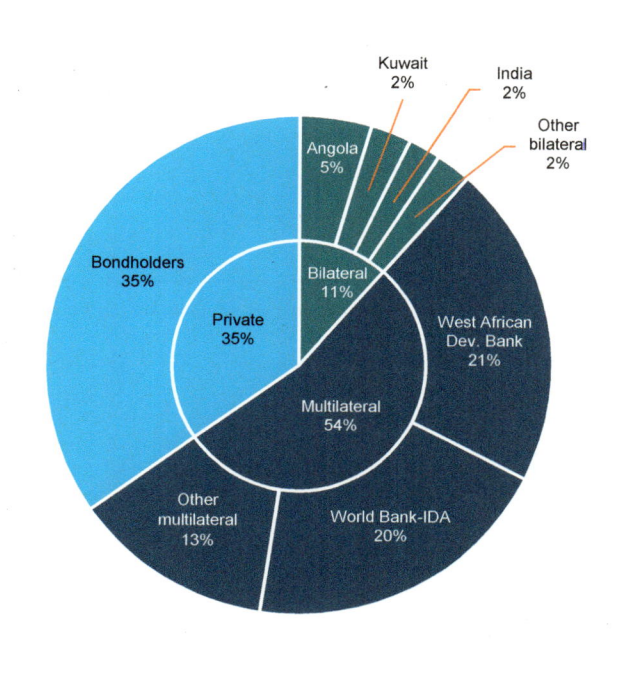

Figure 2 Average terms on new debt commitments from official and private creditors

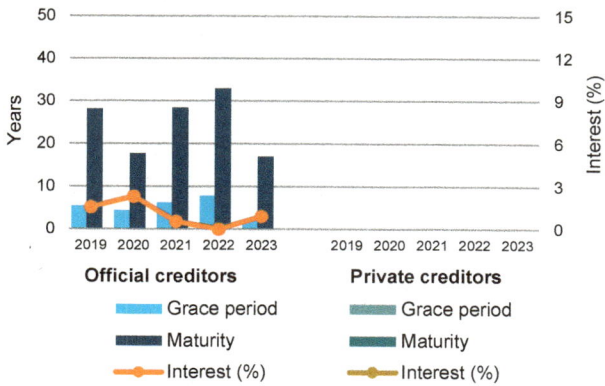

Summary External Debt Data	2010	2019	2020	2021	2022	2023
Total external debt stocks	**1,097**	**657**	**870**	**1,066**	**1,073**	**1,128**
Long-term external debt stocks	**981**	**576**	**789**	**924**	**976**	**1,018**
Public and publicly guaranteed debt from:	*979*	*552*	*789*	*924*	*976*	*1,018*
Official creditors	979	426	553	619	604	646
Multilateral	491	330	458	490	477	522
of which: World Bank	289	126	164	182	187	214
Bilateral	488	96	96	129	127	123
Private creditors	..	126	236	305	372	372
Bondholders	..	126	236	305	372	372
Commercial banks and others	..	..	..	..	..	..
Private nonguaranteed debt from:	*1*	*24*	*0*	*0*	*0*	*0*
Bondholders	..	..	..	..	..	..
Commercial banks and others	1	24	0	0	0	0
Use of IMF credit and SDR allocations	**25**	**50**	**49**	**103**	**95**	**108**
IMF credit	4	31	29	46	41	54
SDR allocations	21	19	20	57	54	55
Short-term external debt stocks	**92**	**31**	**32**	**40**	**1**	**1**
Disbursements, long-term	**9**	**68**	**111**	**81**	**36**	**57**
Public and publicly guaranteed sector	9	68	111	81	36	57
Private sector not guaranteed	..	..	..	..	..	..
Principal repayments, long-term	**9**	**9**	**36**	**23**	**24**	**27**
Public and publicly guaranteed sector	6	8	12	23	24	27
Private sector not guaranteed	3	0	24	..	..	..
Interest payments, long-term	**4**	**12**	**19**	**28**	**31**	**18**
Public and publicly guaranteed sector	4	12	19	28	31	18
Private sector not guaranteed	..	..	..	..	..	..

GUYANA

(US$ million, unless otherwise indicated)

Snapshot	2023
Total external debt stocks	**2,953**
External debt stocks as % of:	
Exports	21
GNI	19
Debt service as % of:	
Exports	3
GNI	2
Net financial flows, debt and equity	8,077
Net debt inflows	879
Net equity inflows	7,198
GNI	**15,206**
Population (thousand)	**814**

Figure 2 Average terms on new debt commitments from official and private creditors

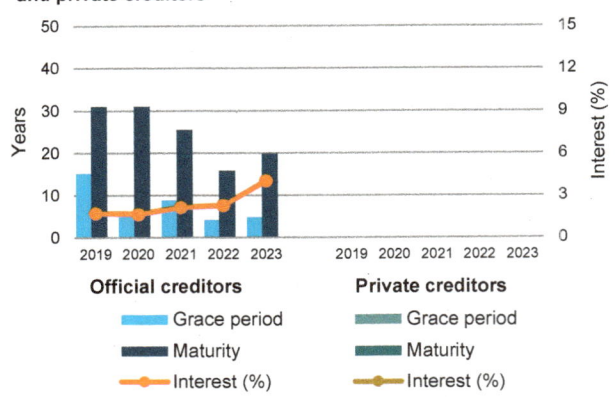

Official creditors
- Grace period
- Maturity
- Interest (%)

Private creditors
- Grace period
- Maturity
- Interest (%)

Figure 1 Public and publicly guaranteed debt, by creditor and creditor type in 2023, including IMF credit

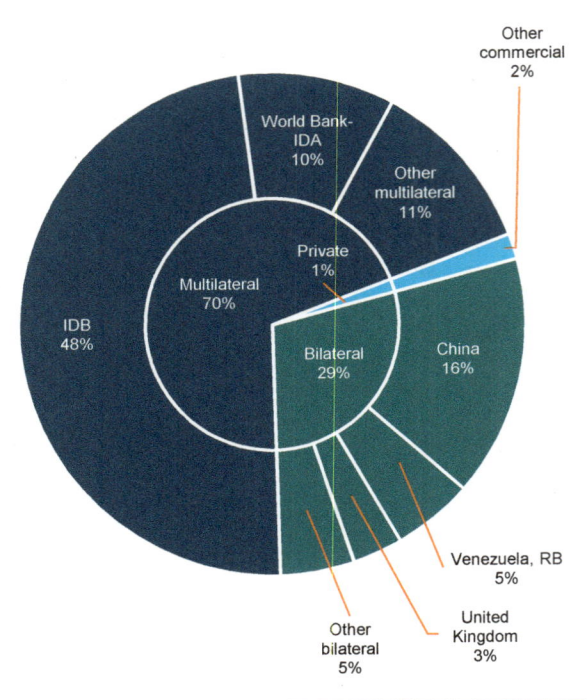

Summary External Debt Data	2010	2019	2020	2021	2022	2023
Total external debt stocks	**1,408**	**1,530**	**1,507**	**1,890**	**2,070**	**2,953**
Long-term external debt stocks	**885**	**1,361**	**1,327**	**1,467**	**1,668**	**2,542**
Public and publicly guaranteed debt from:	*885*	*1,255*	*1,271*	*1,342*	*1,520*	*1,726*
Official creditors	869	1,223	1,240	1,312	1,491	1,698
Multilateral	533	815	825	910	1,092	1,202
of which: World Bank	9	83	90	92	117	172
Bilateral	336	408	415	402	398	496
Private creditors	16	32	31	30	29	28
Bondholders	0	0	0	0	0	0
Commercial banks and others	16	32	31	30	29	28
Private nonguaranteed debt from:	*0*	*106*	*56*	*125*	*148*	*816*
Bondholders	..	..	..	..	..	..
Commercial banks and others	0	106	56	125	148	816
Use of IMF credit and SDR allocations	**190**	**120**	**125**	**366**	**348**	**351**
IMF credit	56	0	0	0	0	0
SDR allocations	134	120	125	366	348	351
Short-term external debt stocks	**333**	**49**	**54**	**57**	**54**	**60**
Disbursements, long-term	**123**	**92**	**48**	**218**	**336**	**1,142**
Public and publicly guaranteed sector	123	92	48	121	262	270
Private sector not guaranteed	0	..	..	97	74	872
Principal repayments, long-term	**16**	**105**	**103**	**85**	**110**	**268**
Public and publicly guaranteed sector	16	54	52	57	60	64
Private sector not guaranteed	..	51	51	28	50	204
Interest payments, long-term	**11**	**33**	**30**	**25**	**27**	**85**
Public and publicly guaranteed sector	11	23	24	23	24	35
Private sector not guaranteed	..	9	6	3	3	50

HAITI

(US$ million, unless otherwise indicated)

Snapshot	2023
Total external debt stocks	**2,638**
External debt stocks as % of:	
Exports	178
GNI	13
Debt service as % of:	
Exports	4
GNI	0
Net financial flows, debt and equity	99
Net debt inflows	67
Net equity inflows	32
GNI	**19,855**
Population (million)	**12**

Figure 1 Public and publicly guaranteed debt, by creditor and creditor type in 2023, including IMF credit

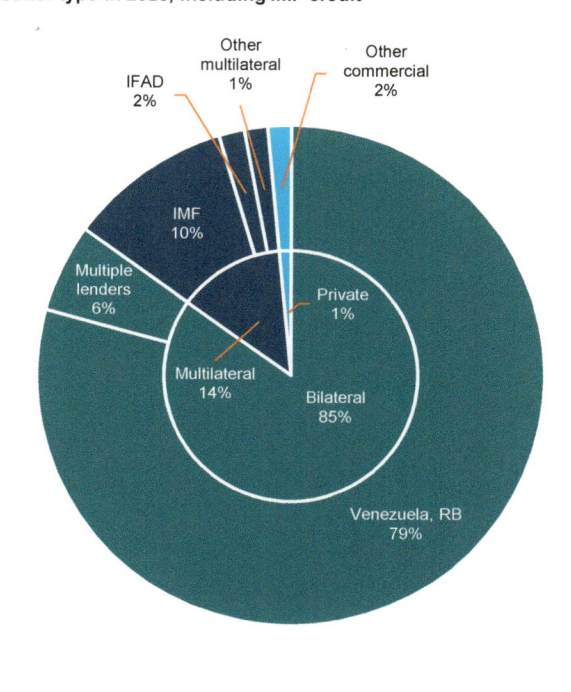

Figure 2 Average terms on new debt commitments from official and private creditors

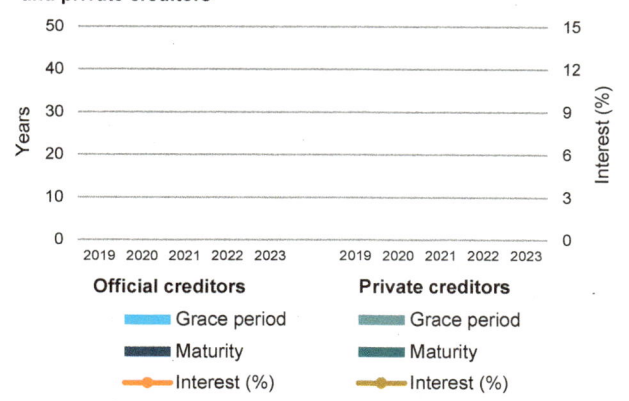

Official creditors	**Private creditors**
Grace period	Grace period
Maturity	Maturity
Interest (%)	Interest (%)

Summary External Debt Data	2010	2019	2020	2021	2022	2023
Total external debt stocks	**959**	**2,214**	**2,318**	**2,605**	**2,562**	**2,638**
Long-term external debt stocks	**824**	**2,012**	**2,027**	**2,103**	**2,117**	**2,085**
Public and publicly guaranteed debt from:	*824*	*2,012*	*2,027*	*2,099*	*2,111*	*2,079*
Official creditors	774	1,968	1,984	2,058	2,074	2,044
Multilateral	557	97	93	87	77	72
of which: World Bank	..	..	..	..	..	..
Bilateral	217	1,872	1,891	1,971	1,997	1,972
Private creditors	50	44	43	41	37	35
Bondholders	..	..	..	..	..	..
Commercial banks and others	50	44	43	41	37	35
Private nonguaranteed debt from:	*..*	*0*	*0*	*4*	*6*	*6*
Bondholders	..	..	..	..	..	..
Commercial banks and others	..	0	0	4	6	6
Use of IMF credit and SDR allocations	**135**	**185**	**291**	**502**	**445**	**553**
IMF credit	13	78	181	171	143	243
SDR allocations	122	107	111	332	301	310
Short-term external debt stocks	**0**	**16**	**0**	**0**	**0**	**0**
Disbursements, long-term	**288**	**3**	**..**	**87**	**32**	**2**
Public and publicly guaranteed sector	288	3	..	83	30	0
Private sector not guaranteed	..	..	..	4	2	2
Principal repayments, long-term	**122**	**7**	**7**	**11**	**11**	**32**
Public and publicly guaranteed sector	122	6	7	11	11	32
Private sector not guaranteed	..	0	..	..	..	..
Interest payments, long-term	**8**	**3**	**2**	**3**	**19**	**8**
Public and publicly guaranteed sector	8	3	2	3	19	8
Private sector not guaranteed	..	0	..	..	..	..

Note: Figure 2 shows no data values because the country did not have new commitments from 2019 to 2023.

HONDURAS

Snapshot	2023
Total external debt stocks	**12,821**
External debt stocks as % of:	
Exports	126
GNI	40
Debt service as % of:	
Exports	17
GNI	5
Net financial flows, debt and equity	1,214
Net debt inflows	168
Net equity inflows	1,047
GNI	**31,873**
Population (million)	**11**

Figure 2 Average terms on new debt commitments from official and private creditors

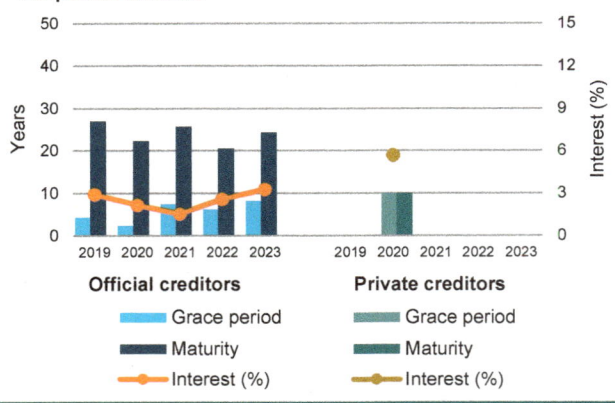

Official creditors
- Grace period
- Maturity
- Interest (%)

Private creditors
- Grace period
- Maturity
- Interest (%)

Figure 1 Public and publicly guaranteed debt, by creditor and creditor type in 2023, including IMF credit

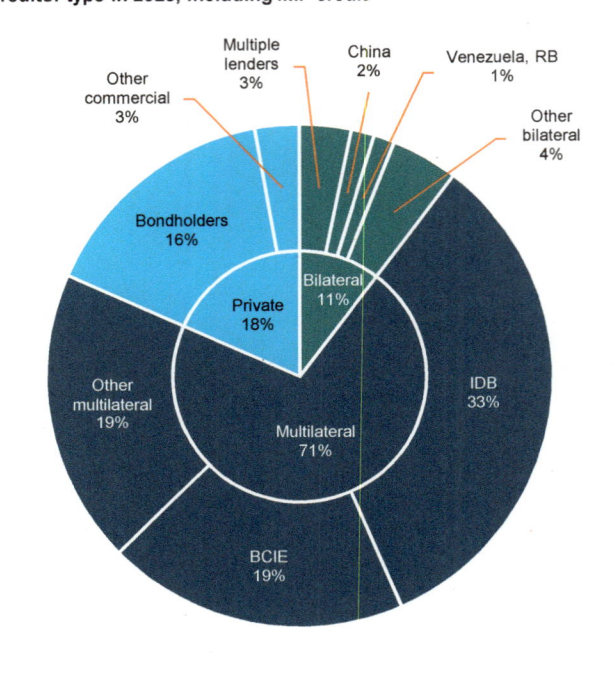

Summary External Debt Data	2010	2019	2020	2021	2022	2023
Total external debt stocks	**4,008**	**9,756**	**11,074**	**12,508**	**12,639**	**12,821**
Long-term external debt stocks	**3,413**	**8,806**	**9,782**	**10,392**	**10,601**	**10,345**
Public and publicly guaranteed debt from:	*2,834*	*7,762*	*8,598*	*8,641*	*9,013*	*8,817*
Official creditors	2,704	5,631	6,401	6,503	7,067	7,085
Multilateral	1,907	4,564	5,404	5,554	6,076	6,106
of which: World Bank	602	908	1,034	1,015	936	970
Bilateral	796	1,067	997	949	991	979
Private creditors	131	2,131	2,197	2,138	1,946	1,732
Bondholders	..	1,700	1,800	1,800	1,633	1,467
Commercial banks and others	131	431	397	338	312	265
Private nonguaranteed debt from:	*579*	*1,044*	*1,184*	*1,751*	*1,588*	*1,528*
Bondholders	..	..	..	300	300	300
Commercial banks and others	579	1,044	1,184	1,451	1,288	1,228
Use of IMF credit and SDR allocations	**220**	**171**	**664**	**1,103**	**1,049**	**1,103**
IMF credit	30	0	486	594	565	615
SDR allocations	191	171	178	508	483	487
Short-term external debt stocks	**374**	**778**	**628**	**1,013**	**989**	**1,373**
Disbursements, long-term	**906**	**1,079**	**2,096**	**1,351**	**1,576**	**864**
Public and publicly guaranteed sector	454	693	1,603	389	872	316
Private sector not guaranteed	452	386	494	962	704	548
Principal repayments, long-term	**453**	**553**	**1,194**	**873**	**1,311**	**1,125**
Public and publicly guaranteed sector	63	276	822	297	444	517
Private sector not guaranteed	390	277	372	576	867	607
Interest payments, long-term	**56**	**328**	**321**	**313**	**337**	**422**
Public and publicly guaranteed sector	46	305	302	247	256	349
Private sector not guaranteed	10	23	19	66	81	72

INDIA

(US$ million, unless otherwise indicated)

Snapshot	2023
Total external debt stocks	**646,787**
External debt stocks as % of:	
Exports	80
GNI	18
Debt service as % of:	
Exports	10
GNI	2
Net financial flows, debt and equity	**80,368**
Net debt inflows	33,421
Net equity inflows	46,947
GNI	**3,497,822**
Population (million)	**1,429**

Figure 2 Average terms on new debt commitments from official and private creditors

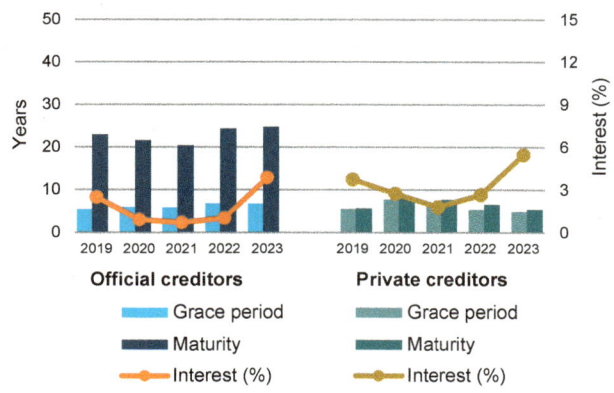

Official creditors
- Grace period
- Maturity
- Interest (%)

Private creditors
- Grace period
- Maturity
- Interest (%)

Figure 1 Public and publicly guaranteed debt, by creditor and creditor type in 2023, including IMF credit

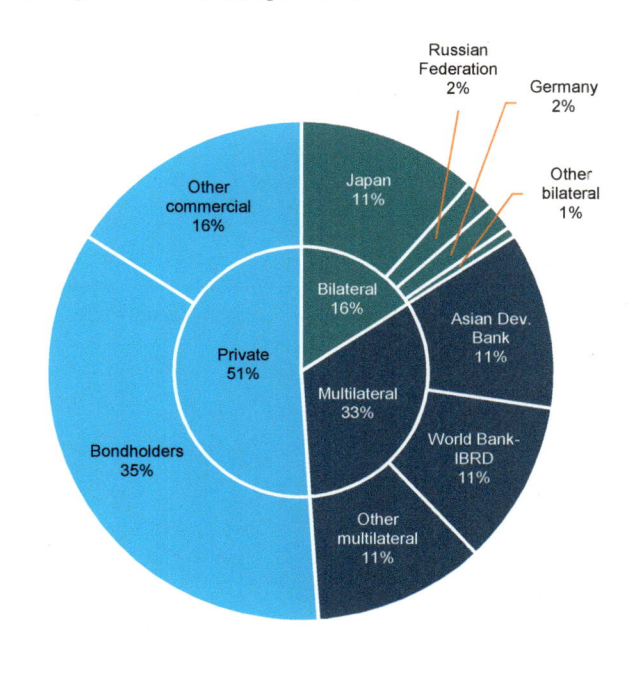

Summary External Debt Data	2010	2019	2020	2021	2022	2023
Total external debt stocks	**290,428**	**561,017**	**564,979**	**611,987**	**615,516**	**646,787**
Long-term external debt stocks	**227,853**	**448,737**	**455,716**	**474,183**	**465,623**	**498,265**
Public and publicly guaranteed debt from:	*100,563*	*192,007*	*192,805*	*205,282*	*205,218*	*214,916*
Official creditors	72,499	84,513	96,151	99,657	101,851	107,188
Multilateral	46,513	56,551	64,454	67,713	70,145	73,705
of which: World Bank	37,068	36,809	39,577	39,742	38,257	39,284
Bilateral	25,986	27,962	31,696	31,944	31,706	33,483
Private creditors	28,065	107,495	96,654	105,625	103,367	107,728
Bondholders	14,700	81,351	71,333	75,093	72,077	74,172
Commercial banks and others	13,364	26,144	25,322	30,531	31,291	33,556
Private nonguaranteed debt from:	*127,290*	*256,729*	*262,911*	*268,902*	*260,404*	*283,350*
Bondholders	13,217	19,197	26,822	32,393	33,698	31,478
Commercial banks and others	114,073	237,532	236,089	236,509	226,706	251,871
Use of IMF credit and SDR allocations	**6,127**	**5,501**	**5,730**	**23,160**	**22,023**	**22,202**
IMF credit	0	0	0	0	0	0
SDR allocations	6,127	5,501	5,730	23,160	22,023	22,202
Short-term external debt stocks	**56,448**	**106,780**	**103,533**	**114,644**	**127,871**	**126,320**
Disbursements, long-term	**43,406**	**71,710**	**67,698**	**61,278**	**44,214**	**86,385**
Public and publicly guaranteed sector	24,337	24,617	22,418	30,078	19,360	27,106
Private sector not guaranteed	19,069	47,093	45,280	31,201	24,854	59,279
Principal repayments, long-term	**19,018**	**34,762**	**63,444**	**38,650**	**47,385**	**51,413**
Public and publicly guaranteed sector	5,164	13,220	24,346	13,693	14,367	15,769
Private sector not guaranteed	13,854	21,543	39,098	24,957	33,018	35,644
Interest payments, long-term	**4,675**	**12,888**	**11,197**	**12,229**	**15,078**	**22,542**
Public and publicly guaranteed sector	1,063	3,284	1,655	2,517	3,246	6,255
Private sector not guaranteed	3,612	9,605	9,543	9,712	11,832	16,287

INDONESIA

(US$ million, unless otherwise indicated)

Snapshot	2023
Total external debt stocks	**406,054**
External debt stocks as % of:	
Exports	136
GNI	30
Debt service as % of:	
Exports	20
GNI	4
Net financial flows, debt and equity	33,520
Net debt inflows	13,113
Net equity inflows	20,407
GNI	**1,335,866**
Population (million)	**278**

Figure 2 Average terms on new debt commitments from official and private creditors

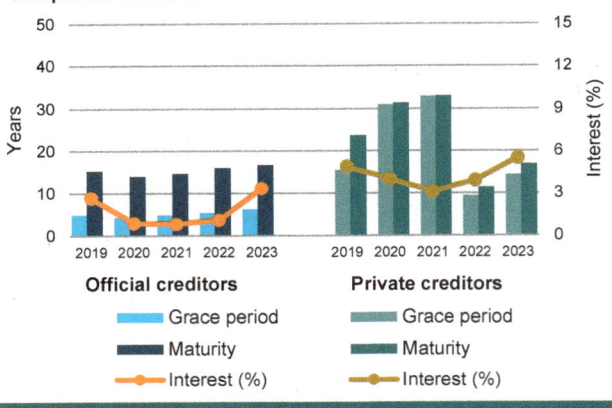

Figure 1 Public and publicly guaranteed debt, by creditor and creditor type in 2023, including IMF credit

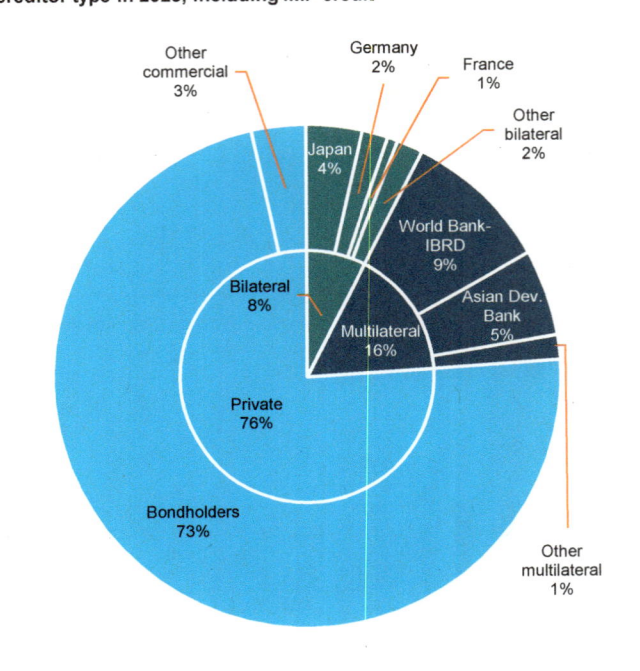

Summary External Debt Data	2010	2019	2020	2021	2022	2023
Total external debt stocks	**198,278**	**402,380**	**417,061**	**417,868**	**396,032**	**406,054**
Long-term external debt stocks	**162,181**	**354,843**	**369,721**	**361,532**	**339,451**	**342,815**
Public and publicly guaranteed debt from:	*102,748*	*233,801*	*247,948*	*242,654*	*226,225*	*234,907*
Official creditors	66,180	52,552	57,983	55,088	53,961	56,316
Multilateral	22,567	31,681	34,326	34,259	35,742	38,551
of which: World Bank	11,367	19,109	19,669	19,622	20,627	22,216
Bilateral	43,613	20,871	23,657	20,829	18,219	17,765
Private creditors	36,568	181,249	189,966	187,566	172,265	178,591
Bondholders	28,698	173,224	182,704	181,413	165,859	170,506
Commercial banks and others	7,870	8,025	7,261	6,153	6,405	8,085
Private nonguaranteed debt from:	*59,433*	*121,041*	*121,773*	*118,878*	*113,226*	*107,909*
Bondholders	8,437	16,515	18,208	20,214	19,999	16,227
Commercial banks and others	50,996	104,526	103,565	98,664	93,227	91,682
Use of IMF credit and SDR allocations	**3,050**	**2,739**	**2,852**	**9,007**	**8,565**	**8,635**
IMF credit	0	0	0	0	0	0
SDR allocations	3,050	2,739	2,852	9,007	8,565	8,635
Short-term external debt stocks	**33,047**	**44,799**	**44,488**	**47,329**	**48,016**	**54,605**
Disbursements, long-term	**34,335**	**94,773**	**65,016**	**50,291**	**52,974**	**48,274**
Public and publicly guaranteed sector	13,695	31,651	30,178	21,249	18,105	25,538
Private sector not guaranteed	20,640	63,122	34,838	29,042	34,869	22,735
Principal repayments, long-term	**26,202**	**68,375**	**52,629**	**55,227**	**61,475**	**41,749**
Public and publicly guaranteed sector	8,072	13,218	18,521	23,292	31,171	16,447
Private sector not guaranteed	18,129	55,157	34,108	31,935	30,304	25,303
Interest payments, long-term	**4,944**	**12,216**	**13,683**	**10,944**	**11,602**	**12,884**
Public and publicly guaranteed sector	3,034	8,037	9,512	7,915	8,433	9,584
Private sector not guaranteed	1,910	4,179	4,170	3,030	3,169	3,300

IRAN, ISLAMIC REPUBLIC OF

(US$ million, unless otherwise indicated)

Snapshot	2023
Total external debt stocks	**9,901**
External debt stocks as % of:	
Exports	9
GNI	2
Debt service as % of:	
Exports	0
GNI	0
Net financial flows, debt and equity	**1,800**
Net debt inflows	378
Net equity inflows	1,422
GNI	**401,036**
Population (million)	**89**

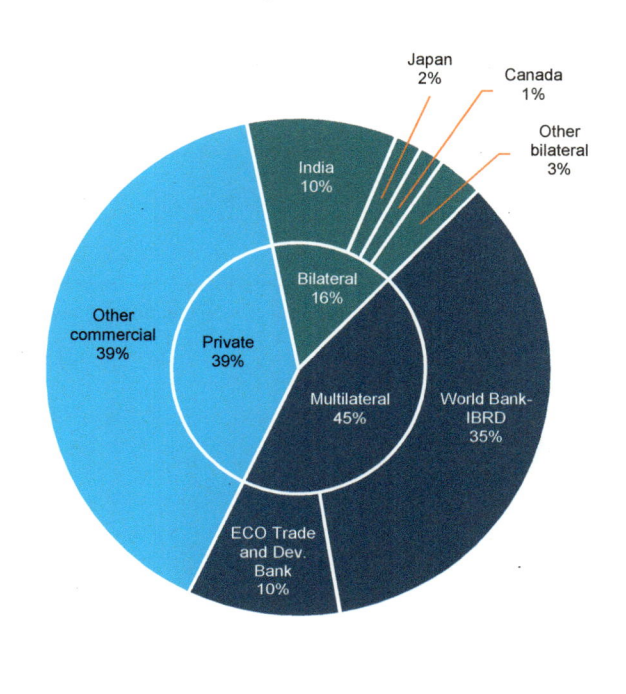

Figure 1 Public and publicly guaranteed debt, by creditor and creditor type in 2023, including IMF credit

Figure 2 Average terms on new debt commitments from official and private creditors

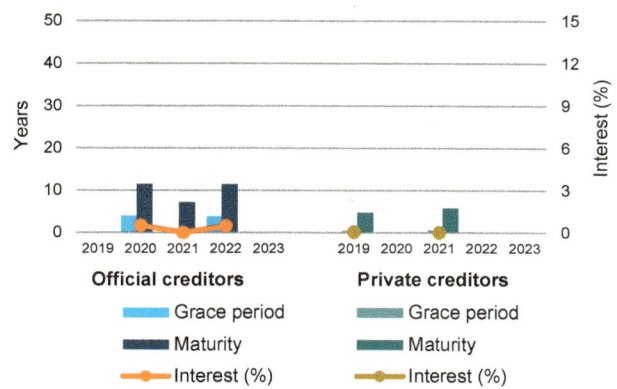

Summary External Debt Data	2010	2019	2020	2021	2022	2023
Total external debt stocks	**19,769**	**4,855**	**5,433**	**10,349**	**9,460**	**9,901**
Long-term external debt stocks	**5,960**	**1,285**	**1,313**	**1,060**	**1,124**	**1,116**
Public and publicly guaranteed debt from:	*5,960*	*370*	*419*	*332*	*397*	*388*
Official creditors	2,068	325	300	225	249	235
Multilateral	833	199	190	119	168	173
of which: World Bank	801	141	132	76	129	135
Bilateral	1,234	126	110	106	81	61
Private creditors	3,892	45	118	107	148	154
Bondholders	..	..	..	..	..	..
Commercial banks and others	3,892	45	118	107	148	154
Private nonguaranteed debt from:	*0*	*915*	*894*	*727*	*727*	*727*
Bondholders	..	..	..	..	..	..
Commercial banks and others	0	915	894	727	727	727
Use of IMF credit and SDR allocations	**2,196**	**1,972**	**2,054**	**6,781**	**6,448**	**6,500**
IMF credit	0	0	0	0	0	0
SDR allocations	2,196	1,972	2,054	6,781	6,448	6,500
Short-term external debt stocks	**11,613**	**1,599**	**2,067**	**2,508**	**1,888**	**2,285**
Disbursements, long-term	**249**	**29**	**116**	**21**	**141**	**43**
Public and publicly guaranteed sector	249	29	116	21	141	43
Private sector not guaranteed	..	..	..	..	..	..
Principal repayments, long-term	**1,532**	**256**	**263**	**254**	**52**	**63**
Public and publicly guaranteed sector	1,532	93	84	88	52	63
Private sector not guaranteed	..	163	178	167	..	..
Interest payments, long-term	**136**	**33**	**26**	**46**	**7**	**13**
Public and publicly guaranteed sector	136	15	15	7	7	13
Private sector not guaranteed	..	18	11	39	..	..

IRAQ

(US$ million, unless otherwise indicated)

Snapshot	2023
Total external debt stocks	**20,331**
External debt stocks as % of:	
Exports	18
GNI	8
Debt service as % of:	
Exports	4
GNI	2
Net financial flows, debt and equity	**-7,574**
Net debt inflows	-2,204
Net equity inflows	-5,370
GNI	**252,097**
Population (million)	**46**

Figure 2 Average terms on new debt commitments from official and private creditors

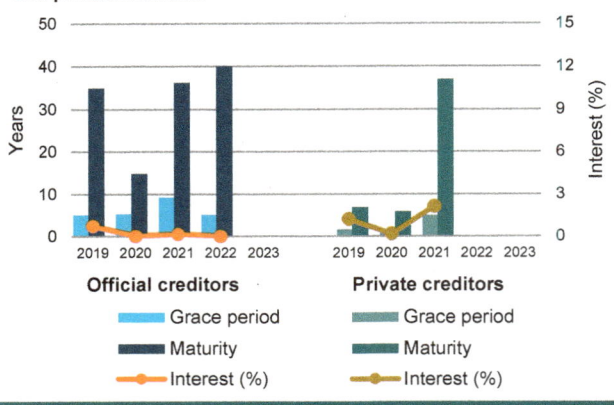

Official creditors
- Grace period
- Maturity
- Interest (%)

Private creditors
- Grace period
- Maturity
- Interest (%)

Figure 1 Public and publicly guaranteed debt, by creditor and creditor type in 2023, including IMF credit

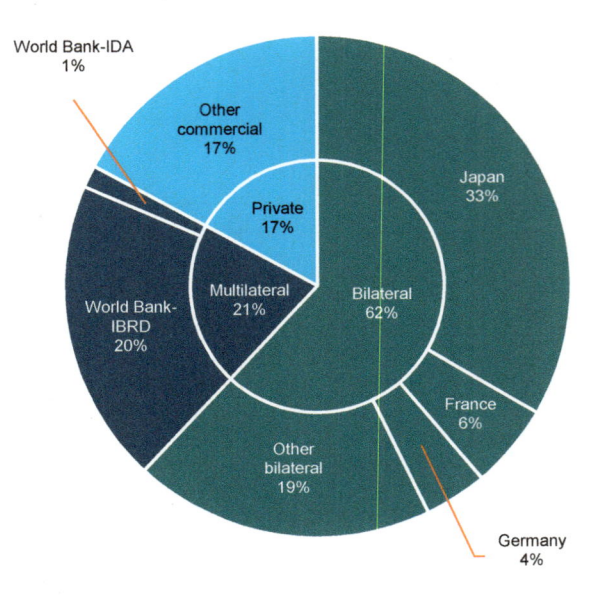

Summary External Debt Data	2010	2019	2020	2021	2022	2023
Total external debt stocks	..	**27,488**	**26,331**	**25,363**	**22,726**	**20,331**
Long-term external debt stocks	..	22,707	22,807	20,617	17,939	15,699
Public and publicly guaranteed debt from:	..	*22,707*	*22,807*	*20,617*	*17,939*	*15,699*
Official creditors	..	16,970	16,834	15,071	13,777	13,025
Multilateral	..	3,568	3,623	3,607	3,463	3,294
of which: World Bank	..	3,550	3,618	3,606	3,460	3,291
Bilateral	..	13,402	13,211	11,464	10,314	9,731
Private creditors	..	5,737	5,973	5,545	4,162	2,674
Bondholders	..	2,000	2,000	2,000	1,000	0
Commercial banks and others	..	3,737	3,973	3,545	3,162	2,674
Private nonguaranteed debt from:	..					
Bondholders	..	..	..	..	..	..
Commercial banks and others	..	..	..	..	..	..
Use of IMF credit and SDR allocations	..	4,019	2,944	4,126	3,632	3,662
IMF credit	..	2,450	1,310	307	0	0
SDR allocations	..	1,569	1,634	3,820	3,632	3,662
Short-term external debt stocks	..	**762**	**580**	**620**	**1,155**	**971**
Disbursements, long-term	..	**1,324**	**1,709**	**826**	**1,622**	**1,662**
Public and publicly guaranteed sector	..	1,324	1,709	826	1,622	1,662
Private sector not guaranteed	..	..	..	..	..	..
Principal repayments, long-term	..	**1,084**	**1,982**	**2,449**	**3,647**	**3,682**
Public and publicly guaranteed sector	..	1,084	1,982	2,449	3,647	3,682
Private sector not guaranteed	..	..	..	..	..	..
Interest payments, long-term	..	**845**	**803**	**675**	**591**	**606**
Public and publicly guaranteed sector	..	845	803	675	591	606
Private sector not guaranteed	..	..	..	..	..	..

JAMAICA

(US$ million, unless otherwise indicated)

Snapshot	2023
Total external debt stocks	**15,349**
External debt stocks as % of:	
Exports	196
GNI	81
Debt service as % of:	
Exports	31
GNI	13
Net financial flows, debt and equity	**-10**
Net debt inflows	-445
Net equity inflows	435
GNI	**18,894**
Population (million)	**3**

Figure 2 Average terms on new debt commitments from official and private creditors

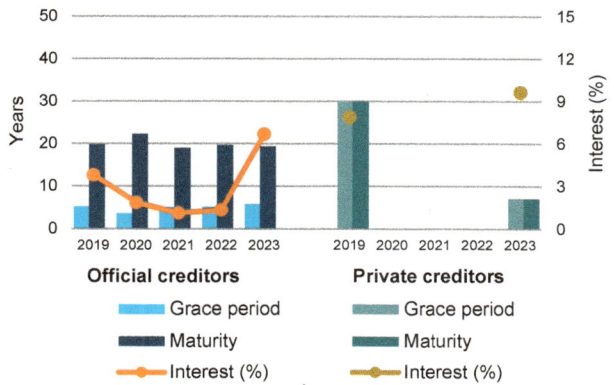

Figure 1 Public and publicly guaranteed debt, by creditor and creditor type in 2023, including IMF credit

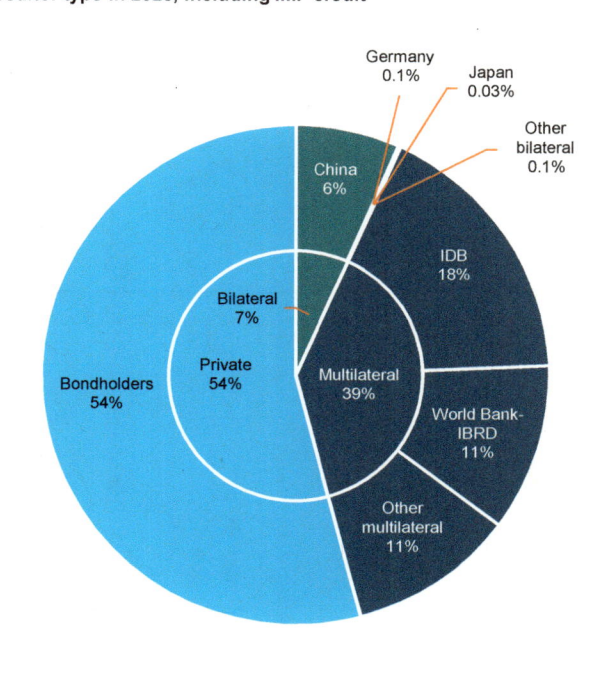

Summary External Debt Data	2010	2019	2020	2021	2022	2023
Total external debt stocks	**14,187**	**14,465**	**14,143**	**16,011**	**15,800**	**15,349**
Long-term external debt stocks	**11,910**	**11,233**	**10,924**	**11,975**	**12,008**	**11,120**
Public and publicly guaranteed debt from:	*7,603*	*9,401*	*9,155*	*9,003*	*8,742*	*8,358*
Official creditors	3,265	3,579	3,570	3,638	3,598	3,415
Multilateral	2,352	2,915	2,947	3,012	2,968	2,798
of which: World Bank	579	886	945	1,062	1,032	988
Bilateral	913	664	623	626	630	617
Private creditors	4,338	5,822	5,585	5,364	5,144	4,942
Bondholders	3,786	5,810	5,585	5,364	5,144	4,942
Commercial banks and others	552	12	0	..	..	..
Private nonguaranteed debt from:	*4,307*	*1,832*	*1,769*	*2,972*	*3,265*	*2,763*
Bondholders	4,290	1,775	1,750	1,750	1,750	1,750
Commercial banks and others	17	57	19	1,222	1,515	1,013
Use of IMF credit and SDR allocations	**1,188**	**978**	**1,449**	**1,792**	**1,580**	**1,611**
IMF credit	785	616	1,072	912	743	768
SDR allocations	403	362	377	880	837	843
Short-term external debt stocks	**1,088**	**2,254**	**1,769**	**2,244**	**2,213**	**2,618**
Disbursements, long-term	**2,360**	**1,609**	**683**	**1,583**	**543**	**418**
Public and publicly guaranteed sector	1,285	1,009	270	380	250	418
Private sector not guaranteed	1,075	600	413	1,203	293	..
Principal repayments, long-term	**345**	**4,637**	**996**	**524**	**503**	**1,290**
Public and publicly guaranteed sector	337	1,355	521	524	503	788
Private sector not guaranteed	9	3,282	475	..	..	502
Interest payments, long-term	**829**	**743**	**690**	**720**	**800**	**801**
Public and publicly guaranteed sector	489	607	552	519	582	612
Private sector not guaranteed	341	136	138	201	219	189

JORDAN

(US$ million, unless otherwise indicated)

Snapshot	2023
Total external debt stocks	**44,630**
External debt stocks as % of:	
Exports	185
GNI	89
Debt service as % of:	
Exports	16
GNI	8
Net financial flows, debt and equity	4,133
Net debt inflows	3,332
Net equity inflows	801
GNI	**50,352**
Population (million)	**11**

Figure 1 Public and publicly guaranteed debt, by creditor and creditor type in 2023, including IMF credit

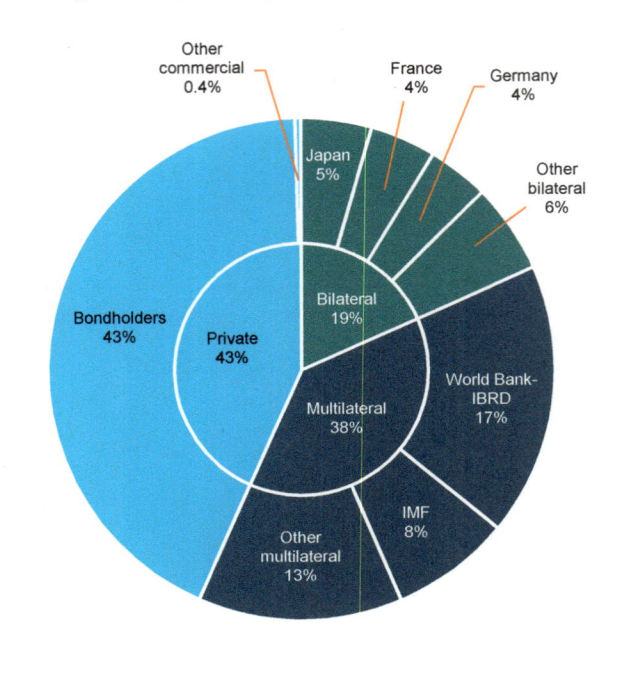

Figure 2 Average terms on new debt commitments from official and private creditors

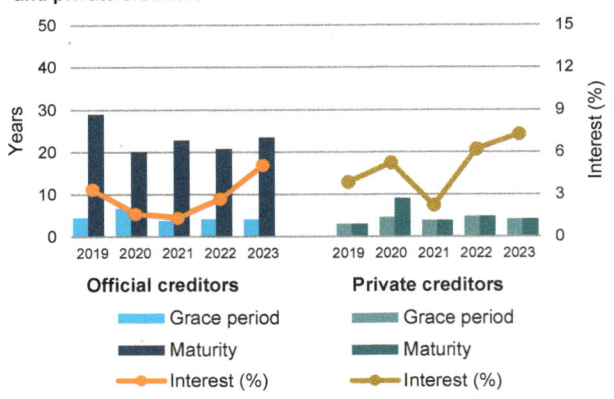

Summary External Debt Data	2010	2019	2020	2021	2022	2023
Total external debt stocks	**16,894**	**33,494**	**38,038**	**41,757**	**41,228**	**44,630**
Long-term external debt stocks	7,588	20,467	22,684	23,936	22,838	26,123
Public and publicly guaranteed debt from:	*6,323*	*16,853*	*18,778*	*19,866*	*19,231*	*22,491*
Official creditors	5,284	8,215	9,449	10,419	10,584	11,933
Multilateral	2,526	4,731	5,491	6,468	6,526	7,448
of which: World Bank	1,040	2,985	3,329	3,723	3,970	4,457
Bilateral	2,757	3,484	3,958	3,951	4,058	4,485
Private creditors	1,040	8,638	9,330	9,447	8,646	10,558
Bondholders	881	8,500	9,198	9,340	8,550	10,470
Commercial banks and others	159	138	132	107	96	88
Private nonguaranteed debt from:	*1,265*	*3,614*	*3,905*	*4,070*	*3,607*	*3,632*
Bondholders	..	..	..	..	..	..
Commercial banks and others	1,265	3,614	3,905	4,070	3,607	3,632
Use of IMF credit and SDR allocations	257	729	1,271	2,215	2,609	2,528
IMF credit	8	505	1,038	1,528	1,955	1,869
SDR allocations	250	224	233	687	653	659
Short-term external debt stocks	9,049	12,297	14,084	15,606	15,782	15,979
Disbursements, long-term	**1,508**	**2,824**	**4,052**	**3,820**	**2,641**	**4,690**
Public and publicly guaranteed sector	1,358	2,049	3,448	3,405	2,641	4,665
Private sector not guaranteed	150	775	604	415	..	25
Principal repayments, long-term	**506**	**1,777**	**2,089**	**2,272**	**3,437**	**1,453**
Public and publicly guaranteed sector	480	1,545	1,775	2,022	2,974	1,453
Private sector not guaranteed	26	231	313	251	463	..
Interest payments, long-term	**161**	**742**	**580**	**645**	**774**	**1,151**
Public and publicly guaranteed sector	145	589	523	604	639	920
Private sector not guaranteed	16	153	56	41	135	231

KAZAKHSTAN

(US$ million, unless otherwise indicated)

Snapshot	2023
Total external debt stocks	**163,155**
External debt stocks as % of:	
Exports	173
GNI	69
Debt service as % of:	
Exports	47
GNI	19
Net financial flows, debt and equity	**14,150**
Net debt inflows	7,951
Net equity inflows	6,198
GNI	**235,419**
Population (million)	**20**

Figure 2 Average terms on new debt commitments from official and private creditors

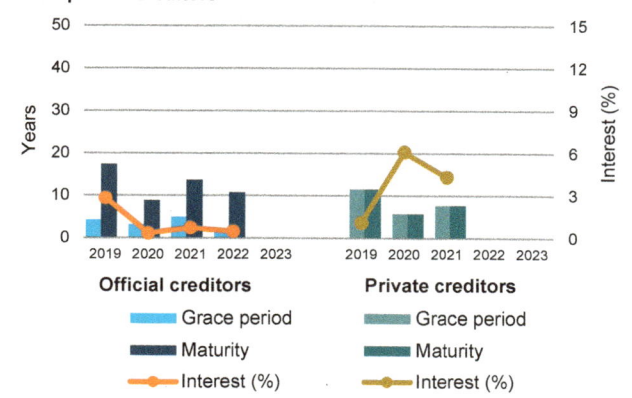

Figure 1 Public and publicly guaranteed debt, by creditor and creditor type in 2023, including IMF credit

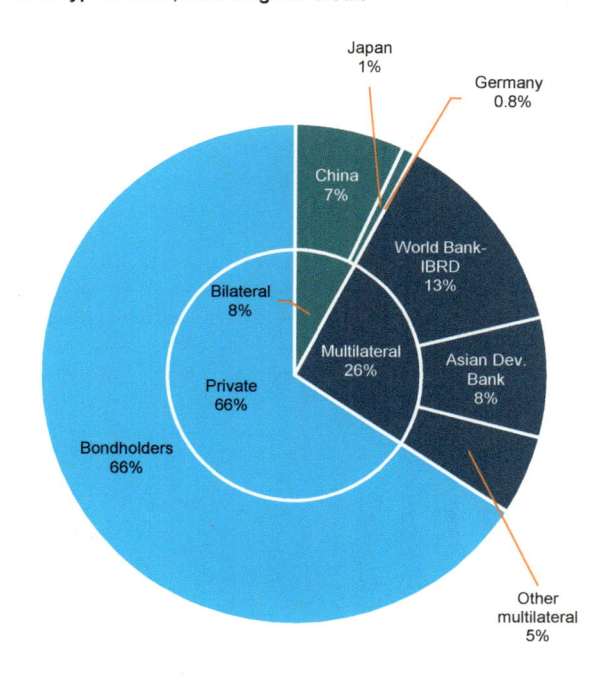

Summary External Debt Data	2010	2019	2020	2021	2022	2023
Total external debt stocks	**119,151**	**159,282**	**161,509**	**161,344**	**160,974**	**163,155**
Long-term external debt stocks	**109,757**	**149,784**	**151,498**	**147,251**	**142,653**	**141,946**
Public and publicly guaranteed debt from:	*3,845*	*25,006*	*26,256*	*28,322*	*26,809*	*25,231*
Official creditors	3,845	7,634	8,097	8,842	8,841	8,611
Multilateral	2,785	6,010	6,265	6,803	6,875	6,636
of which: World Bank	1,830	3,802	3,615	3,463	3,576	3,383
Bilateral	1,060	1,624	1,833	2,039	1,967	1,976
Private creditors	0	17,372	18,159	19,480	17,968	16,620
Bondholders	0	17,372	18,159	19,480	17,968	16,620
Commercial banks and others	..	..	..	..	..	..
Private nonguaranteed debt from:	*105,912*	*124,779*	*125,242*	*118,929*	*115,844*	*116,715*
Bondholders	21,044	6,684	6,361	5,917	3,500	3,478
Commercial banks and others	84,868	118,094	118,881	113,012	112,345	113,237
Use of IMF credit and SDR allocations	**529**	**475**	**495**	**2,035**	**1,935**	**1,951**
IMF credit	0	0	0	0	0	0
SDR allocations	529	475	495	2,035	1,935	1,951
Short-term external debt stocks	**8,864**	**9,022**	**9,516**	**12,058**	**16,386**	**19,258**
Disbursements, long-term	**45,054**	**31,801**	**34,737**	**23,369**	**35,963**	**42,265**
Public and publicly guaranteed sector	1,522	1,975	2,119	2,909	718	501
Private sector not guaranteed	43,532	29,826	32,618	20,460	35,245	41,764
Principal repayments, long-term	**34,639**	**29,334**	**27,125**	**27,289**	**37,927**	**37,219**
Public and publicly guaranteed sector	278	1,433	1,082	461	1,981	1,978
Private sector not guaranteed	34,361	27,901	26,042	26,829	35,946	35,242
Interest payments, long-term	**4,517**	**3,188**	**3,336**	**3,707**	**4,801**	**6,084**
Public and publicly guaranteed sector	54	1,091	1,005	976	1,066	1,237
Private sector not guaranteed	4,463	2,098	2,331	2,732	3,735	4,847

KENYA

(US$ million, unless otherwise indicated)

Snapshot	2023
Total external debt stocks	**42,910**
External debt stocks as % of:	
Exports	334
GNI	41
Debt service as % of:	
Exports	30
GNI	4
Net financial flows, debt and equity	2,039
Net debt inflows	1,570
Net equity inflows	469
GNI	**105,674**
Population (million)	**55**

Figure 2 Average terms on new debt commitments from official and private creditors

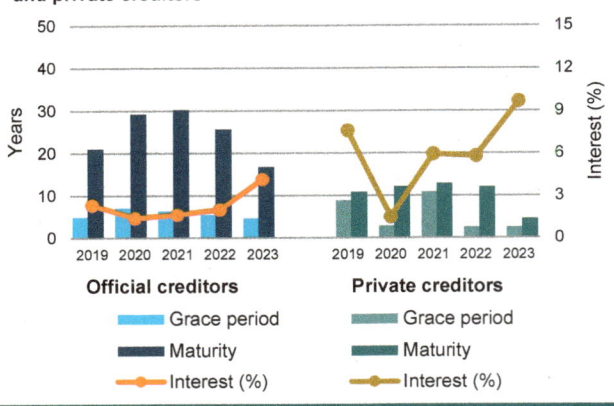

Official creditors
- ▅ Grace period
- ▅ Maturity
- ━●━ Interest (%)

Private creditors
- ▅ Grace period
- ▅ Maturity
- ━●━ Interest (%)

Figure 1 Public and publicly guaranteed debt, by creditor and creditor type in 2023, including IMF credit

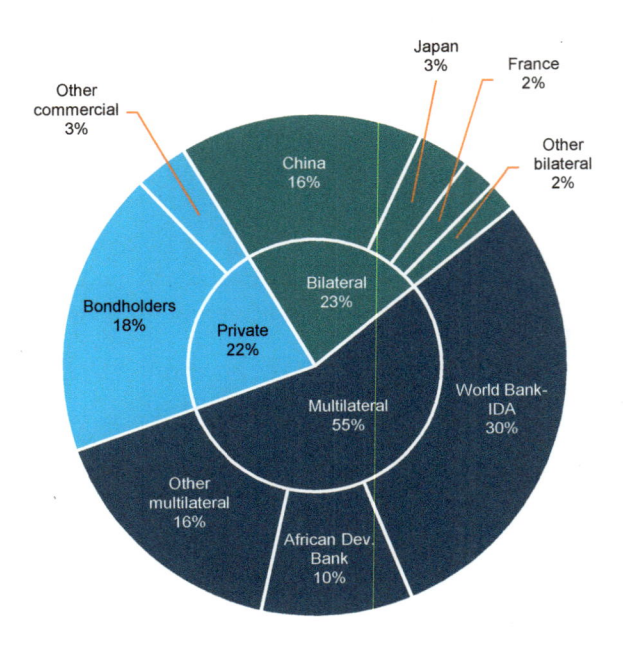

Summary External Debt Data	2010	2019	2020	2021	2022	2023
Total external debt stocks	**8,885**	**34,970**	**38,038**	**41,219**	**41,556**	**42,910**
Long-term external debt stocks	**7,027**	**31,631**	**34,355**	**35,871**	**35,606**	**36,295**
Public and publicly guaranteed debt from:	*7,027*	*30,814*	*33,534*	*35,228*	*35,037*	*35,864*
Official creditors	6,754	23,721	26,135	26,898	26,840	27,445
Multilateral	4,110	12,709	15,111	15,780	16,720	18,594
of which: World Bank	3,238	7,125	9,334	10,228	11,053	12,465
Bilateral	2,644	11,012	11,024	11,118	10,120	8,851
Private creditors	273	7,093	7,399	8,330	8,197	8,419
Bondholders	..	6,100	6,100	7,100	7,100	7,100
Commercial banks and others	273	993	1,299	1,230	1,097	1,319
Private nonguaranteed debt from:	..	*817*	*821*	*644*	*569*	*432*
Bondholders	..	..	..	..	..	..
Commercial banks and others	..	817	821	644	569	432
Use of IMF credit and SDR allocations	**817**	**720**	**1,391**	**2,913**	**3,389**	**3,799**
IMF credit	417	361	1,017	1,821	2,351	2,753
SDR allocations	400	359	374	1,092	1,038	1,046
Short-term external debt stocks	**1,041**	**2,619**	**2,293**	**2,435**	**2,561**	**2,815**
Disbursements, long-term	**532**	**6,722**	**3,417**	**3,405**	**2,957**	**3,111**
Public and publicly guaranteed sector	532	6,712	3,273	3,405	2,881	3,110
Private sector not guaranteed	..	10	144	..	76	1
Principal repayments, long-term	**260**	**3,009**	**1,465**	**1,334**	**2,016**	**2,195**
Public and publicly guaranteed sector	260	2,799	1,310	1,165	1,872	2,056
Private sector not guaranteed	..	210	154	169	143	140
Interest payments, long-term	**90**	**1,242**	**1,195**	**952**	**1,118**	**1,391**
Public and publicly guaranteed sector	90	1,181	1,150	916	1,088	1,348
Private sector not guaranteed	..	61	45	36	29	42

KOSOVO

(US$ million, unless otherwise indicated)

Snapshot	2023
Total external debt stocks	**4,242**
External debt stocks as % of:	
Exports	91
GNI	40
Debt service as % of:	
Exports	6
GNI	2
Net financial flows, debt and equity	**1,264**
Net debt inflows	498
Net equity inflows	766
GNI	**10,636**
Population (million)	**2**

Figure 2 Average terms on new debt commitments from official and private creditors

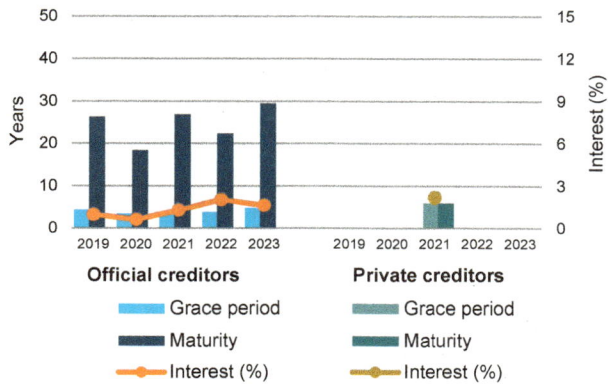

Figure 1 Public and publicly guaranteed debt, by creditor and creditor type in 2023, including IMF credit

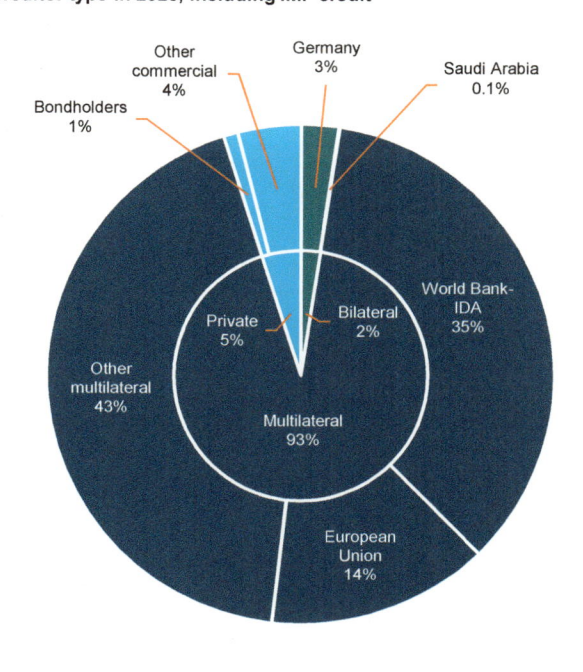

Summary External Debt Data	2010	2019	2020	2021	2022	2023
Total external debt stocks	**1,701**	**2,417**	**3,088**	**3,346**	**3,660**	**4,242**
Long-term external debt stocks	**886**	**1,357**	**1,911**	**1,982**	**2,175**	**2,525**
Public and publicly guaranteed debt from:	*319*	*320*	*517*	*596*	*642*	*694*
Official creditors	319	304	488	557	605	656
Multilateral	319	254	441	521	578	637
of which: World Bank	319	220	314	313	342	373
Bilateral	0	50	46	36	26	19
Private creditors	..	16	30	39	37	38
Bondholders	..	..	..	7	7	7
Commercial banks and others	..	16	30	32	31	31
Private nonguaranteed debt from:	*567*	*1,037*	*1,394*	*1,386*	*1,533*	*1,831*
Bondholders	..	..	..	..	..	..
Commercial banks and others	567	1,037	1,394	1,386	1,533	1,831
Use of IMF credit and SDR allocations	**114**	**225**	**216**	**260**	**234**	**264**
IMF credit	29	148	136	72	55	83
SDR allocations	85	77	80	188	179	181
Short-term external debt stocks	**700**	**835**	**962**	**1,103**	**1,251**	**1,453**
Disbursements, long-term	**169**	**283**	**567**	**647**	**558**	**474**
Public and publicly guaranteed sector	0	44	192	152	118	68
Private sector not guaranteed	169	239	375	495	441	406
Principal repayments, long-term	**76**	**171**	**251**	**327**	**267**	**206**
Public and publicly guaranteed sector	14	24	27	33	39	38
Private sector not guaranteed	61	148	224	293	229	167
Interest payments, long-term	**34**	**47**	**47**	**18**	**15**	**24**
Public and publicly guaranteed sector	11	10	11	11	10	12
Private sector not guaranteed	23	37	36	7	5	12

KYRGYZ REPUBLIC

(US$ million, unless otherwise indicated)

Snapshot	2023
Total external debt stocks	**10,115**
External debt stocks as % of:	
Exports	152
GNI	76
Debt service as % of:	
Exports	18
GNI	9
Net financial flows, debt and equity	853
Net debt inflows	362
Net equity inflows	490
GNI	**13,296**
Population (million)	**7**

Figure 1 Public and publicly guaranteed debt, by creditor and creditor type in 2023, including IMF credit

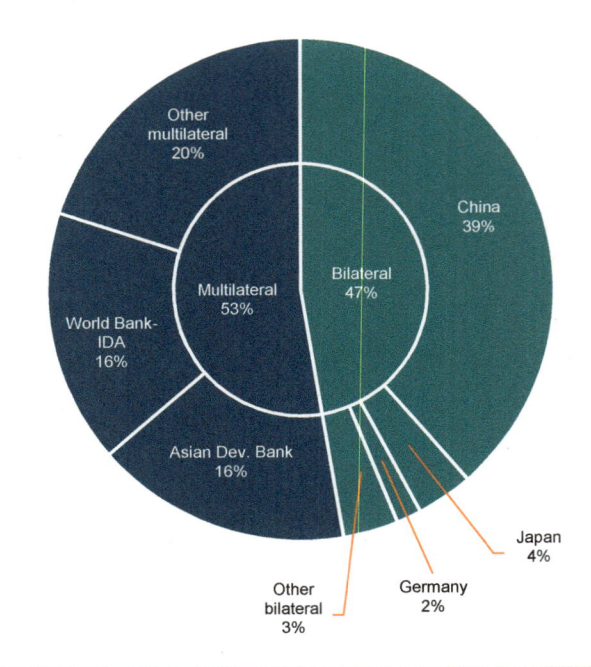

Figure 2 Average terms on new debt commitments from official and private creditors

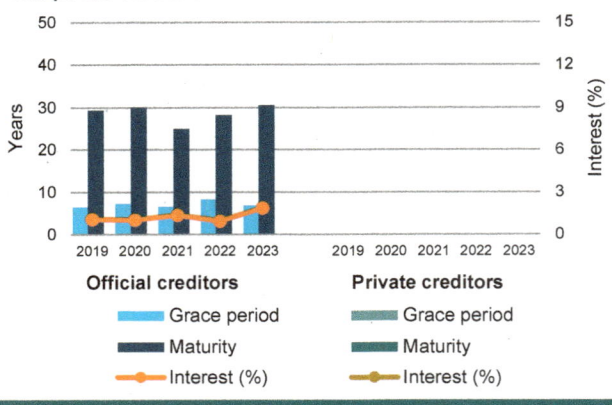

Official creditors	Private creditors
▬ Grace period	▬ Grace period
▬ Maturity	▬ Maturity
━●━ Interest (%)	━●━ Interest (%)

Summary External Debt Data	2010	2019	2020	2021	2022	2023
Total external debt stocks	**4,118**	**8,454**	**8,676**	**9,061**	**9,746**	**10,115**
Long-term external debt stocks	**3,616**	**7,680**	**7,652**	**7,825**	**8,132**	**8,415**
Public and publicly guaranteed debt from:	*2,446*	*3,712*	*3,843*	*3,958*	*4,031*	*4,192*
Official creditors	2,446	3,712	3,843	3,958	4,031	4,192
Multilateral	1,296	1,461	1,588	1,704	1,839	2,098
of which: World Bank	649	657	677	653	636	721
Bilateral	1,150	2,250	2,255	2,255	2,192	2,094
Private creditors	..	..	..	..	..	..
Bondholders	..	..	..	..	..	..
Commercial banks and others	..	..	..	..	..	..
Private nonguaranteed debt from:	*1,171*	*3,968*	*3,809*	*3,866*	*4,101*	*4,222*
Bondholders	..	0	0	0	0	0
Commercial banks and others	1,171	3,968	3,809	3,866	4,101	4,222
Use of IMF credit and SDR allocations	**307**	**258**	**498**	**697**	**642**	**575**
IMF credit	177	140	376	340	302	233
SDR allocations	130	117	122	357	339	342
Short-term external debt stocks	**195**	**517**	**525**	**539**	**972**	**1,125**
Disbursements, long-term	**672**	**898**	**390**	**626**	**755**	**970**
Public and publicly guaranteed sector	151	189	166	289	380	375
Private sector not guaranteed	521	708	224	336	375	595
Principal repayments, long-term	**462**	**630**	**509**	**464**	**327**	**689**
Public and publicly guaranteed sector	38	122	125	117	186	216
Private sector not guaranteed	424	509	384	347	141	474
Interest payments, long-term	**39**	**170**	**104**	**93**	**210**	**328**
Public and publicly guaranteed sector	23	56	55	40	57	60
Private sector not guaranteed	15	114	49	53	153	268

LAO PEOPLE'S DEMOCRATIC REPUBLIC

(US$ million, unless otherwise indicated)

Snapshot	2023
Total external debt stocks	**20,089**
External debt stocks as % of:	
Exports	205
GNI	137
Debt service as % of:	
Exports	12
GNI	8
Net financial flows, debt and equity	2,986
Net debt inflows	1,205
Net equity inflows	1,781
GNI	**14,686**
Population (million)	**8**

Figure 1 Public and publicly guaranteed debt, by creditor and creditor type in 2023, including IMF credit

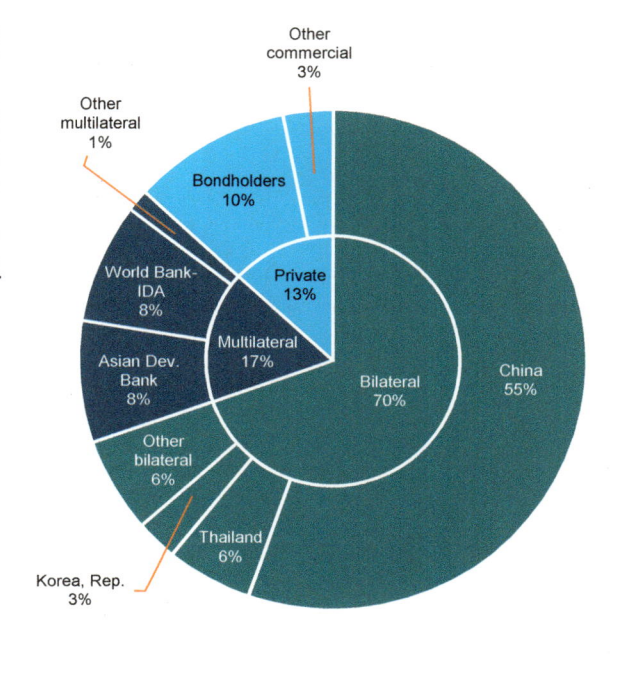

Figure 2 Average terms on new debt commitments from official and private creditors

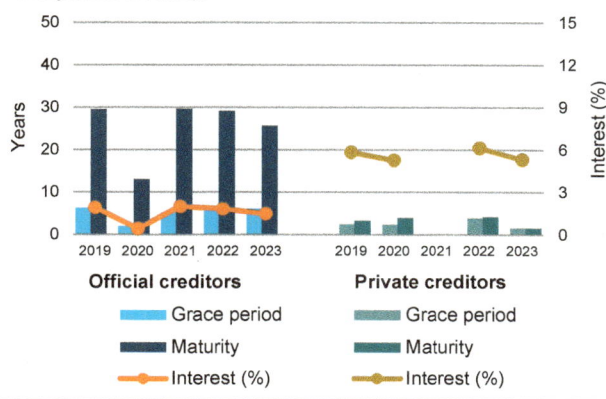

Official creditors — Grace period / Maturity / Interest (%)
Private creditors — Grace period / Maturity / Interest (%)

Summary External Debt Data	2010	2019	2020	2021	2022	2023
Total external debt stocks	**6,554**	**18,974**	**21,014**	**19,225**	**18,879**	**20,089**
Long-term external debt stocks	**6,410**	**18,319**	**19,957**	**18,151**	**17,926**	**19,744**
Public and publicly guaranteed debt from:	*3,751*	*10,202*	*11,464*	*11,083*	*10,914*	*10,772*
Official creditors	3,748	8,134	9,377	9,438	9,317	9,341
Multilateral	2,084	1,710	1,828	1,816	1,780	1,835
of which: World Bank	655	659	717	740	756	836
Bilateral	1,664	6,424	7,549	7,622	7,537	7,506
Private creditors	3	2,068	2,087	1,646	1,596	1,431
Bondholders	..	1,606	1,368	981	1,076	1,088
Commercial banks and others	3	462	719	664	520	343
Private nonguaranteed debt from:	*2,659*	*8,118*	*8,493*	*7,067*	*7,012*	*8,972*
Bondholders	..	691	692	779	1,041	1,149
Commercial banks and others	2,659	7,426	7,801	6,288	5,971	7,824
Use of IMF credit and SDR allocations	**88**	**70**	**73**	**213**	**202**	**204**
IMF credit	10	0	0	0	0	0
SDR allocations	78	70	73	213	202	204
Short-term external debt stocks	**56**	**585**	**985**	**861**	**750**	**140**
Disbursements, long-term	**460**	**3,357**	**2,012**	**468**	**699**	**2,302**
Public and publicly guaranteed sector	267	1,171	1,509	358	432	345
Private sector not guaranteed	193	2,186	503	110	268	1,958
Principal repayments, long-term	**217**	**506**	**568**	**2,047**	**652**	**487**
Public and publicly guaranteed sector	59	504	439	534	335	483
Private sector not guaranteed	159	2	129	1,512	318	4
Interest payments, long-term	**78**	**516**	**333**	**231**	**404**	**698**
Public and publicly guaranteed sector	28	268	201	125	119	149
Private sector not guaranteed	50	248	132	106	285	550

LEBANON

(US$ million, unless otherwise indicated)

Snapshot	2023
Total external debt stocks	**66,296**
External debt stocks as % of:	
Exports	525
GNI	384
Debt service as % of:	
Exports	34
GNI	25
Net financial flows, debt and equity	**-1,876**
Net debt inflows	-2,608
Net equity inflows	732
GNI	**17,253**
Population (million)	**5**

Figure 2 Average terms on new debt commitments from official and private creditors

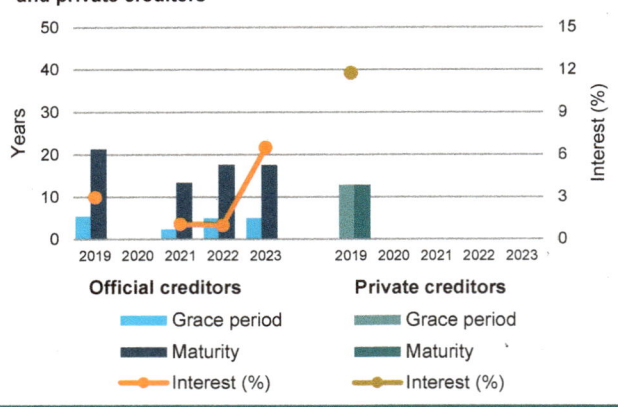

Official creditors
- Grace period
- Maturity
- Interest (%)

Private creditors
- Grace period
- Maturity
- Interest (%)

Figure 1 Public and publicly guaranteed debt, by creditor and creditor type in 2023, including IMF credit

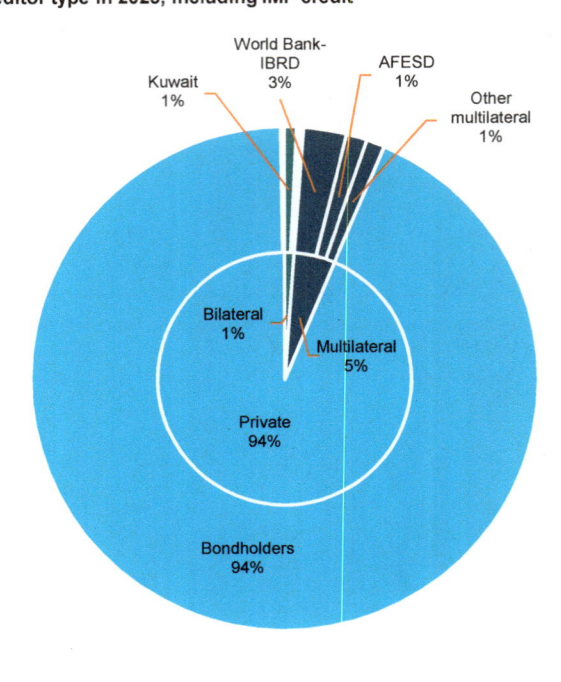

Summary External Debt Data	2010	2019	2020	2021	2022	2023
Total external debt stocks	**47,819**	**73,893**	**68,874**	**66,900**	**67,080**	**66,296**
Long-term external debt stocks	**43,857**	**68,663**	**58,442**	**52,923**	**50,500**	**48,085**
Public and publicly guaranteed debt from:	*20,386*	*33,319*	*33,361*	*33,277*	*33,376*	*33,553*
Official creditors	2,358	1,875	1,938	1,892	1,994	2,169
Multilateral	1,368	1,373	1,461	1,469	1,604	1,755
of which: World Bank	321	536	615	663	846	1,011
Bilateral	990	502	476	423	390	414
Private creditors	18,028	31,444	31,423	31,385	31,381	31,385
Bondholders	17,422	31,314	31,314	31,314	31,314	31,314
Commercial banks and others	606	130	109	71	67	71
Private nonguaranteed debt from:	*23,471*	*35,343*	*25,081*	*19,646*	*17,124*	*14,531*
Bondholders	500	600	600	600	600	300
Commercial banks and others	22,971	34,743	24,481	19,046	16,524	14,231
Use of IMF credit and SDR allocations	**395**	**267**	**278**	**1,120**	**1,065**	**1,074**
IMF credit	98	0	0	0	0	0
SDR allocations	298	267	278	1,120	1,065	1,074
Short-term external debt stocks	**3,567**	**4,963**	**10,154**	**12,857**	**15,515**	**17,138**
Disbursements, long-term	**9,615**	**8,597**	**202**	**145**	**242**	**289**
Public and publicly guaranteed sector	2,186	3,173	202	145	242	289
Private sector not guaranteed	7,430	5,424	..	..	..	..
Principal repayments, long-term	**8,395**	**13,761**	**10,458**	**5,638**	**2,632**	**2,708**
Public and publicly guaranteed sector	2,477	2,917	196	202	111	115
Private sector not guaranteed	5,918	10,844	10,262	5,436	2,521	2,593
Interest payments, long-term	**1,792**	**3,196**	**510**	**342**	**721**	**1,019**
Public and publicly guaranteed sector	1,406	2,142	157	47	32	82
Private sector not guaranteed	386	1,054	353	295	689	937

LESOTHO

(US$ million, unless otherwise indicated)

Snapshot	2023
Total external debt stocks	**1,776**
External debt stocks as % of:	
Exports	121
GNI	74
Debt service as % of:	
Exports	9
GNI	5
Net financial flows, debt and equity	**-69**
Net debt inflows	-38
Net equity inflows	-31
GNI	**2,394**
Population (million)	**2**

Figure 2 Average terms on new debt commitments from official and private creditors

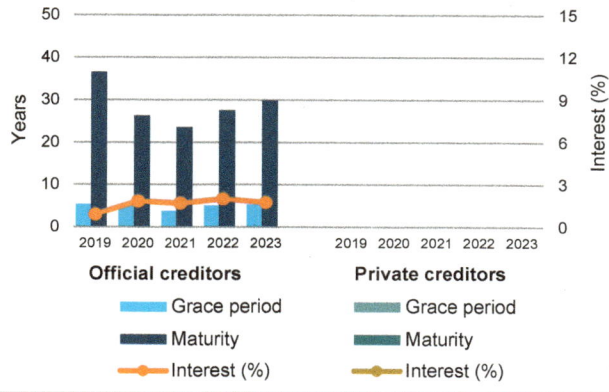

Official creditors
- Grace period
- Maturity
- Interest (%)

Private creditors
- Grace period
- Maturity
- Interest (%)

Figure 1 Public and publicly guaranteed debt, by creditor and creditor type in 2023, including IMF credit

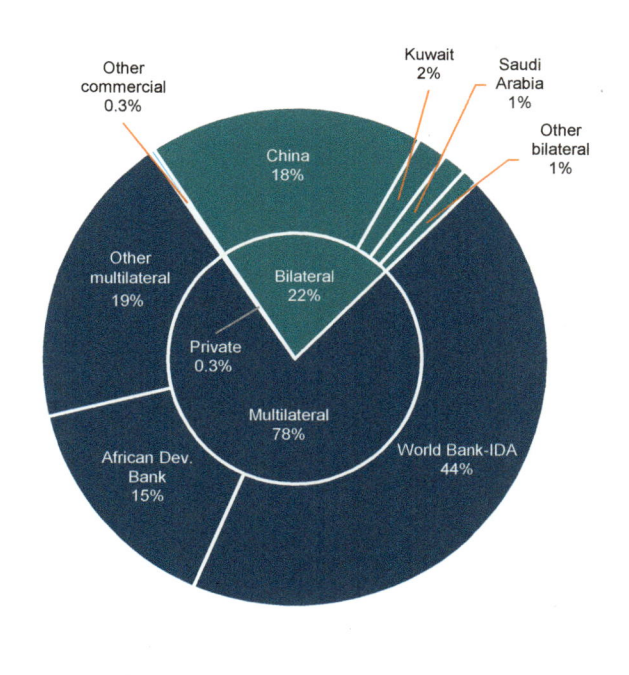

Summary External Debt Data	2010	2019	2020	2021	2022	2023
Total external debt stocks	**788**	**1,583**	**1,738**	**1,833**	**1,809**	**1,776**
Long-term external debt stocks	**709**	**1,504**	**1,616**	**1,633**	**1,613**	**1,595**
Public and publicly guaranteed debt from:	*709*	*856*	*931*	*978*	*968*	*999*
Official creditors	688	852	927	974	965	996
Multilateral	633	722	755	760	742	765
of which: World Bank	330	363	400	424	427	457
Bilateral	55	131	171	215	222	230
Private creditors	21	4	4	4	3	3
Bondholders	..	..	..	..	..	..
Commercial banks and others	21	4	4	4	3	3
Private nonguaranteed debt from:	..	*648*	*685*	*655*	*645*	*597*
Bondholders	..	..	..	..	..	..
Commercial banks and others	..	648	685	655	645	597
Use of IMF credit and SDR allocations	**79**	**79**	**119**	**198**	**182**	**177**
IMF credit	28	34	72	58	49	43
SDR allocations	51	45	47	140	133	134
Short-term external debt stocks	**0**	**0**	**2**	**3**	**14**	**3**
Disbursements, long-term	**45**	**179**	**117**	**106**	**84**	**79**
Public and publicly guaranteed sector	45	91	79	106	84	79
Private sector not guaranteed	..	88	38	..	..	..
Principal repayments, long-term	**19**	**37**	**44**	**66**	**54**	**99**
Public and publicly guaranteed sector	19	37	44	35	45	51
Private sector not guaranteed	..	..	..	31	9	49
Interest payments, long-term	**8**	**24**	**16**	**17**	**18**	**19**
Public and publicly guaranteed sector	8	24	16	17	18	19
Private sector not guaranteed	..	..	..	..	..	..

LIBERIA

(US$ million, unless otherwise indicated)

Snapshot	2023
Total external debt stocks	**2,078**
External debt stocks as % of:	
Exports	179
GNI	51
Debt service as % of:	
Exports	11
GNI	3
Net financial flows, debt and equity	529
Net debt inflows	162
Net equity inflows	367
GNI	**4,058**
Population (million)	**5**

Figure 2 Average terms on new debt commitments from official and private creditors

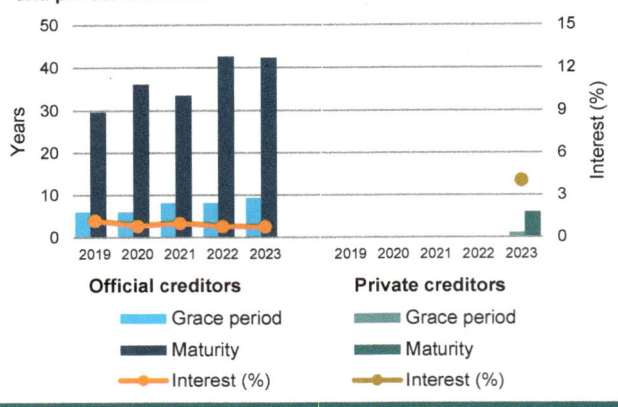

Figure 1 Public and publicly guaranteed debt, by creditor and creditor type in 2023, including IMF credit

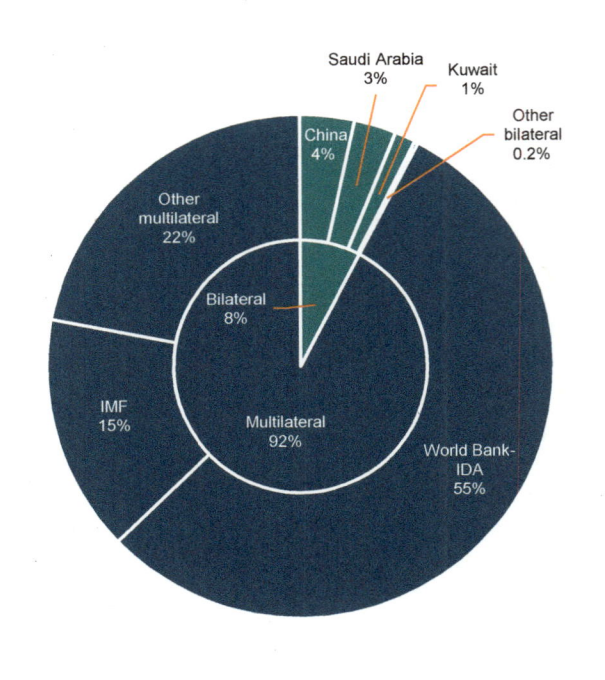

Summary External Debt Data	2010	2019	2020	2021	2022	2023
Total external debt stocks	**419**	**1,267**	**1,462**	**1,849**	**1,904**	**2,078**
Long-term external debt stocks	183	870	989	1,050	1,147	1,351
Public and publicly guaranteed debt from:	*183*	*822*	*948*	*1,017*	*1,109*	*1,274*
Official creditors	183	822	948	1,017	1,109	1,274
Multilateral	63	705	828	898	995	1,158
of which: World Bank	0	455	550	616	703	828
Bilateral	120	117	120	120	114	116
Private creditors	0	..	..	..	..	0
Bondholders	..	..	..	..	..	..
Commercial banks and others	0	..	..	..	..	..
Private nonguaranteed debt from:	*..*	*49*	*41*	*33*	*37*	*77*
Bondholders	..	..	..	..	..	..
Commercial banks and others	..	49	41	33	37	77
Use of IMF credit and SDR allocations	235	396	473	798	757	727
IMF credit	44	225	294	278	263	228
SDR allocations	191	171	179	520	495	499
Short-term external debt stocks	**0**	**0**	**0**	**0**	**0**	**0**
Disbursements, long-term	**8**	**120**	**112**	**99**	**170**	**251**
Public and publicly guaranteed sector	8	119	110	99	148	183
Private sector not guaranteed	..	1	1	..	22	68
Principal repayments, long-term	**4**	**14**	**22**	**18**	**37**	**52**
Public and publicly guaranteed sector	4	6	14	10	19	24
Private sector not guaranteed	..	8	8	8	18	29
Interest payments, long-term	**1**	**8**	**11**	**10**	**13**	**16**
Public and publicly guaranteed sector	1	7	10	9	12	11
Private sector not guaranteed	..	1	1	0	0	5

MADAGASCAR

(US$ million, unless otherwise indicated)

Snapshot	2023
Total external debt stocks	**6,452**
External debt stocks as % of:	
Exports	148
GNI	41
Debt service as % of:	
Exports	6
GNI	2
Net financial flows, debt and equity	**890**
Net debt inflows	476
Net equity inflows	415
GNI	**15,703**
Population (million)	**30**

Figure 1 Public and publicly guaranteed debt, by creditor and creditor type in 2023, including IMF credit

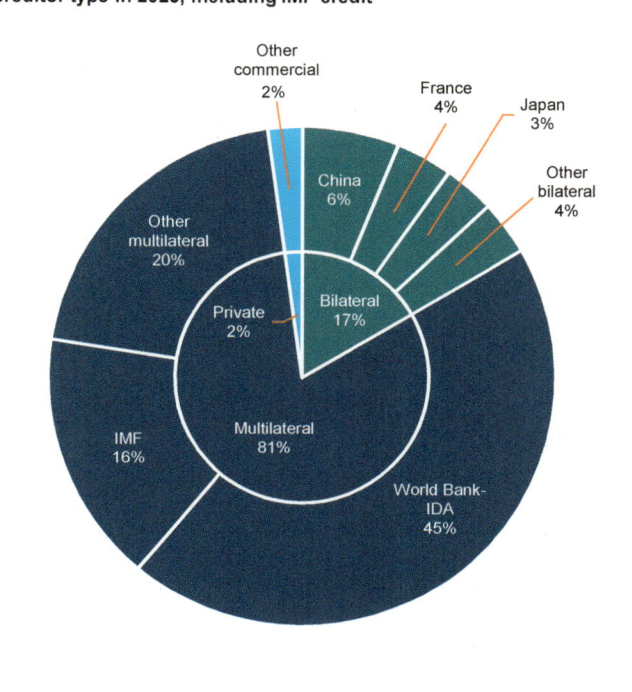

Figure 2 Average terms on new debt commitments from official and private creditors

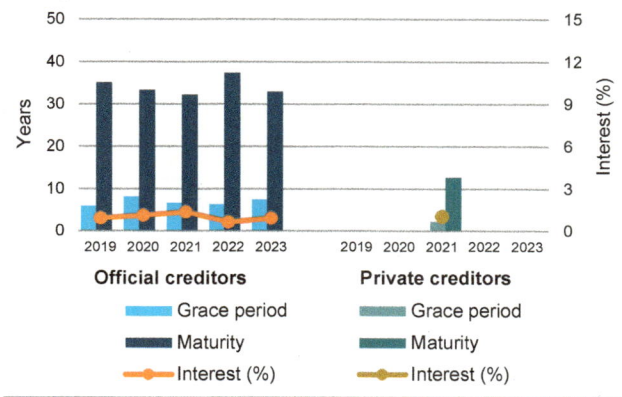

Summary External Debt Data	2010	2019	2020	2021	2022	2023
Total external debt stocks	**2,756**	**4,045**	**4,841**	**5,345**	**5,938**	**6,452**
Long-term external debt stocks	**2,054**	**3,218**	**3,612**	**3,811**	**4,441**	**4,980**
Public and publicly guaranteed debt from:	*2,039*	*3,117*	*3,508*	*3,715*	*3,934*	*4,482*
Official creditors	2,031	2,963	3,362	3,598	3,835	4,364
Multilateral	1,575	2,488	2,809	2,986	3,059	3,478
of which: World Bank	1,161	1,686	1,874	2,010	2,043	2,388
Bilateral	456	475	553	612	776	887
Private creditors	8	154	146	118	99	118
Bondholders	..	..	..	..	..	..
Commercial banks and others	8	154	146	118	99	118
Private nonguaranteed debt from:	*15*	*101*	*104*	*95*	*507*	*498*
Bondholders	..	..	..	..	420	420
Commercial banks and others	15	101	104	95	87	78
Use of IMF credit and SDR allocations	**278**	**545**	**956**	**1,304**	**1,317**	**1,344**
IMF credit	97	383	788	812	850	872
SDR allocations	180	162	169	492	468	471
Short-term external debt stocks	**425**	**281**	**273**	**230**	**180**	**128**
Disbursements, long-term	**198**	**327**	**347**	**413**	**905**	**655**
Public and publicly guaranteed sector	198	300	336	413	485	655
Private sector not guaranteed	..	26	11	..	420	..
Principal repayments, long-term	**39**	**76**	**82**	**105**	**109**	**143**
Public and publicly guaranteed sector	37	67	73	96	100	135
Private sector not guaranteed	1	9	9	9	9	9
Interest payments, long-term	**16**	**36**	**37**	**39**	**72**	**48**
Public and publicly guaranteed sector	16	30	31	32	36	43
Private sector not guaranteed	0	6	6	6	37	5

MALAWI

(US$ million, unless otherwise indicated)

Snapshot	2023
Total external debt stocks	**3,604**
External debt stocks as % of:	
Exports	232
GNI	26
Debt service as % of:	
Exports	10
GNI	1
Net financial flows, debt and equity	**418**
Net debt inflows	243
Net equity inflows	174
GNI	**13,726**
Population (million)	**21**

Figure 1 Public and publicly guaranteed debt, by creditor and creditor type in 2023, including IMF credit

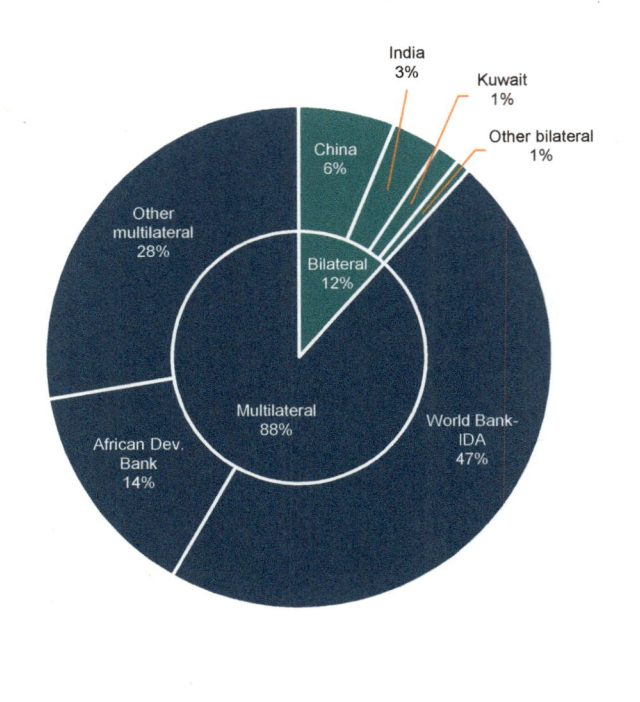

Figure 2 Average terms on new debt commitments from official and private creditors

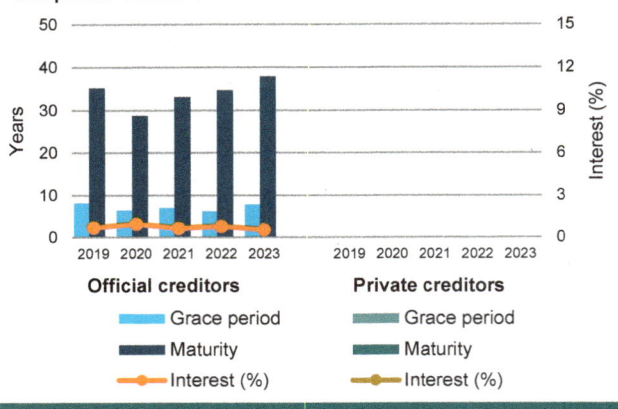

Summary External Debt Data	2010	2019	2020	2021	2022	2023
Total external debt stocks	**1,021**	**2,427**	**2,943**	**3,198**	**3,340**	**3,604**
Long-term external debt stocks	**730**	**2,020**	**2,237**	**2,379**	**2,546**	**2,876**
Public and publicly guaranteed debt from:	*730*	*2,020*	*2,237*	*2,379*	*2,546*	*2,876*
Official creditors	724	2,020	2,237	2,379	2,546	2,876
Multilateral	586	1,600	1,799	1,929	2,119	2,486
of which: World Bank	243	969	1,104	1,177	1,319	1,550
Bilateral	138	419	438	451	427	390
Private creditors	5	..	..	..	..	..
Bondholders	..	..	..	..	..	..
Commercial banks and others	5	..	..	..	..	..
Private nonguaranteed debt from:	..	..	..	..	..	..
Bondholders	..	..	..	..	..	..
Commercial banks and others	..	..	..	..	..	..
Use of IMF credit and SDR allocations	**248**	**339**	**528**	**673**	**704**	**715**
IMF credit	146	248	432	394	438	447
SDR allocations	102	92	96	279	265	268
Short-term external debt stocks	**43**	**68**	**178**	**145**	**91**	**14**
Disbursements, long-term	**81**	**166**	**194**	**245**	**342**	**397**
Public and publicly guaranteed sector	81	166	194	245	342	397
Private sector not guaranteed	..	..	..	..	..	..
Principal repayments, long-term	**13**	**62**	**51**	**60**	**77**	**84**
Public and publicly guaranteed sector	13	62	51	60	77	84
Private sector not guaranteed	..	..	..	..	..	..
Interest payments, long-term	**7**	**17**	**21**	**22**	**24**	**26**
Public and publicly guaranteed sector	7	17	21	22	24	26
Private sector not guaranteed	..	..	..	..	..	..

MALDIVES

(US$ million, unless otherwise indicated)

Snapshot	2023
Total external debt stocks	**4,000**
External debt stocks as % of:	
Exports	81
GNI	69
Debt service as % of:	
Exports	10
GNI	9
Net financial flows, debt and equity	**771**
Net debt inflows	9
Net equity inflows	762
GNI	**5,777**
Population (thousand)	**521**

Figure 1 **Public and publicly guaranteed debt, by creditor and creditor type in 2023, including IMF credit**

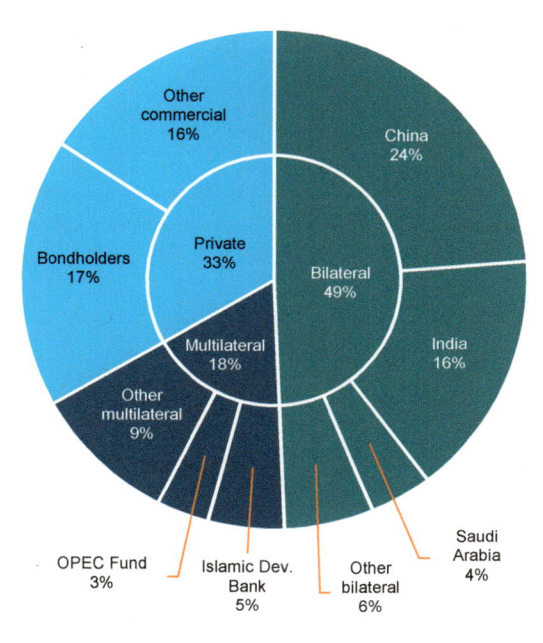

Figure 2 **Average terms on new debt commitments from official and private creditors**

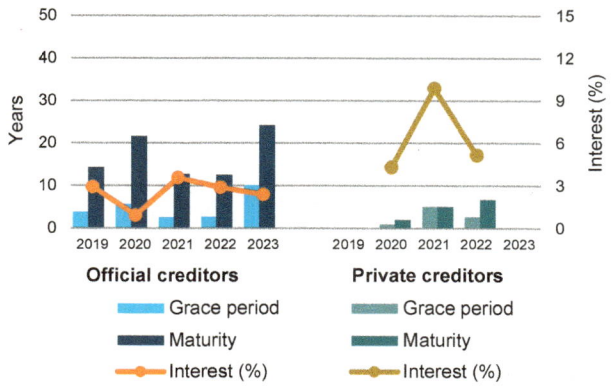

Summary External Debt Data	2010	2019	2020	2021	2022	2023
Total external debt stocks	**914**	**2,675**	**3,661**	**4,099**	**3,993**	**4,000**
Long-term external debt stocks	**743**	**2,330**	**3,211**	**3,545**	**3,476**	**3,836**
Public and publicly guaranteed debt from:	*628*	*2,227*	*2,852*	*3,134*	*3,067*	*3,418*
Official creditors	536	1,444	1,988	1,824	1,907	2,273
Multilateral	301	384	413	443	440	574
of which: World Bank	99	92	106	101	95	98
Bilateral	236	1,061	1,575	1,381	1,466	1,699
Private creditors	92	782	864	1,311	1,161	1,145
Bondholders	..	350	350	850	600	600
Commercial banks and others	92	432	514	461	561	545
Private nonguaranteed debt from:	*115*	*104*	*359*	*411*	*409*	*418*
Bondholders	..	..	..	..	..	..
Commercial banks and others	115	104	359	411	409	418
Use of IMF credit and SDR allocations	**28**	**11**	**42**	**69**	**65**	**66**
IMF credit	16	0	31	30	28	28
SDR allocations	12	11	11	39	37	38
Short-term external debt stocks	**143**	**334**	**409**	**485**	**451**	**98**
Disbursements, long-term	**168**	**612**	**1,070**	**1,037**	**501**	**663**
Public and publicly guaranteed sector	142	561	775	935	450	604
Private sector not guaranteed	26	51	295	102	51	59
Principal repayments, long-term	**60**	**364**	**231**	**706**	**524**	**301**
Public and publicly guaranteed sector	51	331	191	656	470	250
Private sector not guaranteed	9	33	40	50	53	51
Interest payments, long-term	**11**	**84**	**78**	**91**	**150**	**190**
Public and publicly guaranteed sector	9	80	74	85	134	164
Private sector not guaranteed	1	3	5	5	16	27

MALI

(US$ million, unless otherwise indicated)

Snapshot	2023
Total external debt stocks	**6,457**
External debt stocks as % of:	
Exports	104
GNI	32
Debt service as % of:	
Exports	6
GNI	2
Net financial flows, debt and equity	**845**
Net debt inflows	147
Net equity inflows	698
GNI	**19,940**
Population (million)	**23**

Figure 2 Average terms on new debt commitments from official and private creditors

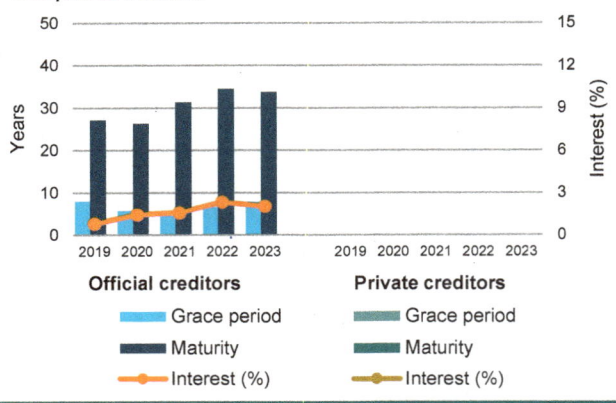

Official creditors
- Grace period
- Maturity
- Interest (%)

Private creditors
- Grace period
- Maturity
- Interest (%)

Figure 1 Public and publicly guaranteed debt, by creditor and creditor type in 2023, including IMF credit

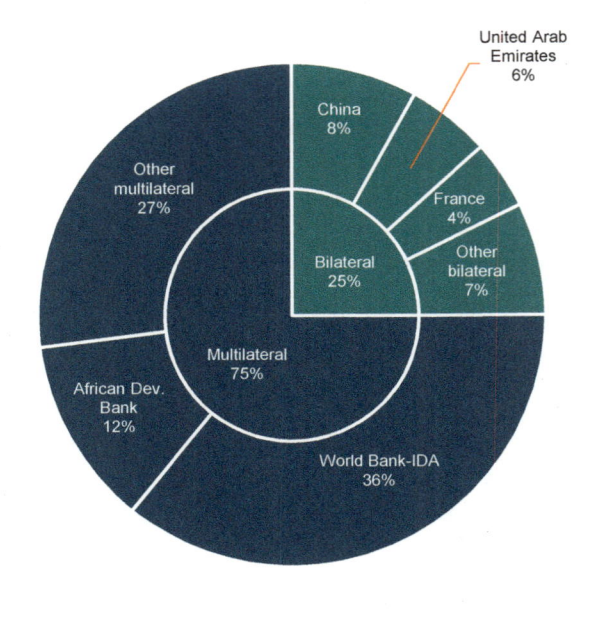

Summary External Debt Data	2010	2019	2020	2021	2022	2023
Total external debt stocks	**2,439**	**4,994**	**5,809**	**6,375**	**6,229**	**6,457**
Long-term external debt stocks	**2,246**	**4,448**	**5,056**	**5,344**	**5,297**	**5,541**
Public and publicly guaranteed debt from:	*2,246*	*4,448*	*5,056*	*5,344*	*5,297*	*5,541*
Official creditors	2,241	4,448	5,056	5,344	5,297	5,541
Multilateral	1,788	3,386	3,790	3,765	3,749	4,034
of which: World Bank	840	1,970	2,146	2,131	2,033	2,166
Bilateral	453	1,061	1,266	1,578	1,548	1,507
Private creditors	5	0	..	..	..	..
Bondholders	..	..	..	..	..	..
Commercial banks and others	5	0	..	..	..	..
Private nonguaranteed debt from:	..	..	..	..	..	..
Bondholders	..	..	..	..	..	..
Commercial banks and others	..	..	..	..	..	..
Use of IMF credit and SDR allocations	**187**	**447**	**681**	**946**	**880**	**851**
IMF credit	49	323	552	571	523	491
SDR allocations	138	124	129	375	357	360
Short-term external debt stocks	**6**	**100**	**72**	**85**	**53**	**65**
Disbursements, long-term	**310**	**607**	**555**	**707**	**424**	**411**
Public and publicly guaranteed sector	310	607	555	707	424	411
Private sector not guaranteed	..	..	..	..	..	..
Principal repayments, long-term	**47**	**158**	**196**	**211**	**224**	**240**
Public and publicly guaranteed sector	47	158	196	211	224	240
Private sector not guaranteed	..	..	..	..	..	..
Interest payments, long-term	**21**	**47**	**37**	**59**	**59**	**66**
Public and publicly guaranteed sector	21	47	37	59	59	66
Private sector not guaranteed	..	..	..	..	..	..

MAURITANIA

(US$ million, unless otherwise indicated)

Snapshot	2023
Total external debt stocks	**4,604**
External debt stocks as % of:	
Exports	119
GNI	44
Debt service as % of:	
Exports	10
GNI	4
Net financial flows, debt and equity	**886**
Net debt inflows	12
Net equity inflows	873
GNI	**10,443**
Population (million)	**5**

Figure 2 Average terms on new debt commitments from official and private creditors

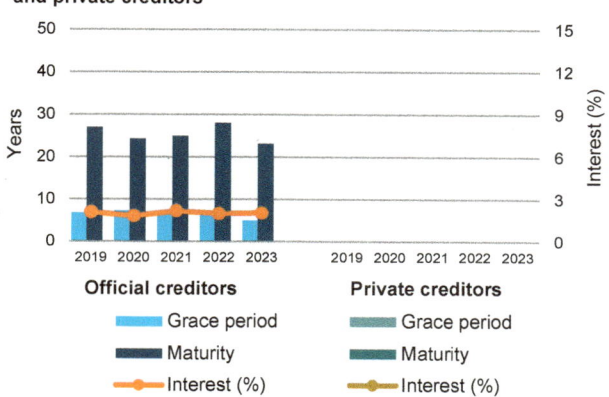

Official creditors
- Grace period
- Maturity
- Interest (%)

Private creditors
- Grace period
- Maturity
- Interest (%)

Figure 1 Public and publicly guaranteed debt, by creditor and creditor type in 2023, including IMF credit

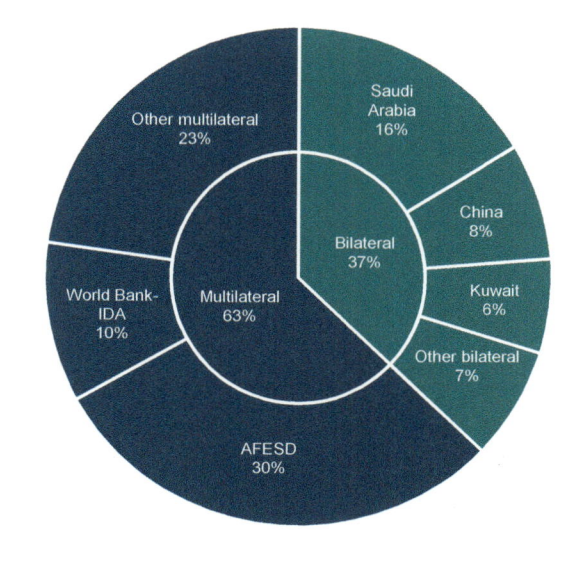

Summary External Debt Data	2010	2019	2020	2021	2022	2023
Total external debt stocks	**3,556**	**5,381**	**5,716**	**4,814**	**4,586**	**4,604**
Long-term external debt stocks	**2,326**	**4,054**	**4,216**	**4,039**	**3,823**	**3,749**
Public and publicly guaranteed debt from:	*2,326*	*4,054*	*4,216*	*4,039*	*3,823*	*3,749*
Official creditors	2,325	4,054	4,216	4,039	3,823	3,749
Multilateral	1,501	2,395	2,489	2,355	2,238	2,231
of which: World Bank	316	388	418	415	385	424
Bilateral	824	1,659	1,727	1,684	1,586	1,519
Private creditors	1	..	..	..	..	..
Bondholders	..	..	..	..	..	..
Commercial banks and others	1	..	..	..	..	..
Private nonguaranteed debt from:	..	..	..	..	..	..
Bondholders	..	..	..	..	..	..
Commercial banks and others	..	..	..	..	..	..
Use of IMF credit and SDR allocations	**145**	**244**	**424**	**594**	**556**	**596**
IMF credit	50	159	336	335	310	348
SDR allocations	95	85	89	259	246	248
Short-term external debt stocks	**1,086**	**1,083**	**1,075**	**180**	**206**	**258**
Disbursements, long-term	**412**	**383**	**223**	**130**	**135**	**202**
Public and publicly guaranteed sector	412	383	223	130	135	202
Private sector not guaranteed	..	..	..	..	..	..
Principal repayments, long-term	**77**	**265**	**212**	**335**	**260**	**277**
Public and publicly guaranteed sector	77	265	212	335	260	277
Private sector not guaranteed	..	..	..	..	..	..
Interest payments, long-term	**35**	**88**	**59**	**57**	**66**	**83**
Public and publicly guaranteed sector	35	88	59	57	66	83
Private sector not guaranteed	..	..	..	..	..	..

MAURITIUS

(US$ million, unless otherwise indicated)

Snapshot	2023
Total external debt stocks	**19,252**
External debt stocks as % of:	
Exports	139
GNI	131
Debt service as % of:	
Exports	14
GNI	13
Net financial flows, debt and equity	5,339
Net debt inflows	1,571
Net equity inflows	3,768
GNI	**14,753**
Population (million)	**1**

Figure 2 Average terms on new debt commitments from official and private creditors

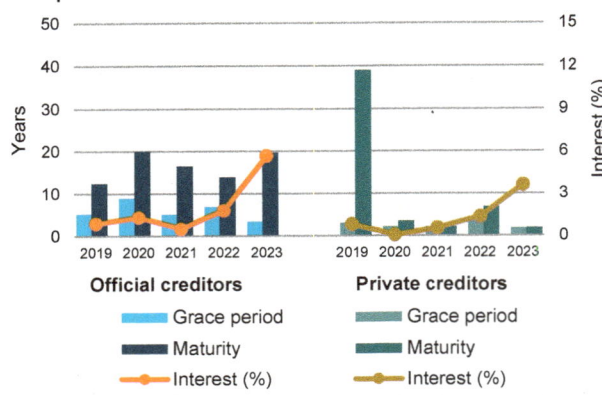

Official creditors
- Grace period
- Maturity
- Interest (%)

Private creditors
- Grace period
- Maturity
- Interest (%)

Figure 1 Public and publicly guaranteed debt, by creditor and creditor type in 2023, including IMF credit

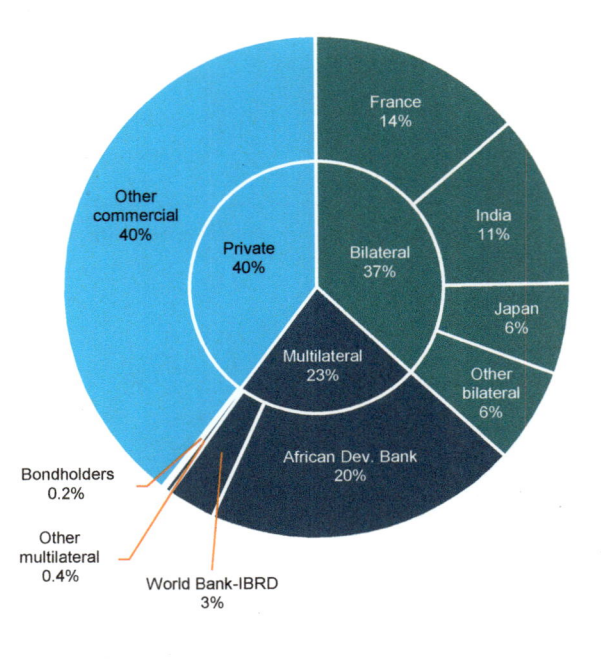

Summary External Debt Data	2010	2019	2020	2021	2022	2023
Total external debt stocks	**7,929**	**12,361**	**12,402**	**14,700**	**17,653**	**19,252**
Long-term external debt stocks	**6,294**	**6,515**	**5,996**	**6,965**	**9,004**	**9,496**
Public and publicly guaranteed debt from:	*1,007*	*1,386*	*1,917*	*2,826*	*3,350*	*3,675*
Official creditors	888	1,366	1,883	2,004	1,943	2,215
Multilateral	501	789	790	702	633	864
of which: World Bank	204	207	189	158	131	113
Bilateral	387	577	1,093	1,302	1,310	1,351
Private creditors	119	20	33	822	1,407	1,461
Bondholders	..	7	8	9	7	8
Commercial banks and others	119	13	26	814	1,400	1,452
Private nonguaranteed debt from:	*5,287*	*5,130*	*4,079*	*4,139*	*5,654*	*5,821*
Bondholders	..	468	399	381	666	1,115
Commercial banks and others	5,287	4,661	3,681	3,757	4,988	4,706
Use of IMF credit and SDR allocations	**149**	**134**	**139**	**326**	**310**	**313**
IMF credit	0	0	0	0	0	0
SDR allocations	149	134	139	326	310	313
Short-term external debt stocks	**1,485**	**5,712**	**6,267**	**7,409**	**8,339**	**9,444**
Disbursements, long-term	**2,568**	**2,794**	**1,636**	**3,164**	**2,418**	**1,978**
Public and publicly guaranteed sector	356	134	784	1,163	772	1,530
Private sector not guaranteed	2,212	2,660	851	2,001	1,646	449
Principal repayments, long-term	**2,118**	**2,499**	**2,243**	**2,390**	**278**	**1,505**
Public and publicly guaranteed sector	69	159	341	164	147	1,223
Private sector not guaranteed	2,049	2,341	1,902	2,227	131	282
Interest payments, long-term	**73**	**622**	**314**	**286**	**483**	**270**
Public and publicly guaranteed sector	17	29	27	20	38	103
Private sector not guaranteed	56	593	287	267	444	167

MEXICO

(US$ million, unless otherwise indicated)

Snapshot	2023
Total external debt stocks	**595,918**
External debt stocks as % of:	
Exports	89
GNI	34
Debt service as % of:	
Exports	8
GNI	3
Net financial flows, debt and equity	38,761
Net debt inflows	12,252
Net equity inflows	26,508
GNI	**1,744,711**
Population (million)	**128**

Figure 2 Average terms on new debt commitments from official and private creditors

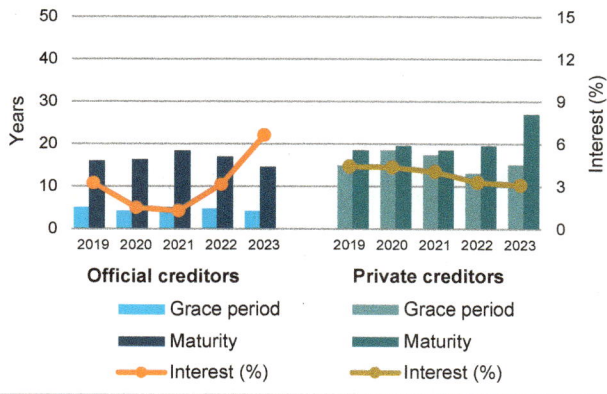

Official creditors / **Private creditors**

- Grace period (Official) / Grace period (Private)
- Maturity (Official) / Maturity (Private)
- Interest (%) (Official) / Interest (%) (Private)

Figure 1 Public and publicly guaranteed debt, by creditor and creditor type in 2023, including IMF credit

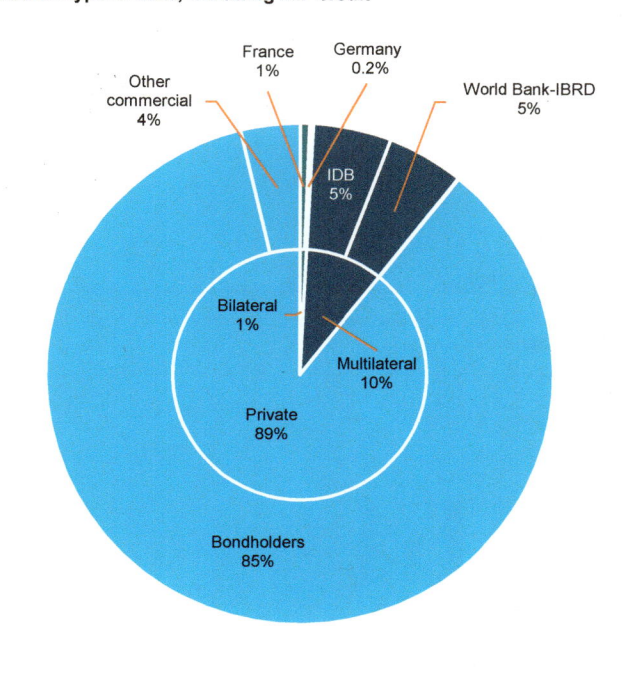

Other commercial 4% · France 1% · Germany 0.2% · World Bank-IBRD 5% · IDB 5% · Bilateral 1% · Multilateral 10% · Private 89% · Bondholders 85%

Summary External Debt Data	2010	2019	2020	2021	2022	2023
Total external debt stocks	**312,338**	**617,450**	**616,686**	**601,474**	**585,464**	**595,918**
Long-term external debt stocks	264,887	558,050	566,202	538,486	515,534	520,492
Public and publicly guaranteed debt from:	*145,925*	*307,413*	*309,061*	*290,868*	*289,397*	*301,048*
Official creditors	25,389	33,476	34,877	33,844	33,597	32,291
Multilateral	21,433	30,989	32,215	31,144	31,234	29,778
of which: World Bank	12,462	14,942	15,714	15,237	15,596	14,618
Bilateral	3,956	2,487	2,662	2,699	2,363	2,513
Private creditors	120,536	273,936	274,184	257,024	255,800	268,756
Bondholders	97,656	258,455	259,213	241,284	241,168	257,410
Commercial banks and others	22,880	15,481	14,971	15,740	14,633	11,346
Private nonguaranteed debt from:	*118,961*	*250,638*	*257,141*	*247,618*	*226,137*	*219,444*
Bondholders	32,898	96,452	102,661	95,854	75,126	71,244
Commercial banks and others	86,063	154,186	154,480	151,764	151,010	148,200
Use of IMF credit and SDR allocations	**4,391**	**3,943**	**4,106**	**15,946**	**15,163**	**15,286**
IMF credit	0	0	0	0	0	0
SDR allocations	4,391	3,943	4,106	15,946	15,163	15,286
Short-term external debt stocks	**43,061**	**55,457**	**46,378**	**47,041**	**54,767**	**60,139**
Disbursements, long-term	**62,651**	**56,168**	**57,419**	**45,700**	**34,519**	**34,743**
Public and publicly guaranteed sector	41,812	38,510	31,660	27,421	24,259	26,624
Private sector not guaranteed	20,839	17,658	25,759	18,278	10,260	8,119
Principal repayments, long-term	**21,683**	**43,237**	**47,968**	**55,814**	**35,280**	**27,863**
Public and publicly guaranteed sector	13,941	25,172	25,548	35,863	13,015	13,496
Private sector not guaranteed	7,742	18,065	22,420	19,951	22,266	14,367
Interest payments, long-term	**8,658**	**22,982**	**21,676**	**21,393**	**18,215**	**23,114**
Public and publicly guaranteed sector	5,859	17,120	16,415	16,155	11,509	13,563
Private sector not guaranteed	2,799	5,862	5,261	5,238	6,707	9,551

MOLDOVA

(US$ million, unless otherwise indicated)

Snapshot	2023
Total external debt stocks	**10,639**
External debt stocks as % of:	
Exports	153
GNI	64
Debt service as % of:	
Exports	19
GNI	8
Net financial flows, debt and equity	1,277
Net debt inflows	847
Net equity inflows	430
GNI	**16,749**
Population (million)	**2**

Figure 2 Average terms on new debt commitments from official and private creditors

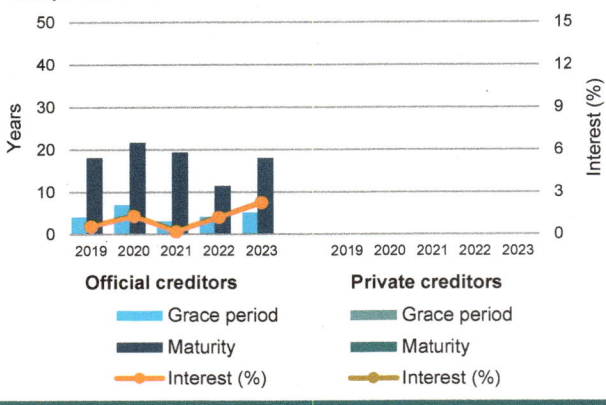

Official creditors
- Grace period
- Maturity
- Interest (%)

Private creditors
- Grace period
- Maturity
- Interest (%)

Figure 1 Public and publicly guaranteed debt, by creditor and creditor type in 2023, including IMF credit

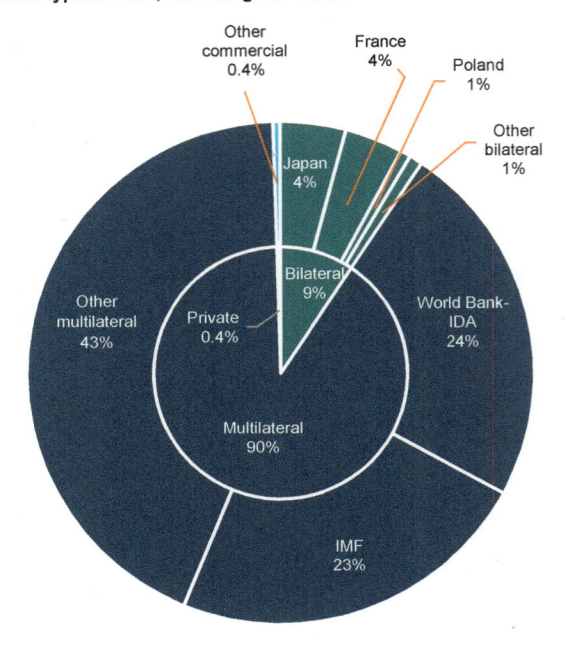

Summary External Debt Data	2010	2019	2020	2021	2022	2023
Total external debt stocks	**4,725**	**7,299**	**7,916**	**9,035**	**9,723**	**10,639**
Long-term external debt stocks	**2,745**	**5,074**	**5,251**	**5,772**	**6,268**	**6,638**
Public and publicly guaranteed debt from:	*839*	*1,464*	*1,761*	*1,819*	*2,260*	*2,630*
Official creditors	816	1,440	1,736	1,799	2,244	2,615
Multilateral	565	1,226	1,574	1,700	2,058	2,293
of which: World Bank	479	716	792	813	928	1,067
Bilateral	251	214	163	99	186	322
Private creditors	23	24	24	20	16	14
Bondholders	..	..	..	..	..	..
Commercial banks and others	23	24	24	20	16	14
Private nonguaranteed debt from:	*1,906*	*3,610*	*3,490*	*3,953*	*4,008*	*4,008*
Bondholders	..	..	..	500	500	500
Commercial banks and others	1,906	3,610	3,490	3,453	3,508	3,508
Use of IMF credit and SDR allocations	**509**	**458**	**669**	**912**	**1,008**	**1,178**
IMF credit	327	295	499	516	631	798
SDR allocations	181	163	170	396	377	380
Short-term external debt stocks	**1,471**	**1,768**	**1,996**	**2,350**	**2,448**	**2,823**
Disbursements, long-term	**464**	**549**	**815**	**1,190**	**1,012**	**1,209**
Public and publicly guaranteed sector	94	130	312	304	640	773
Private sector not guaranteed	370	419	503	886	372	436
Principal repayments, long-term	**306**	**427**	**544**	**508**	**430**	**898**
Public and publicly guaranteed sector	55	101	122	140	113	462
Private sector not guaranteed	251	325	422	368	317	436
Interest payments, long-term	**49**	**63**	**65**	**110**	**109**	**162**
Public and publicly guaranteed sector	16	23	20	21	23	51
Private sector not guaranteed	33	40	45	89	86	111

MONGOLIA

(US$ million, unless otherwise indicated)

Snapshot	2023
Total external debt stocks	**34,321**
External debt stocks as % of:	
Exports	215
GNI	191
Debt service as % of:	
Exports	30
GNI	27
Net financial flows, debt and equity	1,577
Net debt inflows	1,246
Net equity inflows	331
GNI	**17,983**
Population (million)	**3**

Figure 2 Average terms on new debt commitments from official and private creditors

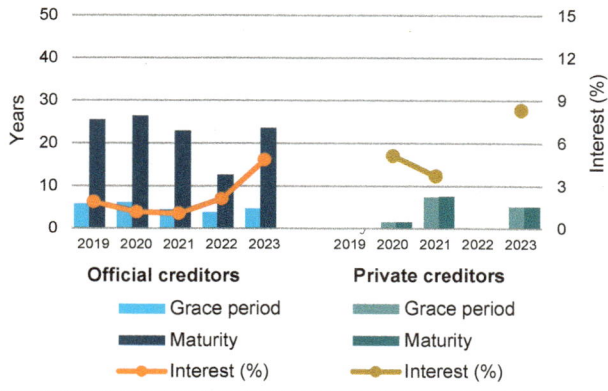

Official creditors
- Grace period
- Maturity
- Interest (%)

Private creditors
- Grace period
- Maturity
- Interest (%)

Figure 1 Public and publicly guaranteed debt, by creditor and creditor type in 2023, including IMF credit

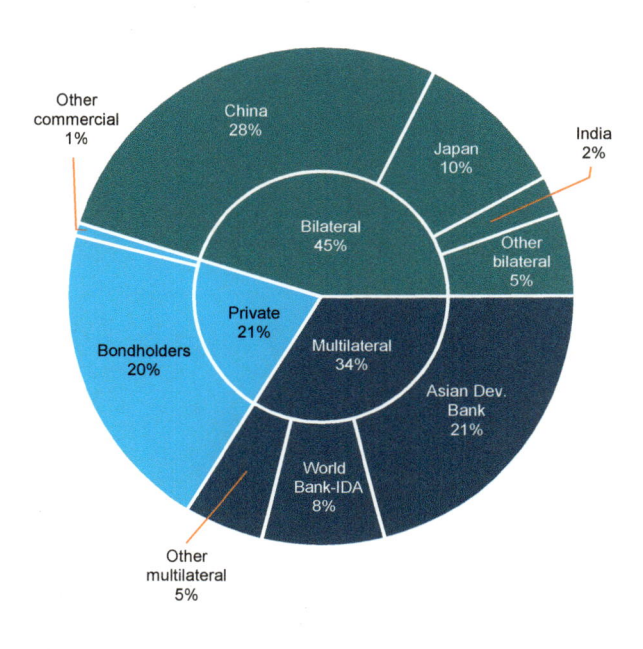

Summary External Debt Data	2010	2019	2020	2021	2022	2023
Total external debt stocks	**5,928**	**33,307**	**32,635**	**34,713**	**33,451**	**34,321**
Long-term external debt stocks	**5,290**	**30,133**	**30,953**	**32,813**	**31,098**	**32,028**
Public and publicly guaranteed debt from:	*1,782*	*10,085*	*11,086*	*11,524*	*9,802*	*9,730*
Official creditors	1,776	6,524	7,588	7,783	7,655	7,651
Multilateral	1,073	2,099	2,692	2,875	3,010	3,154
of which: World Bank	403	579	760	809	798	816
Bilateral	703	4,425	4,897	4,908	4,645	4,497
Private creditors	7	3,562	3,498	3,741	2,147	2,079
Bondholders	0	3,400	3,432	3,637	2,100	2,000
Commercial banks and others	7	162	66	104	47	79
Private nonguaranteed debt from:	*3,508*	*20,048*	*19,866*	*21,288*	*21,296*	*22,298*
Bondholders	..	2,226	1,696	1,774	1,217	550
Commercial banks and others	3,508	17,822	18,171	19,515	20,079	21,749
Use of IMF credit and SDR allocations	**273**	**285**	**401**	**483**	**436**	**380**
IMF credit	198	217	331	318	279	221
SDR allocations	75	67	70	165	157	158
Short-term external debt stocks	**365**	**2,889**	**1,281**	**1,417**	**1,917**	**1,913**
Disbursements, long-term	**2,929**	**12,888**	**3,480**	**4,194**	**3,483**	**5,084**
Public and publicly guaranteed sector	67	521	1,670	1,568	460	1,619
Private sector not guaranteed	2,863	12,367	1,810	2,625	3,024	3,466
Principal repayments, long-term	**139**	**10,646**	**2,176**	**2,256**	**3,370**	**3,775**
Public and publicly guaranteed sector	121	171	817	1,053	1,779	1,602
Private sector not guaranteed	18	10,474	1,359	1,204	1,591	2,173
Interest payments, long-term	**89**	**504**	**464**	**375**	**489**	**872**
Public and publicly guaranteed sector	20	309	320	270	358	309
Private sector not guaranteed	70	196	145	105	131	562

MONTENEGRO

(US$ million, unless otherwise indicated)

Snapshot	2023
Total external debt stocks	**8,616**
External debt stocks as % of:	
Exports	204
GNI	115
Debt service as % of:	
Exports	19
GNI	10
Net financial flows, debt and equity	**188**
Net debt inflows	-234
Net equity inflows	422
GNI	**7,477**
Population (thousand)	**616**

Figure 1 Public and publicly guaranteed debt, by creditor and creditor type in 2023, including IMF credit

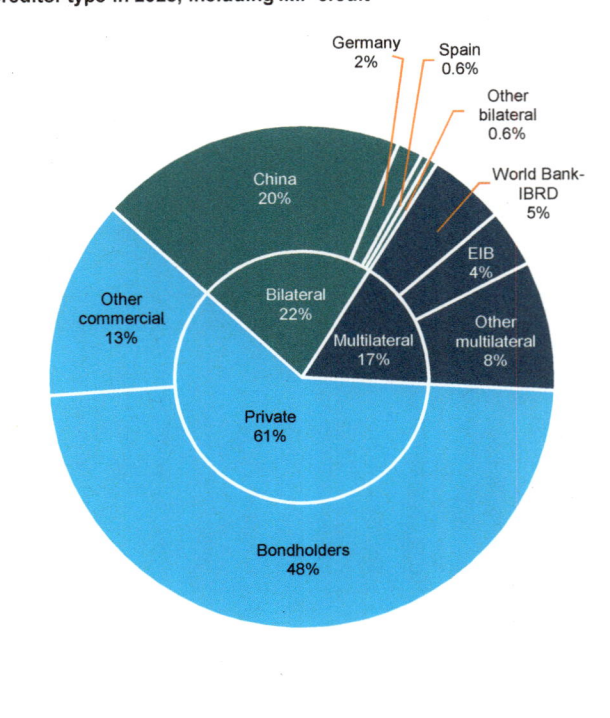

Figure 2 Average terms on new debt commitments from official and private creditors

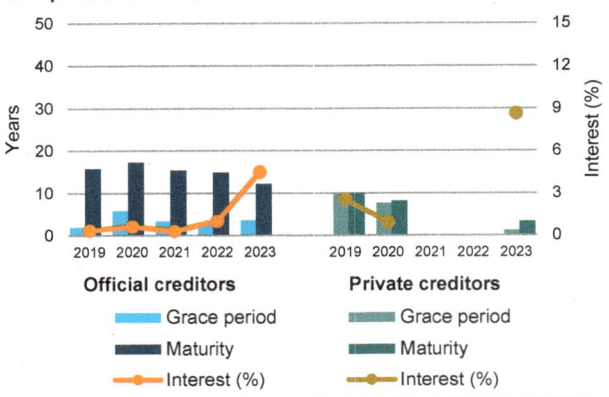

Summary External Debt Data	2010	2019	2020	2021	2022	2023
Total external debt stocks	**4,503**	**8,448**	**10,369**	**9,442**	**8,736**	**8,616**
Long-term external debt stocks	**4,277**	**8,135**	**9,834**	**9,024**	**8,331**	**8,269**
Public and publicly guaranteed debt from:	1,349	3,709	4,826	4,294	3,940	3,966
Official creditors	*818*	*1,534*	*1,658*	*1,658*	*1,597*	*1,519*
Multilateral	546	539	637	650	613	619
of which: World Bank	306	243	252	232	208	204
Bilateral	271	995	1,021	1,008	984	900
Private creditors	531	2,175	3,168	2,636	2,344	2,447
Bondholders	267	1,740	2,427	1,982	1,867	1,934
Commercial banks and others	264	435	741	654	477	514
Private nonguaranteed debt from:	*2,928*	*4,427*	*5,008*	*4,730*	*4,391*	*4,303*
Bondholders	..	..	..	..	..	..
Commercial banks and others	2,928	4,427	5,008	4,730	4,391	4,303
Use of IMF credit and SDR allocations	**40**	**36**	**124**	**202**	**192**	**173**
IMF credit	0	0	87	85	81	61
SDR allocations	40	36	37	117	112	112
Short-term external debt stocks	**186**	**277**	**411**	**216**	**212**	**174**
Disbursements, long-term	**676**	**816**	**1,893**	**222**	**160**	**177**
Public and publicly guaranteed sector	383	787	1,313	213	150	175
Private sector not guaranteed	293	29	580	9	10	3
Principal repayments, long-term	**59**	**454**	**530**	**728**	**646**	**352**
Public and publicly guaranteed sector	59	443	517	452	304	259
Private sector not guaranteed	..	11	13	275	342	93
Interest payments, long-term	**33**	**232**	**171**	**166**	**298**	**391**
Public and publicly guaranteed sector	33	105	108	108	97	121
Private sector not guaranteed	..	127	62	58	200	270

MOROCCO

(US$ million, unless otherwise indicated)

Snapshot	2023
Total external debt stocks	**69,267**
External debt stocks as % of:	
Exports	110
GNI	50
Debt service as % of:	
Exports	9
GNI	4
Net financial flows, debt and equity	**3,921**
Net debt inflows	2,932
Net equity inflows	989
GNI	**138,990**
Population (million)	**38**

Figure 2 Average terms on new debt commitments from official and private creditors

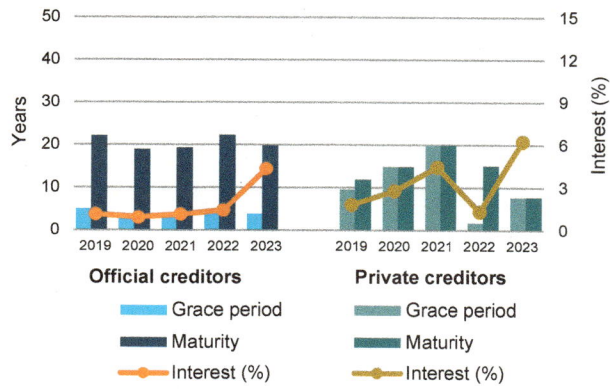

Figure 1 Public and publicly guaranteed debt, by creditor and creditor type in 2023, including IMF credit

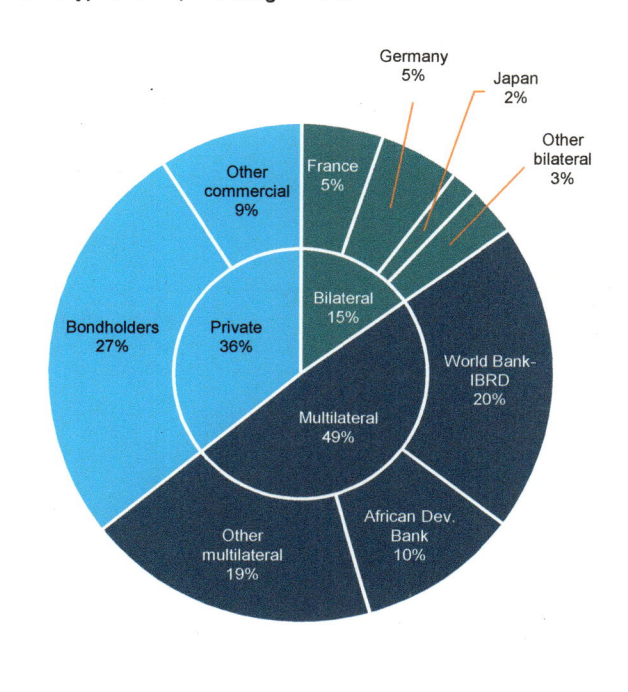

Summary External Debt Data	2010	2019	2020	2021	2022	2023
Total external debt stocks	**27,348**	**55,279**	**66,010**	**65,687**	**64,972**	**69,267**
Long-term external debt stocks	**23,736**	**45,808**	**53,957**	**52,524**	**51,137**	**55,331**
Public and publicly guaranteed debt from:	*21,148*	*36,772*	*43,949*	*42,422*	*41,286*	*45,117*
Official creditors	17,296	23,898	27,404	26,167	27,020	28,260
Multilateral	10,186	16,792	19,816	19,204	19,965	21,093
of which: World Bank	2,518	6,414	7,886	8,118	8,669	9,423
Bilateral	7,110	7,107	7,588	6,963	7,056	7,167
Private creditors	3,852	12,873	16,545	16,255	14,265	16,857
Bondholders	1,336	7,590	10,912	11,602	9,897	12,516
Commercial banks and others	2,515	5,283	5,633	4,653	4,368	4,341
Private nonguaranteed debt from:	*2,589*	*9,036*	*10,008*	*10,102*	*9,851*	*10,214*
Bondholders	..	..	..	..	..	..
Commercial banks and others	2,589	9,036	10,008	10,102	9,851	10,214
Use of IMF credit and SDR allocations	**865**	**776**	**3,906**	**4,085**	**3,884**	**3,916**
IMF credit	0	0	3,098	2,099	1,996	2,012
SDR allocations	865	776	809	1,986	1,888	1,903
Short-term external debt stocks	**2,747**	**8,695**	**8,146**	**9,079**	**9,951**	**10,021**
Disbursements, long-term	**4,999**	**6,767**	**9,315**	**5,401**	**4,550**	**6,430**
Public and publicly guaranteed sector	3,882	5,513	8,197	4,241	4,144	5,195
Private sector not guaranteed	1,116	1,253	1,117	1,160	407	1,235
Principal repayments, long-term	**2,430**	**3,006**	**4,062**	**4,323**	**4,395**	**3,569**
Public and publicly guaranteed sector	1,276	2,127	3,386	3,533	3,710	2,240
Private sector not guaranteed	1,154	880	677	790	686	1,328
Interest payments, long-term	**851**	**1,065**	**1,045**	**1,161**	**1,102**	**1,421**
Public and publicly guaranteed sector	820	959	939	1,020	1,003	1,308
Private sector not guaranteed	31	106	106	141	99	113

MOZAMBIQUE

(US$ million, unless otherwise indicated)

Snapshot	2023
Total external debt stocks	**66,848**
External debt stocks as % of:	
Exports	695
GNI	356
Debt service as % of:	
Exports	45
GNI	23
Net financial flows, debt and equity	2,860
Net debt inflows	2,653
Net equity inflows	208
GNI	**18,787**
Population (million)	**34**

Figure 1 Public and publicly guaranteed debt, by creditor and creditor type in 2023, including IMF credit

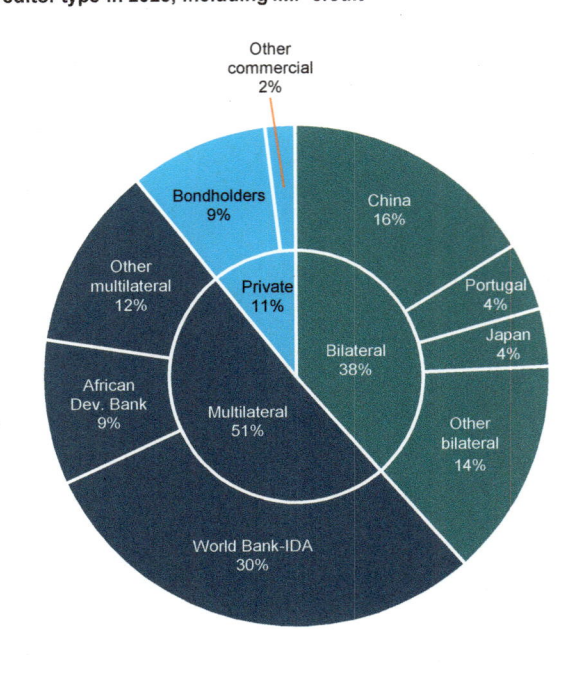

Figure 2 Average terms on new debt commitments from official and private creditors

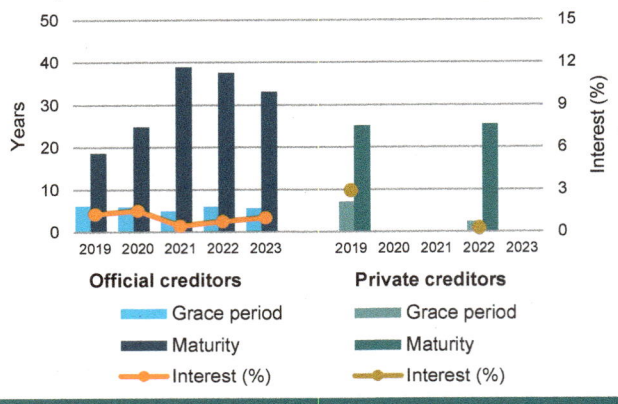

Summary External Debt Data	2010	2019	2020	2021	2022	2023
Total external debt stocks	**11,231**	**54,212**	**58,664**	**62,668**	**64,384**	**66,848**
Long-term external debt stocks	**10,263**	**52,288**	**56,238**	**59,861**	**62,572**	**64,843**
Public and publicly guaranteed debt from:	*3,263*	*10,384*	*10,511*	*10,240*	*9,676*	*9,524*
Official creditors	3,167	8,616	8,949	8,803	8,361	8,432
Multilateral	2,262	4,455	4,746	4,678	4,486	4,525
of which: World Bank	1,491	3,039	3,224	3,147	2,984	3,010
Bilateral	905	4,161	4,202	4,125	3,875	3,907
Private creditors	96	1,769	1,562	1,437	1,316	1,092
Bondholders	..	900	900	900	900	900
Commercial banks and others	96	869	662	537	416	192
Private nonguaranteed debt from:	*7,001*	*41,903*	*45,727*	*49,621*	*52,896*	*55,319*
Bondholders	..	..	..	..	..	..
Commercial banks and others	7,001	41,903	45,727	49,621	52,896	55,319
Use of IMF credit and SDR allocations	**357**	**375**	**689**	**947**	**1,027**	**1,071**
IMF credit	190	225	532	490	592	633
SDR allocations	168	151	157	457	435	438
Short-term external debt stocks	**610**	**1,549**	**1,738**	**1,860**	**785**	**934**
Disbursements, long-term	**3,810**	**4,364**	**4,096**	**10,075**	**6,522**	**3,257**
Public and publicly guaranteed sector	419	503	273	337	274	627
Private sector not guaranteed	3,391	3,861	3,824	9,738	6,248	2,630
Principal repayments, long-term	**39**	**480**	**473**	**6,263**	**3,437**	**651**
Public and publicly guaranteed sector	39	480	473	419	464	444
Private sector not guaranteed	..	..	..	5,844	2,973	206
Interest payments, long-term	**149**	**1,359**	**733**	**798**	**2,305**	**3,647**
Public and publicly guaranteed sector	47	138	158	133	158	137
Private sector not guaranteed	102	1,220	575	665	2,147	3,510

MYANMAR

(US$ million, unless otherwise indicated)

Snapshot	2023
Total external debt stocks	**12,162**
External debt stocks as % of:	
Exports	90
GNI	19
Debt service as % of:	
Exports	7
GNI	1
Net financial flows, debt and equity	**1,489**
Net debt inflows	-197
Net equity inflows	1,686
GNI	**63,664**
Population (million)	**55**

Figure 1 Public and publicly guaranteed debt, by creditor and creditor type in 2023, including IMF credit

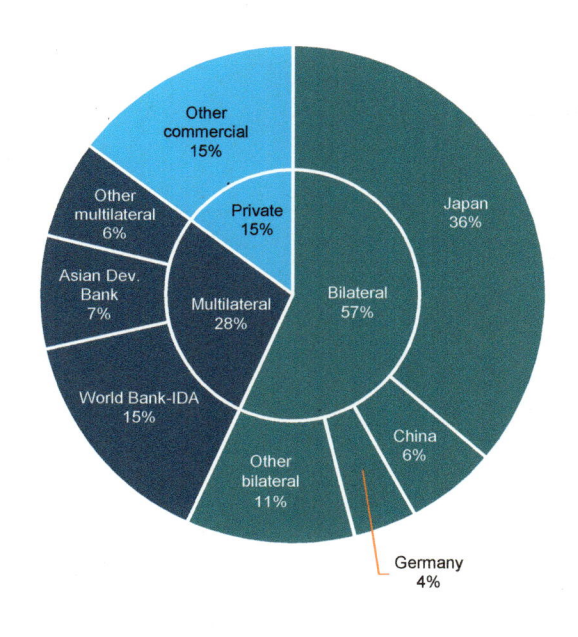

Figure 2 Average terms on new debt commitments from official and private creditors

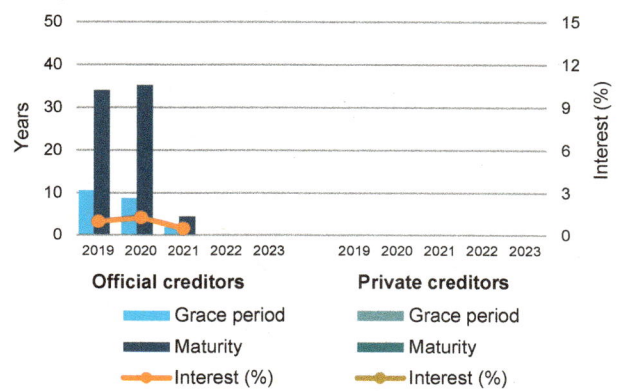

Official creditors
- Grace period
- Maturity
- Interest (%)

Private creditors
- Grace period
- Maturity
- Interest (%)

Summary External Debt Data	2010	2019	2020	2021	2022	2023
Total external debt stocks	**9,990**	**11,182**	**13,407**	**13,759**	**12,538**	**12,162**
Long-term external debt stocks	**8,433**	**10,776**	**12,613**	**11,966**	**10,832**	**10,488**
Public and publicly guaranteed debt from:	*8,433*	*10,748*	*12,578*	*11,805*	*10,458*	*10,036*
Official creditors	7,482	8,369	10,149	9,678	8,702	8,452
Multilateral	1,447	2,086	2,637	2,684	2,493	2,387
of which: World Bank	799	1,468	1,804	1,769	1,641	1,566
Bilateral	6,035	6,283	7,512	6,994	6,209	6,064
Private creditors	952	2,380	2,429	2,127	1,755	1,585
Bondholders	..	..	..	..	..	..
Commercial banks and others	952	2,380	2,429	2,127	1,755	1,585
Private nonguaranteed debt from:	*..*	*28*	*35*	*162*	*374*	*452*
Bondholders	..	..	..	..	..	..
Commercial banks and others	..	28	35	162	374	452
Use of IMF credit and SDR allocations	**378**	**340**	**726**	**1,761**	**1,674**	**1,630**
IMF credit	0	0	372	723	688	636
SDR allocations	378	340	354	1,037	986	994
Short-term external debt stocks	**1,179**	**66**	**68**	**32**	**32**	**44**
Disbursements, long-term	**714**	**1,042**	**1,675**	**697**	**533**	**502**
Public and publicly guaranteed sector	714	977	1,594	499	311	409
Private sector not guaranteed	..	65	81	199	222	93
Principal repayments, long-term	**201**	**506**	**488**	**721**	**753**	**642**
Public and publicly guaranteed sector	201	454	414	637	744	626
Private sector not guaranteed	..	51	74	84	10	16
Interest payments, long-term	**40**	**187**	**112**	**157**	**172**	**154**
Public and publicly guaranteed sector	40	176	98	150	156	140
Private sector not guaranteed	..	10	15	7	15	14

NEPAL

(US$ million, unless otherwise indicated)

Snapshot	2023
Total external debt stocks	**9,968**
External debt stocks as % of:	
Exports	255
GNI	24
Debt service as % of:	
Exports	12
GNI	1
Net financial flows, debt and equity	832
Net debt inflows	758
Net equity inflows	74
GNI	**41,385**
Population (million)	**31**

Figure 1 Public and publicly guaranteed debt, by creditor and creditor type in 2023, including IMF credit

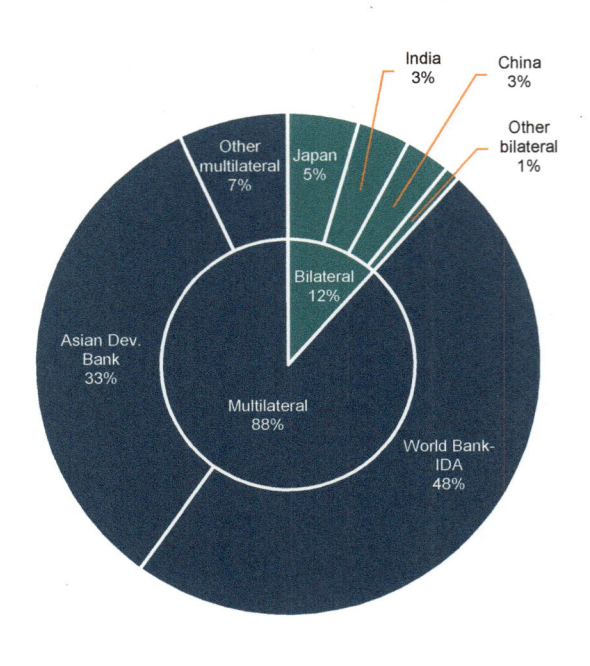

Figure 2 Average terms on new debt commitments from official and private creditors

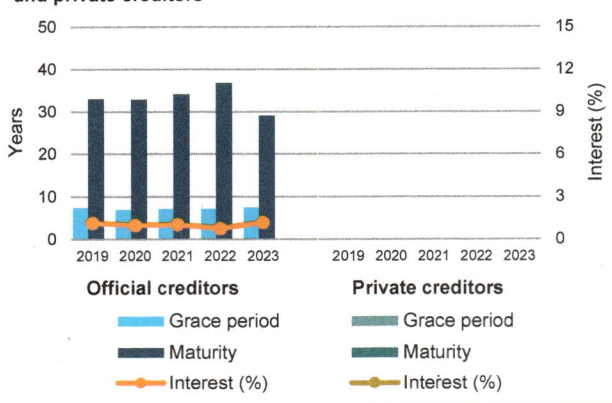

Summary External Debt Data	2010	2019	2020	2021	2022	2023
Total external debt stocks	**3,787**	**6,516**	**7,906**	**8,821**	**9,184**	**9,968**
Long-term external debt stocks	**3,507**	**5,966**	**7,175**	**7,926**	**8,229**	**8,818**
Public and publicly guaranteed debt from:	*3,507*	*5,847*	*7,057*	*7,759*	*7,958*	*8,620*
Official creditors	3,504	5,847	7,056	7,758	7,958	8,619
Multilateral	3,130	5,083	6,157	6,758	6,981	7,556
of which: World Bank	1,426	2,877	3,469	3,966	4,155	4,367
Bilateral	374	765	899	1,001	976	1,063
Private creditors	3	0	1	1	1	1
Bondholders	..	..	..	..	..	..
Commercial banks and others	3	0	1	1	1	1
Private nonguaranteed debt from:	..	*118*	*118*	*166*	*271*	*198*
Bondholders	..	..	..	..	..	..
Commercial banks and others	..	118	118	166	271	198
Use of IMF credit and SDR allocations	**219**	**147**	**370**	**560**	**633**	**733**
IMF credit	114	53	272	255	342	440
SDR allocations	105	94	98	306	291	293
Short-term external debt stocks	**61**	**403**	**361**	**335**	**322**	**418**
Disbursements, long-term	**126**	**1,098**	**1,158**	**1,170**	**940**	**916**
Public and publicly guaranteed sector	126	1,098	1,158	1,122	835	916
Private sector not guaranteed	..	..	..	48	105	..
Principal repayments, long-term	**148**	**205**	**205**	**213**	**243**	**349**
Public and publicly guaranteed sector	148	194	205	213	243	276
Private sector not guaranteed	..	11	..	..	..	73
Interest payments, long-term	**32**	**57**	**59**	**66**	**74**	**84**
Public and publicly guaranteed sector	32	52	54	63	65	74
Private sector not guaranteed	..	6	6	2	9	10

NICARAGUA

(US$ million, unless otherwise indicated)

Snapshot	2023
Total external debt stocks	**15,163**
External debt stocks as % of:	
Exports	177
GNI	90
Debt service as % of:	
Exports	27
GNI	14
Net financial flows, debt and equity	1,194
Net debt inflows	208
Net equity inflows	986
GNI	**16,935**
Population (million)	**7**

Figure 2 Average terms on new debt commitments from official and private creditors

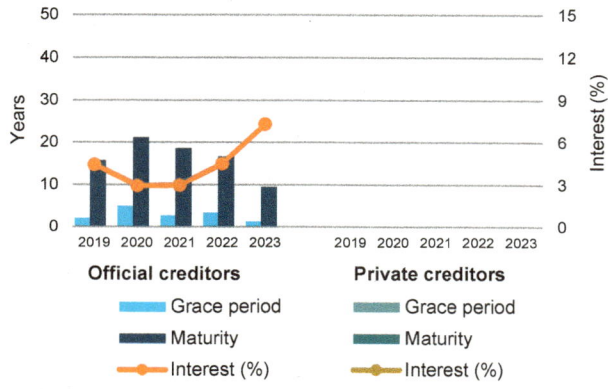

Official creditors
- Grace period
- Maturity
- Interest (%)

Private creditors
- Grace period
- Maturity
- Interest (%)

Figure 1 Public and publicly guaranteed debt, by creditor and creditor type in 2023, including IMF credit

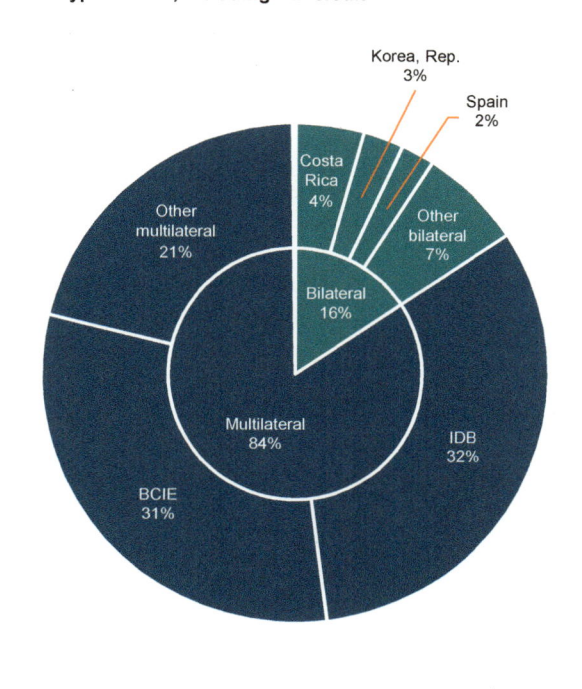

Summary External Debt Data	2010	2019	2020	2021	2022	2023
Total external debt stocks	**7,017**	**13,610**	**13,760**	**14,583**	**14,898**	**15,163**
Long-term external debt stocks	**5,256**	**12,224**	**12,350**	**12,798**	**13,084**	**13,458**
Public and publicly guaranteed debt from:	*2,704*	*5,428*	*5,903*	*6,407*	*6,719*	*7,081*
Official creditors	2,694	5,402	5,879	6,386	6,701	7,065
Multilateral	1,661	4,215	4,653	5,193	5,550	5,929
of which: World Bank	447	692	771	872	886	915
Bilateral	1,033	1,187	1,225	1,193	1,151	1,137
Private creditors	11	26	25	21	18	16
Bondholders	..	..	..	..	..	..
Commercial banks and others	11	26	25	21	18	16
Private nonguaranteed debt from:	*2,552*	*6,796*	*6,446*	*6,391*	*6,365*	*6,376*
Bondholders	..	..	..	..	..	..
Commercial banks and others	2,552	6,796	6,446	6,391	6,365	6,376
Use of IMF credit and SDR allocations	**359**	**181**	**369**	**705**	**670**	**676**
IMF credit	167	9	190	182	173	174
SDR allocations	192	172	179	523	497	501
Short-term external debt stocks	**1,402**	**1,205**	**1,042**	**1,080**	**1,143**	**1,030**
Disbursements, long-term	**1,181**	**2,206**	**1,482**	**2,220**	**2,501**	**2,342**
Public and publicly guaranteed sector	267	509	652	811	660	717
Private sector not guaranteed	914	1,697	830	1,409	1,841	1,625
Principal repayments, long-term	**459**	**1,430**	**1,491**	**1,634**	**2,179**	**1,977**
Public and publicly guaranteed sector	56	176	230	257	295	360
Private sector not guaranteed	403	1,254	1,261	1,377	1,884	1,617
Interest payments, long-term	**103**	**322**	**289**	**197**	**234**	**328**
Public and publicly guaranteed sector	34	119	117	112	133	225
Private sector not guaranteed	70	203	171	85	101	103

NIGER

(US$ million, unless otherwise indicated)

Snapshot	2023
Total external debt stocks	**5,613**
External debt stocks as % of:	
Exports	455
GNI	35
Debt service as % of:	
Exports	16
GNI	1
Net financial flows, debt and equity	1,006
Net debt inflows	40
Net equity inflows	966
GNI	**16,182**
Population (million)	**27**

Figure 1 Public and publicly guaranteed debt, by creditor and creditor type in 2023, including IMF credit

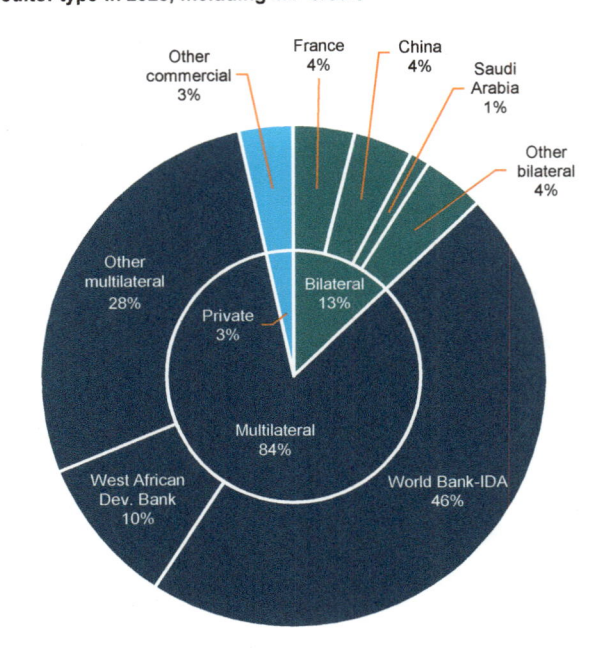

Figure 2 Average terms on new debt commitments from official and private creditors

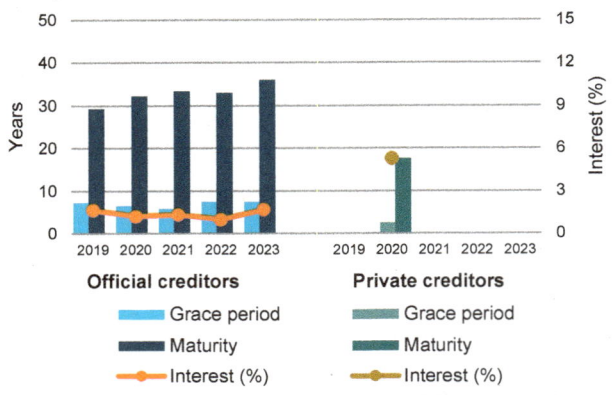

Summary External Debt Data	2010	2019	2020	2021	2022	2023
Total external debt stocks	**1,534**	**3,584**	**4,549**	**4,967**	**5,429**	**5,613**
Long-term external debt stocks	**1,206**	**3,154**	**4,003**	**4,238**	**4,649**	**4,834**
Public and publicly guaranteed debt from:	*1,206*	*3,154*	*4,003*	*4,238*	*4,649*	*4,834*
Official creditors	1,205	3,154	3,784	4,035	4,466	4,652
Multilateral	664	2,451	3,057	3,314	3,765	3,963
of which: World Bank	275	1,347	1,694	1,863	2,310	2,461
Bilateral	541	703	726	721	701	690
Private creditors	1	..	219	202	183	182
Bondholders	..	..	..	..	..	..
Commercial banks and others	1	..	219	202	183	182
Private nonguaranteed debt from:	*0*	*..*	*..*	*..*	*..*	*..*
Bondholders	..	..	..	..	..	..
Commercial banks and others	0	..	..	..	..	..
Use of IMF credit and SDR allocations	**158**	**346**	**498**	**687**	**737**	**736**
IMF credit	61	259	407	423	486	482
SDR allocations	97	87	91	265	252	254
Short-term external debt stocks	**170**	**84**	**48**	**42**	**43**	**43**
Disbursements, long-term	**279**	**423**	**743**	**563**	**818**	**184**
Public and publicly guaranteed sector	279	423	743	563	818	184
Private sector not guaranteed	..	..	..	..	..	..
Principal repayments, long-term	**16**	**95**	**124**	**133**	**193**	**112**
Public and publicly guaranteed sector	9	95	124	133	193	112
Private sector not guaranteed	7	..	..	..	..	..
Interest payments, long-term	**8**	**35**	**50**	**64**	**65**	**36**
Public and publicly guaranteed sector	8	35	50	64	65	36
Private sector not guaranteed	0	..	..	..	..	..

NIGERIA

(US$ million, unless otherwise indicated)

Snapshot	2023
Total external debt stocks	**102,482**
External debt stocks as % of:	
Exports	163
GNI	29
Debt service as % of:	
Exports	15
GNI	3
Net financial flows, debt and equity	2,508
Net debt inflows	-773
Net equity inflows	3,281
GNI	**355,833**
Population (million)	**224**

Figure 2 Average terms on new debt commitments from official and private creditors

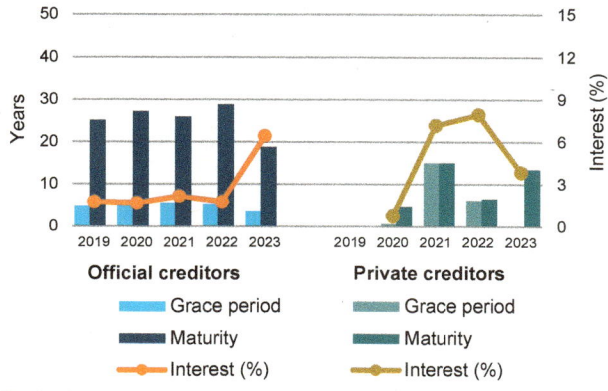

Figure 1 Public and publicly guaranteed debt, by creditor and creditor type in 2023, including IMF credit

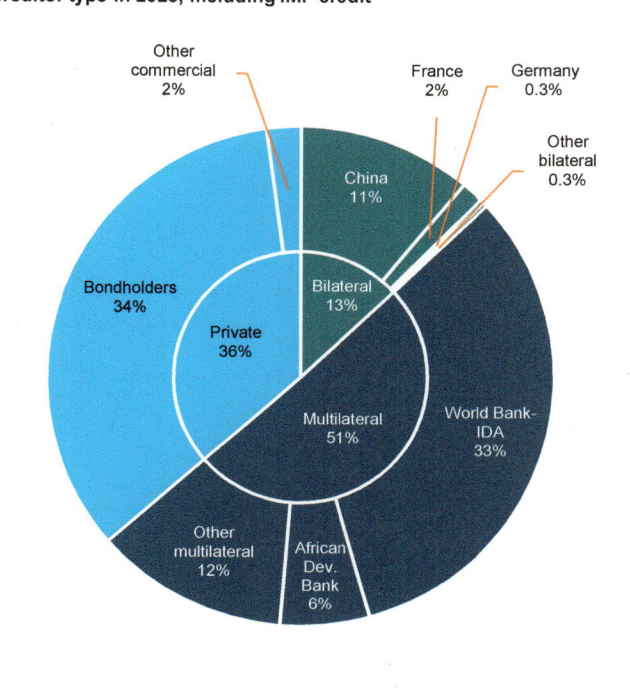

Summary External Debt Data	2010	2019	2020	2021	2022	2023
Total external debt stocks	**29,149**	**81,375**	**87,647**	**96,310**	**103,100**	**102,482**
Long-term external debt stocks	**17,128**	**58,200**	**63,275**	**68,663**	**72,988**	**75,667**
Public and publicly guaranteed debt from:	*4,686*	*27,612*	*32,113*	*36,205*	*40,034*	*44,074*
Official creditors	4,686	16,443	18,573	19,775	22,191	27,167
Multilateral	4,304	12,565	14,328	15,261	17,022	21,087
of which: World Bank	3,705	9,959	11,415	12,310	13,996	15,611
Bilateral	381	3,878	4,246	4,514	5,169	6,080
Private creditors	0	11,168	13,540	16,430	17,843	16,907
Bondholders	..	11,168	11,168	14,668	16,365	15,892
Commercial banks and others	..	..	2,371	1,762	1,478	1,015
Private nonguaranteed debt from:	*12,443*	*30,588*	*31,162*	*32,458*	*32,954*	*31,594*
Bondholders	..	6,367	5,817	5,900	4,550	4,200
Commercial banks and others	12,443	24,221	25,345	26,558	28,404	27,394
Use of IMF credit and SDR allocations	**2,580**	**2,317**	**5,948**	**9,073**	**8,627**	**7,874**
IMF credit	0	0	3,535	3,435	3,267	2,470
SDR allocations	2,580	2,317	2,413	5,637	5,361	5,404
Short-term external debt stocks	**9,441**	**20,858**	**18,424**	**18,574**	**21,485**	**18,940**
Disbursements, long-term	**3,370**	**9,212**	**7,776**	**11,708**	**10,067**	**7,190**
Public and publicly guaranteed sector	1,051	2,695	4,402	6,093	5,953	5,612
Private sector not guaranteed	2,319	6,517	3,373	5,615	4,114	1,577
Principal repayments, long-term	**248**	**4,260**	**3,250**	**5,846**	**5,049**	**4,590**
Public and publicly guaranteed sector	248	295	451	1,527	1,430	1,789
Private sector not guaranteed	..	3,965	2,799	4,319	3,618	2,801
Interest payments, long-term	**212**	**2,095**	**1,949**	**1,862**	**2,350**	**3,050**
Public and publicly guaranteed sector	59	1,096	1,115	1,118	1,485	1,788
Private sector not guaranteed	152	999	834	743	865	1,263

NORTH MACEDONIA

(US$ million, unless otherwise indicated)

Snapshot	2023
Total external debt stocks	**12,614**
External debt stocks as % of:	
Exports	115
GNI	90
Debt service as % of:	
Exports	16
GNI	12
Net financial flows, debt and equity	1,141
Net debt inflows	657
Net equity inflows	485
GNI	**13,952**
Population (million)	**2**

Figure 1 Public and publicly guaranteed debt, by creditor and creditor type in 2023, including IMF credit

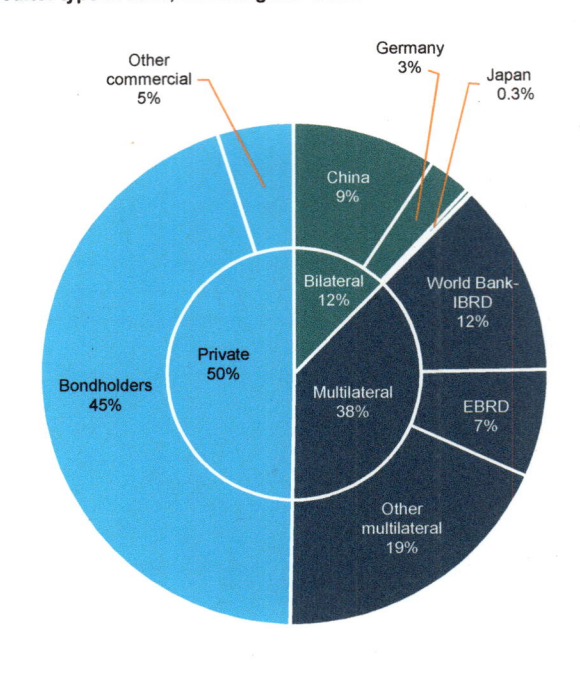

Figure 2 Average terms on new debt commitments from official and private creditors

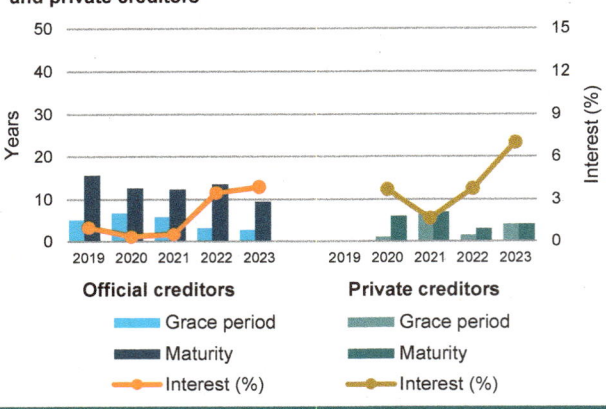

Summary External Debt Data	2010	2019	2020	2021	2022	2023
Total external debt stocks	**5,117**	**8,884**	**10,177**	**10,871**	**11,640**	**12,614**
Long-term external debt stocks	**3,798**	**6,302**	**7,752**	**7,955**	**7,962**	**8,934**
Public and publicly guaranteed debt from:	*1,880*	*4,163*	*5,102*	*5,092*	*5,096*	*5,655*
Official creditors	1,369	2,051	2,390	2,391	2,309	2,717
Multilateral	1,127	1,387	1,735	1,770	1,692	1,986
of which: World Bank	681	732	856	799	761	875
Bilateral	242	665	655	621	617	731
Private creditors	512	2,112	2,712	2,701	2,787	2,938
Bondholders	434	1,829	2,638	2,662	2,507	2,652
Commercial banks and others	77	283	74	39	280	286
Private nonguaranteed debt from:	*1,917*	*2,139*	*2,650*	*2,864*	*2,866*	*3,279*
Bondholders	..	7	8	7	6	7
Commercial banks and others	1,917	2,132	2,642	2,856	2,859	3,272
Use of IMF credit and SDR allocations	**101**	**91**	**297**	**476**	**565**	**523**
IMF credit	0	0	202	196	299	254
SDR allocations	101	91	95	280	266	268
Short-term external debt stocks	**1,218**	**2,491**	**2,128**	**2,440**	**3,113**	**3,158**
Disbursements, long-term	**613**	**845**	**1,806**	**1,965**	**1,153**	**1,944**
Public and publicly guaranteed sector	197	383	1,202	1,178	504	1,130
Private sector not guaranteed	416	461	605	787	649	814
Principal repayments, long-term	**443**	**516**	**951**	**1,241**	**787**	**1,254**
Public and publicly guaranteed sector	98	219	625	829	238	736
Private sector not guaranteed	344	297	326	412	549	518
Interest payments, long-term	**128**	**149**	**151**	**179**	**154**	**223**
Public and publicly guaranteed sector	56	115	112	129	107	155
Private sector not guaranteed	71	34	38	50	47	68

PAKISTAN

(US$ million, unless otherwise indicated)

Snapshot	2023
Total external debt stocks	**130,847**
External debt stocks as % of:	
Exports	352
GNI	39
Debt service as % of:	
Exports	43
GNI	5
Net financial flows, debt and equity	**5,048**
Net debt inflows	3,303
Net equity inflows	1,745
GNI	**332,603**
Population (million)	**240**

Figure 2 Average terms on new debt commitments from official and private creditors

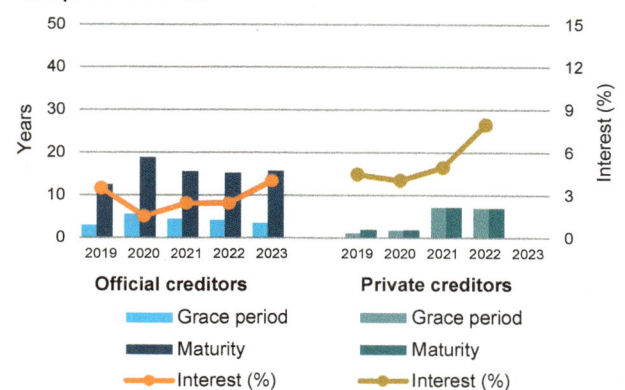

Figure 1 Public and publicly guaranteed debt, by creditor and creditor type in 2023, including IMF credit

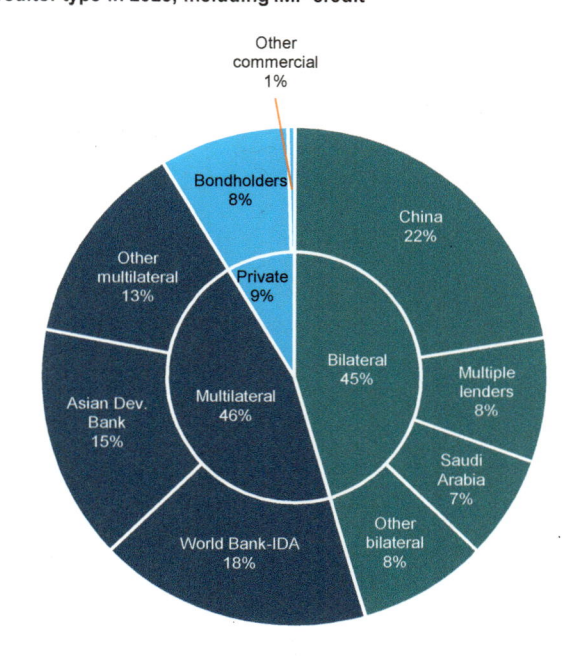

Summary External Debt Data	2010	2019	2020	2021	2022	2023
Total external debt stocks	**63,483**	**110,178**	**118,034**	**130,851**	**127,708**	**130,847**
Long-term external debt stocks	**48,558**	**92,825**	**101,902**	**110,937**	**107,418**	**110,437**
Public and publicly guaranteed debt from:	*44,085*	*78,396*	*86,993*	*95,391*	*91,220*	*92,990*
Official creditors	42,434	69,537	76,823	81,665	80,824	84,250
Multilateral	24,670	30,141	33,340	34,323	36,197	38,582
of which: World Bank	11,806	15,305	17,176	18,262	18,071	19,990
Bilateral	17,764	39,396	43,482	47,342	44,627	45,668
Private creditors	1,651	8,860	10,171	13,726	10,396	8,740
Bondholders	1,550	5,300	5,300	8,300	8,300	8,300
Commercial banks and others	101	3,560	4,871	5,426	2,096	440
Private nonguaranteed debt from:	*4,473*	*14,428*	*14,909*	*15,545*	*16,198*	*17,447*
Bondholders	250	12	12	0	..	..
	4,223	14,416	14,897	15,545	16,198	17,447
Use of IMF credit and SDR allocations	**10,258**	**8,097**	**8,902**	**10,841**	**11,522**	**11,532**
IMF credit	8,736	6,730	7,479	6,733	7,615	7,594
SDR allocations	1,522	1,367	1,424	4,108	3,906	3,938
Short-term external debt stocks	**4,667**	**9,256**	**7,230**	**9,074**	**8,768**	**8,878**
Disbursements, long-term	**3,960**	**15,601**	**14,424**	**18,997**	**11,837**	**12,945**
Public and publicly guaranteed sector	1,869	12,242	13,049	17,477	10,120	10,489
Private sector not guaranteed	2,091	3,358	1,375	1,520	1,718	2,456
Principal repayments, long-term	**3,046**	**7,500**	**7,489**	**8,878**	**12,172**	**9,670**
Public and publicly guaranteed sector	2,163	6,884	6,594	7,994	11,107	8,463
Private sector not guaranteed	883	616	895	883	1,065	1,207
Interest payments, long-term	**891**	**2,705**	**2,258**	**2,181**	**3,201**	**4,327**
Public and publicly guaranteed sector	791	2,166	1,701	1,741	2,661	3,373
Private sector not guaranteed	100	539	557	439	540	954

PAPUA NEW GUINEA

(US$ million, unless otherwise indicated)

Snapshot	2023
Total external debt stocks	**15,321**
External debt stocks as % of:	
Exports	117
GNI	53
Debt service as % of:	
Exports	43
GNI	19
Net financial flows, debt and equity	**-1,313**
Net debt inflows	-1,325
Net equity inflows	12
GNI	**29,106**
Population (million)	**10**

Figure 1 Public and publicly guaranteed debt, by creditor and creditor type in 2023, including IMF credit

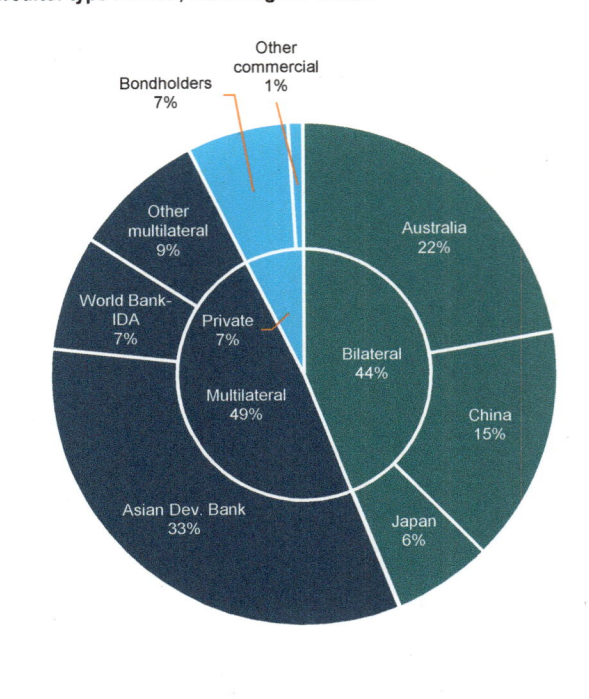

Figure 2 Average terms on new debt commitments from official and private creditors

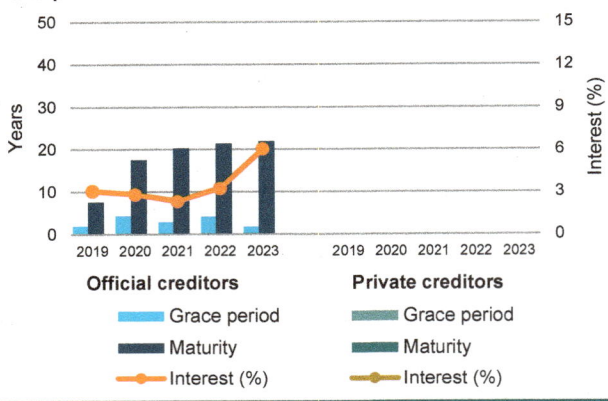

Summary External Debt Data	2010	2019	2020	2021	2022	2023
Total external debt stocks	**5,987**	**18,745**	**18,047**	**19,710**	**19,605**	**15,321**
Long-term external debt stocks	5,380	17,914	17,088	15,903	15,705	14,265
Public and publicly guaranteed debt from:	*1,042*	*4,313*	*5,142*	*6,046*	*6,748*	*7,136*
Official creditors	1,009	3,161	4,210	5,452	6,167	6,564
Multilateral	712	1,853	2,565	2,923	3,159	3,196
of which: World Bank	225	446	480	562	545	569
Bilateral	297	1,307	1,646	2,529	3,008	3,368
Private creditors	33	1,152	931	594	580	572
Bondholders	..	500	500	500	500	500
Commercial banks and others	33	652	431	94	80	72
Private nonguaranteed debt from:	*4,337*	*13,601*	*11,947*	*9,858*	*8,957*	*7,129*
Bondholders	..	..	..	..	..	..
Commercial banks and others	4,337	13,601	11,947	9,858	8,957	7,129
Use of IMF credit and SDR allocations	193	174	560	897	853	1,037
IMF credit	0	0	379	368	350	530
SDR allocations	193	174	181	529	503	507
Short-term external debt stocks	414	657	399	2,910	3,047	19
Disbursements, long-term	**3,153**	**1,501**	**1,538**	**2,552**	**3,060**	**3,565**
Public and publicly guaranteed sector	37	1,201	1,538	1,539	1,192	695
Private sector not guaranteed	3,116	300	..	1,013	1,868	2,870
Principal repayments, long-term	**758**	**1,568**	**2,500**	**3,716**	**3,927**	**4,950**
Public and publicly guaranteed sector	67	281	845	538	239	296
Private sector not guaranteed	691	1,286	1,654	3,178	3,688	4,655
Interest payments, long-term	**50**	**772**	**201**	**332**	**516**	**628**
Public and publicly guaranteed sector	16	149	143	107	130	180
Private sector not guaranteed	33	623	58	226	386	449

PARAGUAY

(US$ million, unless otherwise indicated)

Snapshot	2023
Total external debt stocks	**26,361**
External debt stocks as % of:	
Exports	138
GNI	63
Debt service as % of:	
Exports	10
GNI	4
Net financial flows, debt and equity	**1,804**
Net debt inflows	1,355
Net equity inflows	449
GNI	**41,585**
Population (million)	**7**

Figure 1 Public and publicly guaranteed debt, by creditor and creditor type in 2023, including IMF credit

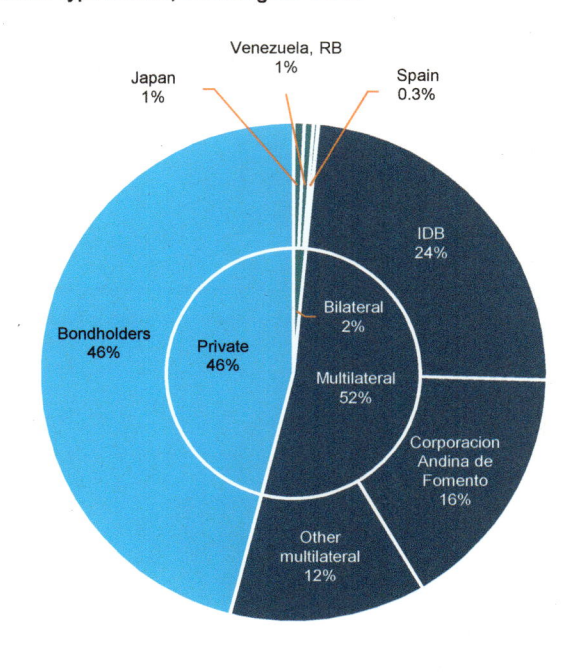

Figure 2 Average terms on new debt commitments from official and private creditors

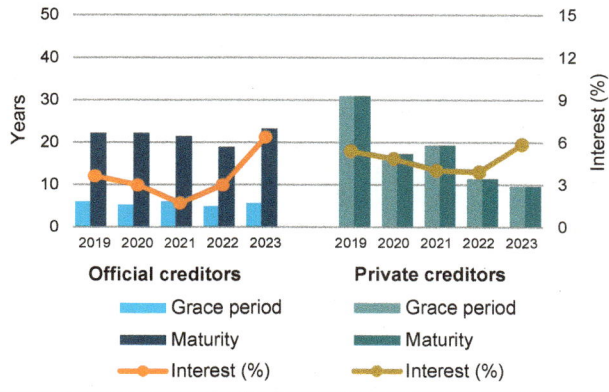

Summary External Debt Data	2010	2019	2020	2021	2022	2023
Total external debt stocks	**16,123**	**17,645**	**20,732**	**22,427**	**25,010**	**26,361**
Long-term external debt stocks	**14,951**	**15,245**	**18,677**	**20,151**	**22,310**	**23,211**
Public and publicly guaranteed debt from:	*2,390*	*7,187*	*10,262*	*11,580*	*13,109*	*14,109*
Official creditors	2,123	3,277	4,902	5,497	6,812	7,619
Multilateral	1,510	3,067	4,657	5,235	6,567	7,398
of which: World Bank	270	619	852	882	887	1,119
Bilateral	613	210	244	263	245	221
Private creditors	267	3,910	5,360	6,082	6,297	6,489
Bondholders	..	3,910	5,360	6,082	6,297	6,489
Commercial banks and others	267	0	0	0	0	0
Private nonguaranteed debt from:	*12,561*	*8,058*	*8,415*	*8,572*	*9,201*	*9,103*
Bondholders	..	600	1,150	1,450	1,150	1,150
Commercial banks and others	12,561	7,458	7,265	7,122	8,051	7,953
Use of IMF credit and SDR allocations	**147**	**132**	**137**	**403**	**384**	**387**
IMF credit	0	0	0	0	0	0
SDR allocations	147	132	137	403	384	387
Short-term external debt stocks	**1,025**	**2,268**	**1,918**	**1,872**	**2,316**	**2,763**
Disbursements, long-term	**2,076**	**1,453**	**4,334**	**2,239**	**2,524**	**1,582**
Public and publicly guaranteed sector	308	994	3,281	1,895	2,088	1,578
Private sector not guaranteed	1,769	459	1,053	344	436	3
Principal repayments, long-term	**314**	**961**	**667**	**740**	**1,358**	**674**
Public and publicly guaranteed sector	240	207	218	552	533	572
Private sector not guaranteed	75	754	449	188	825	102
Interest payments, long-term	**183**	**497**	**460**	**492**	**674**	**959**
Public and publicly guaranteed sector	65	330	359	365	469	693
Private sector not guaranteed	118	167	101	127	206	265

PERU

(US$ million, unless otherwise indicated)

Snapshot	2023
Total external debt stocks	**90,068**
External debt stocks as % of:	
Exports	115
GNI	35
Debt service as % of:	
Exports	18
GNI	5
Net financial flows, debt and equity	**5,517**
Net debt inflows	960
Net equity inflows	4,557
GNI	**253,911**
Population (million)	**34**

Figure 2 Average terms on new debt commitments from official and private creditors

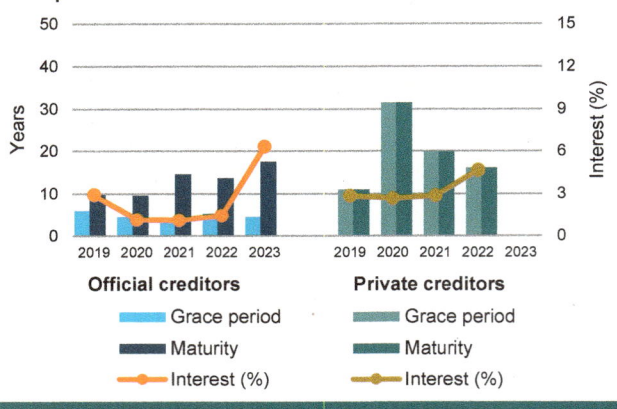

Figure 1 Public and publicly guaranteed debt, by creditor and creditor type in 2023, including IMF credit

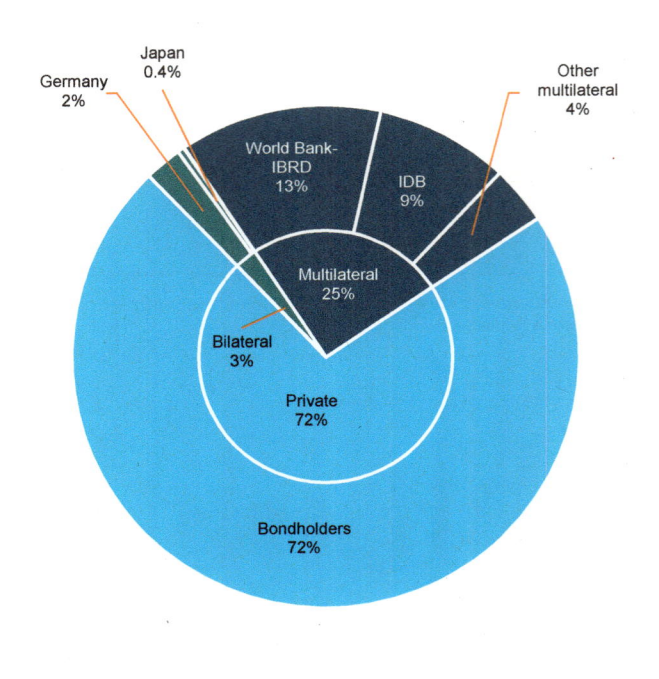

Summary External Debt Data	2010	2019	2020	2021	2022	2023
Total external debt stocks	**42,154**	**64,247**	**73,549**	**86,811**	**88,829**	**90,068**
Long-term external debt stocks	**34,822**	**54,837**	**62,387**	**73,882**	**75,788**	**74,774**
Public and publicly guaranteed debt from:	*20,009*	*18,606*	*28,027*	*40,204*	*41,443*	*40,906*
Official creditors	10,672	4,916	7,174	9,481	10,380	11,470
Multilateral	7,870	3,843	6,123	8,621	9,267	10,308
of which: World Bank	2,965	1,564	3,441	4,685	4,860	5,284
Bilateral	2,802	1,074	1,051	860	1,112	1,163
Private creditors	9,337	13,690	20,853	30,722	31,064	29,436
Bondholders	9,311	13,690	20,853	30,722	31,064	29,436
Commercial banks and others	26	..	..	..	..	..
Private nonguaranteed debt from:	*14,813*	*36,231*	*34,360*	*33,679*	*34,345*	*33,868*
Bondholders	727	16,285	17,800	18,345	17,415	15,725
Commercial banks and others	14,086	19,946	16,560	15,334	16,930	18,143
Use of IMF credit and SDR allocations	**939**	**843**	**878**	**2,644**	**2,514**	**2,534**
IMF credit	0	0	0	0	0	0
SDR allocations	939	843	878	2,644	2,514	2,534
Short-term external debt stocks	**6,393**	**8,567**	**10,284**	**10,285**	**10,527**	**12,759**
Disbursements, long-term	**5,425**	**3,291**	**11,457**	**15,947**	**6,091**	**7,446**
Public and publicly guaranteed sector	3,862	1,866	9,427	12,942	2,439	2,002
Private sector not guaranteed	1,563	1,425	2,030	3,005	3,652	5,444
Principal repayments, long-term	**4,060**	**4,327**	**4,191**	**2,779**	**3,846**	**8,718**
Public and publicly guaranteed sector	3,490	1,356	290	396	860	2,692
Private sector not guaranteed	570	2,972	3,901	2,382	2,986	6,026
Interest payments, long-term	**2,550**	**2,103**	**2,049**	**2,293**	**3,070**	**4,077**
Public and publicly guaranteed sector	1,096	979	919	1,109	1,404	1,885
Private sector not guaranteed	1,454	1,124	1,130	1,184	1,666	2,191

PHILIPPINES

(US$ million, unless otherwise indicated)

Snapshot	2023
Total external debt stocks	**121,402**
External debt stocks as % of:	
Exports	101
GNI	25
Debt service as % of:	
Exports	11
GNI	3
Net financial flows, debt and equity	13,769
Net debt inflows	10,842
Net equity inflows	2,927
GNI	**485,155**
Population (million)	**117**

Figure 1 Public and publicly guaranteed debt, by creditor and creditor type in 2023, including IMF credit

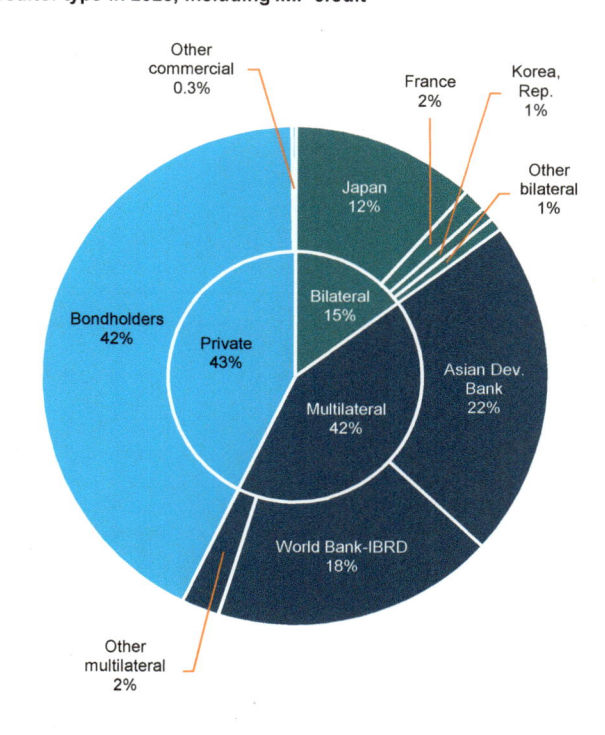

Figure 2 Average terms on new debt commitments from official and private creditors

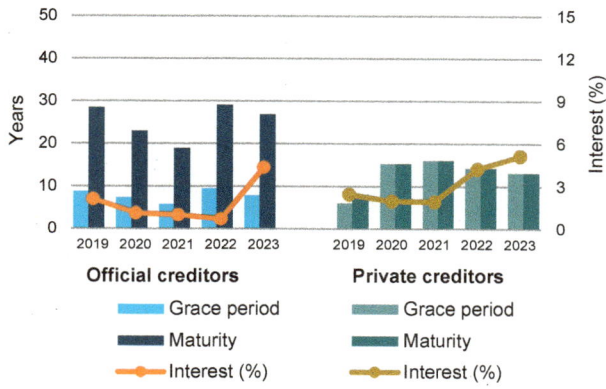

Summary External Debt Data	2010	2019	2020	2021	2022	2023
Total external debt stocks	**65,344**	**83,649**	**98,504**	**106,450**	**111,233**	**121,402**
Long-term external debt stocks	**53,542**	**65,282**	**83,089**	**87,447**	**90,893**	**100,555**
Public and publicly guaranteed debt from:	*45,080*	*41,758*	*56,505*	*59,712*	*62,627*	*68,742*
Official creditors	23,207	21,560	29,422	32,803	35,075	39,377
Multilateral	8,372	13,180	19,672	22,930	25,397	29,107
of which: World Bank	2,738	6,456	8,100	9,740	10,649	12,424
Bilateral	14,835	8,380	9,749	9,873	9,678	10,270
Private creditors	21,873	20,199	27,083	26,909	27,551	29,366
Bondholders	20,590	19,081	26,062	26,256	27,158	29,186
Commercial banks and others	1,283	1,118	1,021	652	393	180
Private nonguaranteed debt from:	*8,462*	*23,524*	*26,584*	*27,735*	*28,266*	*31,813*
Bondholders	1,651	7,041	9,551	10,242	9,867	8,387
Commercial banks and others	6,811	16,483	17,033	17,493	18,399	23,425
Use of IMF credit and SDR allocations	**1,290**	**1,159**	**1,207**	**3,913**	**3,721**	**3,751**
IMF credit	0	0	0	0	0	0
SDR allocations	1,290	1,159	1,207	3,913	3,721	3,751
Short-term external debt stocks	**10,512**	**17,208**	**14,209**	**15,090**	**16,619**	**17,096**
Disbursements, long-term	**10,928**	**11,353**	**21,033**	**16,721**	**12,833**	**18,230**
Public and publicly guaranteed sector	8,251	7,034	15,043	11,937	9,595	10,162
Private sector not guaranteed	2,677	4,320	5,990	4,784	3,238	8,068
Principal repayments, long-term	**8,341**	**7,368**	**6,297**	**9,282**	**5,668**	**7,864**
Public and publicly guaranteed sector	6,813	4,109	3,356	5,653	3,164	2,495
Private sector not guaranteed	1,527	3,259	2,941	3,629	2,504	5,369
Interest payments, long-term	**3,112**	**3,212**	**2,974**	**2,856**	**3,277**	**4,939**
Public and publicly guaranteed sector	2,977	2,416	2,295	2,104	2,339	3,635
Private sector not guaranteed	135	795	679	752	938	1,304

RWANDA

(US$ million, unless otherwise indicated)

Snapshot	2023
Total external debt stocks	**11,384**
External debt stocks as % of:	
Exports	320
GNI	82
Debt service as % of:	
Exports	15
GNI	4
Net financial flows, debt and equity	1,931
Net debt inflows	1,653
Net equity inflows	279
GNI	**13,818**
Population (million)	**14**

Figure 2 **Average terms on new debt commitments from official and private creditors**

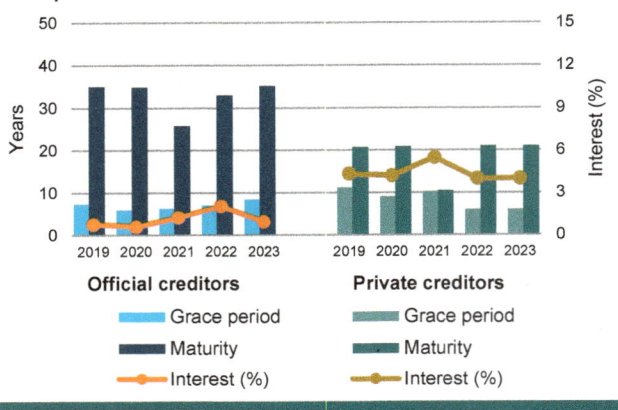

Official creditors / Private creditors
- Grace period
- Maturity
- Interest (%)

Figure 1 **Public and publicly guaranteed debt, by creditor and creditor type in 2023, including IMF credit**

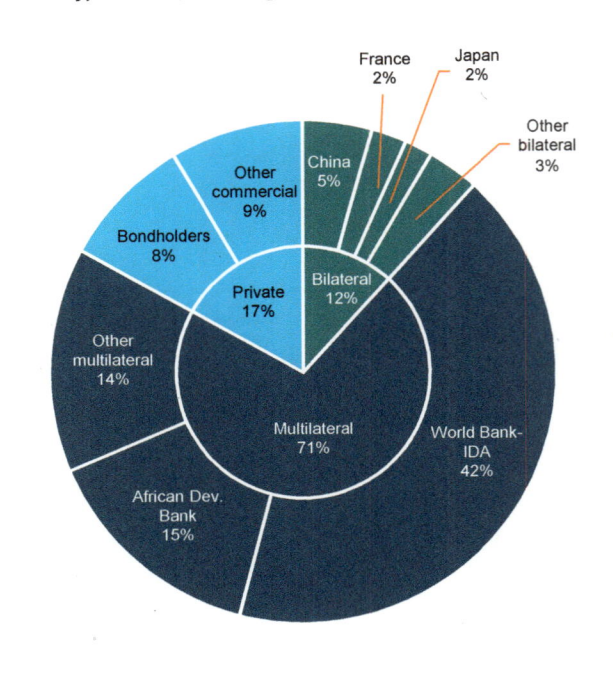

Summary External Debt Data	2010	2019	2020	2021	2022	2023
Total external debt stocks	**1,233**	**6,515**	**8,194**	**9,318**	**9,690**	**11,384**
Long-term external debt stocks	**1,086**	**5,866**	**7,295**	**8,226**	**8,701**	**10,127**
Public and publicly guaranteed debt from:	*759*	*3,929*	*5,122*	*5,794*	*6,145*	*7,231*
Official creditors	759	3,465	4,377	4,739	4,970	5,923
Multilateral	639	2,979	3,737	3,924	4,135	5,009
of which: World Bank	259	1,897	2,432	2,575	2,696	3,270
Bilateral	120	486	640	815	835	914
Private creditors	..	464	745	1,055	1,174	1,308
Bondholders	..	421	475	775	765	651
Commercial banks and others	..	43	270	280	410	658
Private nonguaranteed debt from:	*327*	*1,937*	*2,173*	*2,432*	*2,556*	*2,896*
Bondholders	..	..	..	..	..	..
Commercial banks and others	327	1,937	2,173	2,432	2,556	2,896
Use of IMF credit and SDR allocations	**133**	**306**	**520**	**678**	**613**	**813**
IMF credit	15	199	410	356	306	504
SDR allocations	118	106	111	322	307	309
Short-term external debt stocks	**14**	**343**	**378**	**414**	**376**	**443**
Disbursements, long-term	**182**	**1,044**	**1,368**	**1,483**	**822**	**1,654**
Public and publicly guaranteed sector	63	727	1,086	1,207	659	1,250
Private sector not guaranteed	119	318	282	276	163	404
Principal repayments, long-term	**41**	**185**	**102**	**424**	**124**	**262**
Public and publicly guaranteed sector	8	31	52	406	85	198
Private sector not guaranteed	33	154	50	18	39	64
Interest payments, long-term	**10**	**133**	**148**	**148**	**183**	**222**
Public and publicly guaranteed sector	6	56	61	55	81	106
Private sector not guaranteed	4	78	87	93	102	116

SAMOA

(US$ million, unless otherwise indicated)

Snapshot	2023
Total external debt stocks	**432.5**
External debt stocks as % of:	
Exports	114.1
GNI	46.9
Debt service as % of:	
Exports	10.3
GNI	4.2
Net financial flows, debt and equity	-31.3
Net debt inflows	-35.7
Net equity inflows	4.3
GNI	**922.4**
Population (thousand)	**225.7**

Figure 1 Public and publicly guaranteed debt, by creditor and creditor type in 2023, including IMF credit

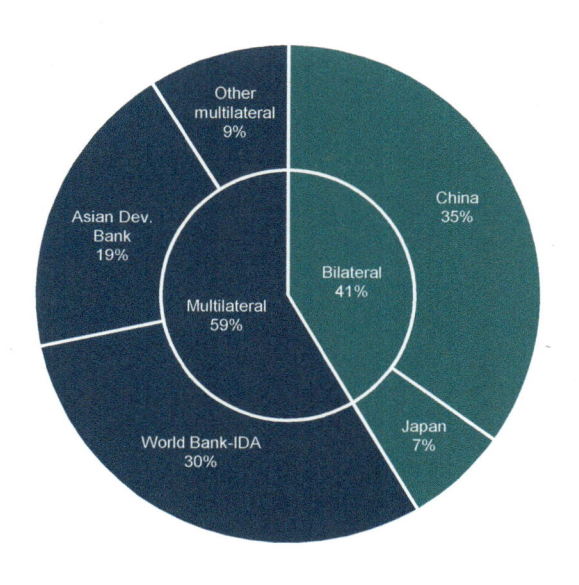

Figure 2 Average terms on new debt commitments from official and private creditors

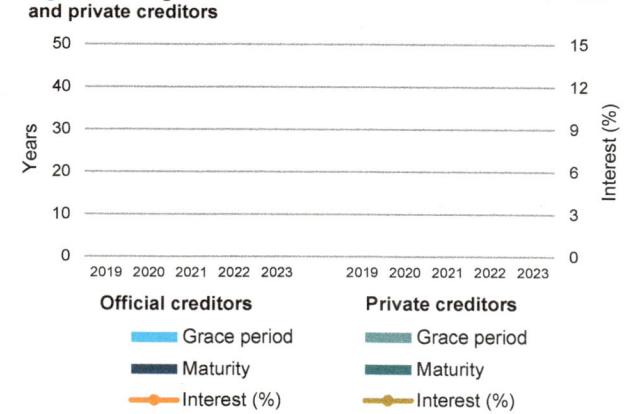

Summary External Debt Data	2010	2019	2020	2021	2022	2023
Total external debt stocks	**325.1**	**434.9**	**477.3**	**505.6**	**470.7**	**432.5**
Long-term external debt stocks	**299.1**	**389.6**	**395.9**	**394.6**	**341.6**	**308.6**
Public and publicly guaranteed debt from:	*299.1*	*387.6*	*393.9*	*381.0*	*328.8*	*296.2*
Official creditors	299.1	387.6	393.9	381.0	328.8	296.2
Multilateral	219.2	205.8	206.1	189.2	173.1	164.6
of which: World Bank	99.3	110.3	114.6	107.8	99.1	96.3
Bilateral	79.9	181.8	187.8	191.8	155.7	131.6
Private creditors	..	..	..	..	..	..
Bondholders	..	..	..	..	..	..
Commercial banks and others	..	..	..	..	..	..
Private nonguaranteed debt from:	*..*	*2.0*	*2.0*	*13.6*	*12.8*	*12.4*
Bondholders	..	..	..	..	..	..
Commercial banks and others	..	2.0	2.0	13.6	12.8	12.4
Use of IMF credit and SDR allocations	**26.0**	**21.0**	**43.5**	**62.4**	**57.8**	**57.4**
IMF credit	8.9	5.6	27.5	25.1	22.3	21.7
SDR allocations	17.1	15.3	16.0	37.3	35.4	35.7
Short-term external debt stocks	**0.0**	**24.3**	**37.9**	**48.7**	**71.3**	**66.4**
Disbursements, long-term	**78.9**	**9.3**	**3.1**	**2.3**	**3.4**	**0.9**
Public and publicly guaranteed sector	78.9	9.3	3.1	0.0	3.4	0.9
Private sector not guaranteed	..	..	0.0	2.3	..	..
Principal repayments, long-term	**7.2**	**22.1**	**18.1**	**12.0**	**29.7**	**30.9**
Public and publicly guaranteed sector	7.2	21.3	18.1	11.3	28.9	30.5
Private sector not guaranteed	..	0.8	..	0.7	0.8	0.4
Interest payments, long-term	**3.3**	**6.0**	**3.9**	**2.7**	**5.2**	**4.5**
Public and publicly guaranteed sector	3.3	5.6	3.8	2.6	5.2	4.5
Private sector not guaranteed	..	0.4	0.1	0.0	0.0	0.1

Note: Figure 2 shows no data values because the country did not have new commitments from 2019 to 2023.

SÃO TOMÉ AND PRÍNCIPE

(US$ million, unless otherwise indicated)

Snapshot	2023
Total external debt stocks	**454.3**
External debt stocks as % of:	
Exports	356.9
GNI	74.4
Debt service as % of:	
Exports	5.1
GNI	1.1
Net financial flows, debt and equity	43.2
Net debt inflows	24.7
Net equity inflows	18.4
GNI	**610.8**
Population (thousand)	**231.9**

Figure 1 Public and publicly guaranteed debt, by creditor and creditor type in 2023, including IMF credit

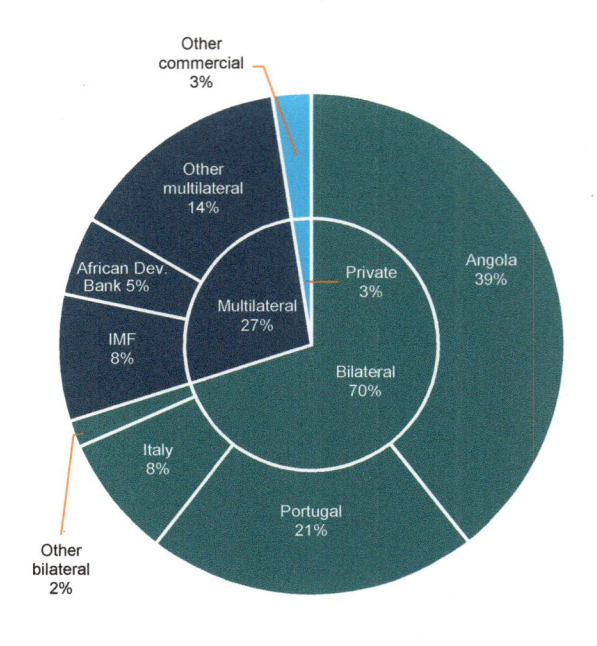

Figure 2 Average terms on new debt commitments from official and private creditors

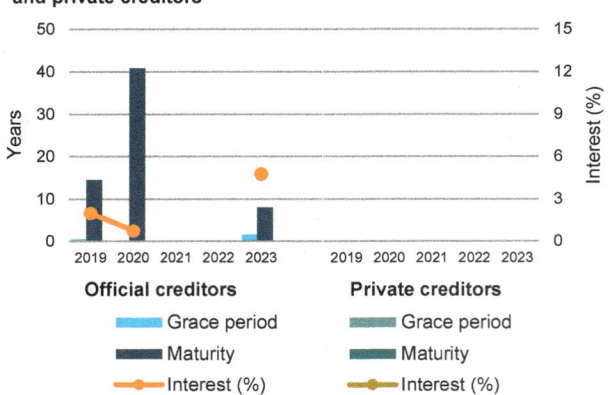

Summary External Debt Data	2010	2019	2020	2021	2022	2023
Total external debt stocks	**181.1**	**277.1**	**316.7**	**331.3**	**421.6**	**454.3**
Long-term external debt stocks	145.3	240.7	256.4	249.4	339.1	370.8
Public and publicly guaranteed debt from:	*145.3*	*240.7*	*256.4*	*249.4*	*339.1*	*370.8*
Official creditors	145.3	230.7	246.4	239.4	329.1	360.8
Multilateral	37.3	48.9	55.9	54.0	51.1	77.7
of which: World Bank	14.2	11.1	11.3	10.7	9.9	9.6
Bilateral	108.0	181.8	190.6	185.4	278.0	283.1
Private creditors	..	10.0	10.0	10.0	10.0	10.0
Bondholders	..	..	..	..	..	..
Commercial banks and others	..	10.0	10.0	10.0	10.0	10.0
Private nonguaranteed debt from:	..	..	..	..	..	..
Bondholders	..	..	..	..	..	..
Commercial banks and others	..	..	..	..	..	..
Use of IMF credit and SDR allocations	15.9	18.8	37.0	60.5	62.0	61.5
IMF credit	4.9	9.0	26.8	30.7	33.6	32.9
SDR allocations	10.9	9.8	10.2	29.8	28.3	28.6
Short-term external debt stocks	19.9	17.6	23.3	21.4	20.5	22.1
Disbursements, long-term	**19.8**	**7.3**	**5.9**	**2.3**	**2.6**	**27.3**
Public and publicly guaranteed sector	19.8	7.3	5.9	2.3	2.6	27.3
Private sector not guaranteed	..	..	..	..	..	..
Principal repayments, long-term	**1.2**	**4.8**	**1.3**	**2.0**	**4.8**	**2.6**
Public and publicly guaranteed sector	1.2	4.8	1.3	2.0	4.8	2.6
Private sector not guaranteed	..	..	..	..	..	..
Interest payments, long-term	**0.3**	**3.4**	**1.2**	**0.6**	**2.2**	**1.7**
Public and publicly guaranteed sector	0.3	3.4	1.2	0.6	2.2	1.7
Private sector not guaranteed	..	..	..	..	..	..

SENEGAL

(US$ million, unless otherwise indicated)

Snapshot	2023
Total external debt stocks	**39,950**
External debt stocks as % of:	
Exports	545
GNI	133
Debt service as % of:	
Exports	37
GNI	9
Net financial flows, debt and equity	**10,005**
Net debt inflows	7,364
Net equity inflows	2,641
GNI	**29,981**
Population (million)	**18**

Figure 2 Average terms on new debt commitments from official and private creditors

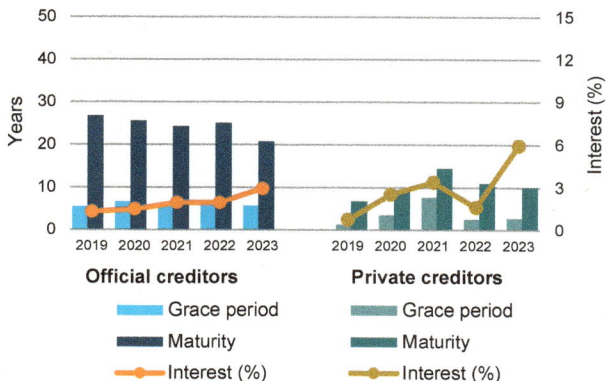

Official creditors
- Grace period
- Maturity
- Interest (%)

Private creditors
- Grace period
- Maturity
- Interest (%)

Figure 1 Public and publicly guaranteed debt, by creditor and creditor type in 2023, including IMF credit

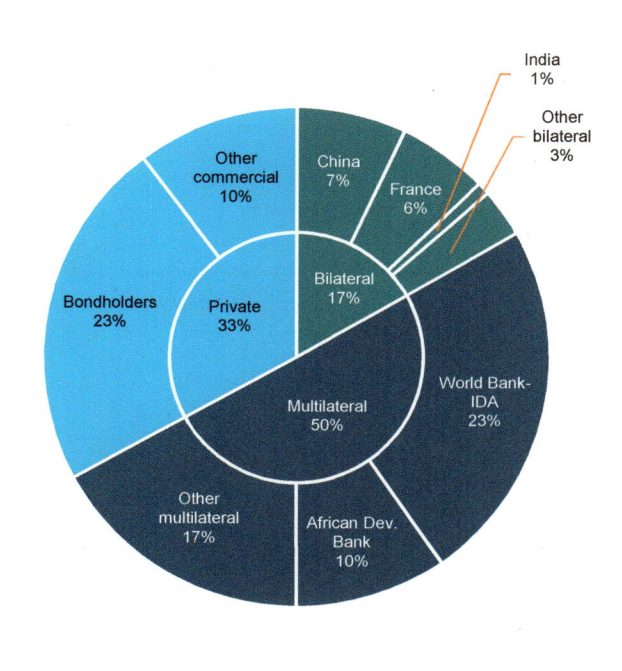

Summary External Debt Data	2010	2019	2020	2021	2022	2023
Total external debt stocks	**4,650**	**19,249**	**23,933**	**28,997**	**32,233**	**39,950**
Long-term external debt stocks	**4,198**	**17,293**	**21,500**	**24,819**	**27,008**	**32,826**
Public and publicly guaranteed debt from:	*3,151*	*12,267*	*14,025*	*14,446*	*14,548*	*16,907*
Official creditors	2,951	7,815	9,360	9,521	9,662	10,753
Multilateral	1,973	4,845	5,932	6,185	6,614	7,666
of which: World Bank	1,023	2,657	3,102	3,257	3,661	4,357
Bilateral	978	2,970	3,428	3,336	3,048	3,087
Private creditors	200	4,452	4,665	4,925	4,886	6,154
Bondholders	200	4,122	4,158	4,235	4,118	4,186
Commercial banks and others	..	330	506	691	768	1,969
Private nonguaranteed debt from:	*1,048*	*5,026*	*7,476*	*10,372*	*12,460*	*15,919*
Bondholders	..	..	..	..	..	..
Commercial banks and others	1,048	5,026	7,476	10,372	12,460	15,919
Use of IMF credit and SDR allocations	**451**	**219**	**689**	**1,285**	**1,609**	**2,266**
IMF credit	213	4	466	634	990	1,643
SDR allocations	238	214	223	651	619	624
Short-term external debt stocks	**0**	**1,737**	**1,743**	**2,894**	**3,616**	**4,858**
Disbursements, long-term	**1,045**	**1,650**	**3,938**	**4,977**	**3,398**	**6,196**
Public and publicly guaranteed sector	355	1,650	1,504	2,081	1,310	2,738
Private sector not guaranteed	690	..	2,433	2,897	2,088	3,458
Principal repayments, long-term	**84**	**806**	**423**	**1,056**	**621**	**715**
Public and publicly guaranteed sector	84	429	423	1,056	621	715
Private sector not guaranteed	..	377	..	..	..	..
Interest payments, long-term	**101**	**497**	**833**	**1,001**	**1,138**	**1,527**
Public and publicly guaranteed sector	64	367	384	379	390	572
Private sector not guaranteed	37	131	449	622	748	955

SERBIA

(US$ million, unless otherwise indicated)

Snapshot	2023
Total external debt stocks	**49,000**
External debt stocks as % of:	
Exports	108
GNI	69
Debt service as % of:	
Exports	13
GNI	9
Net financial flows, debt and equity	7,132
Net debt inflows	3,316
Net equity inflows	3,816
GNI	**71,012**
Population (million)	**7**

Figure 1 Public and publicly guaranteed debt, by creditor and creditor type in 2023, including IMF credit

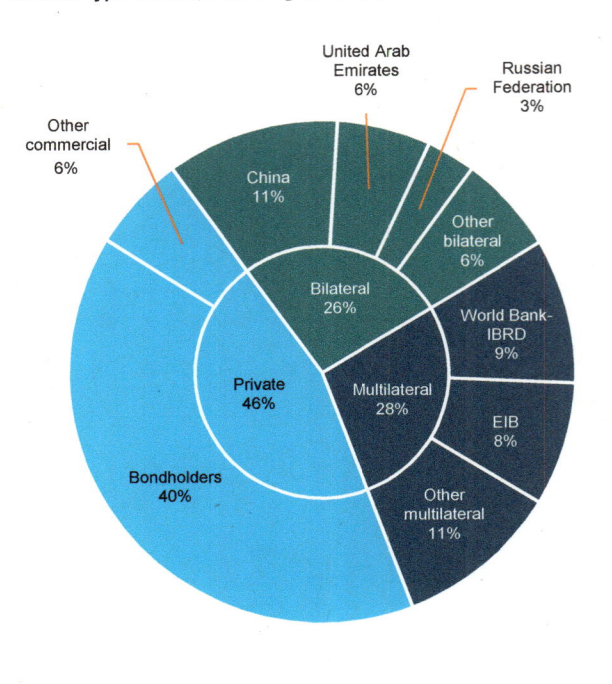

Figure 2 Average terms on new debt commitments from official and private creditors

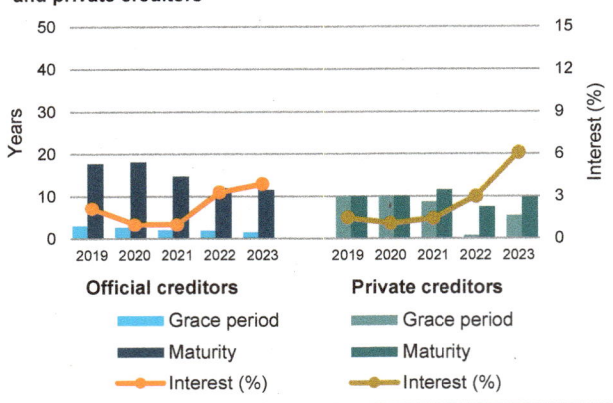

Summary External Debt Data	2010	2019	2020	2021	2022	2023
Total external debt stocks	**32,907**	**32,109**	**38,041**	**41,166**	**44,479**	**49,000**
Long-term external debt stocks	27,389	29,332	35,497	37,671	39,445	45,317
Public and publicly guaranteed debt from:	*9,477*	*15,341*	*18,370*	*20,619*	*21,854*	*25,558*
Official creditors	8,011	11,768	12,046	12,043	13,064	13,727
Multilateral	4,848	5,743	6,064	5,776	5,542	5,894
of which: World Bank	2,499	2,708	2,891	2,655	2,440	2,426
Bilateral	3,163	6,025	5,982	6,267	7,522	7,833
Private creditors	1,466	3,573	6,324	8,575	8,790	11,831
Bondholders	..	3,552	6,303	8,287	8,166	10,249
Commercial banks and others	1,466	21	21	289	624	1,582
Private nonguaranteed debt from:	*17,912*	*13,990*	*17,127*	*17,053*	*17,591*	*19,760*
Bondholders	165	..	..	..	..	..
Commercial banks and others	17,747	13,990	17,127	17,053	17,591	19,760
Use of IMF credit and SDR allocations	2,720	615	641	1,501	2,473	2,713
IMF credit	2,034	0	0	0	1,046	1,274
SDR allocations	685	615	641	1,501	1,428	1,439
Short-term external debt stocks	2,798	2,162	1,902	1,993	2,561	970
Disbursements, long-term	**4,594**	**7,846**	**8,248**	**8,274**	**7,613**	**9,504**
Public and publicly guaranteed sector	1,365	3,125	4,205	5,105	3,250	4,429
Private sector not guaranteed	3,230	4,721	4,043	3,169	4,363	5,075
Principal repayments, long-term	**3,431**	**6,150**	**4,411**	**4,956**	**4,917**	**4,689**
Public and publicly guaranteed sector	351	2,745	2,219	1,713	1,093	1,335
Private sector not guaranteed	3,081	3,406	2,193	3,243	3,825	3,354
Interest payments, long-term	**759**	**718**	**593**	**694**	**773**	**1,239**
Public and publicly guaranteed sector	321	515	479	404	422	770
Private sector not guaranteed	438	203	114	289	350	469

SIERRA LEONE

(US$ million, unless otherwise indicated)

Snapshot	2023
Total external debt stocks	**2,382**
External debt stocks as % of:	
Exports	183
GNI	54
Debt service as % of:	
Exports	12
GNI	4
Net financial flows, debt and equity	**226**
Net debt inflows	-37
Net equity inflows	263
GNI	**4,395**
Population (million)	**9**

Figure 2 Average terms on new debt commitments from official and private creditors

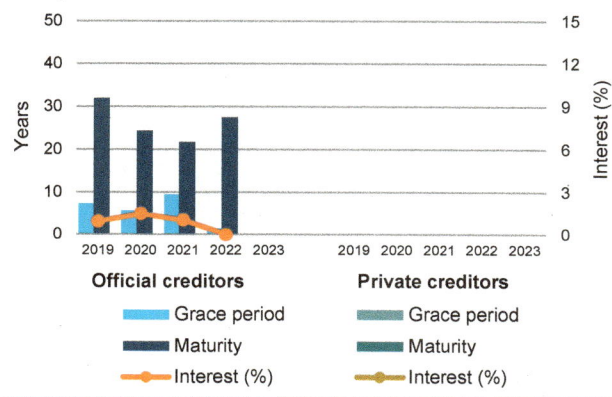

Official creditors
- Grace period
- Maturity
- Interest (%)

Private creditors
- Grace period
- Maturity
- Interest (%)

Figure 1 Public and publicly guaranteed debt, by creditor and creditor type in 2023, including IMF credit

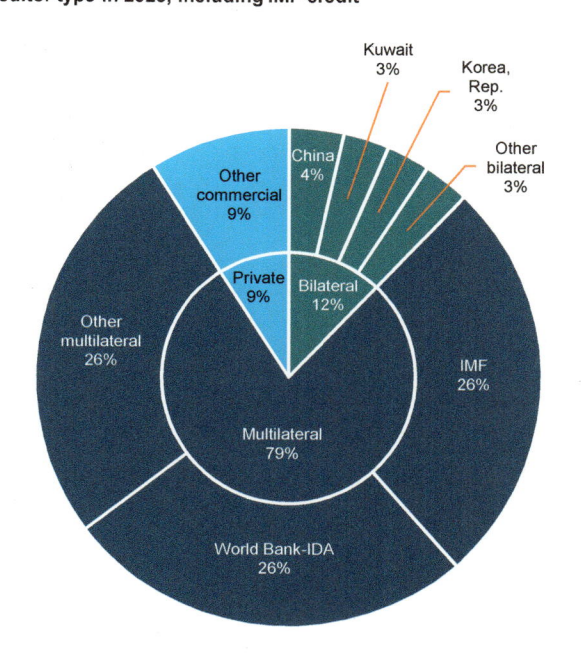

Summary External Debt Data	2010	2019	2020	2021	2022	2023
Total external debt stocks	**931**	**1,930**	**2,195**	**2,532**	**2,400**	**2,382**
Long-term external debt stocks	**661**	**1,241**	**1,360**	**1,387**	**1,347**	**1,345**
Public and publicly guaranteed debt from:	*661*	*1,241*	*1,360*	*1,387*	*1,347*	*1,345*
Official creditors	450	1,054	1,180	1,219	1,182	1,180
Multilateral	371	833	942	967	945	958
of which: World Bank	155	348	432	464	466	479
Bilateral	78	221	238	252	237	221
Private creditors	211	187	179	168	165	165
Bondholders	..	..	..	..	..	..
Commercial banks and others	211	187	179	168	165	165
Private nonguaranteed debt from:	..	..	..	..	..	..
Bondholders	..	..	..	..	..	..
Commercial banks and others	..	..	..	..	..	..
Use of IMF credit and SDR allocations	**266**	**503**	**652**	**959**	**892**	**880**
IMF credit	113	365	509	541	495	480
SDR allocations	153	138	143	417	397	400
Short-term external debt stocks	**4**	**187**	**184**	**186**	**162**	**157**
Disbursements, long-term	**66**	**142**	**135**	**100**	**50**	**51**
Public and publicly guaranteed sector	66	142	135	100	50	51
Private sector not guaranteed	..	..	..	..	..	..
Principal repayments, long-term	**5**	**41**	**46**	**51**	**56**	**58**
Public and publicly guaranteed sector	5	41	46	51	56	58
Private sector not guaranteed	..	..	..	..	..	..
Interest payments, long-term	**4**	**10**	**7**	**7**	**11**	**12**
Public and publicly guaranteed sector	4	10	7	7	11	12
Private sector not guaranteed	..	..	..	..	..	..

SOLOMON ISLANDS

(US$ million, unless otherwise indicated)

Snapshot	2023
Total external debt stocks	**527.8**
External debt stocks as % of:	
Exports	86.2
GNI	31.9
Debt service as % of:	
Exports	4.9
GNI	1.8
Net financial flows, debt and equity	101.8
Net debt inflows	50.6
Net equity inflows	51.2
GNI	**1,656.4**
Population (thousand)	**740**

Figure 1 Public and publicly guaranteed debt, by creditor and creditor type in 2023, including IMF credit

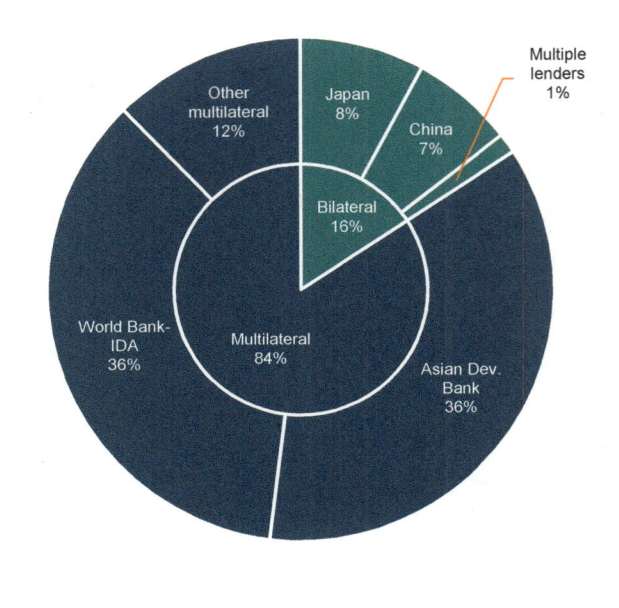

Figure 2 Average terms on new debt commitments from official and private creditors

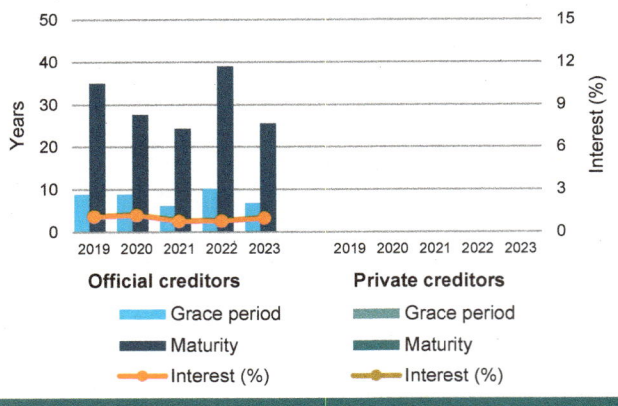

Official creditors
- Grace period
- Maturity
- Interest (%)

Private creditors
- Grace period
- Maturity
- Interest (%)

Summary External Debt Data	2010	2019	2020	2021	2022	2023
Total external debt stocks	**230.8**	**305.0**	**322.6**	**448.6**	**477.4**	**527.8**
Long-term external debt stocks	201.9	253.8	270.5	325.3	350.1	423.4
Public and publicly guaranteed debt from:	*125.3*	*98.1*	*124.0*	*140.8*	*154.8*	*197.6*
Official creditors	125.2	98.1	124.0	140.8	154.8	197.6
Multilateral	105.6	90.7	117.8	113.8	132.0	162.6
of which: World Bank	41.7	38.5	47.8	46.7	58.0	79.0
Bilateral	19.6	7.4	6.3	27.0	22.8	35.0
Private creditors	0.1	..	..	..	..	..
Bondholders	..	..	..	..	..	..
Commercial banks and others	0.1	..	..	..	..	..
Private nonguaranteed debt from:	*76.6*	*155.8*	*146.5*	*184.4*	*195.3*	*225.8*
Bondholders	..	..	..	..	..	..
Commercial banks and others	76.6	155.8	146.5	184.4	195.3	225.8
Use of IMF credit and SDR allocations	24.9	15.0	25.3	71.7	67.9	63.6
IMF credit	9.6	1.3	11.1	29.9	28.2	23.6
SDR allocations	15.3	13.7	14.3	41.8	39.7	40.0
Short-term external debt stocks	4.0	36.2	26.8	51.7	59.3	40.8
Disbursements, long-term	**36.8**	**17.1**	**41.8**	**66.4**	**39.0**	**93.5**
Public and publicly guaranteed sector	0.0	7.6	27.4	25.9	26.1	48.2
Private sector not guaranteed	36.8	9.5	14.4	40.6	12.9	45.3
Principal repayments, long-term	**17.5**	**19.4**	**28.9**	**7.7**	**7.0**	**19.5**
Public and publicly guaranteed sector	8.6	5.1	5.2	5.1	4.9	4.7
Private sector not guaranteed	8.9	14.3	23.7	2.6	2.1	14.8
Interest payments, long-term	**3.2**	**3.0**	**2.2**	**1.8**	**1.9**	**2.1**
Public and publicly guaranteed sector	1.7	1.1	1.1	1.4	1.2	1.5
Private sector not guaranteed	1.5	1.9	1.1	0.5	0.7	0.6

SOMALIA

(US$ million, unless otherwise indicated)

Snapshot	2023
Total external debt stocks	**3,023**
External debt stocks as % of:	
Exports	140
GNI	26
Debt service as % of:	
Exports	17
GNI	3
Net financial flows, debt and equity	**386**
Net debt inflows	-290
Net equity inflows	677
GNI	**11,636**
Population (million)	**18**

Figure 1 Public and publicly guaranteed debt, by creditor and creditor type in 2023, including IMF credit

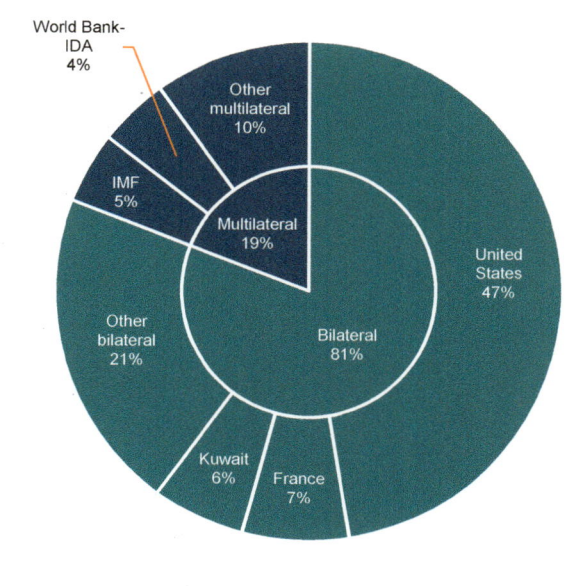

Figure 2 Average terms on new debt commitments from official and private creditors

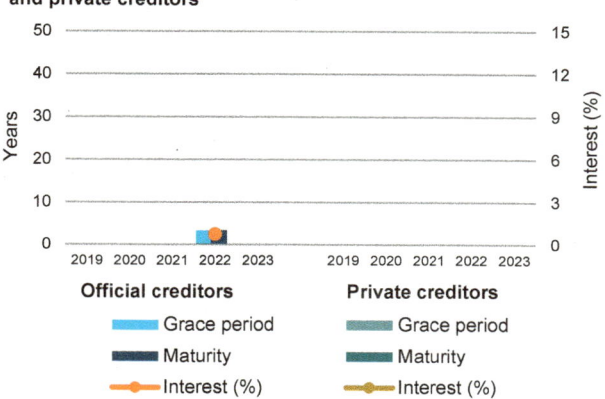

Official creditors
- Grace period
- Maturity
- Interest (%)

Private creditors
- Grace period
- Maturity
- Interest (%)

Summary External Debt Data	2010	2019	2020	2021	2022	2023
Total external debt stocks	**2,934**	**5,374**	**4,592**	**4,143**	**4,089**	**3,023**
Long-term external debt stocks	**1,879**	**2,049**	**2,609**	**2,313**	**2,311**	**1,997**
Public and publicly guaranteed debt from:	*1,879*	*2,049*	*2,609*	*2,313*	*2,311*	*1,997*
Official creditors	1,879	2,049	2,609	2,313	2,311	1,997
Multilateral	773	714	373	366	338	303
of which: World Bank	443	411	138	122	105	94
Bilateral	1,106	1,335	2,236	1,947	1,973	1,694
Private creditors	..	..	..	..	..	..
Bondholders	..	..	..	..	..	..
Commercial banks and others	..	..	..	..	..	..
Private nonguaranteed debt from:						
Bondholders	..	..	..	..	..	..
Commercial banks and others	..	..	..	..	..	..
Use of IMF credit and SDR allocations	**244**	**219**	**444**	**650**	**646**	**375**
IMF credit	172	154	371	360	371	97
SDR allocations	72	64	73	290	276	278
Short-term external debt stocks	**811**	**3,106**	**1,540**	**1,179**	**1,132**	**651**
Disbursements, long-term	**0**	**0**	**0**	**0**	**0**	**0**
Public and publicly guaranteed sector	0	0	0	0	0	0
Private sector not guaranteed	..	..	..	..	..	..
Principal repayments, long-term	**0**	**0**	**350**	**15**	**14**	**15**
Public and publicly guaranteed sector	0	0	350	15	14	15
Private sector not guaranteed	..	..	..	..	..	..
Interest payments, long-term	**0**	**0**	**131**	**1**	**1**	**1**
Public and publicly guaranteed sector	0	0	131	1	1	1
Private sector not guaranteed	..	..	..	..	..	..

SOUTH AFRICA

(US$ million, unless otherwise indicated)

Snapshot	2023
Total external debt stocks	**165,787**
External debt stocks as % of:	
Exports	122
GNI	44
Debt service as % of:	
Exports	17
GNI	6
Net financial flows, debt and equity	**-5,418**
Net debt inflows	-3,939
Net equity inflows	-1,479
GNI	**372,626**
Population (million)	**60**

Figure 1 Public and publicly guaranteed debt, by creditor and creditor type in 2023, including IMF credit

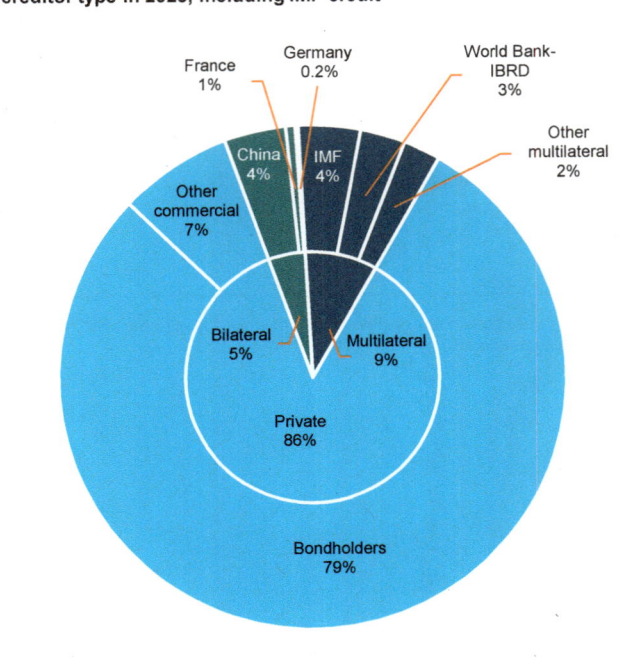

Figure 2 Average terms on new debt commitments from official and private creditors

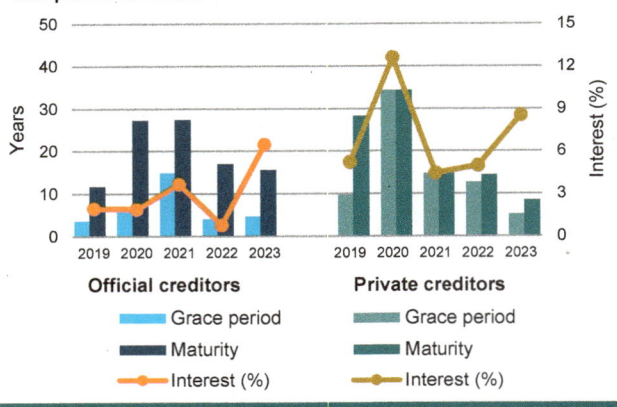

Official creditors
- Grace period
- Maturity
- Interest (%)

Private creditors
- Grace period
- Maturity
- Interest (%)

Summary External Debt Data	2010	2019	2020	2021	2022	2023
Total external debt stocks	**115,322**	**190,738**	**175,417**	**169,438**	**171,723**	**165,787**
Long-term external debt stocks	80,499	143,773	131,374	122,284	118,446	113,667
Public and publicly guaranteed debt from:	*36,329*	*102,054*	*99,435*	*95,178*	*91,237*	*89,473*
Official creditors	1,237	7,708	9,263	10,358	11,424	11,914
Multilateral	1,139	4,870	5,859	6,646	7,290	7,682
of which: World Bank	384	2,239	2,082	1,853	2,787	2,568
Bilateral	99	2,839	3,404	3,712	4,135	4,232
Private creditors	35,092	94,345	90,172	84,820	79,812	77,559
Bondholders	30,676	84,762	81,186	77,723	73,359	71,029
Commercial banks and others	4,416	9,584	8,986	7,097	6,453	6,530
Private nonguaranteed debt from:	*44,170*	*41,719*	*31,939*	*27,106*	*27,209*	*24,194*
Bondholders	8,786	4,737	2,700	2,870	2,823	1,702
Commercial banks and others	35,384	36,982	29,239	24,236	24,386	22,492
Use of IMF credit and SDR allocations	**2,750**	**2,469**	**6,966**	**10,862**	**10,329**	**9,901**
IMF credit	0	0	4,395	4,270	4,061	3,582
SDR allocations	2,750	2,469	2,571	6,592	6,268	6,319
Short-term external debt stocks	**32,073**	**44,496**	**37,077**	**36,292**	**42,949**	**42,219**
Disbursements, long-term	**12,113**	**21,690**	**12,830**	**11,103**	**19,690**	**12,113**
Public and publicly guaranteed sector	8,889	14,551	3,809	3,198	6,017	3,841
Private sector not guaranteed	3,224	7,138	9,020	7,905	13,673	8,273
Principal repayments, long-term	**3,474**	**13,796**	**20,614**	**19,847**	**20,833**	**14,813**
Public and publicly guaranteed sector	1,682	3,392	6,450	7,014	9,576	5,452
Private sector not guaranteed	1,792	10,403	14,163	12,833	11,258	9,361
Interest payments, long-term	**2,177**	**6,563**	**6,243**	**5,904**	**5,590**	**6,149**
Public and publicly guaranteed sector	1,559	4,281	4,664	4,317	4,103	4,600
Private sector not guaranteed	618	2,282	1,579	1,587	1,487	1,549

SRI LANKA

(US$ million, unless otherwise indicated)

Snapshot	2023
Total external debt stocks	**61,706**
External debt stocks as % of:	
Exports	347
GNI	76
Debt service as % of:	
Exports	16
GNI	3
Net financial flows, debt and equity	**2,374**
Net debt inflows	1,870
Net equity inflows	504
GNI	**81,623**
Population (million)	**22**

Figure 2 Average terms on new debt commitments from official and private creditors

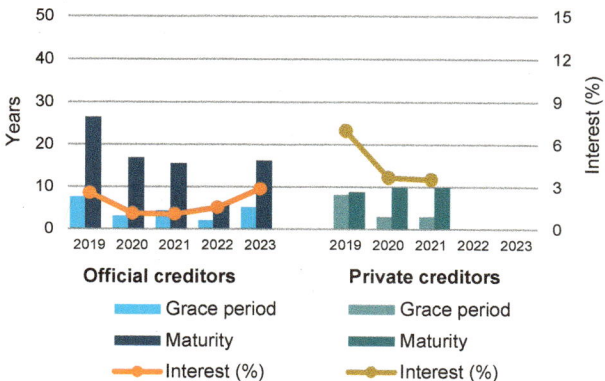

Official creditors
- Grace period
- Maturity
- Interest (%)

Private creditors
- Grace period
- Maturity
- Interest (%)

Figure 1 Public and publicly guaranteed debt, by creditor and creditor type in 2023, including IMF credit

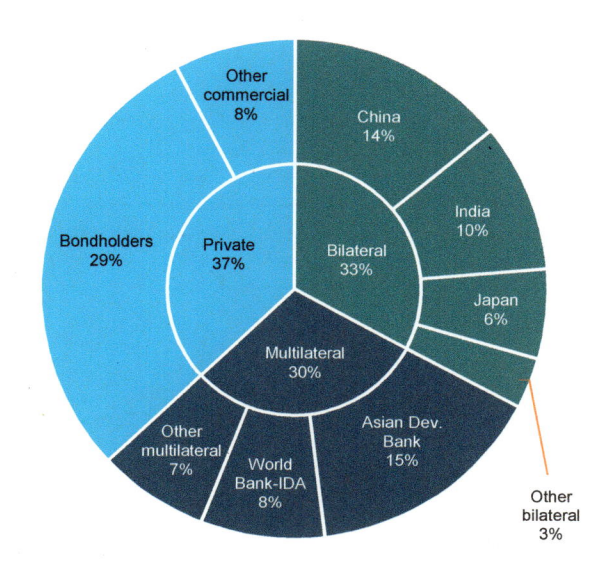

Summary External Debt Data	2010	2019	2020	2021	2022	2023
Total external debt stocks	**21,684**	**56,119**	**56,875**	**58,742**	**58,718**	**61,706**
Long-term external debt stocks	**17,349**	**45,813**	**46,552**	**47,523**	**47,802**	**51,603**
Public and publicly guaranteed debt from:	*16,430*	*36,987*	*37,569*	*38,491*	*38,487*	*41,382*
Official creditors	13,400	19,397	20,743	22,152	22,670	25,502
Multilateral	6,089	8,254	9,135	9,750	10,273	11,462
of which: World Bank	2,531	3,226	3,492	3,740	3,837	4,388
Bilateral	7,311	11,143	11,608	12,402	12,397	14,041
Private creditors	3,029	17,590	16,826	16,339	15,817	15,880
Bondholders	2,000	15,050	14,050	13,050	12,550	12,550
Commercial banks and others	1,029	2,540	2,776	3,289	3,267	3,330
Private nonguaranteed debt from:	*919*	*8,826*	*8,984*	*9,032*	*9,314*	*10,220*
Bondholders	0	175	175	175	175	175
Commercial banks and others	919	8,651	8,809	8,857	9,139	10,045
Use of IMF credit and SDR allocations	**1,920**	**1,864**	**1,927**	**2,593**	**2,326**	**2,854**
IMF credit	1,311	1,317	1,357	1,263	1,062	1,579
SDR allocations	609	547	570	1,330	1,265	1,275
Short-term external debt stocks	**2,416**	**8,442**	**8,396**	**8,626**	**8,590**	**7,249**
Disbursements, long-term	**3,091**	**7,071**	**3,392**	**4,538**	**3,329**	**5,304**
Public and publicly guaranteed sector	2,994	6,235	2,856	4,255	2,503	4,116
Private sector not guaranteed	97	836	536	283	826	1,188
Principal repayments, long-term	**727**	**4,431**	**3,323**	**3,043**	**2,018**	**1,345**
Public and publicly guaranteed sector	582	3,582	2,862	2,808	1,475	1,063
Private sector not guaranteed	145	849	461	235	543	282
Interest payments, long-term	**616**	**1,542**	**1,590**	**1,522**	**787**	**883**
Public and publicly guaranteed sector	596	1,384	1,492	1,337	540	483
Private sector not guaranteed	20	159	97	185	248	400

ST. LUCIA

(US$ million, unless otherwise indicated)

Snapshot	2023
Total external debt stocks	**1,086**
External debt stocks as % of:	
Exports	75
GNI	47
Debt service as % of:	
Exports	5
GNI	3
Net financial flows, debt and equity	**215**
Net debt inflows	106
Net equity inflows	108
GNI	**2,305**
Population (thousand)	**180**

Figure 2 Average terms on new debt commitments from official and private creditors

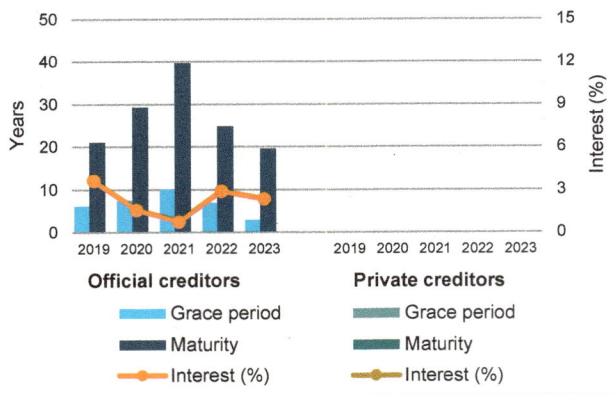

Official creditors — Grace period, Maturity, Interest (%)
Private creditors — Grace period, Maturity, Interest (%)

Figure 1 Public and publicly guaranteed debt, by creditor and creditor type in 2023, including IMF credit

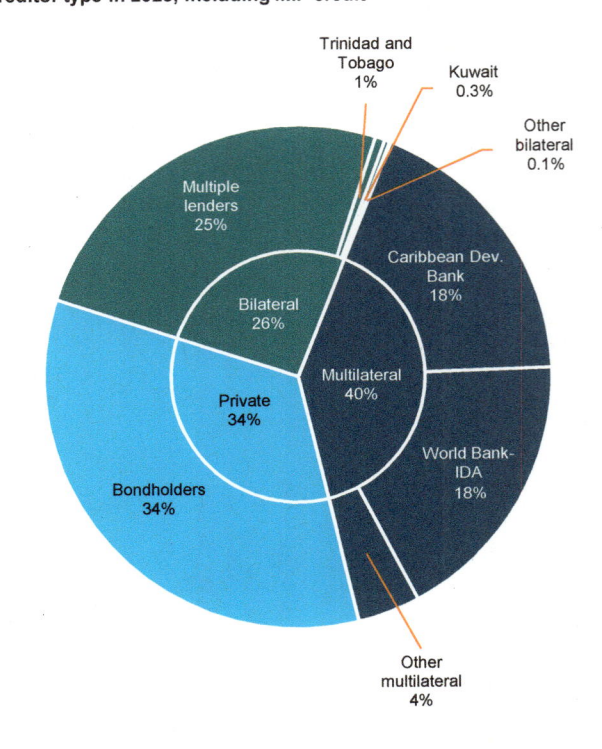

Summary External Debt Data	2010	2019	2020	2021	2022	2023
Total external debt stocks	**585**	**639**	**734**	**893**	**909**	**1,086**
Long-term external debt stocks	**326**	**542**	**604**	**722**	**737**	**930**
Public and publicly guaranteed debt from:	*326*	*542*	*604*	*722*	*737*	*930*
Official creditors	263	271	351	478	481	606
Multilateral	243	223	278	341	344	356
of which: World Bank	80	87	108	150	157	173
Bilateral	21	48	73	137	137	250
Private creditors	63	272	252	244	255	324
Bondholders	63	272	252	244	255	324
Commercial banks and others	..	..	..	..	..	..
Private nonguaranteed debt from:						
Bondholders	..	..	..	..	..	..
Commercial banks and others	..	..	..	..	..	..
Use of IMF credit and SDR allocations	**33**	**22**	**52**	**79**	**75**	**76**
IMF credit	11	2	31	30	28	29
SDR allocations	22	20	21	49	47	47
Short-term external debt stocks	**225**	**75**	**78**	**92**	**98**	**80**
Disbursements, long-term	**36**	**48**	**94**	**148**	**29**	**146**
Public and publicly guaranteed sector	36	48	94	148	29	146
Private sector not guaranteed	..	..	..	..	..	..
Principal repayments, long-term	**30**	**20**	**18**	**19**	**21**	**23**
Public and publicly guaranteed sector	30	20	18	19	21	23
Private sector not guaranteed	..	..	..	..	..	..
Interest payments, long-term	**11**	**26**	**25**	**25**	**28**	**39**
Public and publicly guaranteed sector	11	26	25	25	28	39
Private sector not guaranteed	..	..	..	..	..	..

ST. VINCENT AND THE GRENADINES

(US$ million, unless otherwise indicated)

Snapshot	2023
Total external debt stocks	**628.5**
External debt stocks as % of:	
Exports	176.4
GNI	59.4
Debt service as % of:	
Exports	10.7
GNI	3.6
Net financial flows, debt and equity	**160.0**
Net debt inflows	72.0
Net equity inflows	88.0
GNI	**1,058.6**
Population (thousand)	**103.7**

Figure 2 Average terms on new debt commitments from official and private creditors

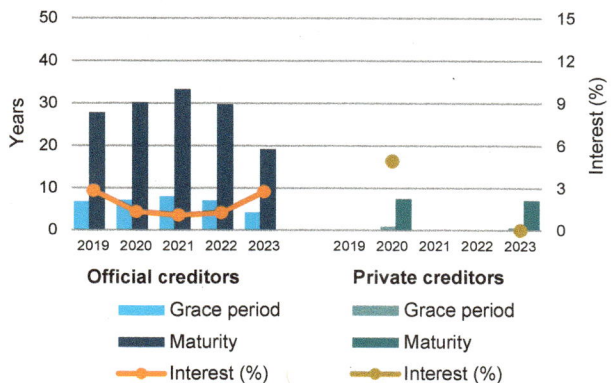

Figure 1 Public and publicly guaranteed debt, by creditor and creditor type in 2023, including IMF credit

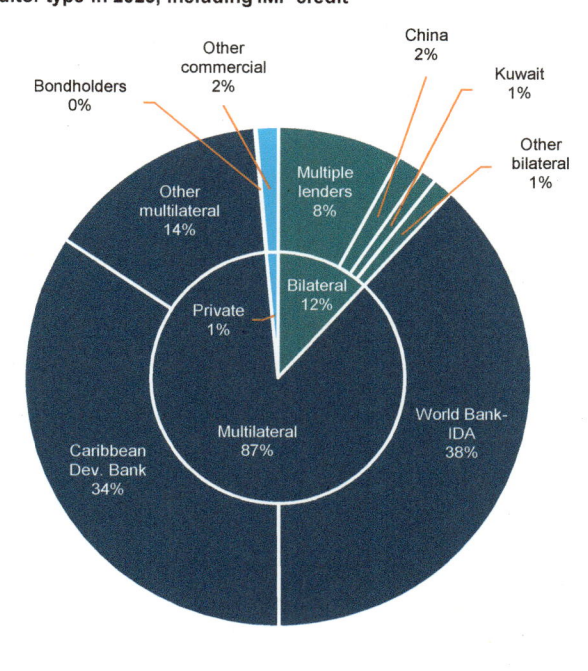

Summary External Debt Data	2010	2019	2020	2021	2022	2023
Total external debt stocks	**295.9**	**337.1**	**395.7**	**505.4**	**553.7**	**628.5**
Long-term external debt stocks	**277.9**	**321.7**	**364.5**	**449.0**	**500.6**	**575.6**
Public and publicly guaranteed debt from:	*277.9*	*321.7*	*364.5*	*449.0*	*500.6*	*575.6*
Official creditors	229.2	302.5	349.8	435.4	490.0	566.6
Multilateral	211.0	254.9	306.7	394.9	434.7	495.0
of which: World Bank	26.5	69.1	117.1	202.0	214.3	229.2
Bilateral	18.2	47.6	43.1	40.6	55.3	71.6
Private creditors	48.7	19.2	14.7	13.6	10.7	9.0
Bondholders	..	7.9	4.0	2.7	1.5	0.4
Commercial banks and others	48.7	11.3	10.7	10.9	9.2	8.5
Private nonguaranteed debt from:	..	..	..	..	..	..
Bondholders	..	..	..	..	..	..
Commercial banks and others	..	..	..	..	..	..
Use of IMF credit and SDR allocations	**17.9**	**15.4**	**31.3**	**56.3**	**53.0**	**52.9**
IMF credit	5.8	4.4	19.9	29.6	27.6	27.2
SDR allocations	12.2	10.9	11.4	26.8	25.5	25.7
Short-term external debt stocks	**0.0**	**0.0**	**0.0**	**0.0**	**0.0**	**0.0**
Disbursements, long-term	**79.4**	**54.7**	**71.9**	**110.4**	**82.2**	**95.5**
Public and publicly guaranteed sector	79.4	54.7	71.9	110.4	82.2	95.5
Private sector not guaranteed	..	..	..	..	..	..
Principal repayments, long-term	**25.9**	**33.8**	**31.8**	**24.1**	**25.9**	**22.9**
Public and publicly guaranteed sector	25.9	33.8	31.8	24.1	25.9	22.9
Private sector not guaranteed	..	..	..	..	..	..
Interest payments, long-term	**9.9**	**9.0**	**7.5**	**6.7**	**7.8**	**13.8**
Public and publicly guaranteed sector	9.9	9.0	7.5	6.7	7.8	13.8
Private sector not guaranteed	..	..	..	..	..	..

SUDAN

(US$ million, unless otherwise indicated)

Snapshot	2023
Total external debt stocks	**22,581**
External debt stocks as % of:	
Exports	..
GNI	21
Debt service as % of:	
Exports	..
GNI	0
Net financial flows, debt and equity	340
Net debt inflows	-208
Net equity inflows	548
GNI	**108,427**
Population (million)	**48**

Figure 1 Public and publicly guaranteed debt, by creditor and creditor type in 2023, including IMF credit

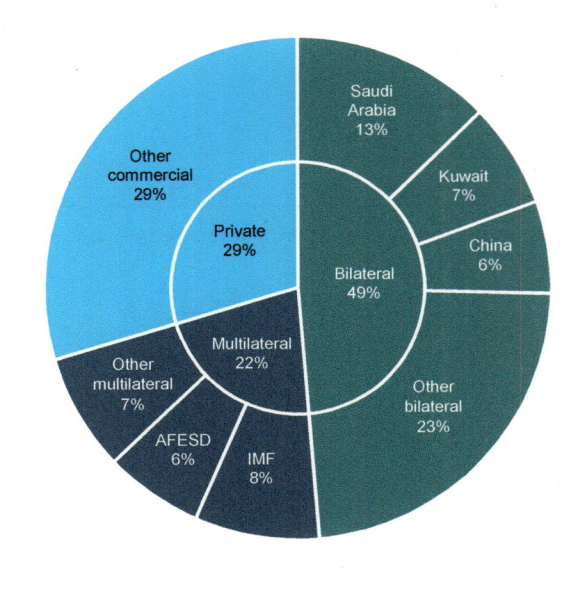

Figure 2 Average terms on new debt commitments from official and private creditors

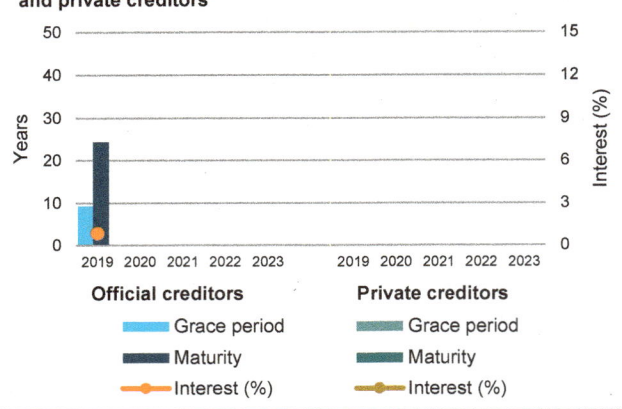

Summary External Debt Data	2010	2019	2020	2021	2022	2023
Total external debt stocks	**22,593**	**22,844**	**23,811**	**22,976**	**22,441**	**22,581**
Long-term external debt stocks	**14,638**	**16,794**	**17,084**	**15,611**	**15,253**	**15,365**
Public and publicly guaranteed debt from:	*14,638*	*16,794*	*17,084*	*15,611*	*15,253*	*15,365*
Official creditors	11,992	12,164	12,258	10,860	10,526	10,432
Multilateral	3,378	3,672	3,747	2,521	2,375	2,308
of which: World Bank	1,290	1,201	1,234	346	294	259
Bilateral	8,614	8,492	8,512	8,339	8,151	8,123
Private creditors	2,645	4,630	4,826	4,751	4,727	4,933
Bondholders	..	..	..	..	..	..
Commercial banks and others	2,645	4,630	4,826	4,751	4,727	4,933
Private nonguaranteed debt from:	..	..	..	..	..	..
Bondholders	..	..	..	..	..	..
Commercial banks and others	..	..	..	..	..	..
Use of IMF credit and SDR allocations	**664**	**528**	**548**	**2,505**	**2,382**	**2,401**
IMF credit	390	282	291	1,388	1,320	1,330
SDR allocations	274	246	256	1,117	1,062	1,071
Short-term external debt stocks	**7,292**	**5,522**	**6,179**	**4,860**	**4,806**	**4,815**
Disbursements, long-term	**935**	**1,152**	**8**	**4**	**0**	**0**
Public and publicly guaranteed sector	935	1,152	8	4	0	0
Private sector not guaranteed	..	..	..	..	..	..
Principal repayments, long-term	**400**	**139**	**111**	**1,238**	**147**	**139**
Public and publicly guaranteed sector	400	139	111	1,238	147	139
Private sector not guaranteed	..	..	..	..	..	..
Interest payments, long-term	**84**	**39**	**30**	**449**	**23**	**21**
Public and publicly guaranteed sector	84	39	30	449	23	21
Private sector not guaranteed	..	..	..	..	..	..

SURINAME

(US$ million, unless otherwise indicated)

Snapshot	2023
Total external debt stocks	**4,048**
External debt stocks as % of:	
Exports	157
GNI	116
Debt service as % of:	
Exports	25
GNI	19
Net financial flows, debt and equity	122
Net debt inflows	44
Net equity inflows	78
GNI	**3,475**
Population (thousand)	**623**

Figure 1 Public and publicly guaranteed debt, by creditor and creditor type in 2023, including IMF credit

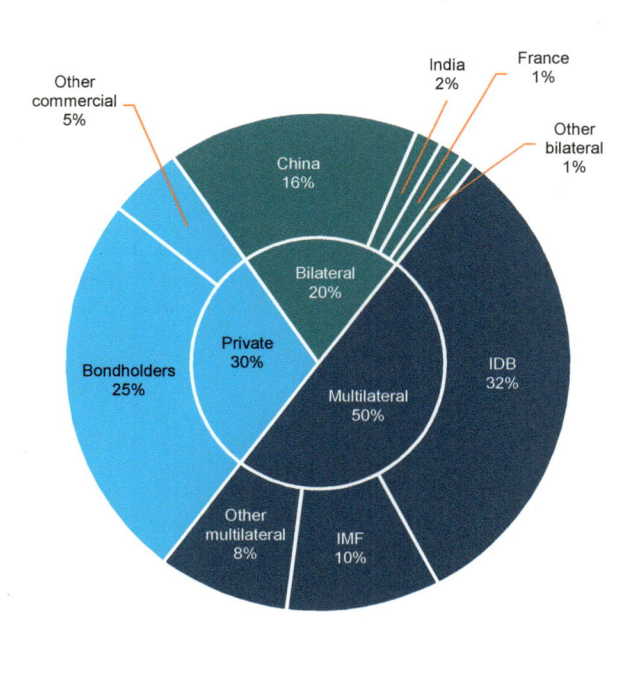

Figure 2 Average terms on new debt commitments from official and private creditors

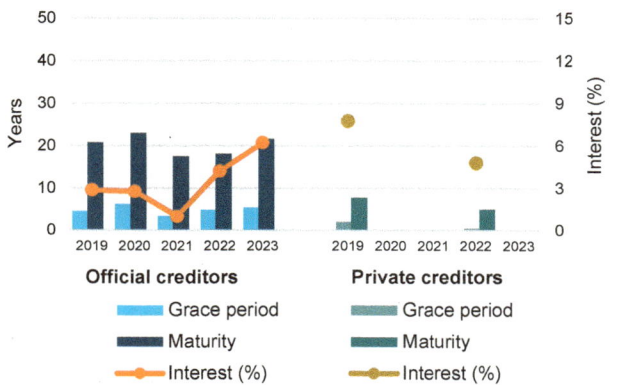

Summary External Debt Data	2010	2019	2020	2021	2022	2023
Total external debt stocks	..	**3,928**	**3,886**	**4,139**	**4,195**	**4,048**
Long-term external debt stocks	..	**3,386**	**3,385**	**3,280**	**3,396**	**3,294**
Public and publicly guaranteed debt from:	..	*1,987*	*2,059*	*2,031*	*2,209*	*2,403*
Official creditors	..	1,158	1,213	1,194	1,396	1,617
Multilateral	..	636	656	632	847	1,073
of which: World Bank	..	0	5	5	6	20
Bilateral	..	522	557	561	548	544
Private creditors	..	829	846	837	813	786
Bondholders	..	675	675	675	675	660
Commercial banks and others	..	154	171	162	138	126
Private nonguaranteed debt from:	..	*1,399*	*1,326*	*1,250*	*1,187*	*891*
Bondholders	..	..	2	2	2	2
Commercial banks and others	..	1,399	1,324	1,248	1,185	889
Use of IMF credit and SDR allocations	..	**182**	**148**	**351**	**387**	**548**
IMF credit	..	60	21	55	105	264
SDR allocations	..	122	127	296	282	284
Short-term external debt stocks	..	**359**	**353**	**508**	**412**	**206**
Disbursements, long-term	..	**738**	**266**	**298**	**471**	**435**
Public and publicly guaranteed sector	..	359	80	43	279	298
Private sector not guaranteed	..	379	186	255	191	137
Principal repayments, long-term	..	**360**	**306**	**318**	**324**	**532**
Public and publicly guaranteed sector	..	82	42	67	70	99
Private sector not guaranteed	..	279	264	251	254	433
Interest payments, long-term	..	**153**	**107**	**50**	**46**	**86**
Public and publicly guaranteed sector	..	101	58	24	19	51
Private sector not guaranteed	..	52	49	26	27	34

SYRIAN ARAB REPUBLIC

(US$ million, unless otherwise indicated)

Snapshot	2023
Total external debt stocks	**4,876**
External debt stocks as % of:	
Exports	..
GNI	..
Debt service as % of:	
Exports	..
GNI	..
Net financial flows, debt and equity	-9
Net debt inflows	-9
Net equity inflows	..
GNI	..
Population (million)	**23**

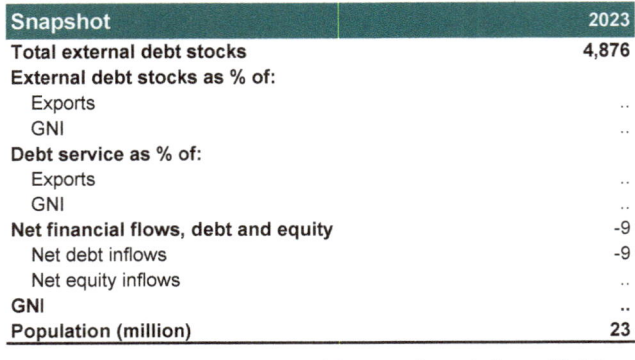

Figure 2 Average terms on new debt commitments from official and private creditors

Official creditors
- Grace period
- Maturity
- Interest (%)

Private creditors
- Grace period
- Maturity
- Interest (%)

Figure 1 Public and publicly guaranteed debt, by creditor and creditor type in 2023, including IMF credit

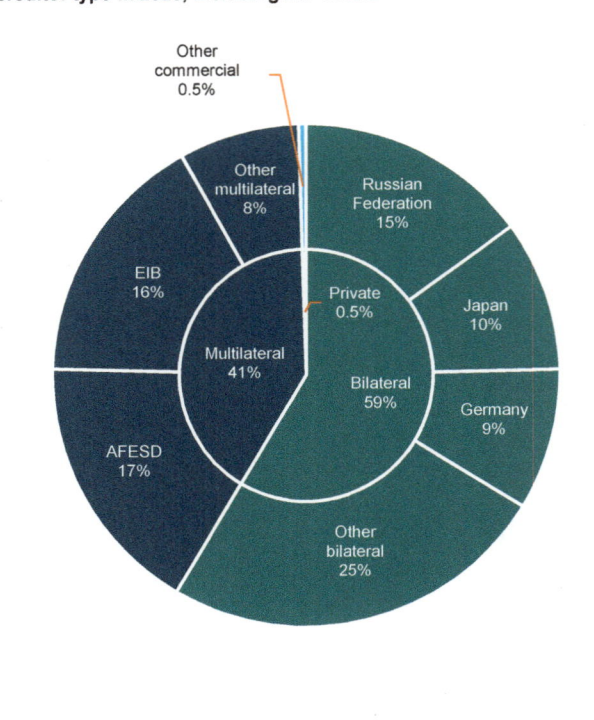

Summary External Debt Data	2010	2019	2020	2021	2022	2023
Total external debt stocks	**5,277**	**4,590**	**4,763**	**5,029**	**4,862**	**4,876**
Long-term external debt stocks	**4,284**	**3,635**	**3,751**	**3,632**	**3,498**	**3,502**
Public and publicly guaranteed debt from:	*4,284*	*3,635*	*3,751*	*3,632*	*3,498*	*3,502*
Official creditors	4,261	3,619	3,734	3,616	3,482	3,485
Multilateral	1,698	1,459	1,529	1,467	1,412	1,435
of which: World Bank	15	14	14	14	14	14
Bilateral	2,563	2,160	2,205	2,149	2,070	2,050
Private creditors	23	16	17	16	16	16
Bondholders	..	..	..	..	..	..
Commercial banks and others	23	16	17	16	16	16
Private nonguaranteed debt from:	..	..	..	..	..	..
Bondholders	..	..	..	..	..	..
Commercial banks and others	..	..	..	..	..	..
Use of IMF credit and SDR allocations	**430**	**386**	**402**	**785**	**746**	**752**
IMF credit	0	0	0	0	0	0
SDR allocations	430	386	402	785	746	752
Short-term external debt stocks	**562**	**569**	**610**	**612**	**618**	**622**
Disbursements, long-term	**286**	**0**	**0**	**0**	**0**	**0**
Public and publicly guaranteed sector	286	0	0	0	0	0
Private sector not guaranteed	..	..	..	..	..	..
Principal repayments, long-term	**509**	**1**	**0**	**0**	**0**	**0**
Public and publicly guaranteed sector	509	1	0	0	0	0
Private sector not guaranteed	..	..	..	..	..	..
Interest payments, long-term	**111**	**0**	**0**	**0**	**0**	**0**
Public and publicly guaranteed sector	111	0	0	0	0	0
Private sector not guaranteed	..	..	..	..	..	..

Note: Figure 2 shows no data values because the country did not have new commitments from 2019 to 2023.

TAJIKISTAN

(US$ million, unless otherwise indicated)

Snapshot	2023
Total external debt stocks	**6,873**
External debt stocks as % of:	
Exports	126
GNI	45
Debt service as % of:	
Exports	11
GNI	4
Net financial flows, debt and equity	**239**
Net debt inflows	141
Net equity inflows	97
GNI	**15,144**
Population (million)	**10**

Figure 2 Average terms on new debt commitments from official and private creditors

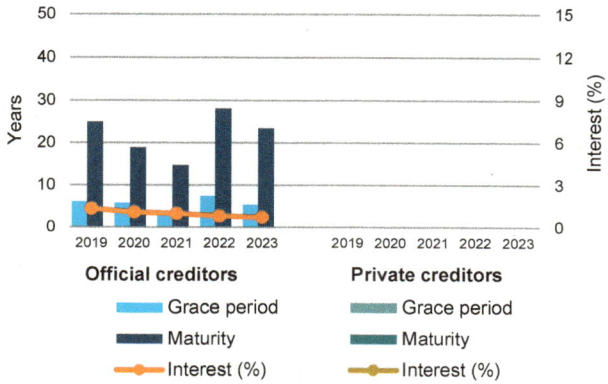

Official creditors
- Grace period
- Maturity
- Interest (%)

Private creditors
- Grace period
- Maturity
- Interest (%)

Figure 1 Public and publicly guaranteed debt, by creditor and creditor type in 2023, including IMF credit

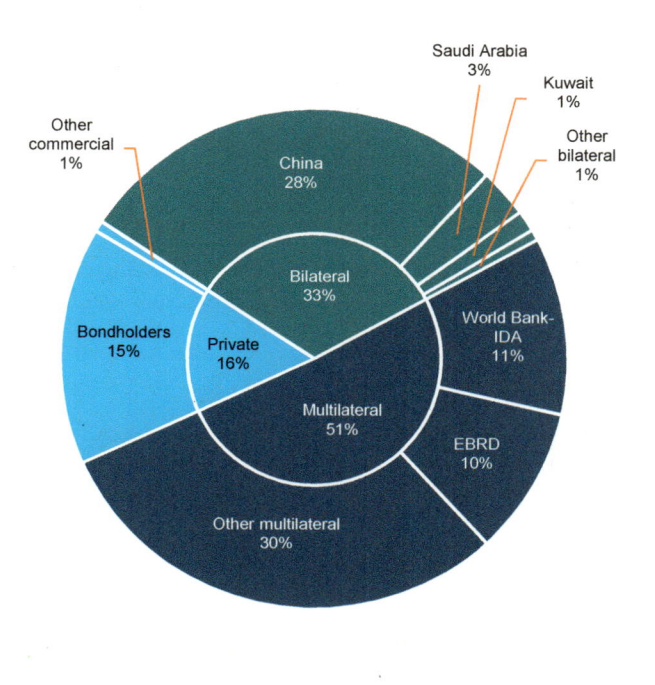

Summary External Debt Data	2010	2019	2020	2021	2022	2023
Total external debt stocks	**3,561**	**6,633**	**6,904**	**6,591**	**6,724**	**6,873**
Long-term external debt stocks	**2,733**	**5,125**	**5,451**	**5,538**	**5,582**	**5,674**
Public and publicly guaranteed debt from:	*1,806*	*2,827*	*3,065*	*3,142*	*3,070*	*3,091*
Official creditors	1,800	2,304	2,540	2,619	2,549	2,569
Multilateral	943	1,035	1,229	1,333	1,386	1,490
of which: World Bank	377	342	356	358	369	375
Bilateral	856	1,269	1,311	1,286	1,163	1,078
Private creditors	6	522	525	523	521	522
Bondholders	..	500	500	500	500	500
Commercial banks and others	6	22	25	23	21	22
Private nonguaranteed debt from:	*927*	*2,298*	*2,387*	*2,396*	*2,511*	*2,583*
Bondholders	..	..	..	..	..	..
Commercial banks and others	927	2,298	2,387	2,396	2,511	2,583
Use of IMF credit and SDR allocations	**227**	**144**	**330**	**545**	**516**	**521**
IMF credit	101	31	212	197	185	187
SDR allocations	126	114	118	348	331	334
Short-term external debt stocks	**601**	**1,364**	**1,122**	**508**	**625**	**678**
Disbursements, long-term	**924**	**454**	**484**	**513**	**394**	**476**
Public and publicly guaranteed sector	251	121	275	242	191	195
Private sector not guaranteed	673	332	209	271	204	281
Principal repayments, long-term	**631**	**383**	**228**	**373**	**353**	**387**
Public and publicly guaranteed sector	37	129	103	143	190	178
Private sector not guaranteed	593	254	124	230	162	208
Interest payments, long-term	**54**	**109**	**91**	**114**	**119**	**134**
Public and publicly guaranteed sector	23	75	61	77	79	87
Private sector not guaranteed	31	33	30	37	41	48

TANZANIA

(US$ million, unless otherwise indicated)

Snapshot	2023
Total external debt stocks	**34,598**
External debt stocks as % of:	
Exports	244
GNI	44
Debt service as % of:	
Exports	16
GNI	3
Net financial flows, debt and equity	5,460
Net debt inflows	4,122
Net equity inflows	1,339
GNI	**77,758**
Population (million)	**67**

Figure 1 Public and publicly guaranteed debt, by creditor and creditor type in 2023, including IMF credit

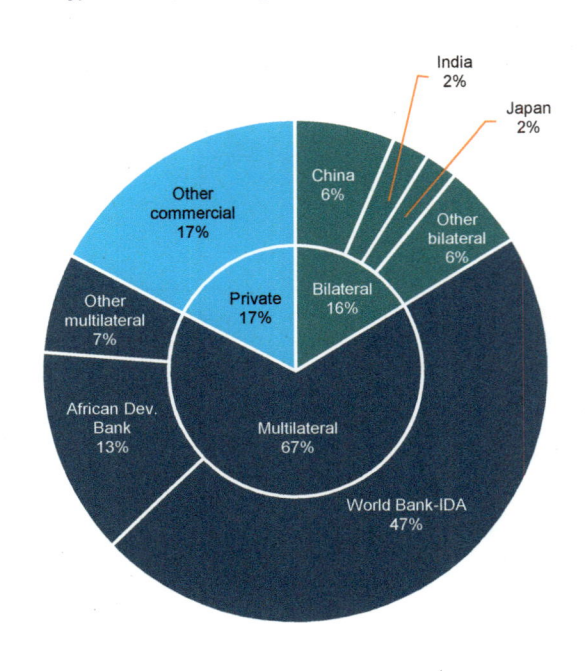

Figure 2 Average terms on new debt commitments from official and private creditors

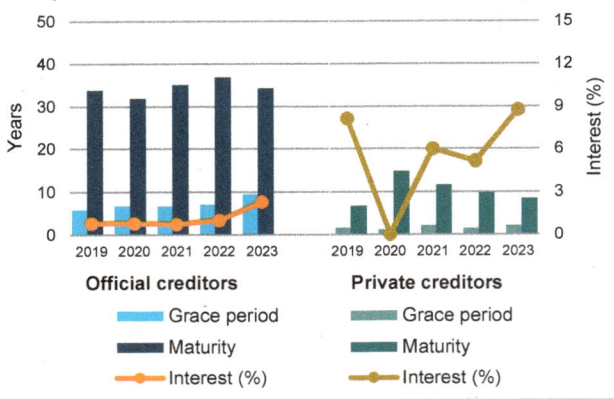

Summary External Debt Data	2010	2019	2020	2021	2022	2023
Total external debt stocks	**8,937**	**24,184**	**25,566**	**28,526**	**30,379**	**34,598**
Long-term external debt stocks	6,922	21,092	22,141	23,606	24,626	28,461
Public and publicly guaranteed debt from:	*5,698*	*16,864*	*17,649*	*18,954*	*19,646*	*22,575*
Official creditors	5,563	14,295	15,324	15,508	16,380	18,500
Multilateral	4,412	10,099	11,187	11,464	12,571	14,657
of which: World Bank	3,248	7,341	8,148	8,290	9,228	10,989
Bilateral	1,152	4,197	4,137	4,045	3,809	3,843
Private creditors	135	2,569	2,325	3,446	3,266	4,075
Bondholders	..	..	..	..	..	..
Commercial banks and others	135	2,569	2,325	3,446	3,266	4,075
Private nonguaranteed debt from:	*1,224*	*4,228*	*4,491*	*4,651*	*4,981*	*5,886*
Bondholders	..	..	..	..	..	..
Commercial banks and others	1,224	4,228	4,491	4,651	4,981	5,886
Use of IMF credit and SDR allocations	647	301	274	1,357	1,444	1,760
IMF credit	354	37	0	557	683	993
SDR allocations	293	263	274	800	761	767
Short-term external debt stocks	1,368	2,792	3,151	3,563	4,309	4,377
Disbursements, long-term	**1,347**	**2,504**	**1,450**	**3,033**	**3,089**	**5,294**
Public and publicly guaranteed sector	1,131	2,361	1,171	2,848	2,406	4,123
Private sector not guaranteed	216	143	279	184	683	1,171
Principal repayments, long-term	**132**	**785**	**867**	**1,244**	**1,543**	**1,582**
Public and publicly guaranteed sector	52	765	852	1,220	1,189	1,317
Private sector not guaranteed	79	20	15	25	353	266
Interest payments, long-term	**51**	**382**	**351**	**324**	**416**	**605**
Public and publicly guaranteed sector	33	375	349	321	363	550
Private sector not guaranteed	17	6	2	4	52	56

THAILAND

(US$ million, unless otherwise indicated)

Snapshot	2023
Total external debt stocks	**193,626**
External debt stocks as % of:	
Exports	55
GNI	39
Debt service as % of:	
Exports	12
GNI	8
Net financial flows, debt and equity	**-8,872**
Net debt inflows	-7,304
Net equity inflows	-1,569
GNI	**502,921**
Population (million)	**72**

Figure 2 Average terms on new debt commitments from official and private creditors

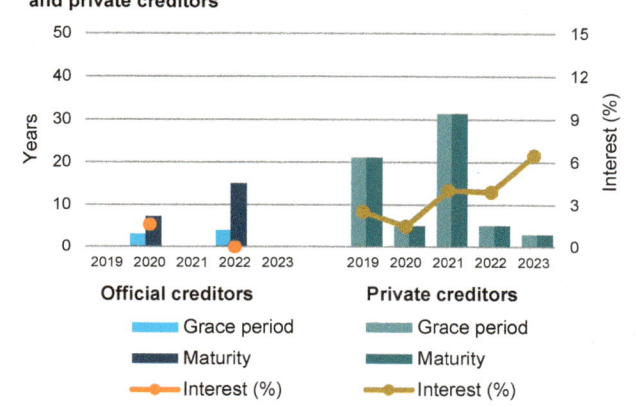

Figure 1 Public and publicly guaranteed debt, by creditor and creditor type in 2023, including IMF credit

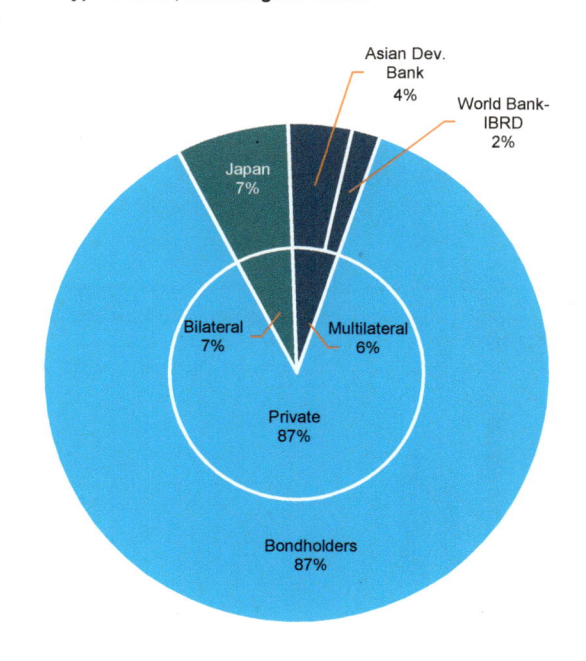

Summary External Debt Data	2010	2019	2020	2021	2022	2023
Total external debt stocks	107,166	168,600	186,866	196,676	201,051	193,626
Long-term external debt stocks	55,015	116,444	120,719	128,241	127,350	120,420
Public and publicly guaranteed debt from:	*16,737*	*40,884*	*35,824*	*36,815*	*35,678*	*32,419*
Official creditors	6,881	4,438	4,422	5,353	5,043	4,239
Multilateral	187	1,191	1,068	2,440	2,316	1,902
of which: World Bank	128	927	837	750	666	583
Bilateral	6,693	3,248	3,353	2,913	2,728	2,337
Private creditors	9,856	36,446	31,403	31,462	30,635	28,180
Bondholders	8,812	36,446	31,403	31,462	30,635	28,180
Commercial banks and others	1,045	..	..	..	..	..
Private nonguaranteed debt from:	*38,278*	*75,560*	*84,895*	*91,426*	*91,672*	*88,001*
Bondholders	4,265	13,193	15,840	17,747	17,080	14,419
Commercial banks and others	34,012	62,367	69,055	73,679	74,592	73,581
Use of IMF credit and SDR allocations	**1,494**	**1,342**	**1,397**	**5,667**	**5,388**	**5,432**
IMF credit	0	0	0	0	0	0
SDR allocations	1,494	1,342	1,397	5,667	5,388	5,432
Short-term external debt stocks	**50,657**	**50,814**	**64,749**	**62,768**	**68,312**	**67,775**
Disbursements, long-term	**17,539**	**28,608**	**24,053**	**25,569**	**22,136**	**27,822**
Public and publicly guaranteed sector	5,941	4,560	542	2,430	882	169
Private sector not guaranteed	11,597	24,049	23,512	23,140	21,254	27,653
Principal repayments, long-term	**9,386**	**29,047**	**19,995**	**14,700**	**22,588**	**34,588**
Public and publicly guaranteed sector	803	1,185	5,771	1,134	1,612	3,254
Private sector not guaranteed	8,582	27,862	14,223	13,566	20,976	31,334
Interest payments, long-term	**1,079**	**1,695**	**1,630**	**774**	**1,067**	**2,507**
Public and publicly guaranteed sector	202	1,114	1,059	92	276	1,788
Private sector not guaranteed	877	581	571	682	792	719

TIMOR-LESTE

(US$ million, unless otherwise indicated)

Snapshot	2023
Total external debt stocks	**307.4**
External debt stocks as % of:	
Exports	25.2
GNI	11.9
Debt service as % of:	
Exports	2.1
GNI	1.0
Net financial flows, debt and equity	-31.0
Net debt inflows	19.1
Net equity inflows	-50.1
GNI	**2,581.3**
Population (million)	**1.4**

Figure 1 **Public and publicly guaranteed debt, by creditor and creditor type in 2023, including IMF credit**

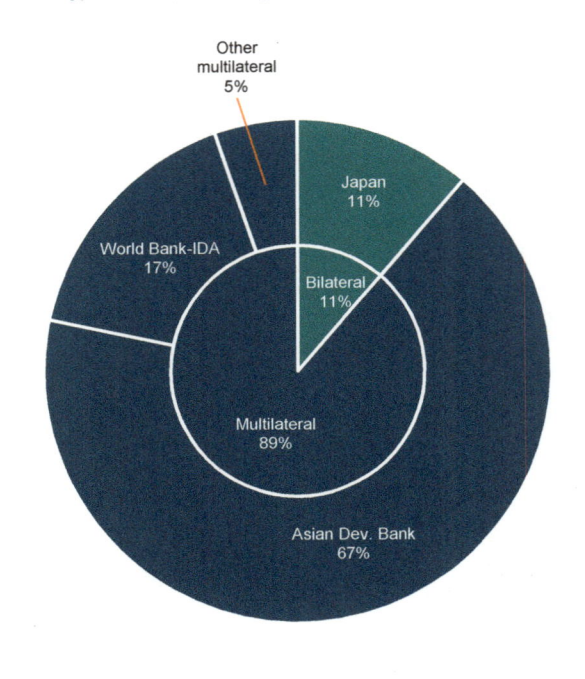

Figure 2 **Average terms on new debt commitments from official and private creditors**

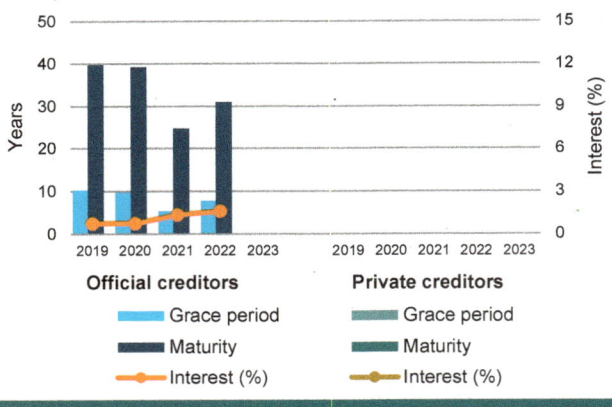

Summary External Debt Data	2010	2019	2020	2021	2022	2023
Total external debt stocks	..	**203.4**	**231.8**	**278.6**	**289.7**	**307.4**
Long-term external debt stocks	..	**191.2**	**220.2**	**232.4**	**246.4**	**254.8**
Public and publicly guaranteed debt from:	..	*191.2*	*220.2*	*232.4*	*246.4*	*254.8*
Official creditors	..	191.2	220.2	232.4	246.4	254.8
Multilateral	..	166.3	189.4	200.6	214.0	225.9
of which: World Bank	..	43.2	47.6	50.7	53.0	55.2
Bilateral	..	24.9	30.9	31.8	32.5	28.9
Private creditors	..	..	..	..	..	..
Bondholders	..	..	..	..	..	..
Commercial banks and others	..	..	..	..	..	..
Private nonguaranteed debt from:	..	..	..	..	..	..
Bondholders	..	..	..	..	..	..
Commercial banks and others	..	..	..	..	..	..
Use of IMF credit and SDR allocations	..	**10.7**	**11.1**	**45.2**	**42.9**	**43.3**
IMF credit	..	0.0	0.0	0.0	0.0	0.0
SDR allocations	..	10.7	11.1	45.2	42.9	43.3
Short-term external debt stocks	..	**1.5**	**0.4**	**1.1**	**0.3**	**9.3**
Disbursements, long-term	..	**49.7**	**30.1**	**22.6**	**31.0**	**24.7**
Public and publicly guaranteed sector	..	49.7	30.1	22.6	31.0	24.7
Private sector not guaranteed	..	..	..	..	..	..
Principal repayments, long-term	..	**3.3**	**3.9**	**6.4**	**10.5**	**14.6**
Public and publicly guaranteed sector	..	3.3	3.9	6.4	10.5	14.6
Private sector not guaranteed	..	..	..	..	..	..
Interest payments, long-term	..	**3.8**	**4.1**	**3.2**	**4.0**	**8.3**
Public and publicly guaranteed sector	..	3.8	4.1	3.2	4.0	8.3
Private sector not guaranteed	..	..	..	..	..	..

TOGO

(US$ million, unless otherwise indicated)

Snapshot	2023
Total external debt stocks	**3,375**
External debt stocks as % of:	
Exports	148
GNI	37
Debt service as % of:	
Exports	11
GNI	3
Net financial flows, debt and equity	**144**
Net debt inflows	110
Net equity inflows	34
GNI	**9,211**
Population (million)	**9**

Figure 1 Public and publicly guaranteed debt, by creditor and creditor type in 2023, including IMF credit

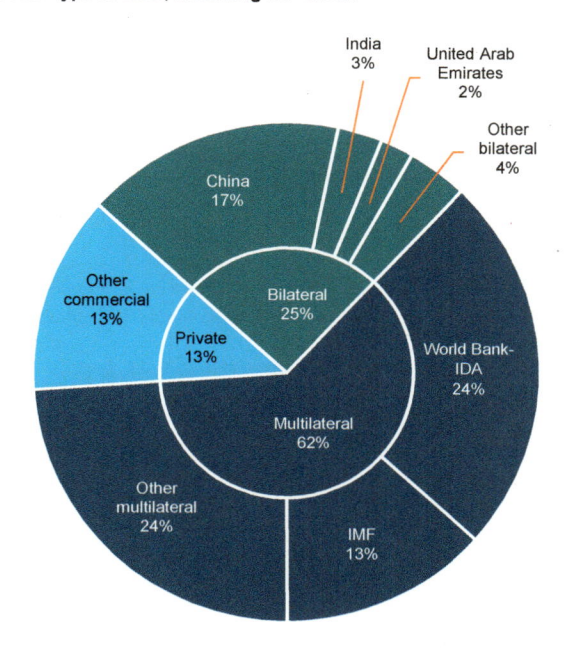

Figure 2 Average terms on new debt commitments from official and private creditors

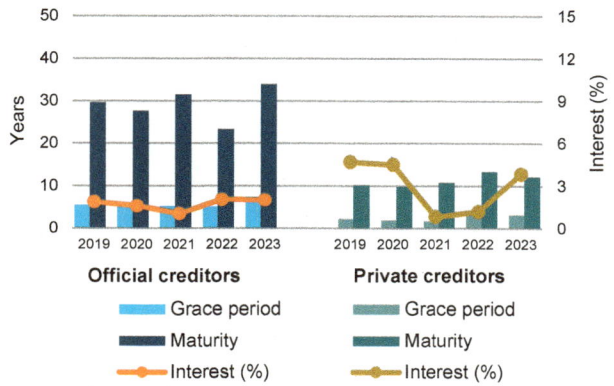

Summary External Debt Data	2010	2019	2020	2021	2022	2023
Total external debt stocks	**1,285**	**1,996**	**2,546**	**3,495**	**3,220**	**3,375**
Long-term external debt stocks	**1,005**	**1,353**	**1,767**	**2,451**	**2,443**	**2,680**
Public and publicly guaranteed debt from:	*1,005*	*1,353*	*1,767*	*1,801*	*1,793*	*2,030*
Official creditors	1,005	1,237	1,458	1,515	1,528	1,731
Multilateral	858	632	823	859	918	1,137
of which: World Bank	554	165	265	288	360	575
Bilateral	147	604	635	657	610	594
Private creditors	..	116	309	286	265	299
Bondholders	..	..	..	..	..	..
Commercial banks and others	..	116	309	286	265	299
Private nonguaranteed debt from:	..	..	..	*650*	*650*	*650*
Bondholders	..	..	..	650	650	650
Commercial banks and others	..	..	..	..	..	..
Use of IMF credit and SDR allocations	**241**	**319**	**459**	**642**	**607**	**595**
IMF credit	133	222	358	347	326	312
SDR allocations	108	97	101	295	281	283
Short-term external debt stocks	**39**	**324**	**320**	**402**	**170**	**100**
Disbursements, long-term	**94**	**264**	**367**	**820**	**220**	**333**
Public and publicly guaranteed sector	94	264	367	170	220	333
Private sector not guaranteed	..	..	..	650	..	..
Principal repayments, long-term	**28**	**60**	**54**	**71**	**143**	**136**
Public and publicly guaranteed sector	28	60	54	71	143	136
Private sector not guaranteed	..	..	..	..	..	..
Interest payments, long-term	**8**	**26**	**33**	**89**	**92**	**91**
Public and publicly guaranteed sector	8	26	33	37	40	39
Private sector not guaranteed	..	..	..	52	52	52

TONGA

(US$ million, unless otherwise indicated)

Snapshot	2023
Total external debt stocks	**196.5**
External debt stocks as % of:	
Exports	106.3
GNI	..
Debt service as % of:	
Exports	9.5
GNI	..
Net financial flows, debt and equity	12.0
Net debt inflows	-12.3
Net equity inflows	24.3
GNI	..
Population (thousand)	**107.8**

Figure 1 Public and publicly guaranteed debt, by creditor and creditor type in 2023, including IMF credit

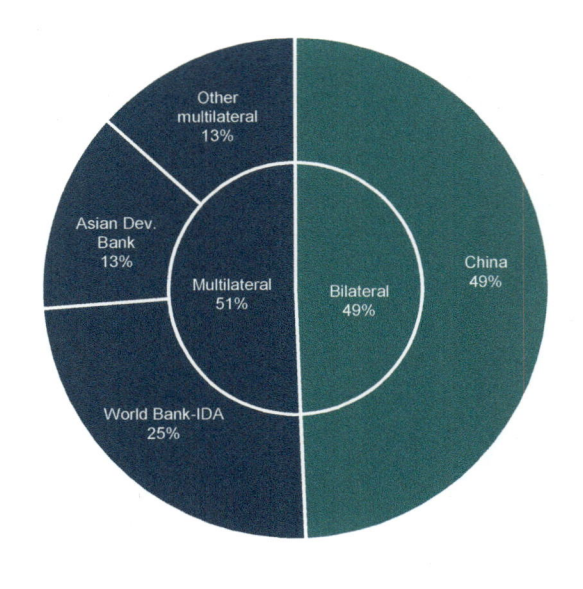

Figure 2 Average terms on new debt commitments from official and private creditors

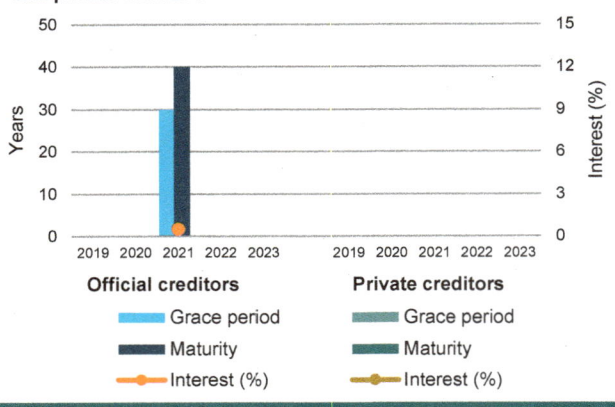

Summary External Debt Data	2010	2019	2020	2021	2022	2023
Total external debt stocks	**153.7**	**186.6**	**194.6**	**223.6**	**209.9**	**196.5**
Long-term external debt stocks	**143.5**	**177.5**	**185.1**	**186.2**	**165.2**	**151.4**
Public and publicly guaranteed debt from:	*143.5*	*177.5*	*185.1*	*186.2*	*165.2*	*151.4*
Official creditors	142.4	177.5	185.1	186.2	165.2	151.4
Multilateral	70.8	75.9	77.5	73.7	67.8	67.5
of which: World Bank	23.6	42.9	45.0	43.6	40.8	41.5
Bilateral	71.7	101.6	107.6	112.6	97.4	83.9
Private creditors	1.1	..	..	..	..	..
Bondholders	..	..	..	..	..	..
Commercial banks and others	1.1	..	..	..	..	..
Private nonguaranteed debt from:	..	..	..	..	..	..
Bondholders	..	..	..	..	..	..
Commercial banks and others	..	..	..	..	..	..
Use of IMF credit and SDR allocations	**10.1**	**9.1**	**9.5**	**37.4**	**44.7**	**45.1**
IMF credit	0.0	0.0	0.0	9.7	18.4	18.5
SDR allocations	10.1	9.1	9.5	27.7	26.4	26.6
Short-term external debt stocks	**0.0**	**0.0**	**0.0**	**0.0**	**0.0**	**0.0**
Disbursements, long-term	**40.9**	**4.9**	**1.3**	**1.0**	**0.3**	**1.7**
Public and publicly guaranteed sector	40.9	4.9	1.3	1.0	0.3	1.7
Private sector not guaranteed	..	..	..	..	..	..
Principal repayments, long-term	**2.7**	**2.7**	**4.7**	**2.7**	**8.1**	**14.1**
Public and publicly guaranteed sector	2.7	2.7	4.7	2.7	8.1	14.1
Private sector not guaranteed	..	..	..	..	..	..
Interest payments, long-term	**2.4**	**2.7**	**1.3**	**2.1**	**2.7**	**2.5**
Public and publicly guaranteed sector	2.4	2.7	1.3	2.1	2.7	2.5
Private sector not guaranteed	..	..	..	..	..	..

TUNISIA

(US$ million, unless otherwise indicated)

Snapshot	2023
Total external debt stocks	**41,279**
External debt stocks as % of:	
Exports	180
GNI	87
Debt service as % of:	
Exports	23
GNI	11
Net financial flows, debt and equity	**622**
Net debt inflows	-146
Net equity inflows	768
GNI	**47,220**
Population (million)	**12**

Figure 1 Public and publicly guaranteed debt, by creditor and creditor type in 2023, including IMF credit

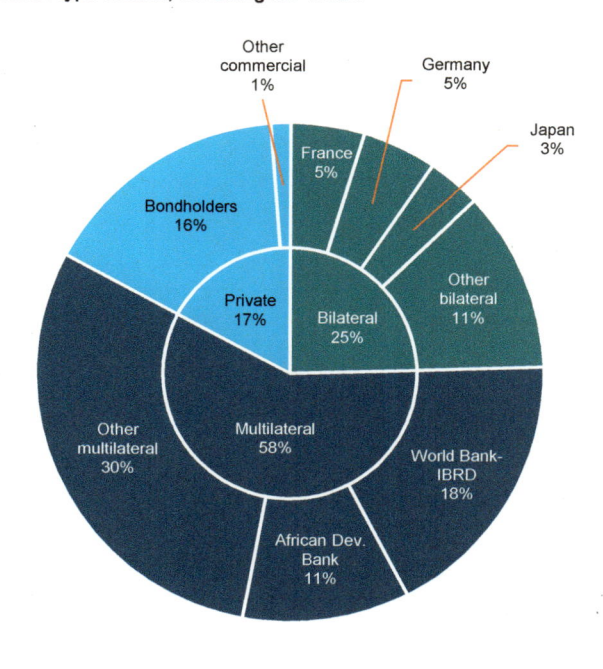

Figure 2 Average terms on new debt commitments from official and private creditors

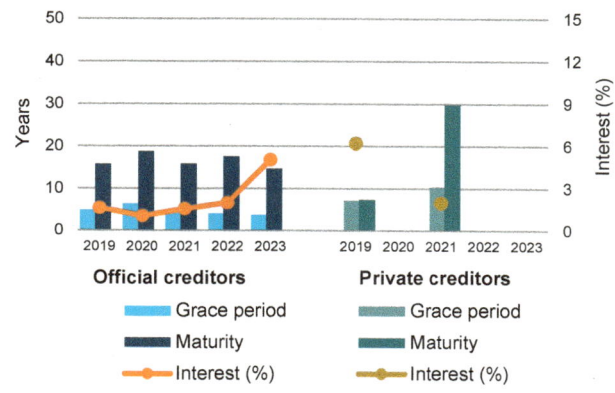

Summary External Debt Data	2010	2019	2020	2021	2022	2023
Total external debt stocks	**22,659**	**40,225**	**41,977**	**43,022**	**41,002**	**41,279**
Long-term external debt stocks	**17,260**	**26,662**	**28,521**	**26,137**	**24,209**	**24,796**
Public and publicly guaranteed debt from:	*14,858*	*23,783*	*25,778*	*23,152*	*21,635*	*22,663*
Official creditors	10,383	15,854	18,274	17,372	16,745	18,474
Multilateral	6,978	11,300	12,809	12,055	11,691	12,510
of which: World Bank	1,399	3,489	4,196	4,063	4,136	4,315
Bilateral	3,404	4,554	5,465	5,317	5,054	5,964
Private creditors	4,476	7,928	7,503	5,780	4,891	4,189
Bondholders	4,003	7,416	7,022	5,406	4,598	3,885
Commercial banks and others	472	513	481	374	292	304
Private nonguaranteed debt from:	*2,402*	*2,879*	*2,744*	*2,985*	*2,574*	*2,133*
Bondholders	..	..	..	..	..	..
Commercial banks and others	2,402	2,879	2,744	2,985	2,574	2,133
Use of IMF credit and SDR allocations	**420**	**2,132**	**2,824**	**3,396**	**3,109**	**2,711**
IMF credit	0	1,755	2,431	2,283	2,050	1,644
SDR allocations	420	377	393	1,113	1,058	1,067
Short-term external debt stocks	**4,979**	**11,431**	**10,632**	**13,489**	**13,683**	**13,772**
Disbursements, long-term	**1,671**	**4,357**	**2,519**	**2,327**	**2,025**	**2,981**
Public and publicly guaranteed sector	1,574	3,374	2,344	1,810	1,975	2,921
Private sector not guaranteed	97	983	175	517	50	60
Principal repayments, long-term	**1,631**	**1,936**	**2,161**	**3,452**	**2,720**	**2,795**
Public and publicly guaranteed sector	1,411	1,936	1,815	2,950	2,259	2,294
Private sector not guaranteed	220	..	346	501	461	501
Interest payments, long-term	**672**	**682**	**661**	**624**	**634**	**1,093**
Public and publicly guaranteed sector	548	573	583	555	530	984
Private sector not guaranteed	124	109	78	69	104	109

TÜRKIYE

(US$ million, unless otherwise indicated)

Snapshot	2023
Total external debt stocks	**499,842**
External debt stocks as % of:	
Exports	137
GNI	46
Debt service as % of:	
Exports	21
GNI	7
Net financial flows, debt and equity	47,490
Net debt inflows	37,339
Net equity inflows	10,151
GNI	**1,096,809**
Population (million)	**85**

Figure 1 **Public and publicly guaranteed debt, by creditor and creditor type in 2023, including IMF credit**

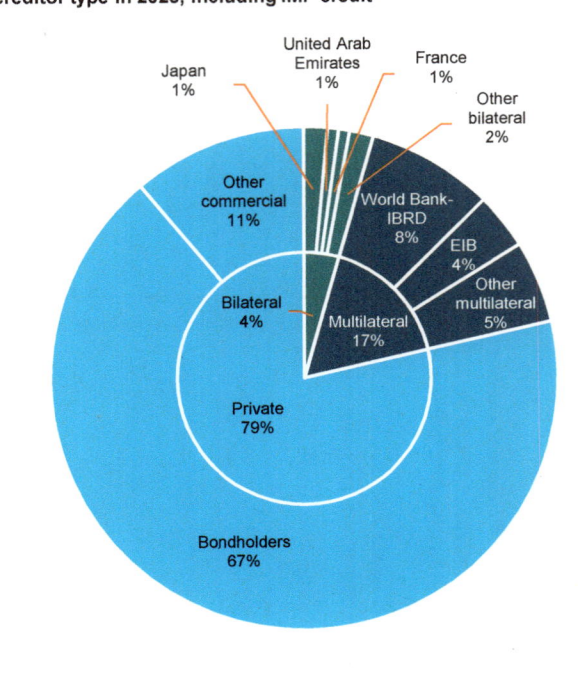

Figure 2 **Average terms on new debt commitments from official and private creditors**

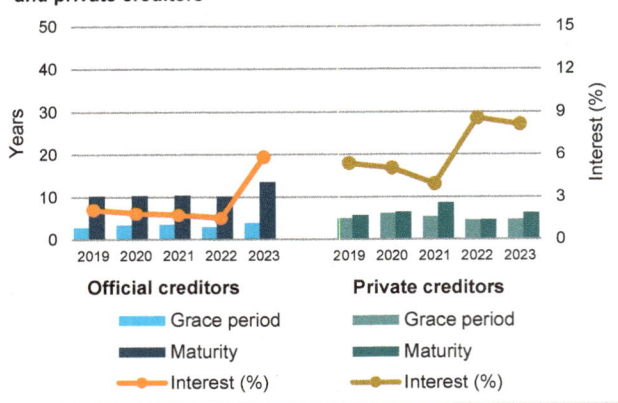

Summary External Debt Data	2010	2019	2020	2021	2022	2023
Total external debt stocks	**316,657**	**414,870**	**429,770**	**436,370**	**457,917**	**499,842**
Long-term external debt stocks	216,379	317,518	316,633	310,271	301,948	318,391
Public and publicly guaranteed debt from:	*93,299*	*129,104*	*138,145*	*139,197*	*140,204*	*149,369*
Official creditors	26,941	34,632	35,037	32,654	31,706	32,117
Multilateral	19,932	27,133	27,984	25,820	24,780	25,460
of which: World Bank	11,605	11,362	11,925	11,179	11,262	12,037
Bilateral	7,009	7,499	7,053	6,834	6,927	6,657
Private creditors	66,358	94,472	103,109	106,544	108,498	117,252
Bondholders	45,774	83,806	89,850	91,612	94,200	100,669
Commercial banks and others	20,584	10,666	13,259	14,932	14,297	16,583
Private nonguaranteed debt from:	*123,080*	*188,413*	*178,488*	*171,074*	*161,744*	*169,021*
Bondholders	6,202	36,115	34,660	34,011	27,241	27,615
Commercial banks and others	116,878	152,298	143,828	137,063	134,503	141,406
Use of IMF credit and SDR allocations	**7,277**	**1,481**	**1,543**	**7,749**	**7,368**	**7,428**
IMF credit	5,627	0	0	0	0	0
SDR allocations	1,650	1,481	1,543	7,749	7,368	7,428
Short-term external debt stocks	**93,001**	**95,871**	**111,594**	**118,350**	**148,601**	**174,024**
Disbursements, long-term	**48,834**	**60,915**	**59,778**	**56,408**	**50,973**	**65,450**
Public and publicly guaranteed sector	14,795	19,246	18,109	20,718	18,914	24,152
Private sector not guaranteed	34,039	41,669	41,669	35,690	32,059	41,298
Principal repayments, long-term	**45,504**	**69,330**	**68,878**	**56,366**	**51,469**	**53,534**
Public and publicly guaranteed sector	6,028	13,017	12,574	16,186	15,055	16,059
Private sector not guaranteed	39,476	56,313	56,303	40,179	36,414	37,475
Interest payments, long-term	**8,869**	**12,678**	**12,773**	**11,867**	**11,749**	**15,386**
Public and publicly guaranteed sector	4,693	5,549	5,749	6,065	6,311	8,150
Private sector not guaranteed	4,177	7,129	7,024	5,802	5,437	7,237

TURKMENISTAN

(US$ million, unless otherwise indicated)

Snapshot	2023
Total external debt stocks	**3,918**
External debt stocks as % of:	
Exports	..
GNI	7
Debt service as % of:	
Exports	..
GNI	2
Net financial flows, debt and equity	656
Net debt inflows	-722
Net equity inflows	1,378
GNI	**59,382**
Population (million)	**7**

Figure 2 Average terms on new debt commitments from official and private creditors

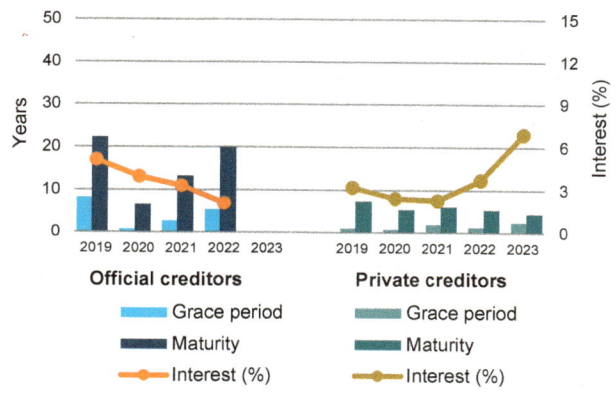

Figure 1 Public and publicly guaranteed debt, by creditor and creditor type in 2023, including IMF credit

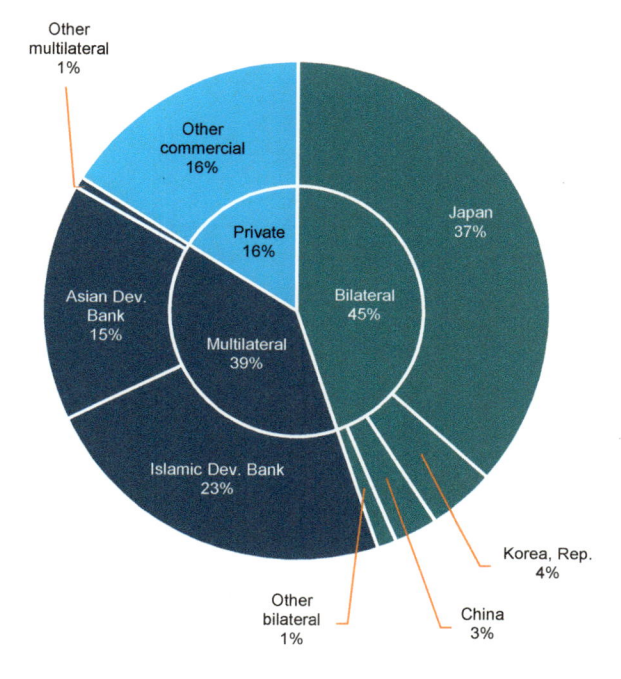

Summary External Debt Data	2010	2019	2020	2021	2022	2023
Total external debt stocks	**1,682**	**6,650**	**5,771**	**4,986**	**4,645**	**3,918**
Long-term external debt stocks	**1,520**	**6,554**	**5,529**	**4,569**	**4,148**	**3,517**
Public and publicly guaranteed debt from:	*1,513*	*6,511*	*5,477*	*4,522*	*4,123*	*3,502*
Official creditors	1,513	6,010	4,861	3,913	3,509	2,937
Multilateral	96	606	808	941	1,246	1,372
of which: World Bank	11	..	..	15	20	20
Bilateral	1,417	5,404	4,053	2,973	2,263	1,565
Private creditors	0	501	616	608	614	565
Bondholders	..	..	..	..	..	..
Commercial banks and others	..	501	616	608	614	565
Private nonguaranteed debt from:	*7*	*43*	*51*	*47*	*25*	*16*
Bondholders	..	..	..	..	..	..
Commercial banks and others	7	43	51	47	25	16
Use of IMF credit and SDR allocations	**108**	**97**	**101**	**418**	**397**	**400**
IMF credit	0	0	0	0	0	0
SDR allocations	108	97	101	418	397	400
Short-term external debt stocks	**54**	**0**	**142**	**0**	**100**	**0**
Disbursements, long-term	**1,051**	**604**	**747**	**552**	**611**	**313**
Public and publicly guaranteed sector	1,044	584	729	540	611	313
Private sector not guaranteed	8	20	18	12	..	..
Principal repayments, long-term	**148**	**1,804**	**1,850**	**1,446**	**943**	**935**
Public and publicly guaranteed sector	135	1,793	1,839	1,423	919	924
Private sector not guaranteed	13	12	11	23	24	11
Interest payments, long-term	**50**	**355**	**240**	**205**	**185**	**210**
Public and publicly guaranteed sector	50	354	239	204	184	210
Private sector not guaranteed	0	1	1	1	0	0

UGANDA

(US$ million, unless otherwise indicated)

Snapshot	2023
Total external debt stocks	**19,393**
External debt stocks as % of:	
Exports	211
GNI	40
Debt service as % of:	
Exports	26
GNI	5
Net financial flows, debt and equity	1,762
Net debt inflows	-1,129
Net equity inflows	2,891
GNI	**48,300**
Population (million)	**49**

Figure 2 Average terms on new debt commitments from official and private creditors

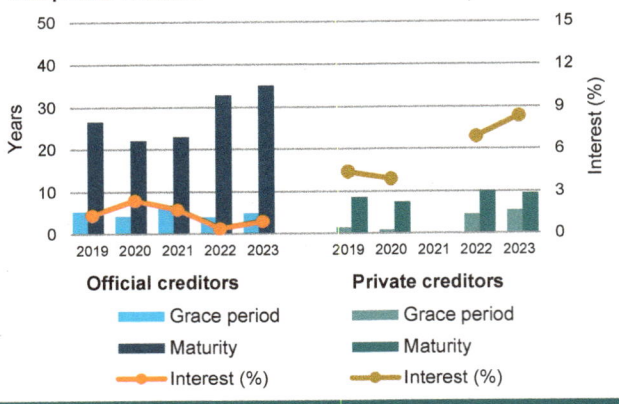

Official creditors
- Grace period
- Maturity
- Interest (%)

Private creditors
- Grace period
- Maturity
- Interest (%)

Figure 1 Public and publicly guaranteed debt, by creditor and creditor type in 2023, including IMF credit

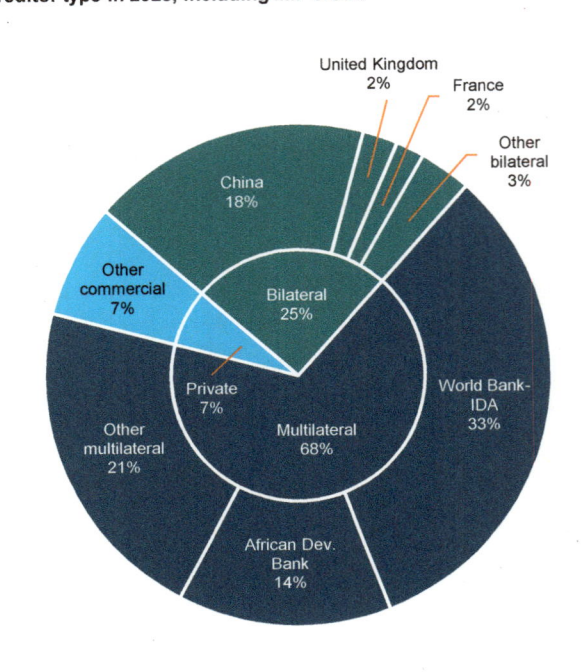

Summary External Debt Data	2010	2019	2020	2021	2022	2023
Total external debt stocks	**2,975**	**13,993**	**17,236**	**19,974**	**20,407**	**19,393**
Long-term external debt stocks	**2,673**	**12,802**	**15,276**	**16,718**	**17,152**	**17,001**
Public and publicly guaranteed debt from:	*2,673*	*8,660*	*11,364*	*12,028*	*11,955*	*13,158*
Official creditors	2,673	8,577	10,845	11,541	11,546	12,110
Multilateral	2,416	5,675	7,241	7,887	7,886	8,485
of which: World Bank	1,682	3,443	4,300	4,453	4,464	4,675
Bilateral	257	2,902	3,604	3,654	3,660	3,625
Private creditors	0	83	519	487	410	1,048
Bondholders	..	..	..	..	..	..
Commercial banks and others	0	83	519	487	410	1,048
Private nonguaranteed debt from:	..	*4,142*	*3,911*	*4,690*	*5,197*	*3,842*
Bondholders	..	..	..	..	..	..
Commercial banks and others	..	4,142	3,911	4,690	5,197	3,842
Use of IMF credit and SDR allocations	**275**	**239**	**769**	**1,484**	**1,532**	**1,907**
IMF credit	9	0	520	758	841	1,211
SDR allocations	267	239	249	726	691	696
Short-term external debt stocks	**26**	**952**	**1,191**	**1,772**	**1,724**	**485**
Disbursements, long-term	**489**	**1,420**	**2,494**	**2,120**	**1,381**	**1,740**
Public and publicly guaranteed sector	489	1,143	2,494	1,341	874	1,740
Private sector not guaranteed	..	277	..	778	507	..
Principal repayments, long-term	**40**	**166**	**403**	**342**	**469**	**1,992**
Public and publicly guaranteed sector	40	166	172	342	469	638
Private sector not guaranteed	..	..	231	..	..	1,354
Interest payments, long-term	**21**	**115**	**266**	**397**	**377**	**326**
Public and publicly guaranteed sector	21	115	141	270	210	296
Private sector not guaranteed	..	..	125	128	166	29

UKRAINE

(US$ million, unless otherwise indicated)

Snapshot	2023
Total external debt stocks	**176,645**
External debt stocks as % of:	
Exports	279
GNI	96
Debt service as % of:	
Exports	12
GNI	4
Net financial flows, debt and equity	32,580
Net debt inflows	28,296
Net equity inflows	4,284
GNI	**184,268**
Population (million)	**37**

Figure 2 Average terms on new debt commitments from official and private creditors

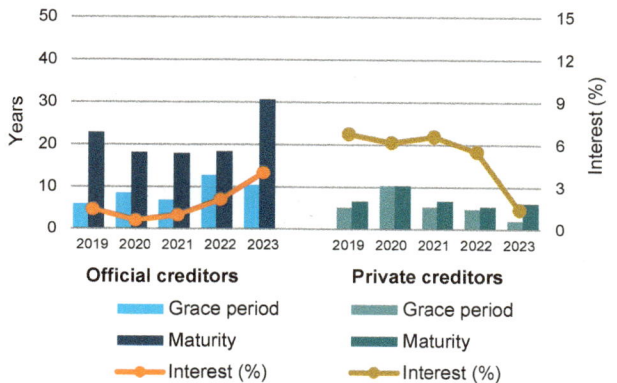

Official creditors
- Grace period
- Maturity
- Interest (%)

Private creditors
- Grace period
- Maturity
- Interest (%)

Figure 1 Public and publicly guaranteed debt, by creditor and creditor type in 2023, including IMF credit

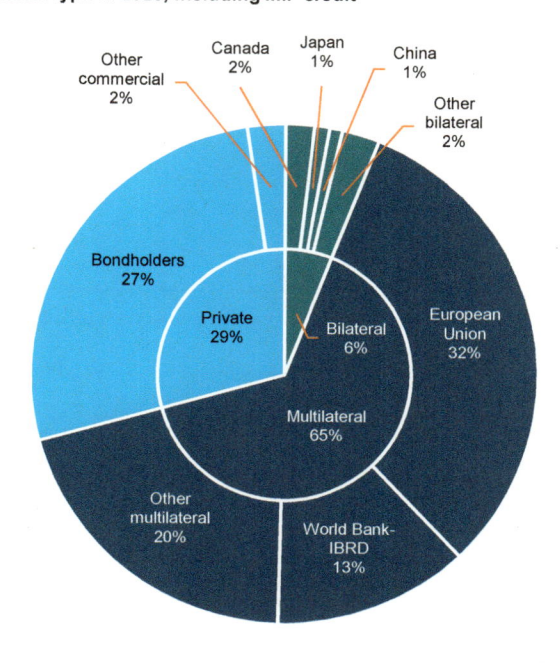

Summary External Debt Data	2010	2019	2020	2021	2022	2023
Total external debt stocks	**124,527**	**125,725**	**133,406**	**136,908**	**143,318**	**176,645**
Long-term external debt stocks	**81,001**	**91,771**	**96,426**	**99,159**	**112,690**	**139,131**
Public and publicly guaranteed debt from:	*25,327*	*39,434*	*42,529*	*44,918*	*61,592*	*87,664*
Official creditors	14,961	13,381	14,920	15,942	32,447	58,469
Multilateral	13,560	10,704	12,404	13,551	26,541	52,474
of which: World Bank	3,212	5,360	5,741	6,623	8,773	13,584
Bilateral	1,400	2,677	2,516	2,391	5,906	5,996
Private creditors	10,366	26,053	27,609	28,976	29,145	29,195
Bondholders	9,058	24,483	25,613	26,944	26,655	26,765
Commercial banks and others	1,308	1,569	1,996	2,031	2,490	2,430
Private nonguaranteed debt from:	*55,674*	*52,337*	*53,897*	*54,241*	*51,098*	*51,467*
Bondholders	4,313	5,635	5,294	4,833	4,654	4,666
Commercial banks and others	51,361	46,702	48,603	49,409	46,444	46,801
Use of IMF credit and SDR allocations	**16,262**	**11,328**	**12,824**	**14,505**	**14,434**	**16,477**
IMF credit	14,245	9,518	10,938	9,974	10,125	12,133
SDR allocations	2,017	1,811	1,886	4,531	4,309	4,344
Short-term external debt stocks	**27,264**	**22,625**	**24,156**	**23,243**	**16,194**	**21,037**
Disbursements, long-term	**32,240**	**11,203**	**16,500**	**12,820**	**19,842**	**27,173**
Public and publicly guaranteed sector	7,969	5,367	7,056	6,373	18,524	25,645
Private sector not guaranteed	24,272	5,836	9,444	6,447	1,318	1,528
Principal repayments, long-term	**22,885**	**8,350**	**12,445**	**8,992**	**6,229**	**2,210**
Public and publicly guaranteed sector	1,446	3,075	4,987	2,940	1,129	949
Private sector not guaranteed	21,439	5,275	7,458	6,052	5,100	1,262
Interest payments, long-term	**3,532**	**3,187**	**3,372**	**3,649**	**1,974**	**1,594**
Public and publicly guaranteed sector	594	1,699	1,893	2,126	1,270	963
Private sector not guaranteed	2,938	1,488	1,479	1,523	704	631

UZBEKISTAN

(US$ million, unless otherwise indicated)

Snapshot	2023
Total external debt stocks	**59,184**
External debt stocks as % of:	
Exports	211
GNI	66
Debt service as % of:	
Exports	30
GNI	9
Net financial flows, debt and equity	11,581
Net debt inflows	10,335
Net equity inflows	1,246
GNI	**90,128**
Population (million)	**36**

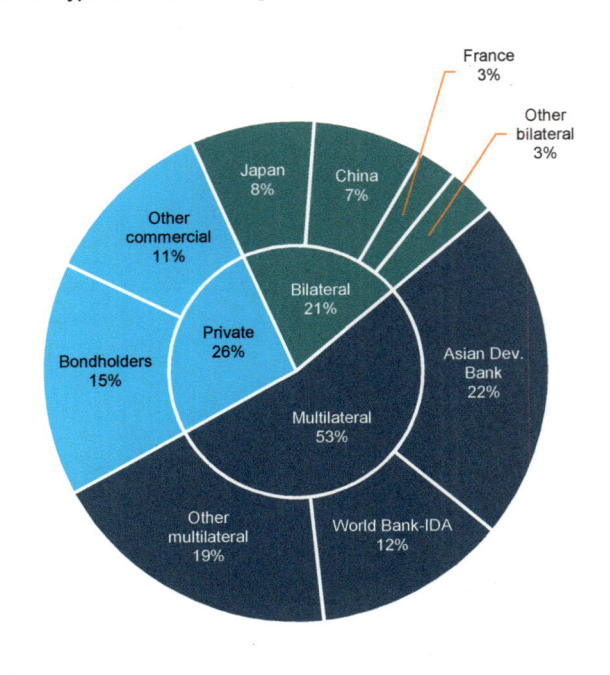

Figure 1 Public and publicly guaranteed debt, by creditor and creditor type in 2023, including IMF credit

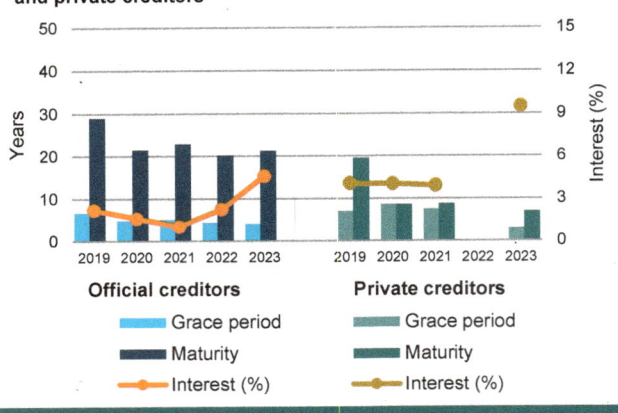

Figure 2 Average terms on new debt commitments from official and private creditors

Official creditors
- Grace period
- Maturity
- Interest (%)

Private creditors
- Grace period
- Maturity
- Interest (%)

Summary External Debt Data	2010	2019	2020	2021	2022	2023
Total external debt stocks	**7,981**	**22,958**	**33,711**	**40,606**	**48,993**	**59,184**
Long-term external debt stocks	**7,154**	**21,921**	**30,560**	**35,551**	**41,296**	**50,996**
Public and publicly guaranteed debt from:	*3,423*	*13,343*	*18,731*	*21,689*	*24,659*	*28,887*
Official creditors	3,197	11,560	14,728	16,022	18,555	21,219
Multilateral	1,210	7,030	9,246	10,086	12,884	15,214
of which: World Bank	373	2,723	3,734	4,328	5,528	6,572
Bilateral	1,987	4,530	5,481	5,936	5,672	6,006
Private creditors	226	1,783	4,003	5,667	6,103	7,667
Bondholders	..	1,000	2,048	3,383	3,383	4,391
Commercial banks and others	226	783	1,955	2,284	2,720	3,276
Private nonguaranteed debt from:	*3,730*	*8,579*	*11,829*	*13,862*	*16,637*	*22,109*
Bondholders	..	300	600	900	900	1,000
Commercial banks and others	3,730	8,279	11,229	12,962	15,737	21,109
Use of IMF credit and SDR allocations	**405**	**363**	**775**	**1,493**	**1,420**	**1,370**
IMF credit	0	0	397	386	367	308
SDR allocations	405	363	378	1,107	1,053	1,061
Short-term external debt stocks	**423**	**673**	**2,376**	**3,562**	**6,278**	**6,819**
Disbursements, long-term	**1,191**	**7,331**	**9,359**	**10,144**	**11,996**	**15,789**
Public and publicly guaranteed sector	455	4,485	5,637	4,075	4,241	5,372
Private sector not guaranteed	736	2,846	3,722	6,069	7,755	10,417
Principal repayments, long-term	**493**	**1,950**	**2,363**	**3,689**	**5,754**	**5,936**
Public and publicly guaranteed sector	370	429	520	740	774	1,050
Private sector not guaranteed	123	1,521	1,842	2,950	4,980	4,886
Interest payments, long-term	**118**	**669**	**756**	**826**	**1,104**	**2,056**
Public and publicly guaranteed sector	63	257	303	350	484	961
Private sector not guaranteed	55	412	453	476	619	1,095

VANUATU

(US$ million, unless otherwise indicated)

Snapshot	2023
Total external debt stocks	**470.7**
External debt stocks as % of:	
Exports	100.9
GNI	36.7
Debt service as % of:	
Exports	5.5
GNI	2.0
Net financial flows, debt and equity	**25.5**
Net debt inflows	16.2
Net equity inflows	9.3
GNI	**1,281.0**
Population (thousand)	**334.5**

Figure 1 Public and publicly guaranteed debt, by creditor and creditor type in 2023, including IMF credit

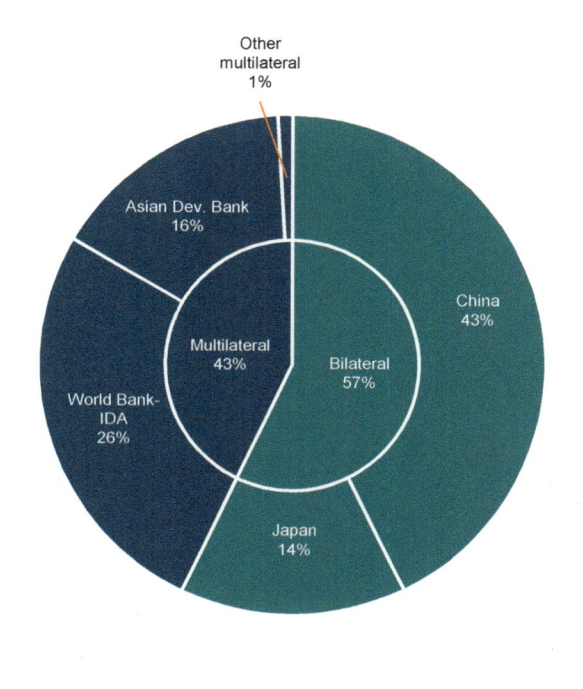

Figure 2 Average terms on new debt commitments from official and private creditors

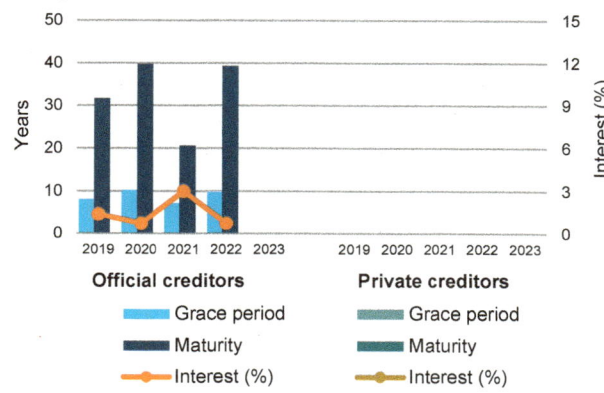

Summary External Debt Data	2010	2019	2020	2021	2022	2023
Total external debt stocks	**177.7**	**424.7**	**439.9**	**476.7**	**463.4**	**470.7**
Long-term external debt stocks	**102.6**	**345.5**	**367.1**	**373.9**	**374.0**	**362.3**
Public and publicly guaranteed debt from:	*102.6*	*345.5*	*367.1*	*373.9*	*374.0*	*362.3*
Official creditors	102.6	345.5	367.1	373.9	374.0	362.3
Multilateral	68.8	135.0	145.2	148.4	151.1	153.4
of which: World Bank	11.7	83.0	91.6	97.9	98.2	96.0
Bilateral	33.8	210.4	221.9	225.4	222.9	208.9
Private creditors	..	..	..	..	..	..
Bondholders	..	..	..	..	..	..
Commercial banks and others	..	..	..	..	..	..
Private nonguaranteed debt from:	..	..	..	..	..	..
Bondholders	..	..	..	..	..	..
Commercial banks and others	..	..	..	..	..	..
Use of IMF credit and SDR allocations	**25.1**	**37.2**	**34.4**	**63.0**	**57.7**	**55.9**
IMF credit	0.0	14.7	11.0	8.3	5.7	3.4
SDR allocations	25.1	22.5	23.4	54.7	52.0	52.4
Short-term external debt stocks	**50.0**	**42.1**	**38.4**	**39.9**	**31.8**	**52.5**
Disbursements, long-term	**3.3**	**55.0**	**10.7**	**25.5**	**46.0**	**11.3**
Public and publicly guaranteed sector	3.3	55.0	10.7	25.5	46.0	11.3
Private sector not guaranteed	..	..	..	..	..	..
Principal repayments, long-term	**3.6**	**21.4**	**8.1**	**10.5**	**13.8**	**13.6**
Public and publicly guaranteed sector	3.6	21.4	8.1	10.5	13.8	13.6
Private sector not guaranteed	..	..	..	..	..	..
Interest payments, long-term	**1.6**	**4.3**	**4.1**	**4.2**	**4.6**	**4.5**
Public and publicly guaranteed sector	1.6	4.3	4.1	4.2	4.6	4.5
Private sector not guaranteed	..	..	..	..	..	..

VIET NAM

(US$ million, unless otherwise indicated)

Snapshot	2023
Total external debt stocks	**141,850**
External debt stocks as % of:	
Exports	37
GNI	35
Debt service as % of:	
Exports	8
GNI	7
Net financial flows, debt and equity	13,575
Net debt inflows	-4,178
Net equity inflows	17,753
GNI	**407,254**
Population (million)	**99**

Figure 2 Average terms on new debt commitments from official and private creditors

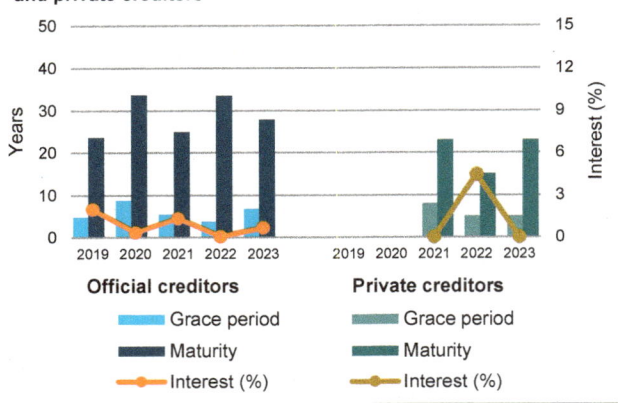

Official creditors
- Grace period
- Maturity
- Interest (%)

Private creditors
- Grace period
- Maturity
- Interest (%)

Figure 1 Public and publicly guaranteed debt, by creditor and creditor type in 2023, including IMF credit

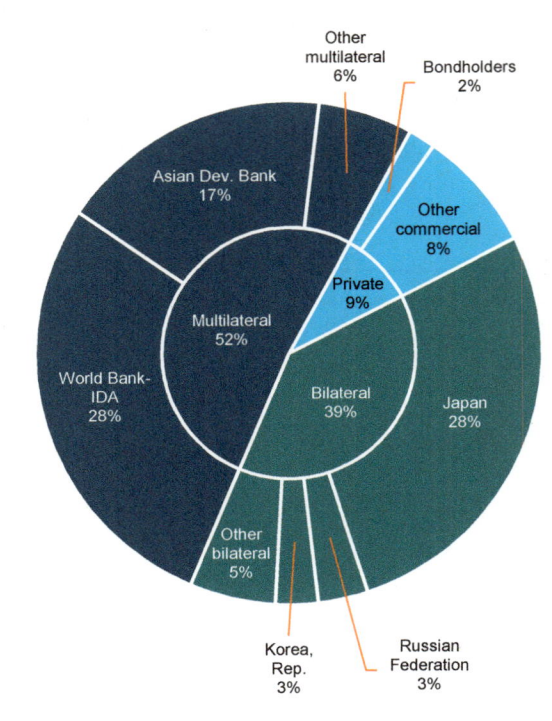

Summary External Debt Data	2010	2019	2020	2021	2022	2023
Total external debt stocks	**45,022**	**122,496**	**129,479**	**139,853**	**146,627**	**141,850**
Long-term external debt stocks	**37,560**	**97,664**	**102,422**	**104,632**	**106,583**	**104,835**
Public and publicly guaranteed debt from:	*32,805*	*55,825*	*55,651*	*51,374*	*46,466*	*43,894*
Official creditors	27,320	47,822	49,185	45,796	41,571	39,730
Multilateral	12,573	24,110	25,383	24,656	23,348	22,667
of which: World Bank	7,743	15,327	16,378	16,008	15,109	14,532
Bilateral	14,746	23,712	23,802	21,140	18,223	17,063
Private creditors	5,485	8,003	6,467	5,578	4,894	4,164
Bondholders	2,020	1,506	756	751	746	741
Commercial banks and others	3,465	6,497	5,711	4,827	4,148	3,423
Private nonguaranteed debt from:	*4,755*	*41,839*	*46,771*	*53,258*	*60,118*	*60,941*
Bondholders	..	1,014	1,094	1,444	1,769	1,734
Commercial banks and others	4,755	40,825	45,677	51,814	58,349	59,208
Use of IMF credit and SDR allocations	**529**	**435**	**453**	**1,987**	**1,890**	**1,905**
IMF credit	45	0	0	0	0	0
SDR allocations	485	435	453	1,987	1,890	1,905
Short-term external debt stocks	**6,932**	**24,397**	**26,604**	**33,233**	**38,154**	**35,109**
Disbursements, long-term	**6,965**	**18,633**	**17,327**	**23,264**	**28,470**	**21,833**
Public and publicly guaranteed sector	5,643	2,355	2,125	1,746	1,779	1,643
Private sector not guaranteed	1,322	16,278	15,202	21,518	26,692	20,190
Principal repayments, long-term	**1,055**	**13,607**	**14,389**	**18,780**	**23,490**	**22,966**
Public and publicly guaranteed sector	1,055	3,188	4,117	3,752	3,661	3,600
Private sector not guaranteed	..	10,420	10,273	15,028	19,829	19,366
Interest payments, long-term	**699**	**2,935**	**2,020**	**1,595**	**2,017**	**4,198**
Public and publicly guaranteed sector	554	1,257	995	756	739	1,047
Private sector not guaranteed	145	1,679	1,025	839	1,278	3,150

YEMEN, REPUBLIC OF

(US$ million, unless otherwise indicated)

Snapshot	2023
Total external debt stocks	**7,283**
External debt stocks as % of:	
Exports	..
GNI	..
Debt service as % of:	
Exports	..
GNI	..
Net financial flows, debt and equity	**-96**
Net debt inflows	-96
Net equity inflows	..
GNI	..
Population (million)	**34**

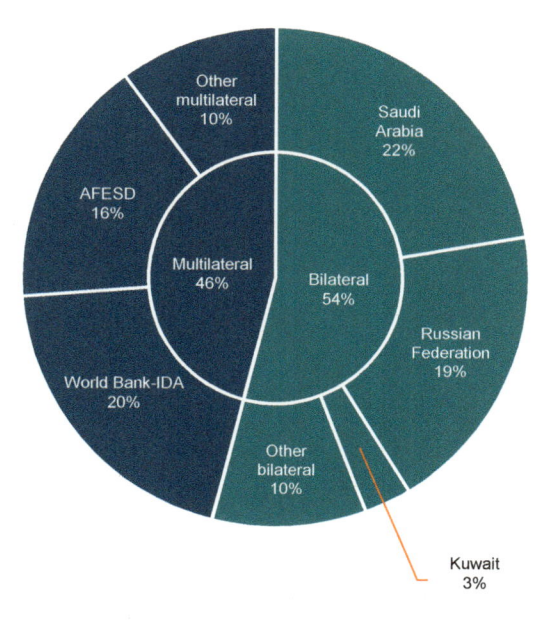

Figure 1 Public and publicly guaranteed debt, by creditor and creditor type in 2023, including IMF credit

Figure 2 Average terms on new debt commitments from official and private creditors

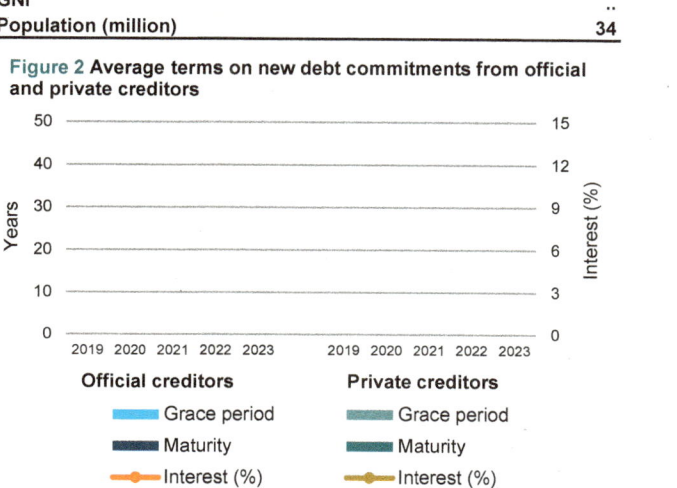

Official creditors
- Grace period
- Maturity
- Interest (%)

Private creditors
- Grace period
- Maturity
- Interest (%)

Summary External Debt Data	2010	2019	2020	2021	2022	2023
Total external debt stocks	**6,504**	**7,055**	**7,121**	**7,602**	**7,351**	**7,283**
Long-term external debt stocks	**5,945**	**6,188**	**6,251**	**6,108**	**5,896**	**5,815**
Public and publicly guaranteed debt from:	*5,945*	*6,188*	*6,251*	*6,108*	*5,896*	*5,815*
Official creditors	5,941	6,188	6,251	6,108	5,896	5,815
Multilateral	3,294	2,987	3,027	2,910	2,739	2,669
of which: World Bank	2,180	1,505	1,488	1,368	1,225	1,155
Bilateral	2,647	3,201	3,224	3,198	3,157	3,146
Private creditors	3	..	..	..	..	..
Bondholders	..	..	..	..	..	..
Commercial banks and others	3	..	..	..	..	..
Private nonguaranteed debt from:	..	..	..	..	..	..
Bondholders	..	..	..	..	..	..
Commercial banks and others	..	..	..	..	..	..
Use of IMF credit and SDR allocations	**436**	**440**	**410**	**1,021**	**956**	**951**
IMF credit	78	119	75	43	26	13
SDR allocations	358	321	335	978	930	938
Short-term external debt stocks	**124**	**427**	**460**	**473**	**499**	**517**
Disbursements, long-term	**297**	**66**	**38**	**13**	**9**	**0**
Public and publicly guaranteed sector	297	66	38	13	9	0
Private sector not guaranteed	..	..	..	..	..	..
Principal repayments, long-term	**155**	**72**	**75**	**80**	**78**	**79**
Public and publicly guaranteed sector	155	72	75	80	78	79
Private sector not guaranteed	..	..	..	..	..	..
Interest payments, long-term	**74**	**12**	**11**	**11**	**9**	**9**
Public and publicly guaranteed sector	74	12	11	11	9	9
Private sector not guaranteed	..	..	..	..	..	..

Note: Figure 2 shows no data values because the country did not have new commitments from 2019 to 2023.

ZAMBIA

(US$ million, unless otherwise indicated)

Snapshot	2023
Total external debt stocks	**29,579**
External debt stocks as % of:	
Exports	257
GNI	109
Debt service as % of:	
Exports	8
GNI	4
Net financial flows, debt and equity	810
Net debt inflows	616
Net equity inflows	194
GNI	**27,020**
Population (million)	**21**

Figure 2 Average terms on new debt commitments from official and private creditors

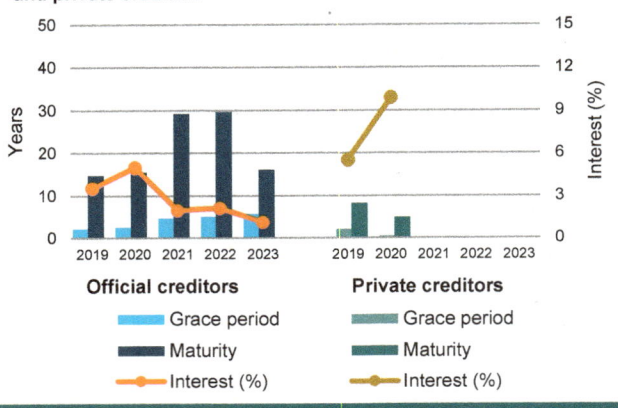

Official creditors
- Grace period
- Maturity
- Interest (%)

Private creditors
- Grace period
- Maturity
- Interest (%)

Figure 1 Public and publicly guaranteed debt, by creditor and creditor type in 2023, including IMF credit

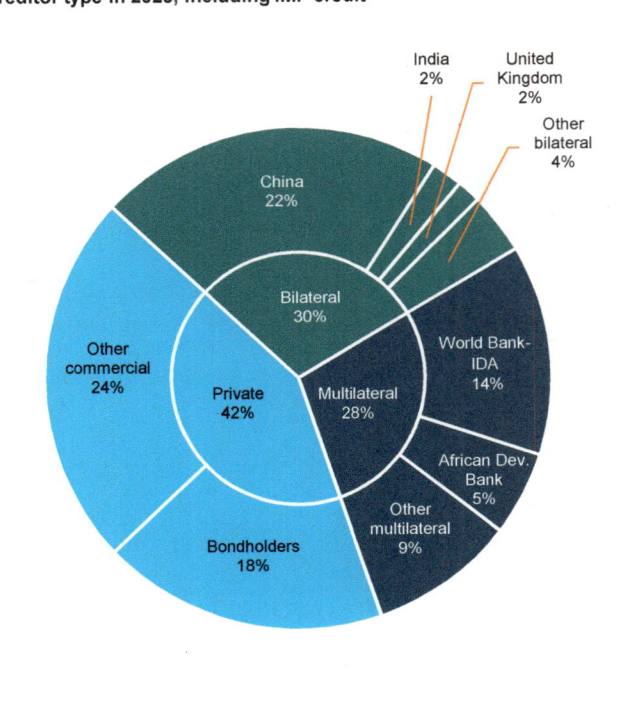

Summary External Debt Data	2010	2019	2020	2021	2022	2023
Total external debt stocks	**4,325**	**29,445**	**29,642**	**26,941**	**28,339**	**29,579**
Long-term external debt stocks	**2,058**	**27,939**	**28,233**	**23,593**	**23,677**	**23,701**
Public and publicly guaranteed debt from:	*1,264*	*13,208*	*15,167*	*15,293*	*15,755*	*15,868*
Official creditors	1,207	6,485	7,874	8,088	8,778	8,931
Multilateral	877	2,204	3,043	3,140	3,861	4,075
of which: World Bank	430	1,108	1,296	1,377	2,047	2,221
Bilateral	331	4,281	4,831	4,948	4,917	4,856
Private creditors	56	6,723	7,293	7,205	6,976	6,938
Bondholders	..	3,000	3,000	3,000	3,000	3,000
Commercial banks and others	56	3,723	4,293	4,205	3,976	3,938
Private nonguaranteed debt from:	*794*	*14,731*	*13,066*	*8,301*	*7,922*	*7,832*
Bondholders	..	..	..	..	..	..
Commercial banks and others	794	14,731	13,066	8,301	7,922	7,832
Use of IMF credit and SDR allocations	**1,117**	**667**	**678**	**1,969**	**2,058**	**2,450**
IMF credit	395	18	3	0	186	563
SDR allocations	722	649	676	1,969	1,872	1,887
Short-term external debt stocks	**1,150**	**839**	**731**	**1,379**	**2,604**	**3,428**
Disbursements, long-term	**251**	**6,584**	**3,309**	**491**	**1,427**	**591**
Public and publicly guaranteed sector	224	2,713	2,166	491	996	341
Private sector not guaranteed	27	3,871	1,143	..	431	250
Principal repayments, long-term	**92**	**1,834**	**1,552**	**1,515**	**1,158**	**610**
Public and publicly guaranteed sector	52	553	363	281	349	271
Private sector not guaranteed	40	1,282	1,188	1,234	809	339
Interest payments, long-term	**31**	**837**	**467**	**246**	**220**	**166**
Public and publicly guaranteed sector	12	503	335	118	88	80
Private sector not guaranteed	18	334	132	127	132	85

ZIMBABWE

(US$ million, unless otherwise indicated)

Snapshot	2023
Total external debt stocks	**14,213**
External debt stocks as % of:	
Exports	187
GNI	54
Debt service as % of:	
Exports	15
GNI	4
Net financial flows, debt and equity	836
Net debt inflows	247
Net equity inflows	588
GNI	**26,187**
Population (million)	**17**

Figure 2 Average terms on new debt commitments from official and private creditors

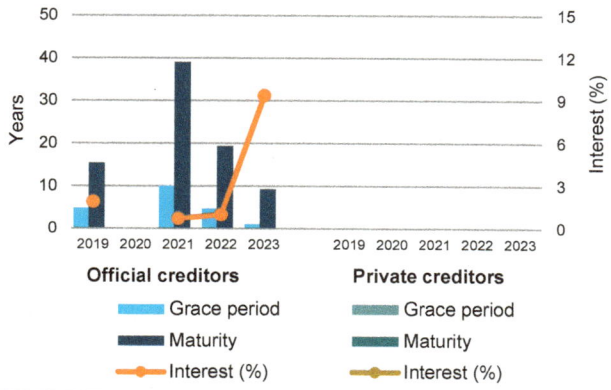

Official creditors
- Grace period
- Maturity
- Interest (%)

Private creditors
- Grace period
- Maturity
- Interest (%)

Figure 1 Public and publicly guaranteed debt, by creditor and creditor type in 2023, including IMF credit

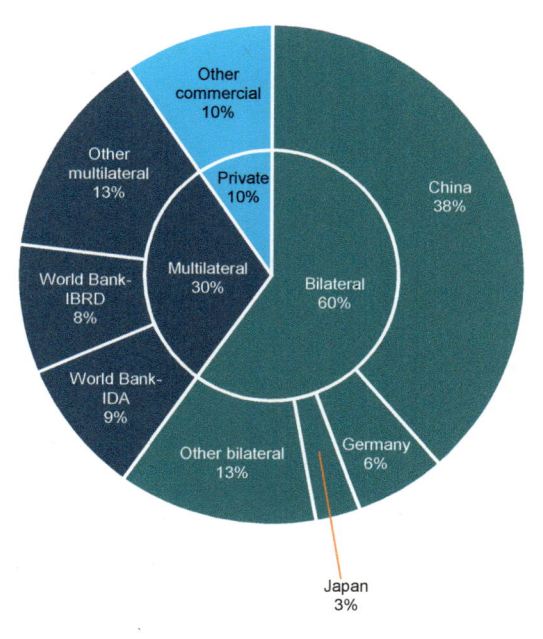

Summary External Debt Data	2010	2019	2020	2021	2022	2023
Total external debt stocks	**6,764**	**12,249**	**12,742**	**13,818**	**13,830**	**14,213**
Long-term external debt stocks	**4,405**	**8,254**	**8,397**	**8,655**	**8,495**	**8,911**
Public and publicly guaranteed debt from:	*3,800*	*4,358*	*4,565*	*4,583*	*4,671*	*5,109*
Official creditors	3,231	3,844	4,023	4,073	4,194	4,618
Multilateral	1,614	1,202	1,235	1,201	1,166	1,559
of which: World Bank	976	890	910	893	867	869
Bilateral	1,618	2,643	2,788	2,872	3,028	3,059
Private creditors	569	514	542	510	476	490
Bondholders	0	0	0	0	0	0
Commercial banks and others	569	514	542	510	476	490
Private nonguaranteed debt from:	*605*	*3,896*	*3,832*	*4,072*	*3,825*	*3,802*
Bondholders	..	..	..	..	..	..
Commercial banks and others	605	3,896	3,832	4,072	3,825	3,802
Use of IMF credit and SDR allocations	**529**	**468**	**488**	**1,422**	**1,352**	**1,363**
IMF credit	110	0	0	0	0	0
SDR allocations	419	468	488	1,422	1,352	1,363
Short-term external debt stocks	**1,830**	**3,527**	**3,858**	**3,741**	**3,982**	**3,939**
Disbursements, long-term	**847**	**972**	**906**	**914**	**316**	**1,013**
Public and publicly guaranteed sector	4	91	60	209	295	473
Private sector not guaranteed	843	881	845	706	20	540
Principal repayments, long-term	**338**	**1,224**	**934**	**551**	**290**	**621**
Public and publicly guaranteed sector	2	61	25	85	23	59
Private sector not guaranteed	336	1,163	910	466	266	562
Interest payments, long-term	**32**	**313**	**22**	**29**	**45**	**358**
Public and publicly guaranteed sector	14	13	17	25	12	49
Private sector not guaranteed	18	301	5	4	32	309

APPENDIX

Data Sources

The principal sources of information for the tables in *International Debt Report 2024* are from the International Debt Statistics database, which is based on reports to the World Bank through the World Bank's Debtor Reporting System (DRS) from member countries that have received either International Bank for Reconstruction and Development loans or International Development Association credits. The DRS has its origin in the World Bank's need to monitor and assess the financial position of its borrowers. Since 1951, borrowers have been required to provide statistics on their public external debt and private sector debt that benefit from a public guarantee. Reporting countries submit reports on the annual status, transactions, and terms of the long-term external debt of public agencies and that of private ones guaranteed by a public agency in the debtor country. The DRS maintains these records on a loan-by-loan basis. In 1973, coverage of the DRS was expanded to include private sector nonguaranteed borrowing; however, for this category of debt, data are provided by borrowers in aggregate rather than loan by loan.

Data submitted to the DRS are processed in the World Bank External Debt system, along with additional information received from the African Development Bank, the Asian Development Bank, the European Bank for Reconstruction and Development, the Inter-American Development Bank, the International Monetary Fund, and institutions of the World Bank Group (International Bank for Reconstruction and Development and International Development Association). The World Bank External Debt is an internal system of the World Bank. Among its outputs is the International Debt Statistics database, from which the tables and data visualizations in this publication and the online database are produced.

Data on exports and imports (on a balance of payments basis), international reserves, current account balances, foreign direct investment on equity, portfolio equity flows, and primary income on foreign direct investment are drawn mainly from the International Monetary Fund, supplemented by UN Trade and Development reports and country data. Balance of payments data are presented according to the sixth edition of the International Monetary Fund's *Balance of Payments Manual*. Official aid flows come from data collected and published by the Development Assistance Committee of the Organisation for Economic Co-operation and Development. Short-term external debt data are as reported by debtor countries or are estimates based on the Bank for International Settlements quarterly series of commercial banks' claims on low- and middle-income countries. For some countries, estimates were prepared by pooling creditor and debtor information. Data on the gross national income of most low- and middle-income countries are collected from national statistical organizations or central banks by visiting and resident World Bank missions.

Every effort has been made to ensure the accuracy and completeness of the external debt statistics. Coverage has been improved through the efforts of the reporting agencies and close collaboration between the World Bank and its partners, the Commonwealth Secretariat and UN Trade and Development, which provide debt recording and reporting systems across the globe, as well as through the work of the World Bank missions, which visit member countries to gather data and to provide technical assistance on debt issues. Nevertheless, quality and coverage vary among debtors and may also vary for the same debtor from year to year. Data on long-term external debt reported by member countries are checked against, and supplemented by, data from several other sources. Among these sources are the statements and reports of several regional development banks, government lending agencies, and official government websites.

Country Groups

Regional Groups

East Asia and Pacific
Cambodia (A)
China (P)
Fiji (A)
Indonesia (A)
Lao PDR (A)
Mongolia (A)
Myanmar (A)
Papua New Guinea (A)
Philippines (A)
Samoa (A)
Solomon Islands (A)
Thailand (A)
Timor-Leste (A)
Tonga (A)
Vanuatu (A)
Viet Nam (A)

Europe and Central Asia
Albania (A)
Armenia (A)
Azerbaijan (A)
Belarus (E)
Bosnia and Herzegovina[a] (A)
Georgia (A)
Kazakhstan (A)
Kosovo (A)
Kyrgyz Republic (A)
Moldova (A)
Montenegro (A)
North Macedonia (A)
Serbia[a,b] (A)
Tajikistan (A)
Türkiye (A)
Turkmenistan (A)
Ukraine (A)
Uzbekistan (A)

Latin America and the Caribbean[c]
Argentina (A)
Belize (A)
Bolivia (A)
Brazil (P)
Colombia (A)
Costa Rica (A)
Dominica (A)
Dominican Republic (A)
Ecuador (A)
El Salvador (A)
Grenada (A)
Guatemala (A)
Haiti (A)
Honduras (A)
Jamaica (A)
Mexico (A)
Nicaragua (A)
Paraguay (A)
Peru (A)
St. Lucia (A)
St. Vincent and the Grenadines (A)
Suriname (A)

Middle East and North Africa
Algeria (A)
Djibouti (A)
Egypt, Arab Rep. (A)
Iran, Islamic Rep. (E)
Iraq (A)
Jordan (A)
Lebanon (A)
Morocco (A)
Syrian Arab Republic (E)
Tunisia (A)
Yemen, Rep. (E)

South Asia
Afghanistan (E)
Bangladesh (A)
Bhutan (A)
India (A)
Maldives (A)
Nepal (A)
Pakistan (A)
Sri Lanka (A)

Sub-Saharan Africa
Angola (A)
Benin (A)
Botswana (A)
Burkina Faso (A)
Burundi (A)
Cabo Verde (A)
Cameroon (A)
Central African Republic (A)
Chad (P)
Comoros (A)
Congo, Dem. Rep. (A)
Congo, Rep. (A)
Côte d'Ivoire (A)
Eritrea (E)
Eswatini (A)
Ethiopia (A)
Gabon (A)
Gambia, The (A)
Ghana (A)
Guinea (A)
Guinea-Bissau (A)
Kenya (A)
Lesotho (A)
Liberia (A)
Madagascar (A)
Malawi (A)
Mali (A)
Mauritania (A)
Mauritius (A)
Mozambique (A)
Niger (A)
Nigeria (A)
Rwanda (A)
São Tomé and Príncipe (A)
Senegal (A)
Sierra Leone (A)
Somalia (A)
South Africa (A)
Sudan (E)
Tanzania (A)
Togo (A)
Uganda (A)
Zambia (A)
Zimbabwe (A)

Source: World Bank Debtor Reporting System.
Note: Letters in parentheses indicate Debtor Reporting System reporters' status: (A) as reported, (P) preliminary, and (E) estimated. The status "as reported" indicates that the country was fully current in its reporting under the Debtor Reporting System and that World Bank staff are satisfied that the reported data give an adequate and fair representation of the country's total public debt. "Preliminary" data are based on reported or collected information; however, because of incompleteness or other reasons, an element of staff estimation is included. "Estimated" data indicate that countries are not current in their reporting and that a significant element of staff estimation has been necessary in producing the data tables.
a. For Bosnia and Herzegovina, total debt before 1999, excluding International Bank for Reconstruction and Development and International Monetary Fund obligations and short-term debt, is included under Serbia.
b. Data before 2006 include Montenegro.
c. Guyana's data are reported and included in this report because the country is eligible for International Development Association resources. However, because it is classified as a high-income country, its data are excluded from the regional aggregates.

Income Groups

Low-income countries	Middle-income countries		
Afghanistan	Albania	Georgia	Pakistan
Burkina Faso	Algeria	*Ghana*	Papua New Guinea
Burundi	Angola	Grenada	Paraguay
Central African Republic	Argentina	Guatemala	Peru
Chad	Armenia	*Guinea*	Philippines
Congo, Dem. Rep.	Azerbaijan	*Haiti*	*Samoa*
Eritrea	*Bangladesh*	*Honduras*	*São Tomé and Príncipe*
Ethiopia	Belarus	India	*Senegal*
Gambia, The	Belize	Indonesia	Serbia
Guinea-Bissau	*Benin*	Iran, Islamic Rep.	*Solomon Islands*
Liberia	*Bhutan*	Iraq	South Africa
Madagascar	Bolivia	Jamaica	*Sri Lanka*
Malawi	Bosnia and Herzegovina	Jordan	St. Lucia
Mali	Botswana	Kazakhstan	St. Vincent and the Grenadines
Mozambique	Brazil	Kenya	Suriname
Niger	Cabo Verde	*Kosovo*	*Tajikistan*
Rwanda	*Cambodia*	*Kyrgyz Republic*	*Tanzania*
Sierra Leone	Cameroon	*Lao PDR*	Thailand
Somalia	China	Lebanon	Timor-Leste
Sudan	Colombia	*Lesotho*	*Tonga*
Syrian Arab Republic	Comoros	*Maldives*	Tunisia
Togo	Congo, Rep.	*Mauritania*	Türkiye
Uganda	Costa Rica	Mauritius	Turkmenistan
Yemen, Rep.	*Côte d'Ivoire*	Mexico	Ukraine
	Djibouti	Moldova	Uzbekistan
	Dominica	Mongolia	*Vanuatu*
	Dominican Republic	Montenegro	Viet Nam
	Ecuador	Morocco	*Zambia*
	Egypt, Arab Rep.	*Myanmar*	Zimbabwe
	El Salvador	*Nepal*	
	Eswatini	*Nicaragua*	
	Fiji	Nigeria	
	Gabon	North Macedonia	

Source: World Bank.

Note: Low-income countries are those with a GNI per capita of US$1,145 or less in 2023. Middle-income countries are those with a GNI per capita equal to or more than US$1,146 but equal to or less than US$14,005. Italicized countries are IDA-only countries as of July 1, 2024; IDA-only excludes blend and IBRD countries. Guyana is classified as a high-income country as of July 1, 2024, so it does not appear in this table or in the low- and middle-income countries' aggregates; however, as an IDA-only country, its data are included in this report. República Bolivariana de Venezuela is unclassified according to the World Bank FY2025 income classification owing to a lack of available data; thus, it is not included in this report or the International Debt Statistics database. FY = fiscal year; GNI = gross national income; IBRD = International Bank for Reconstruction and Development; IDA = International Development Association.

Glossary

This list provides general descriptions, not precise legal definitions, of the terms commonly used in this report. However, the descriptions include legal and policy elements relevant to how these terms are understood and applied in practice.

Blue bond is a debt instrument issued by governments, development banks, or other entities to raise capital from impact investors to finance marine- and ocean-based projects that yield positive environmental, economic, and climate benefits.

Bonds are debt instruments issued by public and publicly guaranteed or private debtors with durations of one year or longer. Bonds usually give the holder the unconditional right to fixed money income or contractually determined, variable money income.

Central bank is a country's financial institution that exercises control over key aspects of the financial system. It carries out activities such as issuing currency, managing international reserves, transacting with the International Monetary Fund, and providing credit to deposit-taking corporations.

Commitments of public and publicly guaranteed debt constitute the total amount of new long-term loans to public sector borrowers or borrowers with a public sector guarantee extended by official and private lenders and for which contracts were signed in the year specified.

Common Framework for debt treatment beyond the Debt Service Suspension Initiative is an initiative launched in 2022 and endorsed by the Group of Twenty. It is designed to support, in a structural manner, low-income countries with unsustainable debt.

Concessional debt conveys information about the borrower's receipt of aid from official lenders at concessional terms as defined by the World Bank, that is, loans with an original grant element of 35 percent or more. Loans from major regional development banks—the African Development Bank, Asian Development Bank, and Inter-American Development Bank—are classified as concessional according to World Bank classification.

Debt-for-climate swaps are agreements that convert debts into commitments related to climate adaptation or conservation measures.

Debt buyback is the repurchase by a debtor of its own debt, either at a discount price or at par value. In the event of a buyback of long-term debt, the face value of the debt bought back will be recorded as a decline in stock outstanding of long-term debt, and the cash amount received by creditors will be recorded as a principal repayment.

Debt distress, as defined under the debt sustainability framework, is caused by unsustainable debt, wherein a country is unable to fulfill its financial obligations and debt restructuring is required.

Debt restructurings are revisions to debt service obligations agreed on by creditors and debtors. Such agreements change the amount and timing of future principal and interest payments. Debt restructuring is a complex process that requires the agreement of domestic and foreign creditors and involves burden sharing between different parties (for example, between residents and banks in most domestic restructurings).

Debt service is the sum of principal repayments and interest paid on total long-term debt (public and publicly guaranteed debt and private nonguaranteed debt).

Debt Service Suspension Initiative (DSSI) took effect on May 1, 2020, and allowed 73 eligible countries to apply for a temporary suspension of debt service payments owed to official bilateral creditors. The suspension period, originally set to end on December 31, 2020, was extended through December 2021.

Debt sustainability is the condition under which a country (or its government) does not, in the future, need to default or renegotiate or restructure its debt, or make implausibly large policy adjustments.

Debt swap (conversion) is an exchange of debt—typically at a discount—for a nondebt claim (such as equity) or for counterpart funds that can be used to finance a particular project or policy. In essence, public sector debt is extinguished and a nondebt liability created in a debt conversion.

Debt transparency results in readily available data on public debt, allowing governments to make informed decisions about macroeconomic policy and debt sustainability.

Disbursements are drawings during the year specified on loan commitments contracted by the borrower.

Eurobond is a type of bond issued by governments or corporations outside of their home country and is denominated in a currency different from that of the issuer. Eurobonds are typically long-term debt instruments and are commonly denominated in US dollars. They can also be denominated in other currencies such as the euro, pound, Japanese yen, and Swiss franc.

External debt flows are debt-related transactions during the year specified. They include disbursements, principal repayments, and interest payments.

External debt stocks comprise public and publicly guaranteed long-term external debt, private nonguaranteed long-term external debt, use of International Monetary Fund credit and special drawing rights allocation, and short-term external debt.

Debt stock to exports is the ratio of outstanding external debt to the value of exports of goods and services and receipts of primary income from abroad.

Debt-to-GNI ratio is the ratio of outstanding external debt to gross national income (GNI).

Fiscal sustainability refers to the future implications of current fiscal policies and, more precisely, to the question of whether the government can continue to pursue its set of budgetary policies without endangering its solvency.

Foreign direct investment (FDI) refers to direct investment equity flows in the reporting economy. It is the sum of equity capital, reinvestment earnings, and other capital. Direct investment is a category of cross-border investment associated with a resident in one economy having control or a significant degree of influence on the management of an enterprise that is resident in another economy. Ownership of 10 percent or more of the ordinary shares or voting stock is the criterion for determining the existence of a direct investment relationship.

Grace period is the time between the date on which a loan is committed and the date on which the first principal payment is due. The information presented in the International Debt Statistics database is the average grace period on all public and publicly guaranteed debt committed during the specified period.

Grants are legally binding commitments that obligate a specific value of funds available for disbursement for which there is no payment requirement. They include debt forgiveness grants and grants from bilateral and multilateral agencies (such as the International Development Association).

Green bonds are bonds that finance green projects and provide investors with regular or fixed income payments.

Gross national income (GNI) is the sum of value added by all resident producers, plus any product taxes (less subsidies) not included in the valuation of output, plus net receipts of primary income compensation of employees and property income from abroad. Yearly average exchange rates are used to convert GNI from local currency to US dollars.

The Group of Seven (G-7) is the collection of seven industrialized countries—Canada, France, Germany, Italy, Japan, the United Kingdom, and the United States—that meets annually to discuss issues such as global economic governance, international security, and, most recently, artificial intelligence.

The Group of Twenty (G-20) is the collection of 19 of the world's largest economies—Argentina, Australia, Brazil, Canada, China, France, Germany, India, Indonesia, Italy, Japan, the Republic of Korea, Mexico, the Russian Federation, Saudi Arabia, South Africa, Türkiye, the United Kingdom, and the United States, and two regional bodies—the African Union and European Union—established to discuss international economic and financial stability.

Heavily Indebted Poor Country (HIPC) Initiative is a program of the World Bank and the International Monetary Fund to provide debt relief to qualifying countries with unsustainable debt burdens.

IDA-eligible countries are the countries that are eligible to receive International Development Association (IDA) resources. Eligibility for IDA support depends on a country's relative poverty, defined as gross national income per capita below an established threshold, which is updated annually.

Imports of goods, services, and primary income constitute the total value of goods and services imported and income payable to nonresidents.

Inflation is the rate of increase in prices over a given period in an economy.

Interest payments are the amounts of interest paid in foreign currency, goods, or services in the year specified.

Interest payment-to-GNI ratio is the ratio of interest payment to gross national income (GNI).

Interest rate is the interest rate applicable to a loan commitment as specified in the loan contract. The information presented in the International Debt Statistics database is the average interest on all public and publicly guaranteed debt committed during the specified period.

International reserves constitute the sum of a country's monetary authority's holdings of special drawing rights, its reserve position in the International Monetary Fund, its holdings of foreign exchange, and its holdings of gold (valued at year-end London prices).

Lender of last resort is an institution, often a multilateral creditor or a country's central bank, that offers loans to banks or other eligible institutions that are experiencing financial difficulty or are considered highly risky or near collapse. Loans from such lenders can happen in periods of financial turmoil, when banks may have doubts about lending to each other and depositors may suddenly seek to withdraw their money from their bank account.

Long-term external debt is debt that has an original or extended maturity of more than one year and that is owed to nonresidents by residents of an economy and is repayable in currency, goods, or services.

Maturity is the date on which the final principal repayment on a loan is due. It is the sum of the grace and repayment periods. The information presented in the International Debt Statistics database is the average maturity on all public and publicly guaranteed debt committed during the specified period.

Monetary policy is used by central banks to manage economic fluctuations and achieve price stability with low and stable inflation. Central banks conduct monetary policy by adjusting the supply of money, usually through buying or selling securities in the open market. When central banks lower interest rates, monetary policy is easing. When they raise interest rates, monetary policy is tightening.

Multilateral Debt Relief Initiative (MDRI) is a program of the World Bank, the International Monetary Fund, the Inter-American Development Bank, and the African Development Bank that provides additional debt relief to countries that have completed the Heavily Indebted Poor Country Initiative process.

Multilateral official creditors are official agencies owned or governed by more than one country and that provide loan financing. They include international financial institutions such as the World Bank, regional development banks, and other intergovernmental agencies.

Multilateral to external debt stock is the ratio of the stock of debt owed to multilateral creditors to total external debt.

Net debt flow is gross disbursements minus principal payments.

Net transfers on external debt are net flows minus interest payments during the year; negative transfers show net transfers made by the borrower to the creditor during the year.

Official creditors are governments or other bilateral public entities (such as export-import agencies or development agencies) and multilateral financial institutions (such as the World Bank and regional development banks).

Panda bond is a bond denominated in renminbi that is issued by a non-Chinese entity and sold within mainland China.

Paris Club is an informal group of official creditors whose role is to find coordinated and sustainable solutions to the payment difficulties experienced by debtor countries. Paris Club creditors provide appropriate debt treatment as debtor countries undertake reforms to stabilize and restore their macroeconomic and financial situations.

Portfolio equity is the category of international investment that refers to portfolio equity inflows and covers investment in equity securities. Equity securities include shares, stocks, participation, or similar documents (such as US depositary receipts) that usually denote ownership of equity.

Primary income on FDI (foreign direct investment) is payments of direct investment income (debit side) that consist of income on equity (dividends, branch profits, and reinvested earnings) and income on the intercompany debt (interest).

Principal repayments are the amounts of principal (amortization) paid in currency, goods, or services in the year specified with respect to long-term external debt.

Private creditors are bondholders, commercial banks, and other trade-related lenders.

Private nonguaranteed (PNG) debt is debt owed by private sector borrowers to external creditors on loans that do not benefit from a public sector guarantee by the debtor country.

Public and publicly guaranteed (PPG) debt comprises public debt (an external obligation of a public debtor, such as the general government or agency, the central bank, a political subdivision or agency, or an autonomous public body) and publicly guaranteed external debt (an external obligation of a private debtor that is guaranteed for repayment by a public entity).

Public debt is an external obligation of a public debtor, including all levels of government, the central bank, state-owned enterprises, public corporations, development banks, and any other autonomous public bodies of government.

Repurchase agreement/loan is a transaction in which the borrower temporarily lends a security to the lender for cash with an agreement to buy it back in the future at a predetermined price. Ownership of the security does not change hands in a repurchase transaction. For that reason, these agreements are treated as collateralized loans.

Samurai bond is a corporate bond denominated in yen that is issued by foreign companies in the Japanese market and is subject to Japanese regulations.

SDR allocations are reserve-related liabilities, distributed to member countries in proportion to their quota shares at the International Monetary Fund. The SDR (special drawing right) allocations are included in the gross external debt position and classified as long-term debt.

Short-term external debt has an original maturity of one year or less. Available data permit no distinctions among public, publicly guaranteed, and private nonguaranteed short-term external debt.

Short-term debt stock to total debt stock is the ratio of total short-term debt to total debt stock.

Sovereign credit ratings indicate the capacity and willingness of rated governments to repay commercial debt obligations in full and on time.

Treasury bonds are long-term debt securities with a maturity period of 20 or 30 years. They are considered low-risk and are generally free of risk when held until maturity.

Variable-rate loans are loans for which the interest fluctuates according to changes in market interest rates.